2002. 2.28

↑
2002 Zensa
Clear Poster, draft

← Doodle ①

This Ito looks
very different
from the one
above.

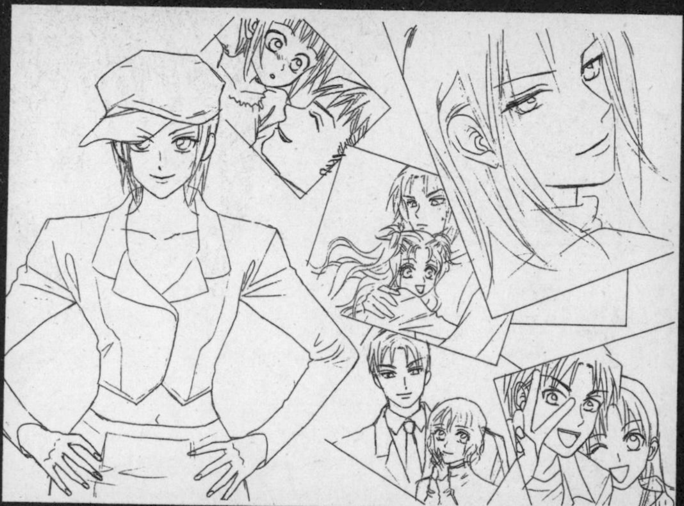

↑ 2002 Hana to Yume No. 13 splash page, draft (B5 size)

↓ 2002 Hana to Yume No. 19 bonus gift, drafts (B4 size)

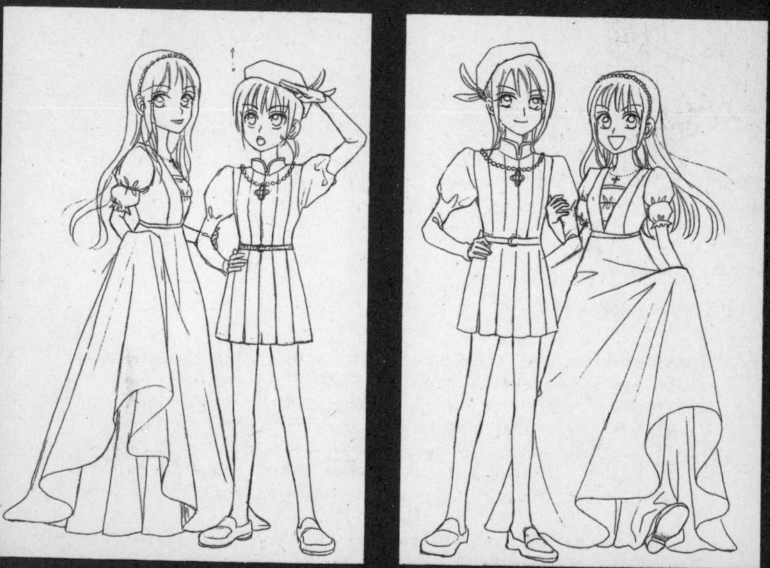

W Juliet ™

Volume 13

Story & Art by Emura

W Juliet
Volume 13

Story and Art by Emura

Translation & English Adaptation/Naomi Kokubo & Jeff Carlson
Touch-up Art & Lettering/Krysta Lau, Imaginary Friends Studios
Graphic Design/Hidemi Sahara
Editor/Carrie Shepherd

Managing Editor/Megan Bates
Editorial Director/Elizabeth Kawasaki
Editor in Chief/Alvin Lu
Sr. Director of Acquisitions/Rika Inouye
Sr. VP of Marketing/Liza Coppola
Exec. VP of Sales & Marketing/John Easum
Publisher/Hyoe Narita

Published by VIZ Media, LLC
P.O. Box 77010
San Francisco, CA 94107

10 9 8 7 6 5 4 3 2 1
First printing, November 2006

www.viz.com
store.viz.com

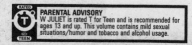

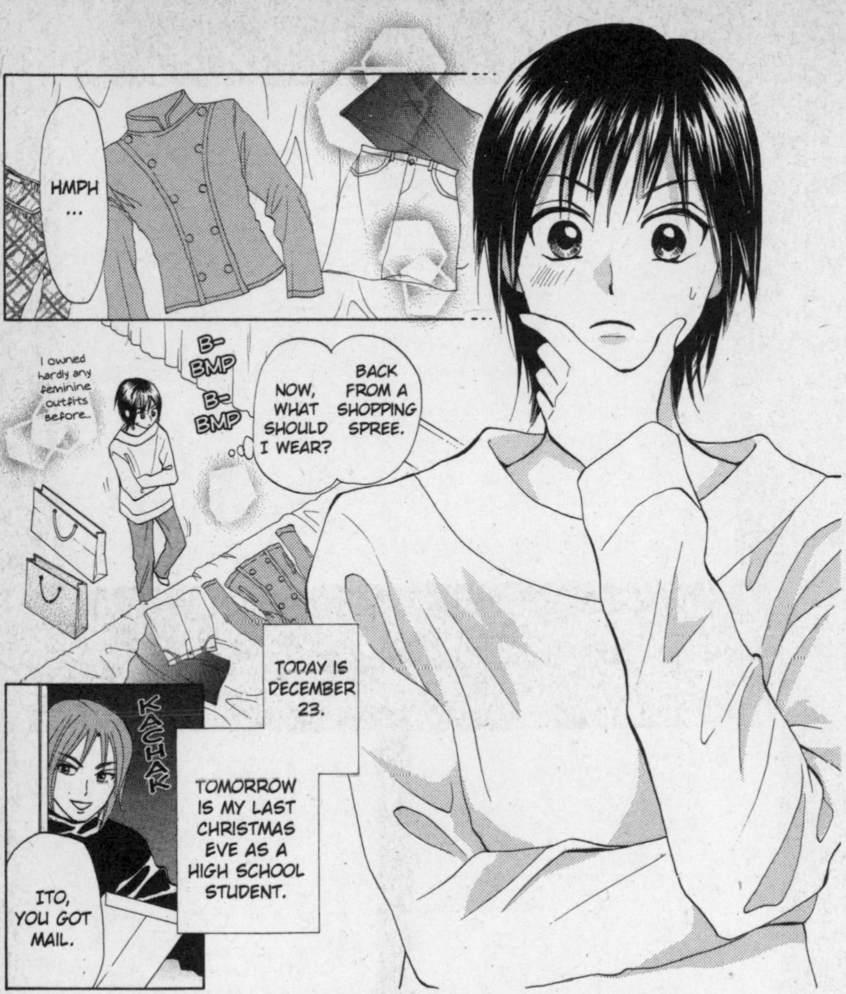
HMPH ...
BACK FROM A SHOPPING SPREE.
NOW, WHAT SHOULD I WEAR?
B-BMP B-BMP
I owned hardly any feminine outfits before...
TODAY IS DECEMBER 23.
TOMORROW IS MY LAST CHRISTMAS EVE AS A HIGH SCHOOL STUDENT.
KACHAK
ITO, YOU GOT MAIL.

—Behind the Scenes Story ①—

Come to think of it, Ito always shows her belly button... I mean, she always wears that style of clothes. No doubt, it's my taste, but I won't wear them myself. ♪ I just enjoy looking at them—like a middle-aged man. "I understand why Mako dragged the doll with him, but why did Ito do that?!" (pages 26 and 27) I received a fair number of letters asking about it. Well, I sort of got carried away (laugh), and before I knew it, I already drew it. Incidentally, these two dolls are supposed to be a couple.

They were torn apart!! I hope they were put back together properly.

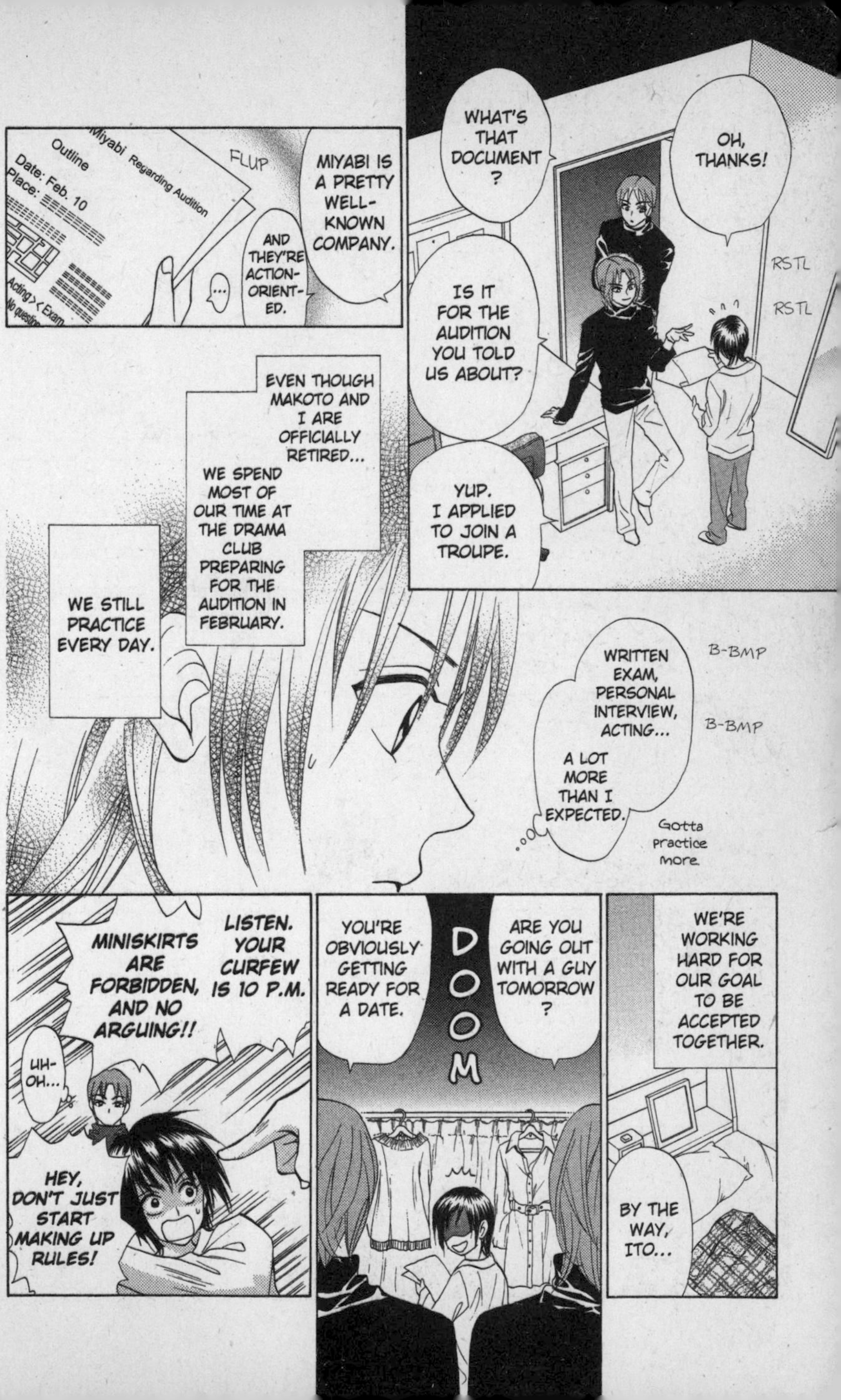
OH, THANKS!
WHAT'S THAT DOCUMENT?
RSTL
RSTL
IS IT FOR THE AUDITION YOU TOLD US ABOUT?
YUP. I APPLIED TO JOIN A TROUPE.
MIYABI IS A PRETTY WELL-KNOWN COMPANY.
FLUP
AND THEY'RE ACTION-ORIENTED.
...
Miyabi Regarding Audition
Outline
Date: Feb. 10
Place:
Acting >< Exam
WRITTEN EXAM, PERSONAL INTERVIEW, ACTING...
A LOT MORE THAN I EXPECTED.
B-BMP
B-BMP
Gotta practice more.
EVEN THOUGH MAKOTO AND I ARE OFFICIALLY RETIRED...
WE SPEND MOST OF OUR TIME AT THE DRAMA CLUB PREPARING FOR THE AUDITION IN FEBRUARY.
WE STILL PRACTICE EVERY DAY.
WE'RE WORKING HARD FOR OUR GOAL TO BE ACCEPTED TOGETHER.
BY THE WAY, ITO...
ARE YOU GOING OUT WITH A GUY TOMORROW?
DOOM
YOU'RE OBVIOUSLY GETTING READY FOR A DATE.
LISTEN. YOUR CURFEW IS 10 P.M.
MINISKIRTS ARE FORBIDDEN, AND NO ARGUING!!
UH-OH...
HEY, DON'T JUST START MAKING UP RULES!

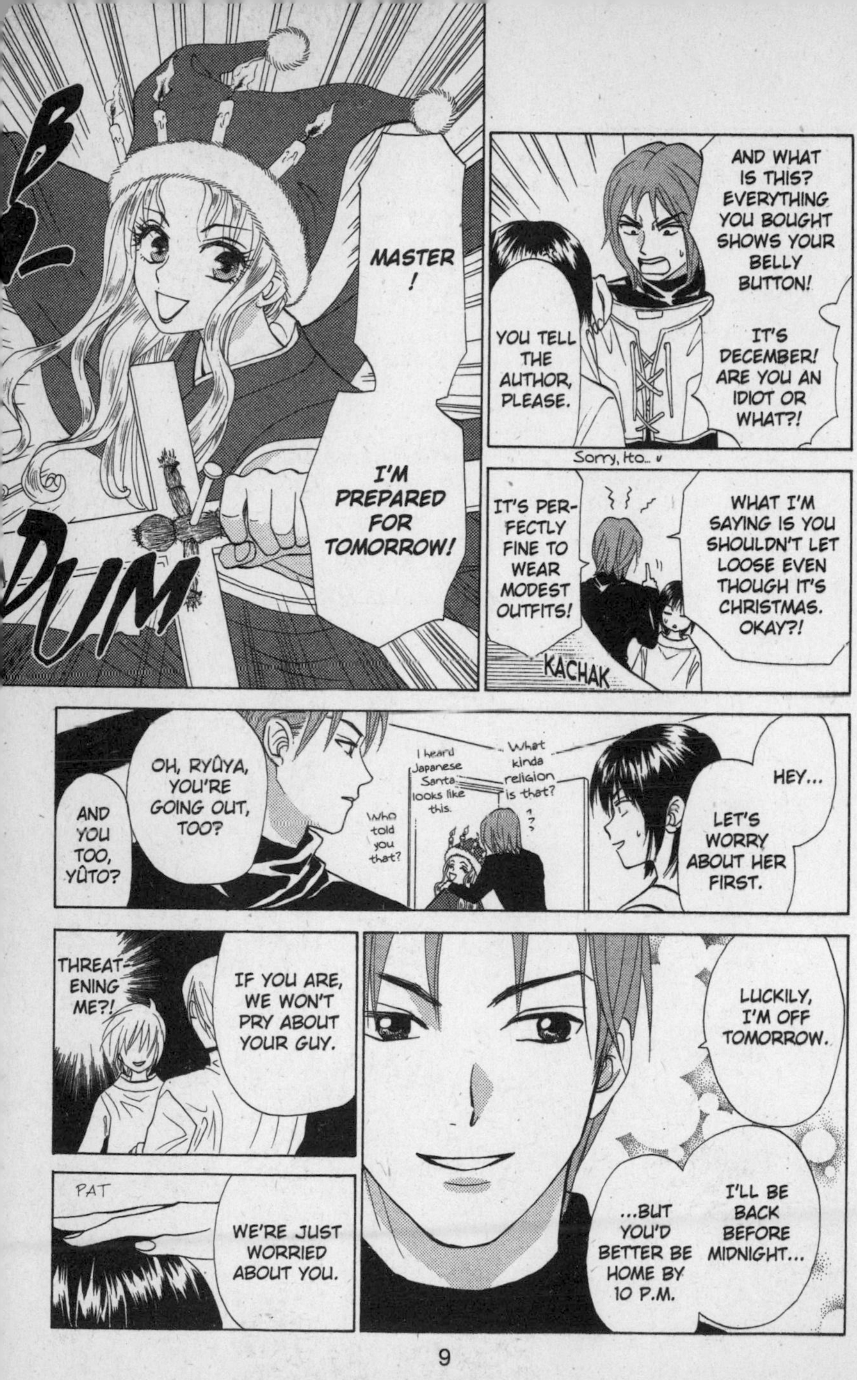
AND WHAT IS THIS? EVERYTHING YOU BOUGHT SHOWS YOUR BELLY BUTTON!
IT'S DECEMBER! ARE YOU AN IDIOT OR WHAT?!
YOU TELL THE AUTHOR, PLEASE.
Sorry, Ito...
WHAT I'M SAYING IS YOU SHOULDN'T LET LOOSE EVEN THOUGH IT'S CHRISTMAS. OKAY?!
IT'S PERFECTLY FINE TO WEAR MODEST OUTFITS!
KACHAK
B-DUM
MASTER!
I'M PREPARED FOR TOMORROW!
HEY...
LET'S WORRY ABOUT HER FIRST.
What kinda religion is that?
I heard Japanese Santa looks like this.
Who told you that?
OH, RYÛYA, YOU'RE GOING OUT, TOO?
AND YOU TOO, YÛTO?
LUCKILY, I'M OFF TOMORROW.
I'LL BE BACK BEFORE MIDNIGHT...
...BUT YOU'D BETTER BE HOME BY 10 P.M.
IF YOU ARE, WE WON'T PRY ABOUT YOUR GUY.
THREATENING ME?!
PAT
WE'RE JUST WORRIED ABOUT YOU.

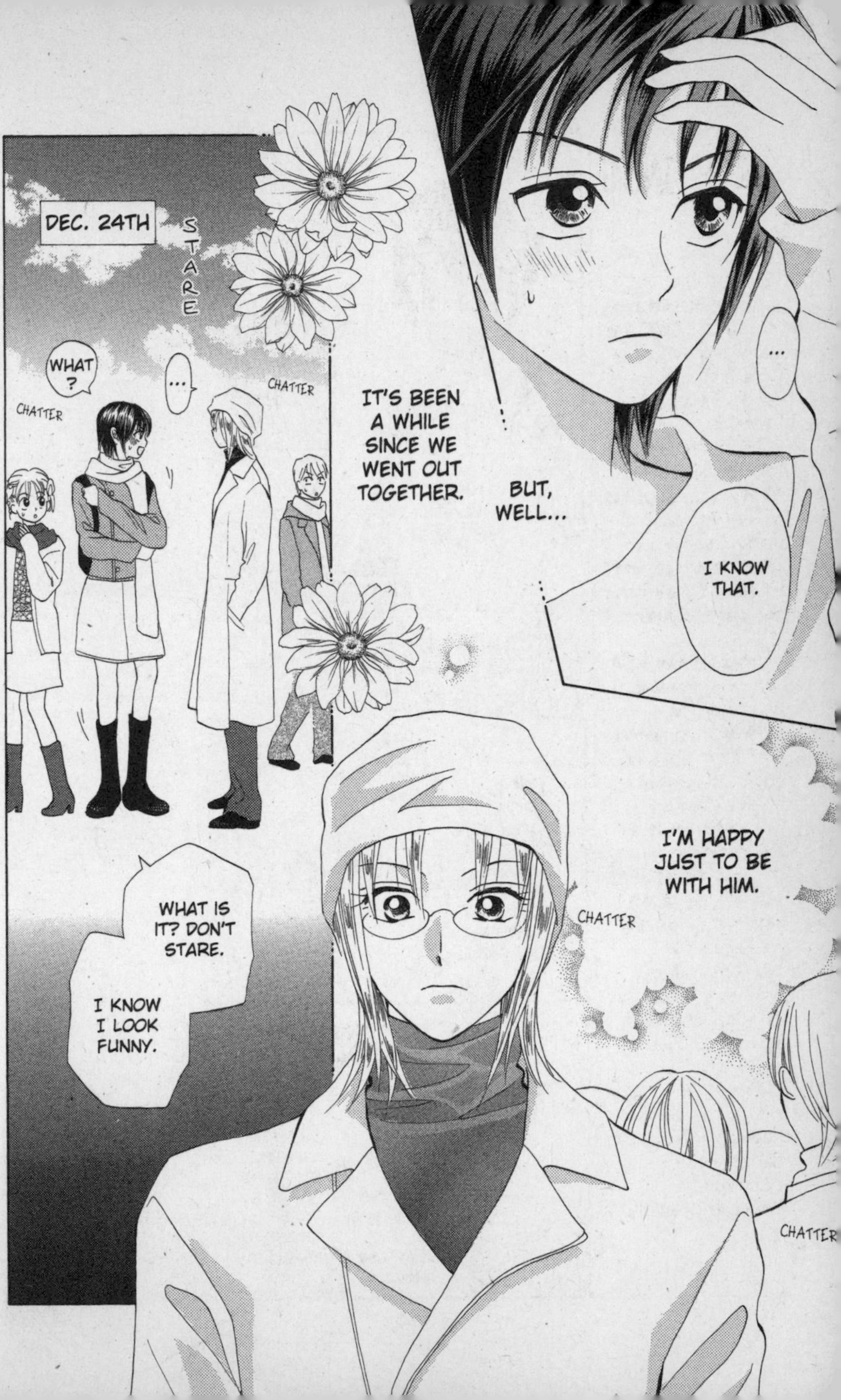
DEC. 24TH
STARE
WHAT?
...
CHATTER
CHATTER
WHAT IS IT? DON'T STARE.
I KNOW I LOOK FUNNY.
...
I KNOW THAT.
BUT, WELL...
IT'S BEEN A WHILE SINCE WE WENT OUT TOGETHER.
I'M HAPPY JUST TO BE WITH HIM.
CHATTER
CHATTER

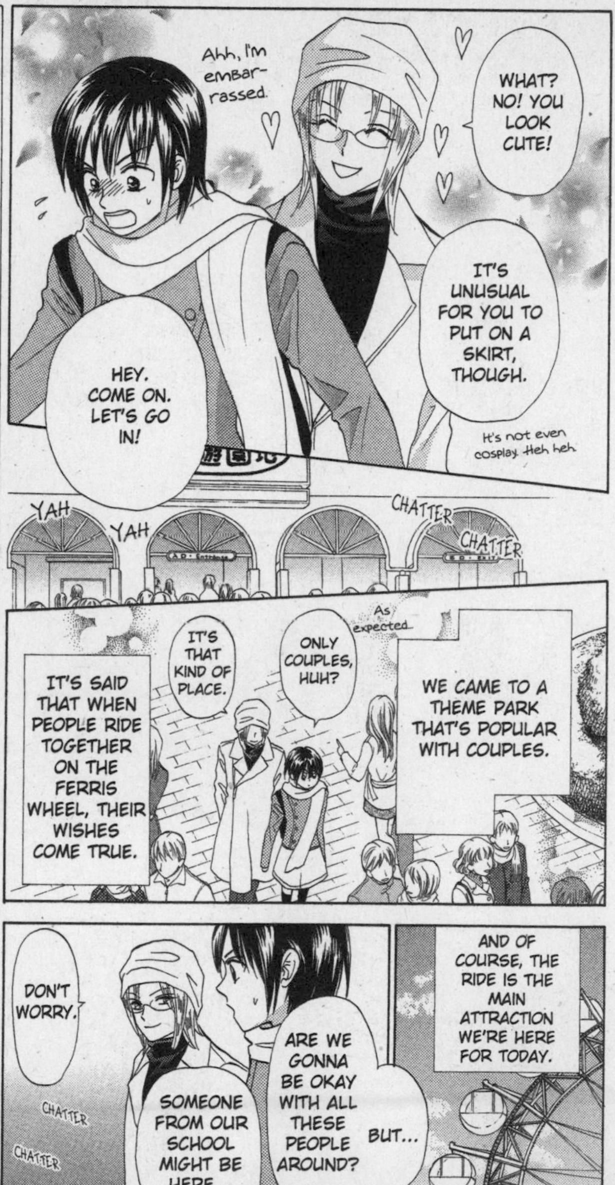
WHAT? NO! YOU LOOK CUTE!
Ahh, I'm embarrassed.
IT'S UNUSUAL FOR YOU TO PUT ON A SKIRT, THOUGH.
HEY. COME ON. LET'S GO IN!
It's not even cosplay. Heh heh.
CHATTER
CHATTER
YAH
YAH
WE CAME TO A THEME PARK THAT'S POPULAR WITH COUPLES.
As expected
ONLY COUPLES, HUH?
IT'S THAT KIND OF PLACE.
IT'S SAID THAT WHEN PEOPLE RIDE TOGETHER ON THE FERRIS WHEEL, THEIR WISHES COME TRUE.
AND OF COURSE, THE RIDE IS THE MAIN ATTRACTION WE'RE HERE FOR TODAY.
BUT...
ARE WE GONNA BE OKAY WITH ALL THESE PEOPLE AROUND?
SOMEONE FROM OUR SCHOOL MIGHT BE HERE...
DON'T WORRY.
CHATTER
CHATTER

GREETINGS

Hello, this is Emura. : It snowed yesterday (Dec. 9, 2002) in Kanagawa Prefecture. It shocked me, because that hadn't happened for a long while. But I was shut up in my room, working, and I didn't notice until noon. It was over by then. (Laugh)

In the latter half of this volume, Ito and the others go skiing in February with tons of snow. But in fact, I worked on it in midsummer. August! It's strange, isn't it? ^^; At least volume 13 will be released in January, which matches the season in the story. ♥

By the way, I plan on filling up the column space with Question Corner.
Now, let's go! ♪

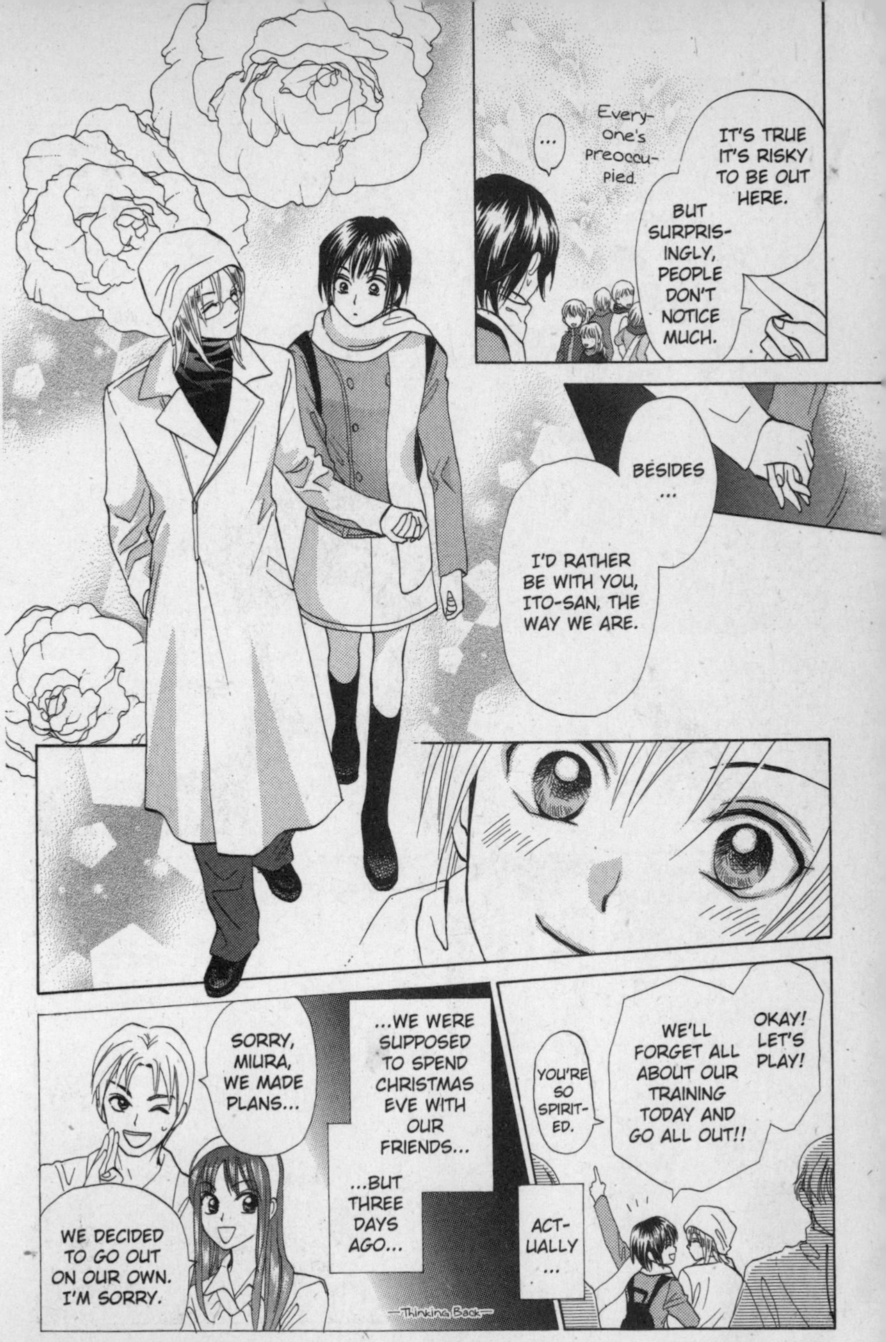
IT'S TRUE IT'S RISKY TO BE OUT HERE.
BUT SURPRISINGLY, PEOPLE DON'T NOTICE MUCH.
Everyone's preoccupied.
...
BESIDES...
I'D RATHER BE WITH YOU, ITO-SAN, THE WAY WE ARE.
OKAY! LET'S PLAY!
WE'LL FORGET ALL ABOUT OUR TRAINING TODAY AND GO ALL OUT!!
YOU'RE SO SPIRITED.
ACTUALLY...
...WE WERE SUPPOSED TO SPEND CHRISTMAS EVE WITH OUR FRIENDS...
...BUT THREE DAYS AGO...
SORRY, MIURA, WE MADE PLANS...
WE DECIDED TO GO OUT ON OUR OWN. I'M SORRY.
—Thinking Back—

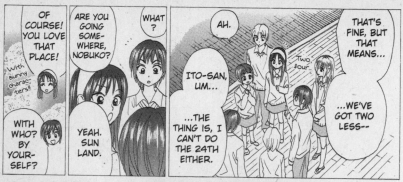

THAT'S FINE, BUT THAT MEANS...
Two, four...
...WE'VE GOT TWO LESS--
AH.
ITO-SAN, UM...
...THE THING IS, I CAN'T DO THE 24TH EITHER.
WHAT ?
ARE YOU GOING SOME-WHERE, NOBUKO?
YEAH. SUN LAND.
OF COURSE! YOU LOVE THAT PLACE!
With bunny charac-ters!!
WITH WHO? BY YOUR-SELF?
WITH TOKI-SEMPAI.
—Done Thinking Back—
THAT'S HOW WE ALL ENDED UP DOING OUR OWN THING TODAY.
BEING ALONE WITH MAKOTO IS MORE THAN I COULD'VE WISHED FOR, BUT--
YAAH
KYAAH
WUM
Eeek, I'm dizzy.
You okay?
WUM
WHO WOULD'VE THOUGHT NOBUKO AND TOKI-CHAN WOULD--
SHE SAID HE'S LIKE A DAD A WHILE BACK.
LOOKS LIKE THEY BECAME AWARE OF EACH OTHER AFTER WHAT HAPPENED AT THE CULTURAL FESTIVAL.
I MEAN, IT'S A SURPRISE, YOU KNOW...
Map

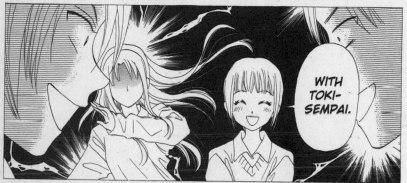

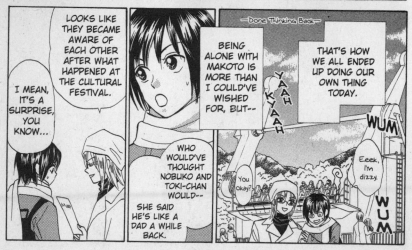

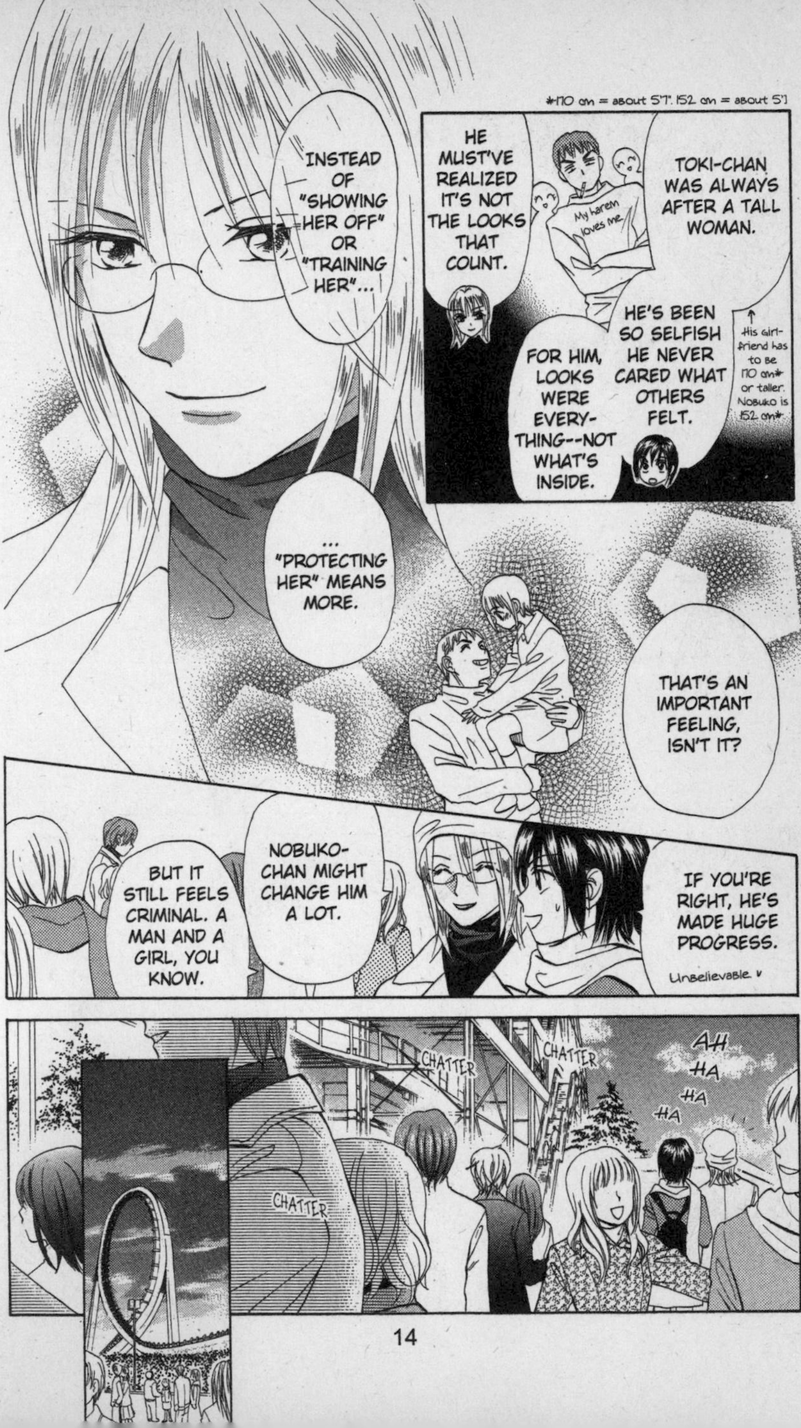
*170 cm = about 5'7". 152 cm = about 5'1"
TOKI-CHAN WAS ALWAYS AFTER A TALL WOMAN.
↑ His girlfriend has to be 170 cm* or taller. Nobuko is 152 cm*
My harem loves me.
HE MUST'VE REALIZED IT'S NOT THE LOOKS THAT COUNT.
HE'S BEEN SO SELFISH HE NEVER CARED WHAT OTHERS FELT.
FOR HIM, LOOKS WERE EVERY-THING--NOT WHAT'S INSIDE.
INSTEAD OF "SHOWING HER OFF" OR "TRAINING HER"...
... "PROTECTING HER" MEANS MORE.
THAT'S AN IMPORTANT FEELING, ISN'T IT?
IF YOU'RE RIGHT, HE'S MADE HUGE PROGRESS.
Unbelievable. ♥
NOBUKO-CHAN MIGHT CHANGE HIM A LOT.
BUT IT STILL FEELS CRIMINAL. A MAN AND A GIRL, YOU KNOW.
AH HA HA HA
CHATTER
CHATTER
CHATTER

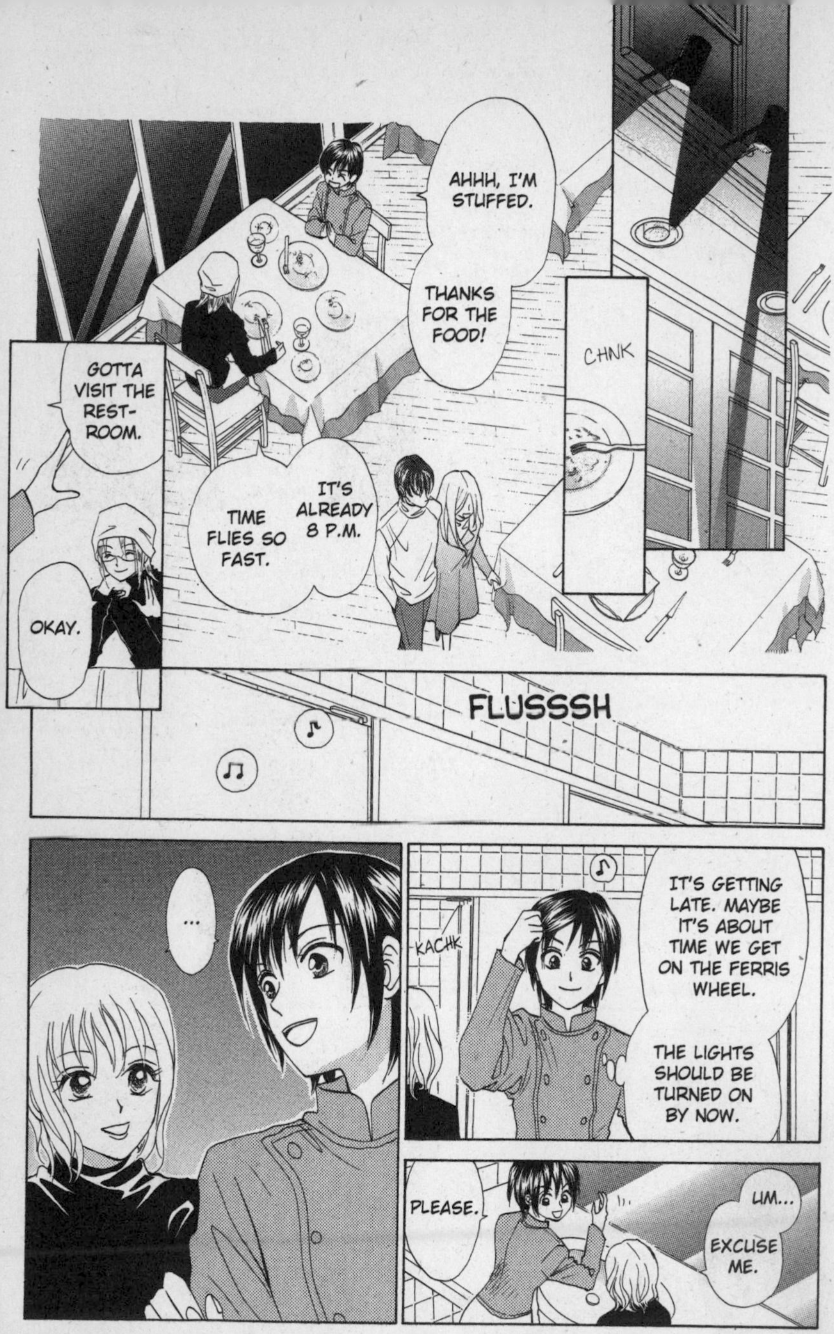
CHNK
AHHH, I'M STUFFED.
THANKS FOR THE FOOD!
IT'S ALREADY 8 P.M.
TIME FLIES SO FAST.
GOTTA VISIT THE REST-ROOM.
OKAY.
FLUSSSH
KACHK
IT'S GETTING LATE. MAYBE IT'S ABOUT TIME WE GET ON THE FERRIS WHEEL.
THE LIGHTS SHOULD BE TURNED ON BY NOW.
UM...
EXCUSE ME.
PLEASE.
...

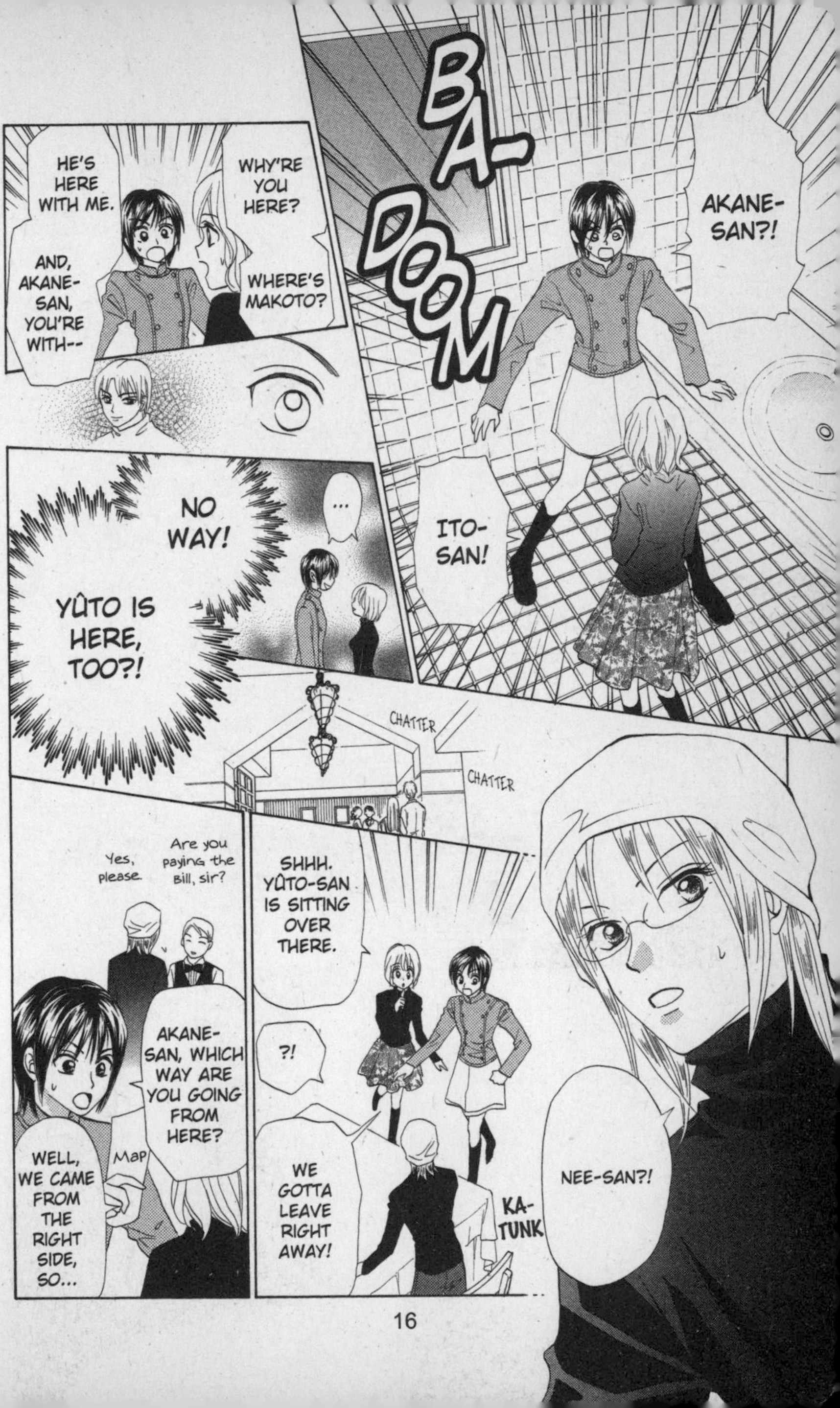
BA-DOOM
AKANE-SAN?!
ITO-SAN!
WHY'RE YOU HERE?
WHERE'S MAKOTO?
HE'S HERE WITH ME.
AND, AKANE-SAN, YOU'RE WITH--
...
NO WAY!
YÛTO IS HERE, TOO?!
CHATTER
CHATTER
NEE-SAN?!
KA-TUNK
SHHH. YÛTO-SAN IS SITTING OVER THERE.
?!
WE GOTTA LEAVE RIGHT AWAY!
Are you paying the bill, sir?
Yes, please.
AKANE-SAN, WHICH WAY ARE YOU GOING FROM HERE?
Map
WELL, WE CAME FROM THE RIGHT SIDE, SO...

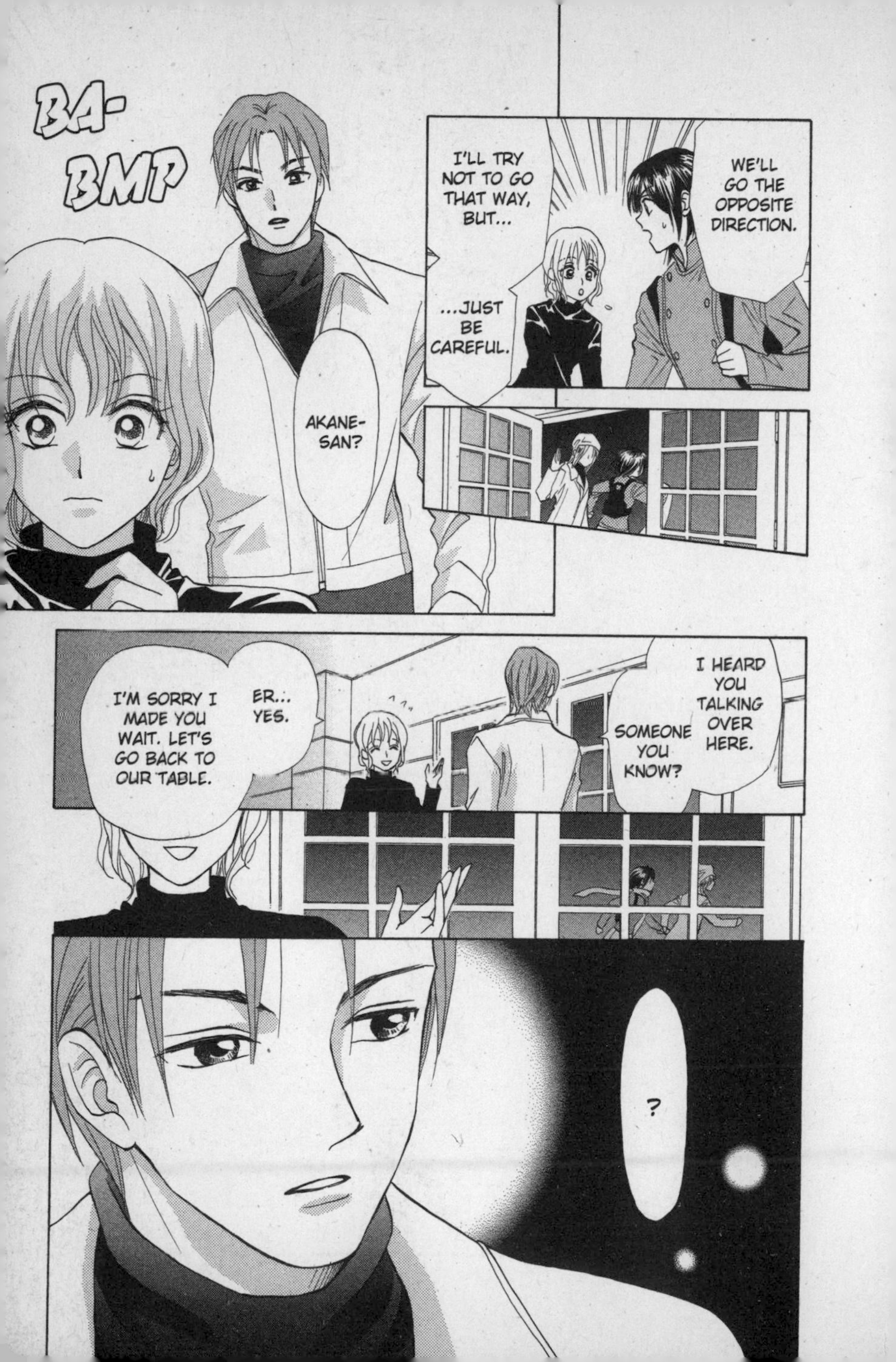
WE'LL GO THE OPPOSITE DIRECTION.
I'LL TRY NOT TO GO THAT WAY, BUT...
...JUST BE CAREFUL.
BA-BMP
AKANE-SAN?
I HEARD YOU TALKING OVER HERE.
SOMEONE YOU KNOW?
ER... YES.
I'M SORRY I MADE YOU WAIT. LET'S GO BACK TO OUR TABLE.
?

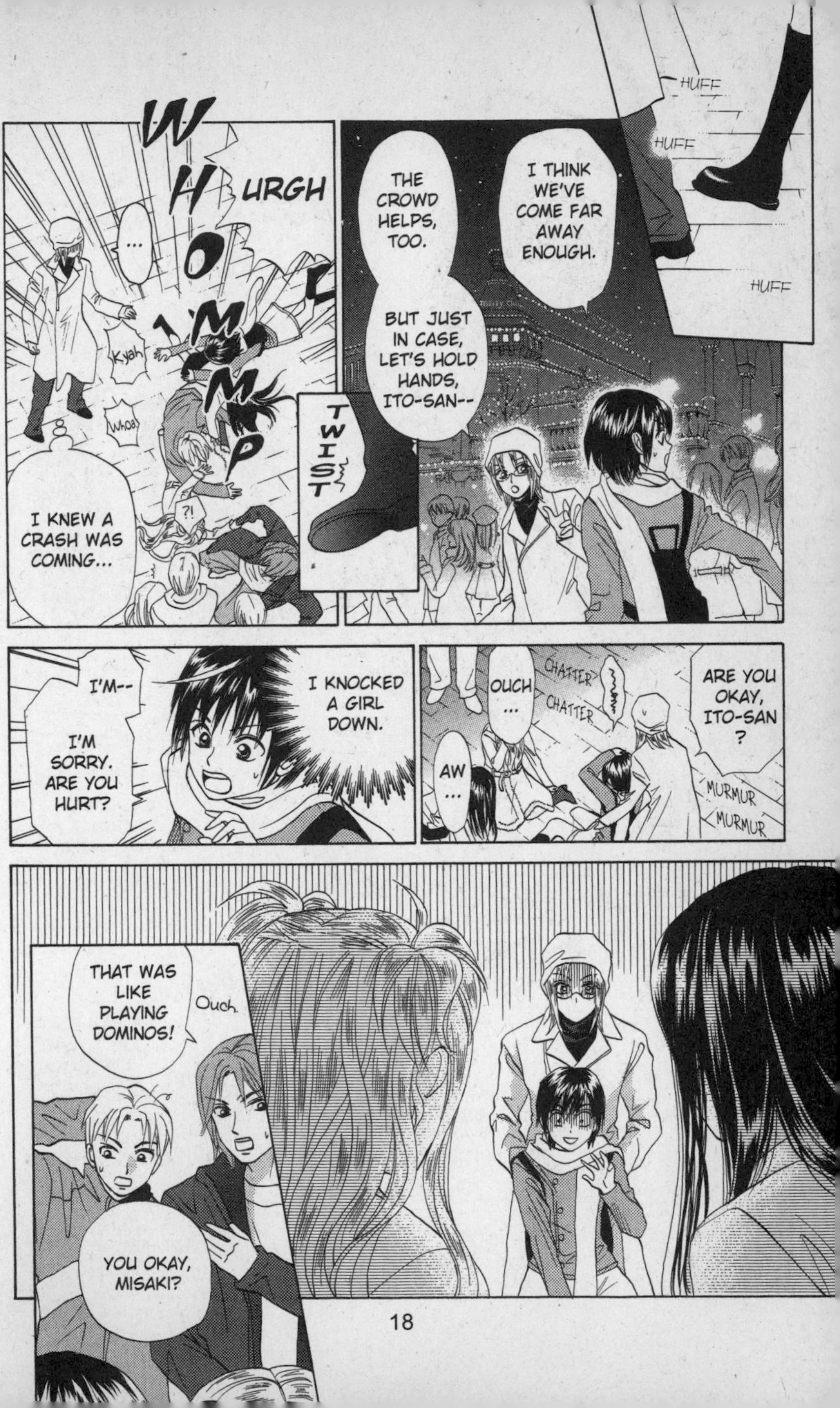
HUFF
HUFF
HUFF
I THINK WE'VE COME FAR AWAY ENOUGH.
THE CROWD HELPS, TOO.
BUT JUST IN CASE, LET'S HOLD HANDS, ITO-SAN--
TWIST
WHOMP
URGH
...
Kyah
Whoa
?!
I KNEW A CRASH WAS COMING...
ARE YOU OKAY, ITO-SAN?
MURMUR
MURMUR
CHATTER
CHATTER
OUCH...
AW...
I KNOCKED A GIRL DOWN.
I'M--
I'M SORRY. ARE YOU HURT?
THAT WAS LIKE PLAYING DOMINOS!
Ouch.
YOU OKAY, MISAKI?

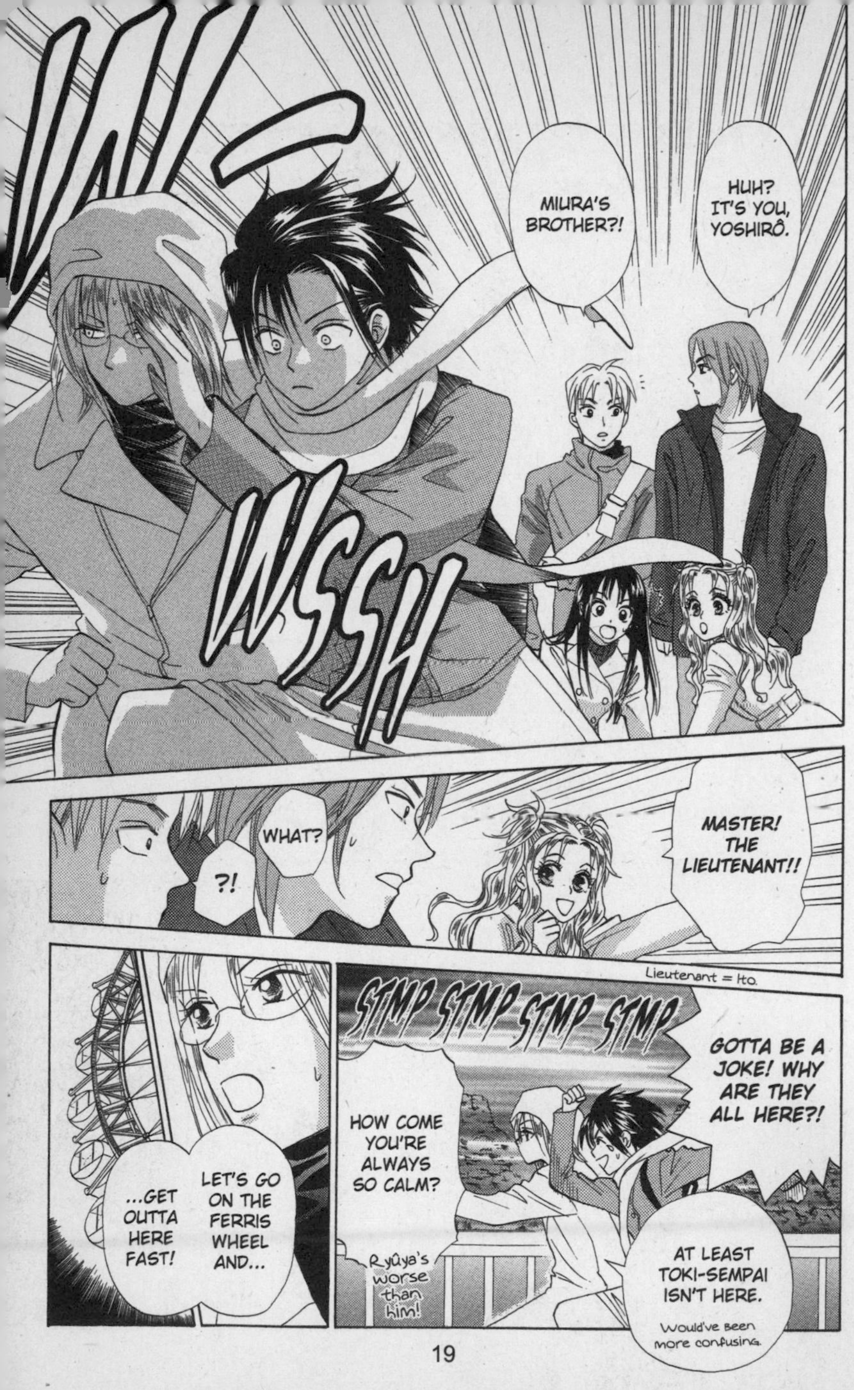
HUH? IT'S YOU, YOSHIRÔ.
MIURA'S BROTHER?!
WSSH
MASTER! THE LIEUTENANT!!
WHAT?
?!
Lieutenant = Ito.
STMP STMP STMP STMP
GOTTA BE A JOKE! WHY ARE THEY ALL HERE?!
HOW COME YOU'RE ALWAYS SO CALM?
AT LEAST TOKI-SEMPAI ISN'T HERE.
Would've been more confusing.
Ryûya's worse than him!
LET'S GO ON THE FERRIS WHEEL AND...
...GET OUTTA HERE FAST!

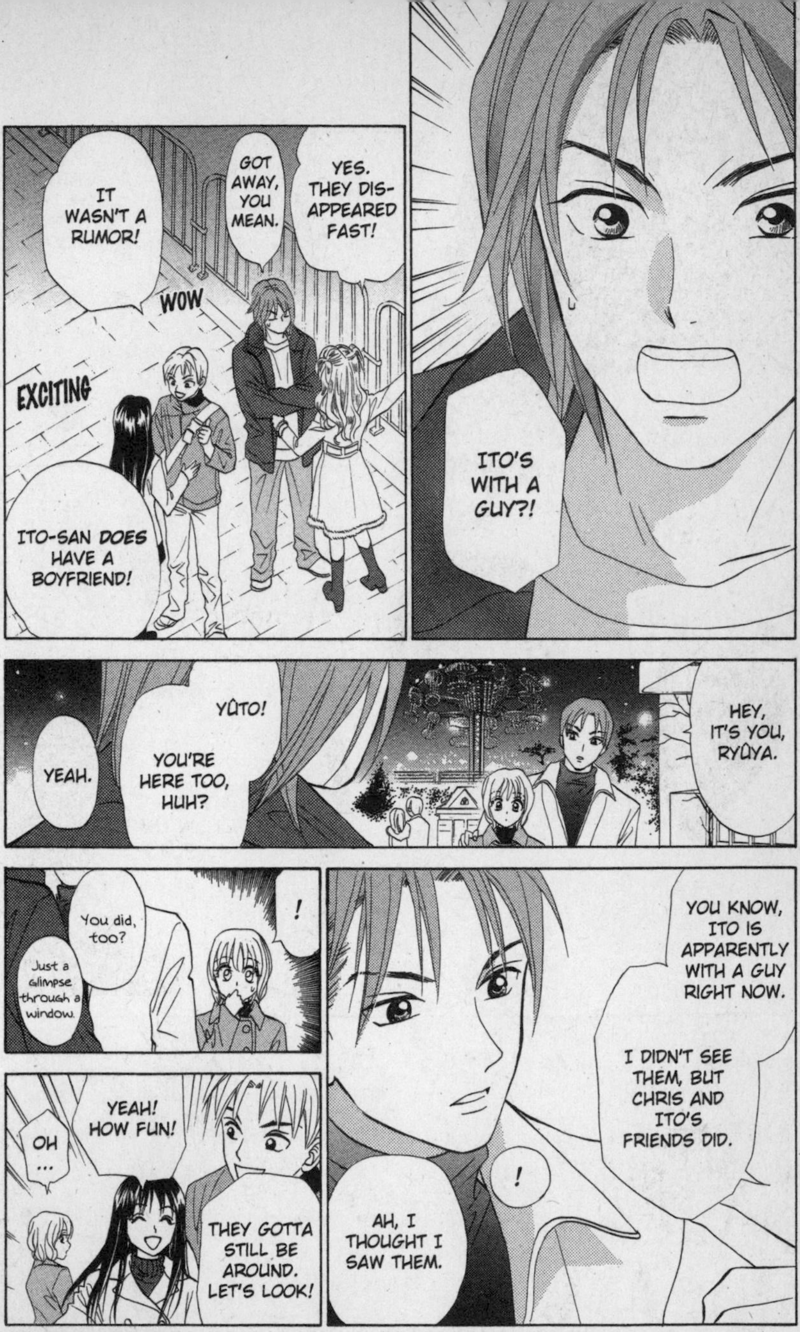
ITO'S WITH A GUY?!
YES. THEY DIS-APPEARED FAST!
GOT AWAY, YOU MEAN.
IT WASN'T A RUMOR!
WOW
EXCITING
ITO-SAN DOES HAVE A BOYFRIEND!
HEY, IT'S YOU, RYÛYA.
YÛTO!
YOU'RE HERE TOO, HUH?
YEAH.
YOU KNOW, ITO IS APPARENTLY WITH A GUY RIGHT NOW.
I DIDN'T SEE THEM, BUT CHRIS AND ITO'S FRIENDS DID.
!
AH, I THOUGHT I SAW THEM.
!
You did, too?
Just a glimpse through a window.
YEAH! HOW FUN!
OH ...
THEY GOTTA STILL BE AROUND. LET'S LOOK!

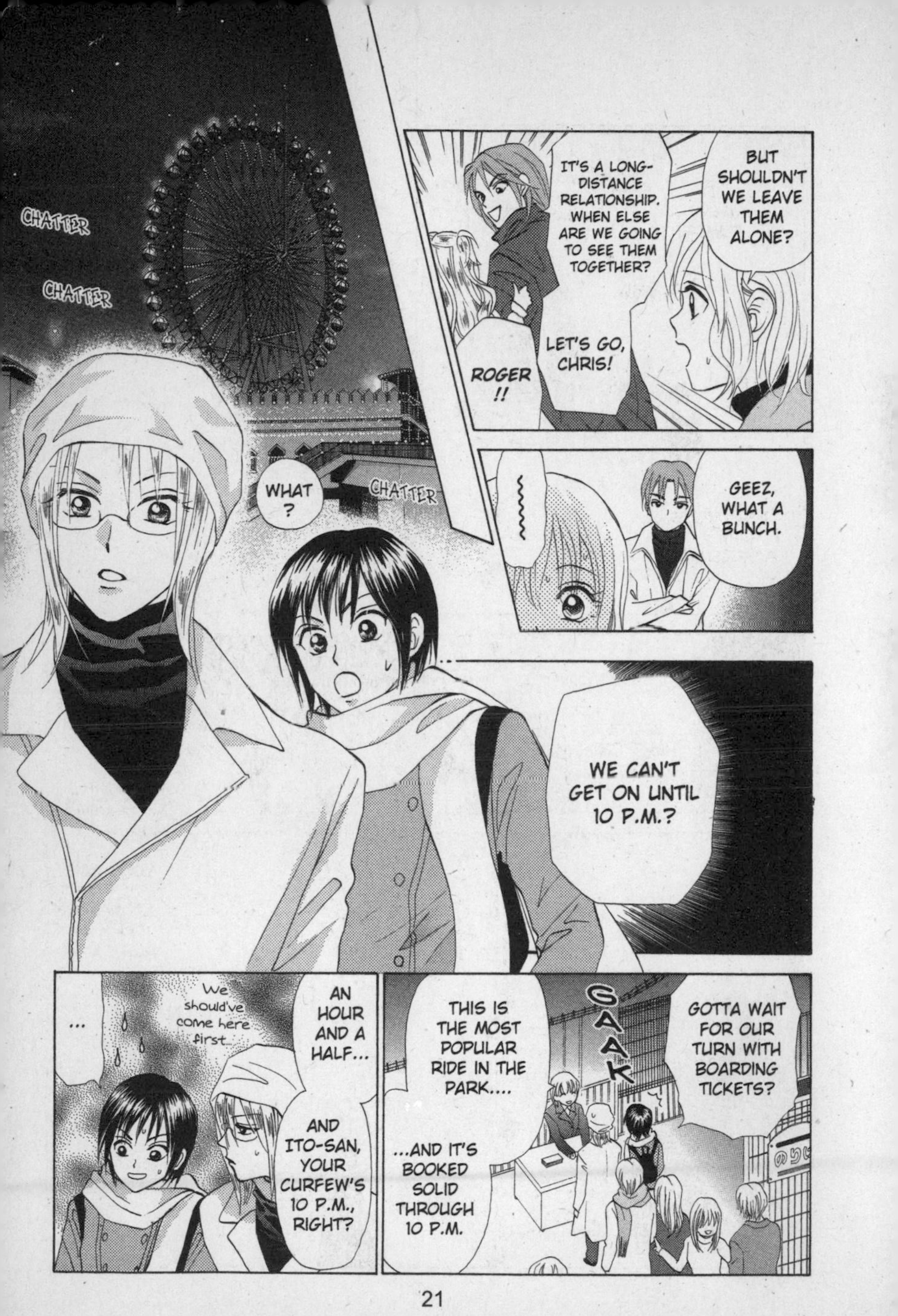
BUT SHOULDN'T WE LEAVE THEM ALONE?
IT'S A LONG-DISTANCE RELATIONSHIP. WHEN ELSE ARE WE GOING TO SEE THEM TOGETHER?
LET'S GO, CHRIS!
ROGER !!
GEEZ, WHAT A BUNCH.
...
WE CAN'T GET ON UNTIL 10 P.M.?
CHATTER
CHATTER
WHAT ?
CHATTER
GOTTA WAIT FOR OUR TURN WITH BOARDING TICKETS?
GAAK
THIS IS THE MOST POPULAR RIDE IN THE PARK....
...AND IT'S BOOKED SOLID THROUGH 10 P.M.
AN HOUR AND A HALF...
We should've come here first...
...
AND ITO-SAN, YOUR CURFEW'S 10 P.M., RIGHT?

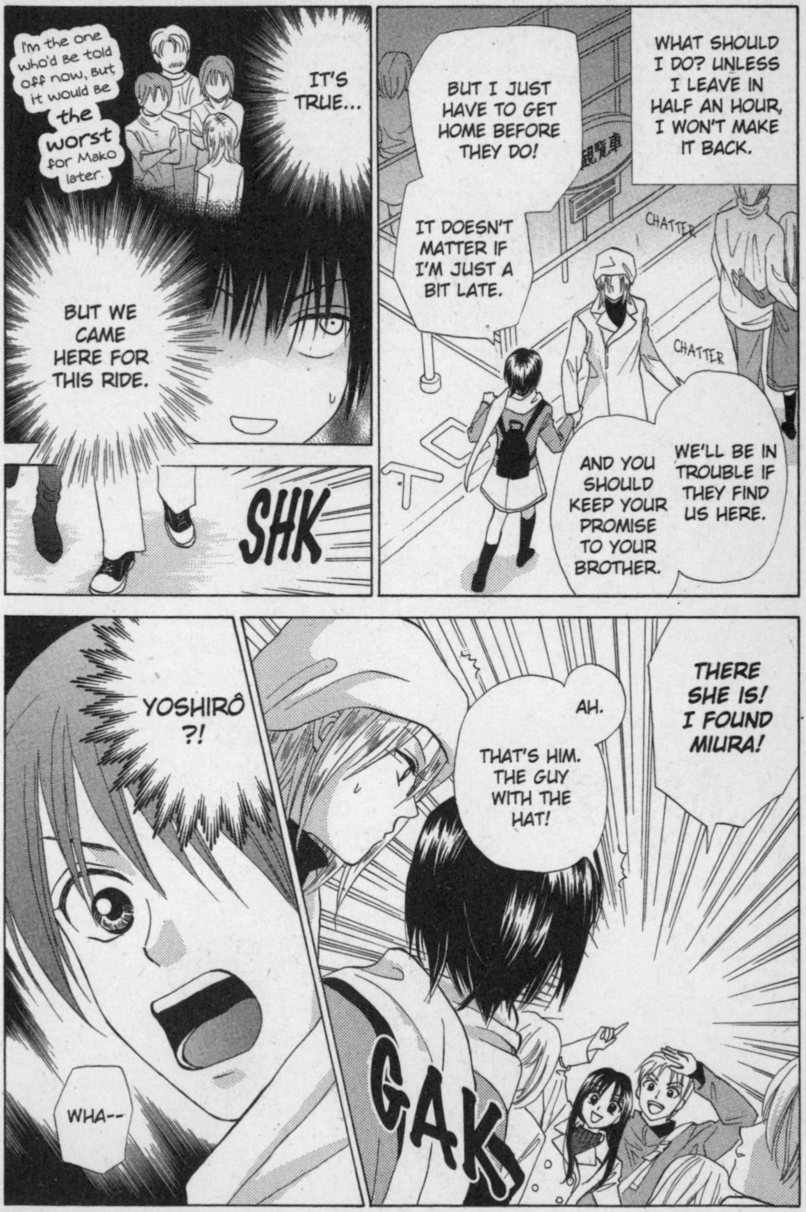
WHAT SHOULD I DO? UNLESS I LEAVE IN HALF AN HOUR, I WON'T MAKE IT BACK.
BUT I JUST HAVE TO GET HOME BEFORE THEY DO!
IT DOESN'T MATTER IF I'M JUST A BIT LATE.
CHATTER
CHATTER
WE'LL BE IN TROUBLE IF THEY FIND US HERE.
AND YOU SHOULD KEEP YOUR PROMISE TO YOUR BROTHER.
IT'S TRUE...
I'm the one who'd be told off now, but it would be the worst for Mako later.
BUT WE CAME HERE FOR THIS RIDE.
SHK
THERE SHE IS! I FOUND MIURA!
AH.
THAT'S HIM. THE GUY WITH THE HAT!
GAK
YOSHIRÔ ?!
WHA--

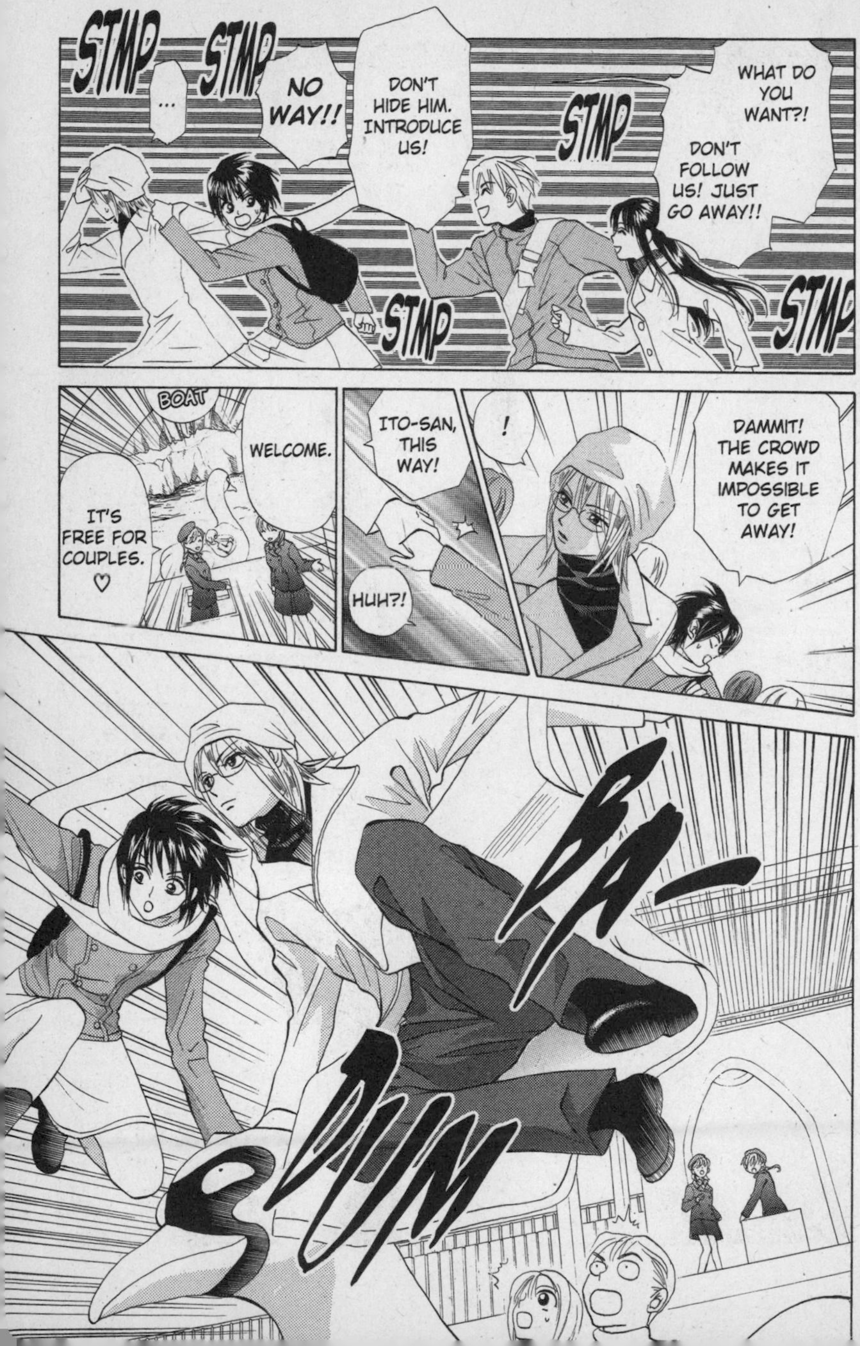
STMP
WHAT DO YOU WANT?!
DON'T FOLLOW US! JUST GO AWAY!!
STMP
DON'T HIDE HIM. INTRODUCE US!
STMP
NO WAY!!
STMP
...
STMP
DAMMIT! THE CROWD MAKES IT IMPOSSIBLE TO GET AWAY!
!
ITO-SAN, THIS WAY!
HUH?!
BOAT
WELCOME.
IT'S FREE FOR COUPLES. ♡
BA-

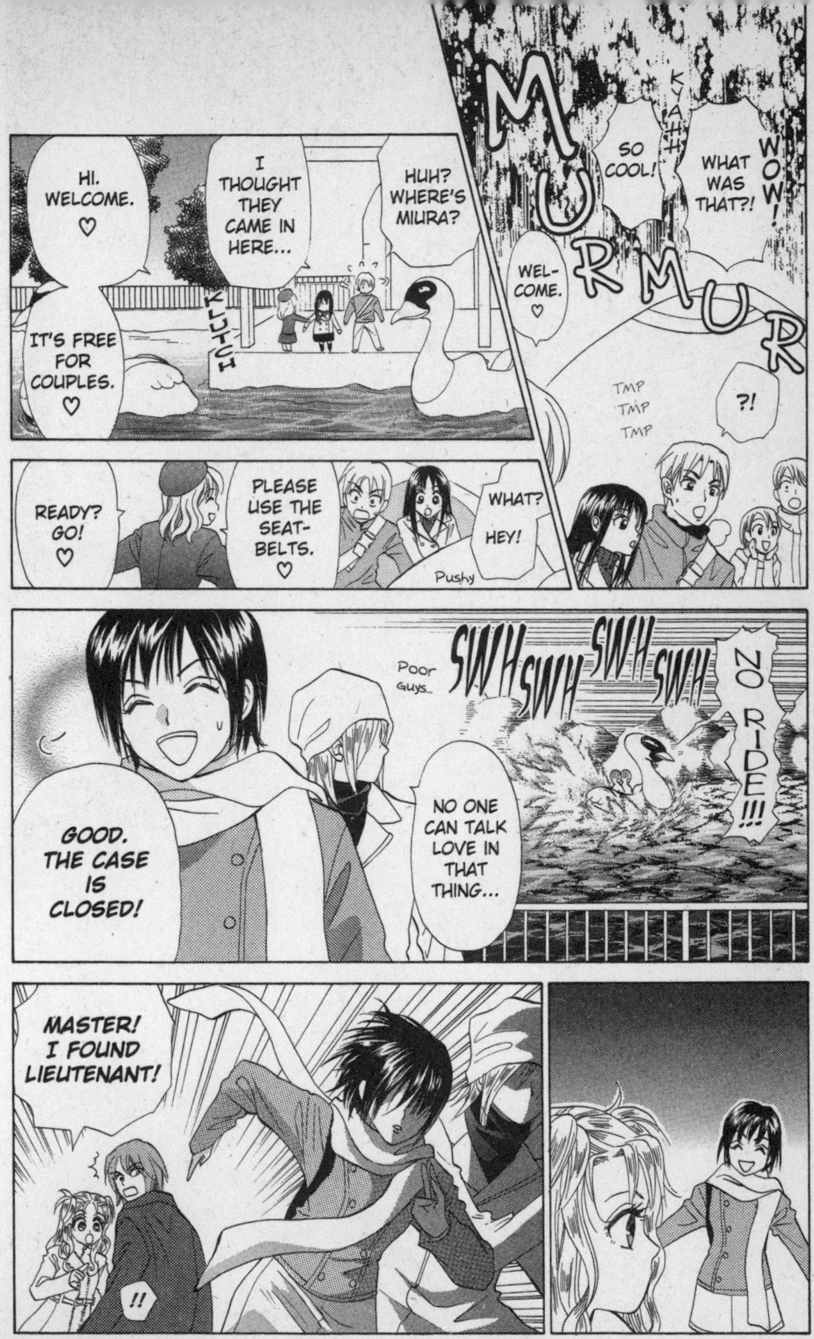

WOW!
WHAT WAS THAT?!
KYAHH
SO COOL!
MURMUR
WEL-COME. ♡
TMP TMP TMP
?!
HUH? WHERE'S MIURA?
I THOUGHT THEY CAME IN HERE...
KLUTCH
HI. WELCOME. ♡
IT'S FREE FOR COUPLES. ♡
WHAT? HEY!
Pushy
PLEASE USE THE SEAT-BELTS. ♡
READY? GO! ♡
NO RIDE!!!
SWH SWH SWH SWH
Poor Guys...
NO ONE CAN TALK LOVE IN THAT THING...
GOOD. THE CASE IS CLOSED!
MASTER! I FOUND LIEUTENANT!
!!

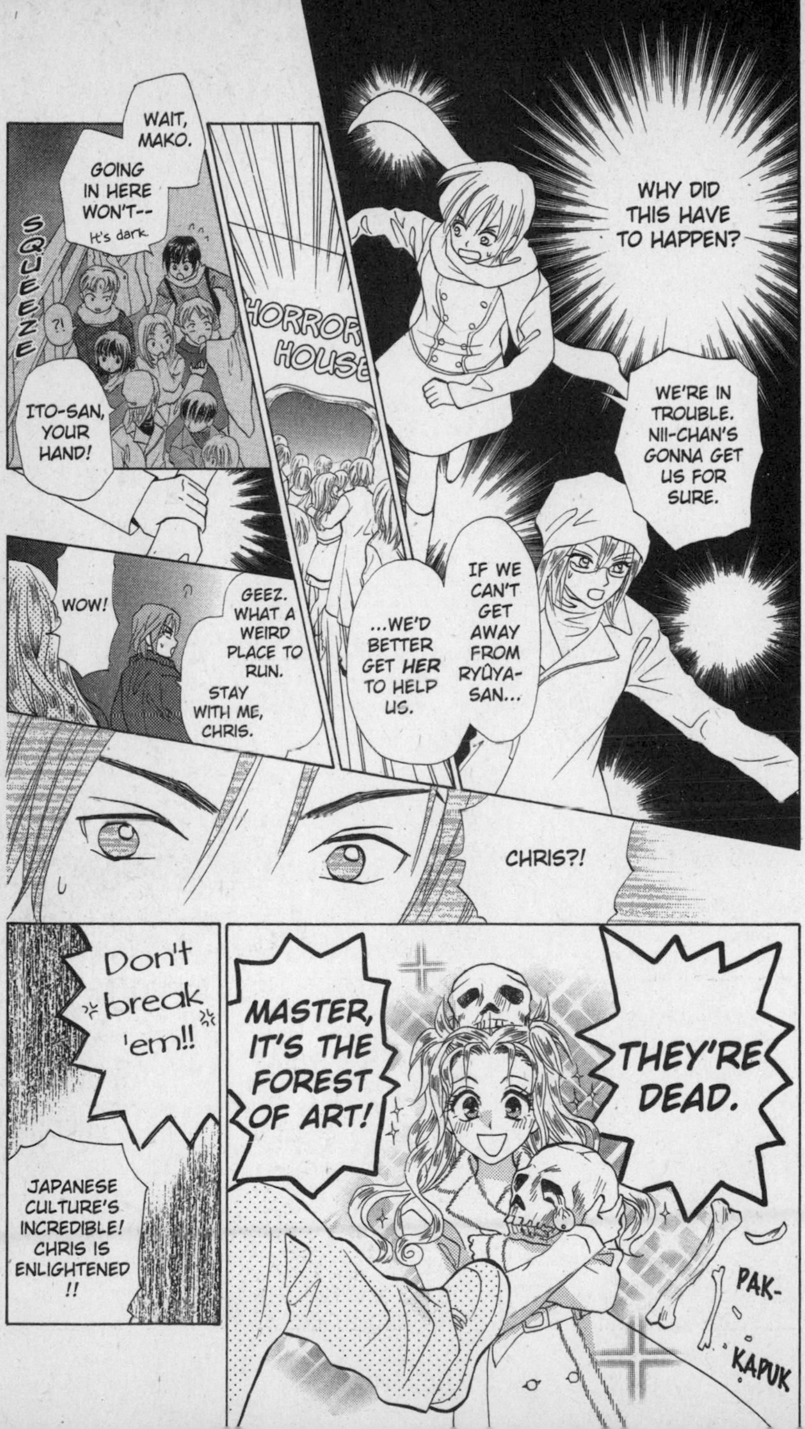
WHY DID THIS HAVE TO HAPPEN?
WE'RE IN TROUBLE. NII-CHAN'S GONNA GET US FOR SURE.
IF WE CAN'T GET AWAY FROM RYŪYA-SAN...
...WE'D BETTER GET HER TO HELP US.
HORROR HOUSE
WAIT, MAKO.
GOING IN HERE WON'T--
It's dark.
SQUEEZE
?!
ITO-SAN, YOUR HAND!
GEEZ. WHAT A WEIRD PLACE TO RUN.
STAY WITH ME, CHRIS.
WOW!
CHRIS?!
THEY'RE DEAD.
MASTER, IT'S THE FOREST OF ART!
PAK-
KAPUK
Don't break 'em!!
JAPANESE CULTURE'S INCREDIBLE! CHRIS IS ENLIGHTENED!!

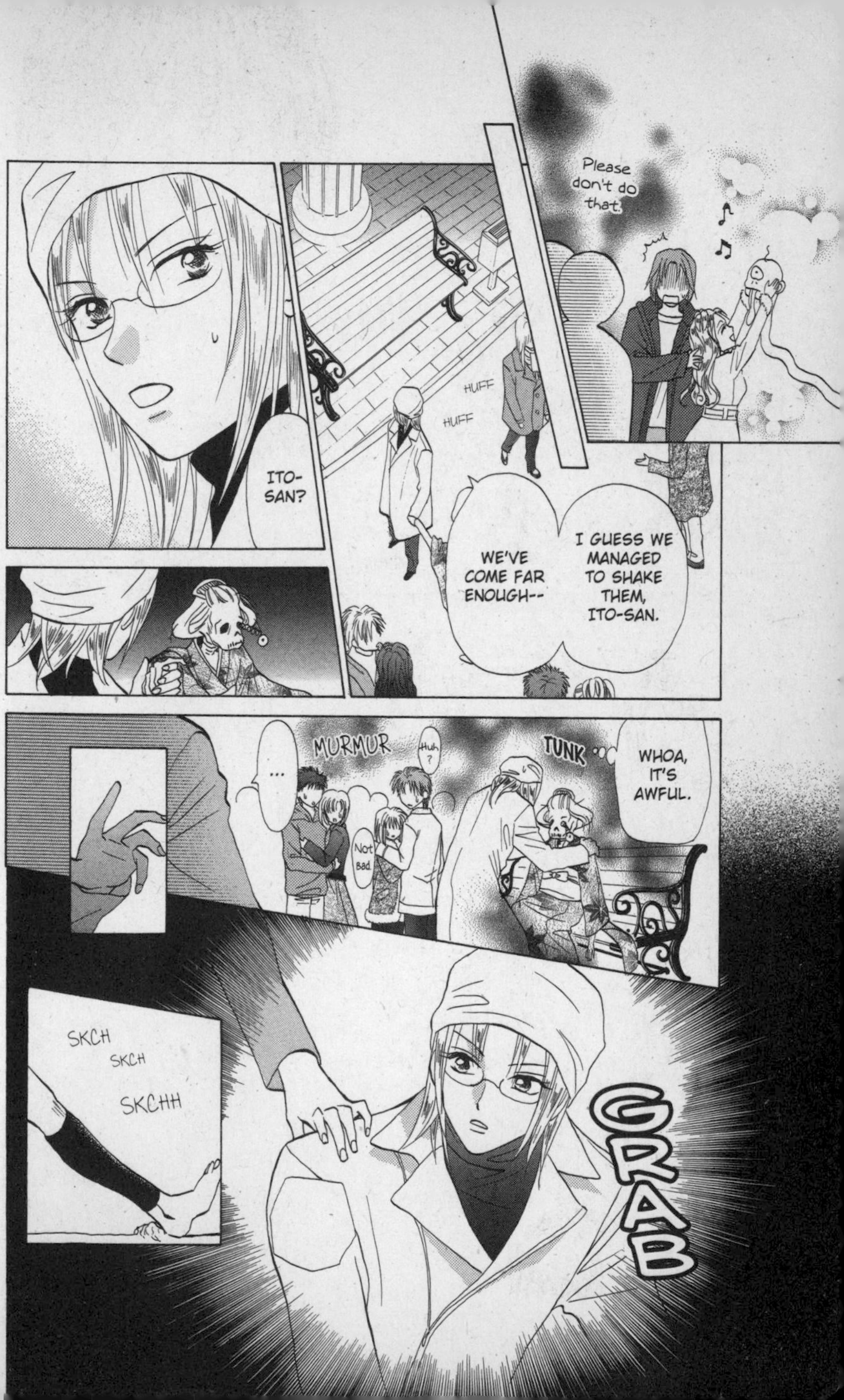
Please don't do that.
HUFF
HUFF
WE'VE COME FAR ENOUGH--
I GUESS WE MANAGED TO SHAKE THEM, ITO-SAN.
ITO-SAN?
WHOA, IT'S AWFUL.
TUNK
Huh?
MURMUR
Not bad.
...
GRAB
SKCH
SKCH
SKCHH

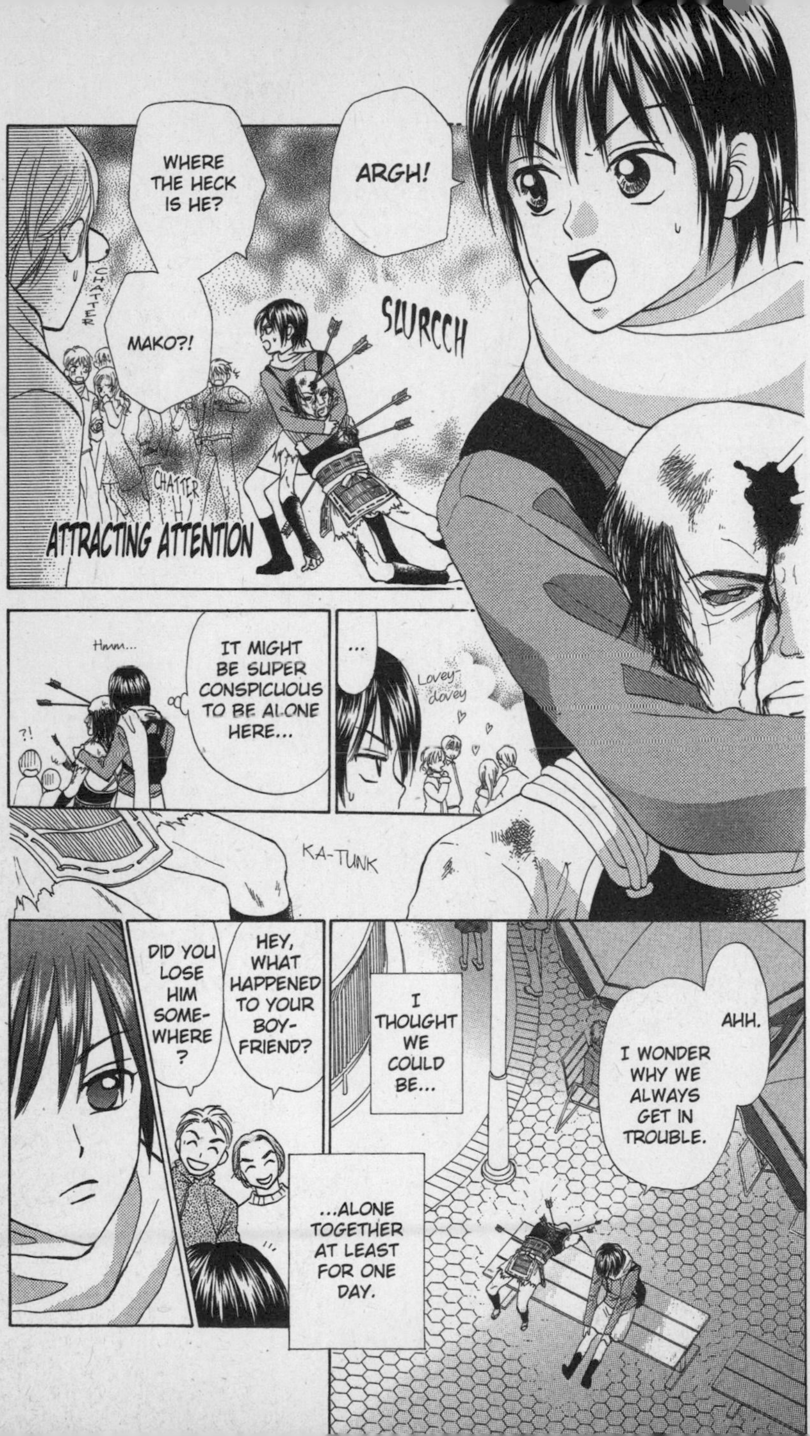
ARGH!
WHERE THE HECK IS HE?
SLURCCH
MAKO?!
CHATTER
CHATTER
ATTRACTING ATTENTION
...
Lovey-dovey
Hmm...
IT MIGHT BE SUPER CONSPICUOUS TO BE ALONE HERE...
?!
KA-TUNK
AHH.
I WONDER WHY WE ALWAYS GET IN TROUBLE.
I THOUGHT WE COULD BE...
...ALONE TOGETHER AT LEAST FOR ONE DAY.
HEY, WHAT HAPPENED TO YOUR BOY-FRIEND?
DID YOU LOSE HIM SOME-WHERE?

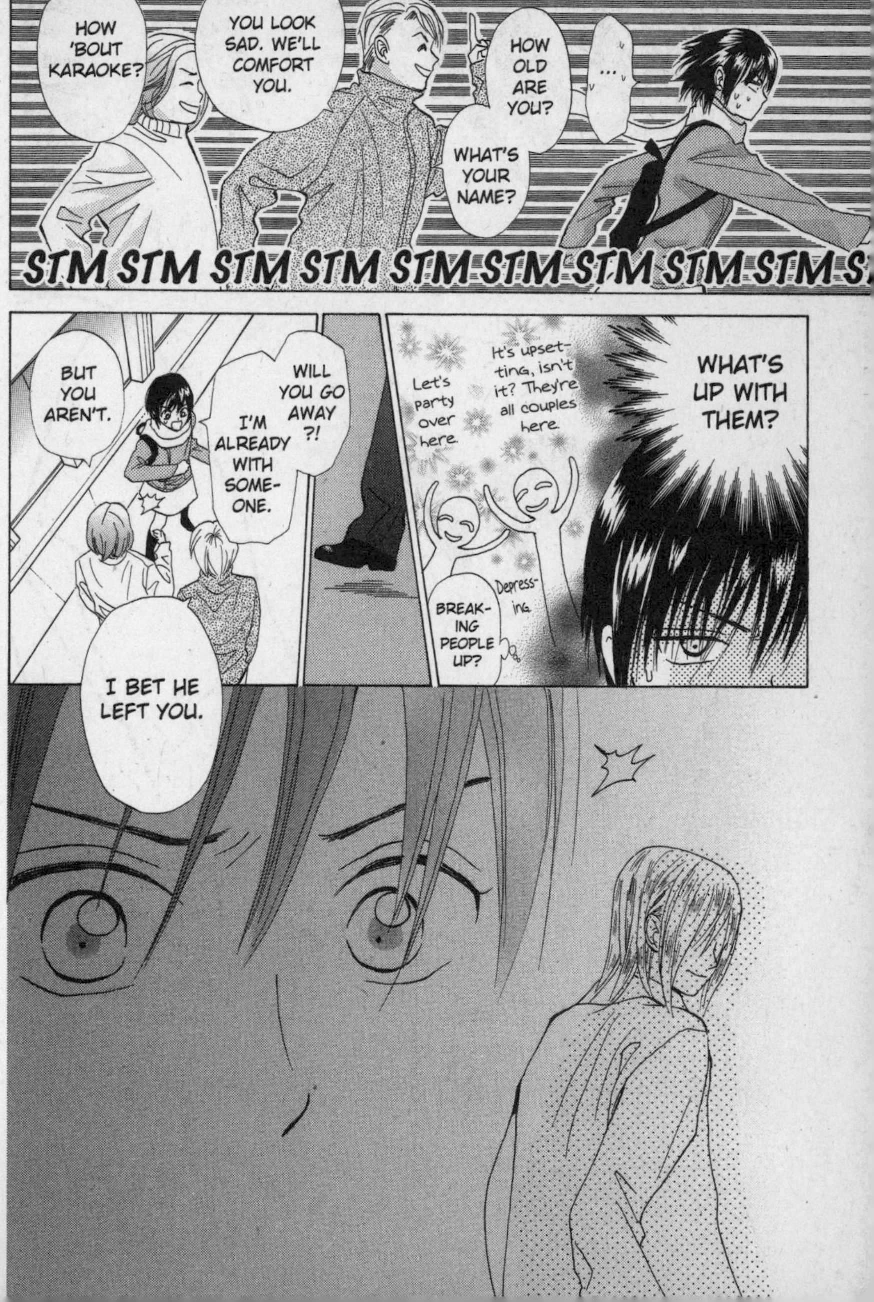
...
HOW OLD ARE YOU?
WHAT'S YOUR NAME?
YOU LOOK SAD. WE'LL COMFORT YOU.
HOW 'BOUT KARAOKE?
STM STM STM STM STM STM STM STM STM S
WHAT'S UP WITH THEM?
It's upsetting, isn't it? They're all couples here.
Let's party over here.
Depressing.
BREAKING PEOPLE UP?
WILL YOU GO AWAY?!
I'M ALREADY WITH SOMEONE.
BUT YOU AREN'T.
I BET HE LEFT YOU.

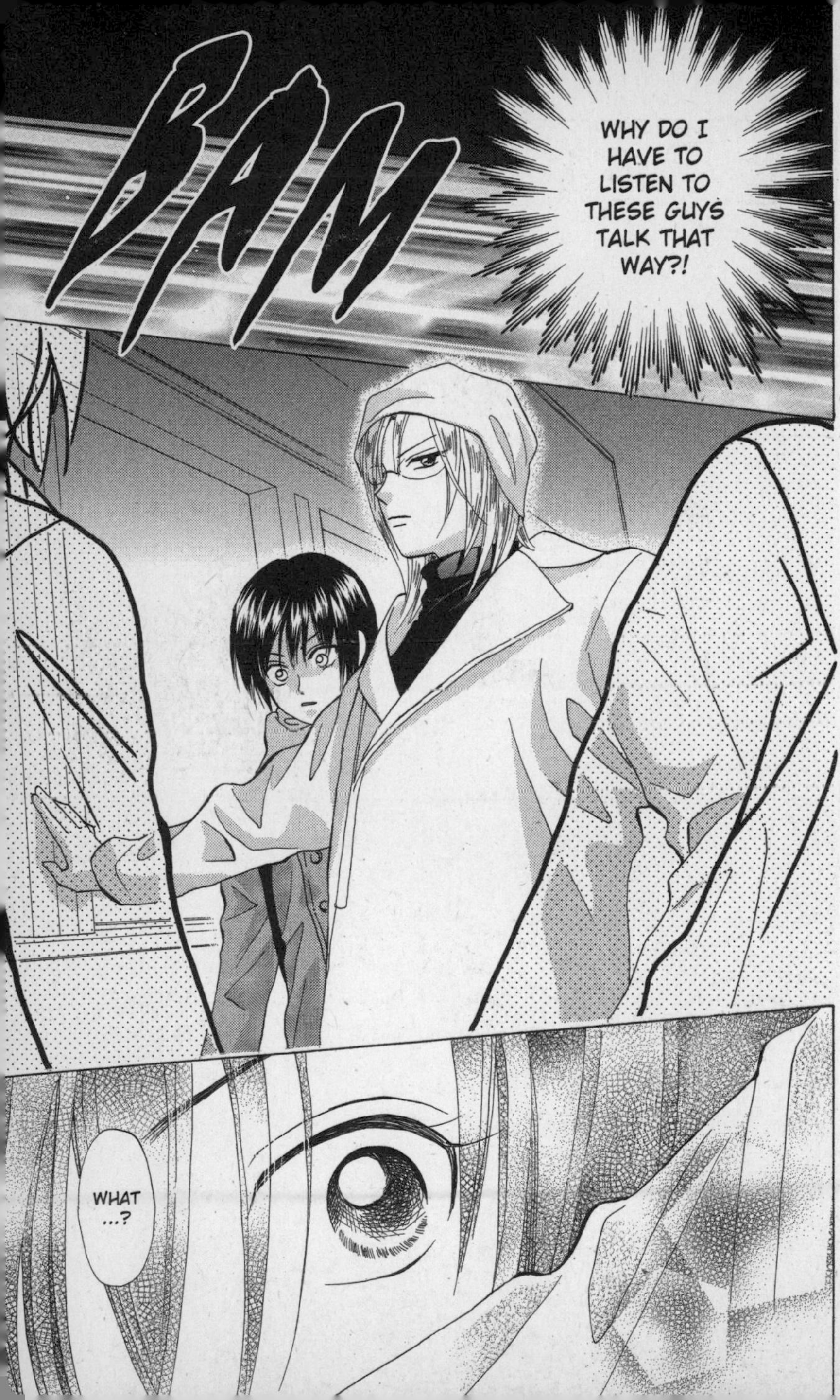
BAM
WHY DO I HAVE TO LISTEN TO THESE GUYS TALK THAT WAY?!
WHAT ...?

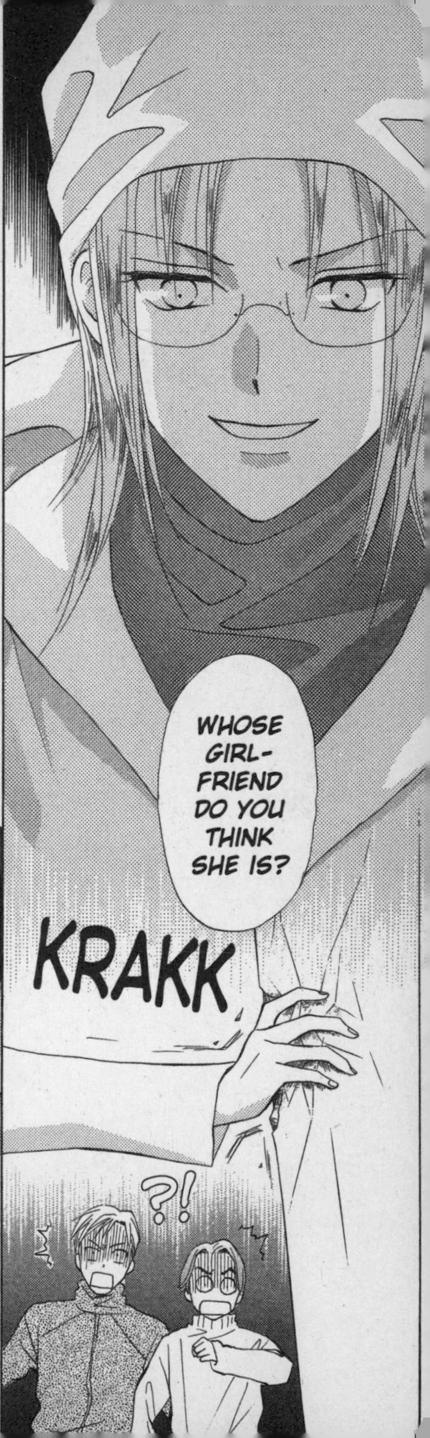
WHOSE GIRL-FRIEND DO YOU THINK SHE IS?
KRAKK
?!

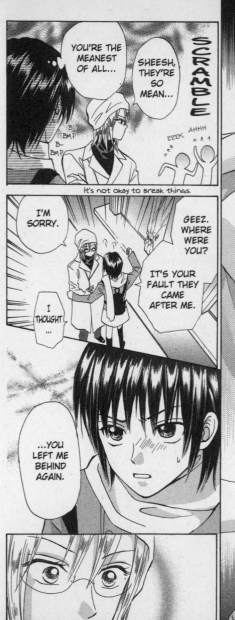

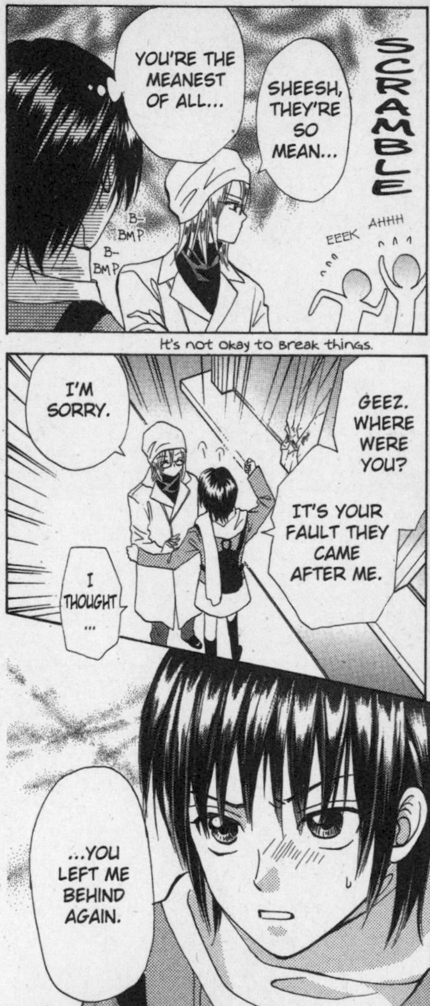
SCRAMBLE
SHEESH, THEY'RE SO MEAN...
YOU'RE THE MEANEST OF ALL...
AHHH
EEEK
B-BMP B-BMP
It's not okay to break things.
GEEZ. WHERE WERE YOU?
IT'S YOUR FAULT THEY CAME AFTER ME.
I'M SORRY.
I THOUGHT...
...YOU LEFT ME BEHIND AGAIN.

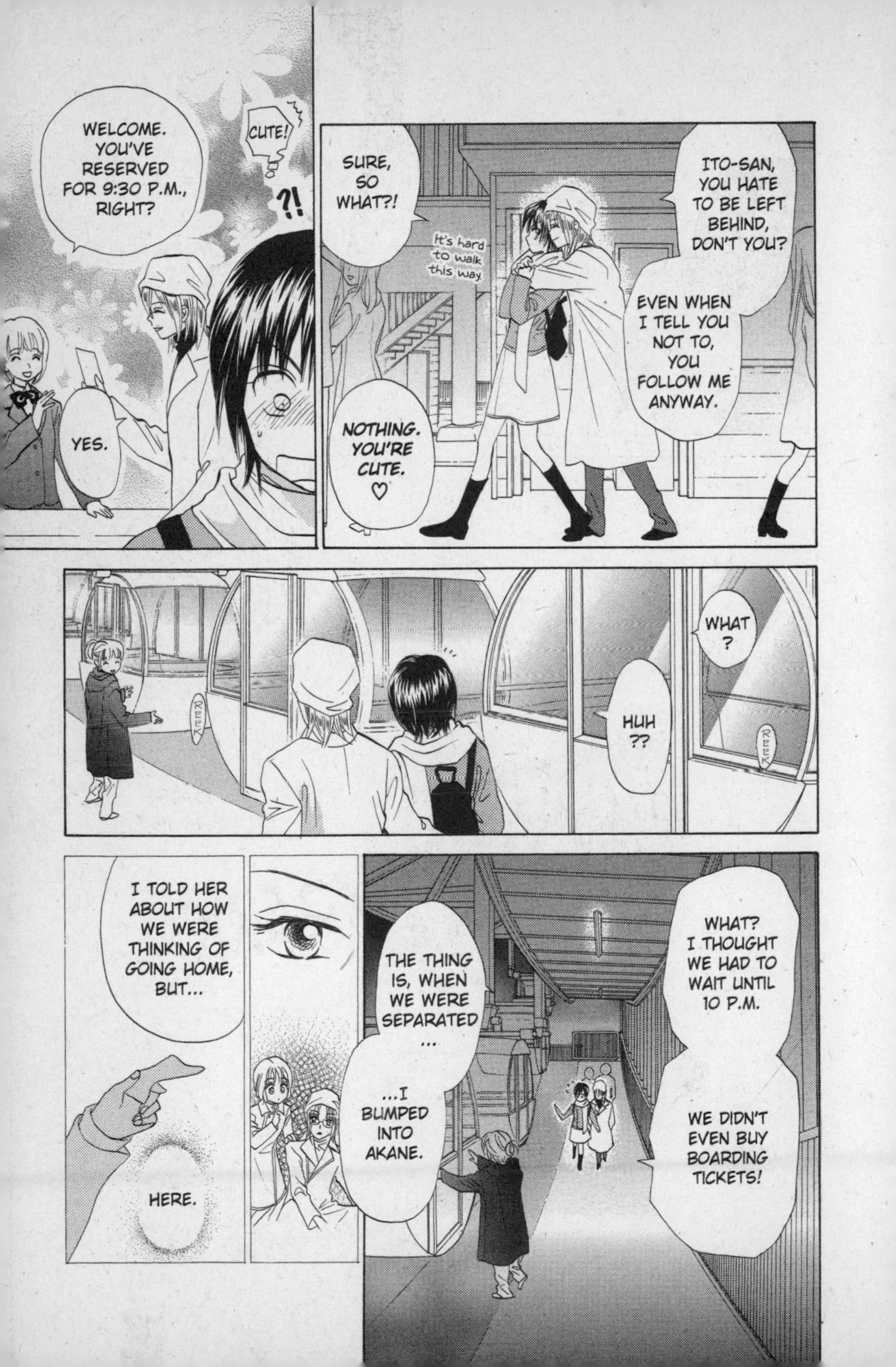
ITO-SAN, YOU HATE TO BE LEFT BEHIND, DON'T YOU?
EVEN WHEN I TELL YOU NOT TO, YOU FOLLOW ME ANYWAY.
SURE, SO WHAT?!
It's hard to walk this way.
NOTHING. YOU'RE CUTE. ♡
CUTE!
?!
WELCOME. YOU'VE RESERVED FOR 9:30 P.M., RIGHT?
YES.
WHAT ?
HUH ??
REEK
REEK
WHAT? I THOUGHT WE HAD TO WAIT UNTIL 10 P.M.
WE DIDN'T EVEN BUY BOARDING TICKETS!
THE THING IS, WHEN WE WERE SEPARATED ...
...I BUMPED INTO AKANE.
I TOLD HER ABOUT HOW WE WERE THINKING OF GOING HOME, BUT...
HERE.

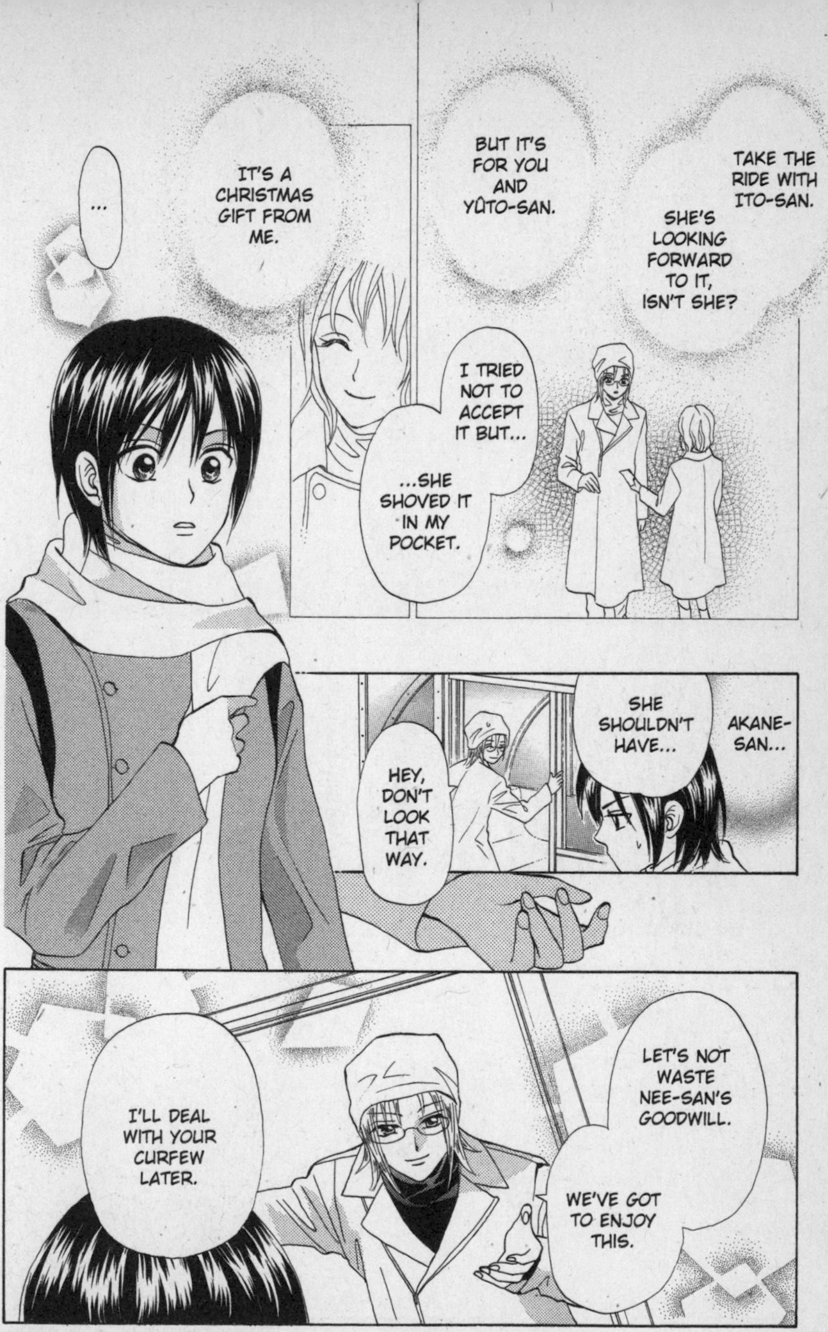
TAKE THE RIDE WITH ITO-SAN.
BUT IT'S FOR YOU AND YÛTO-SAN.
SHE'S LOOKING FORWARD TO IT, ISN'T SHE?
I TRIED NOT TO ACCEPT IT BUT...
...SHE SHOVED IT IN MY POCKET.
IT'S A CHRISTMAS GIFT FROM ME.
...
AKANE-SAN...
SHE SHOULDN'T HAVE...
HEY, DON'T LOOK THAT WAY.
LET'S NOT WASTE NEE-SAN'S GOODWILL.
WE'VE GOT TO ENJOY THIS.
I'LL DEAL WITH YOUR CURFEW LATER.

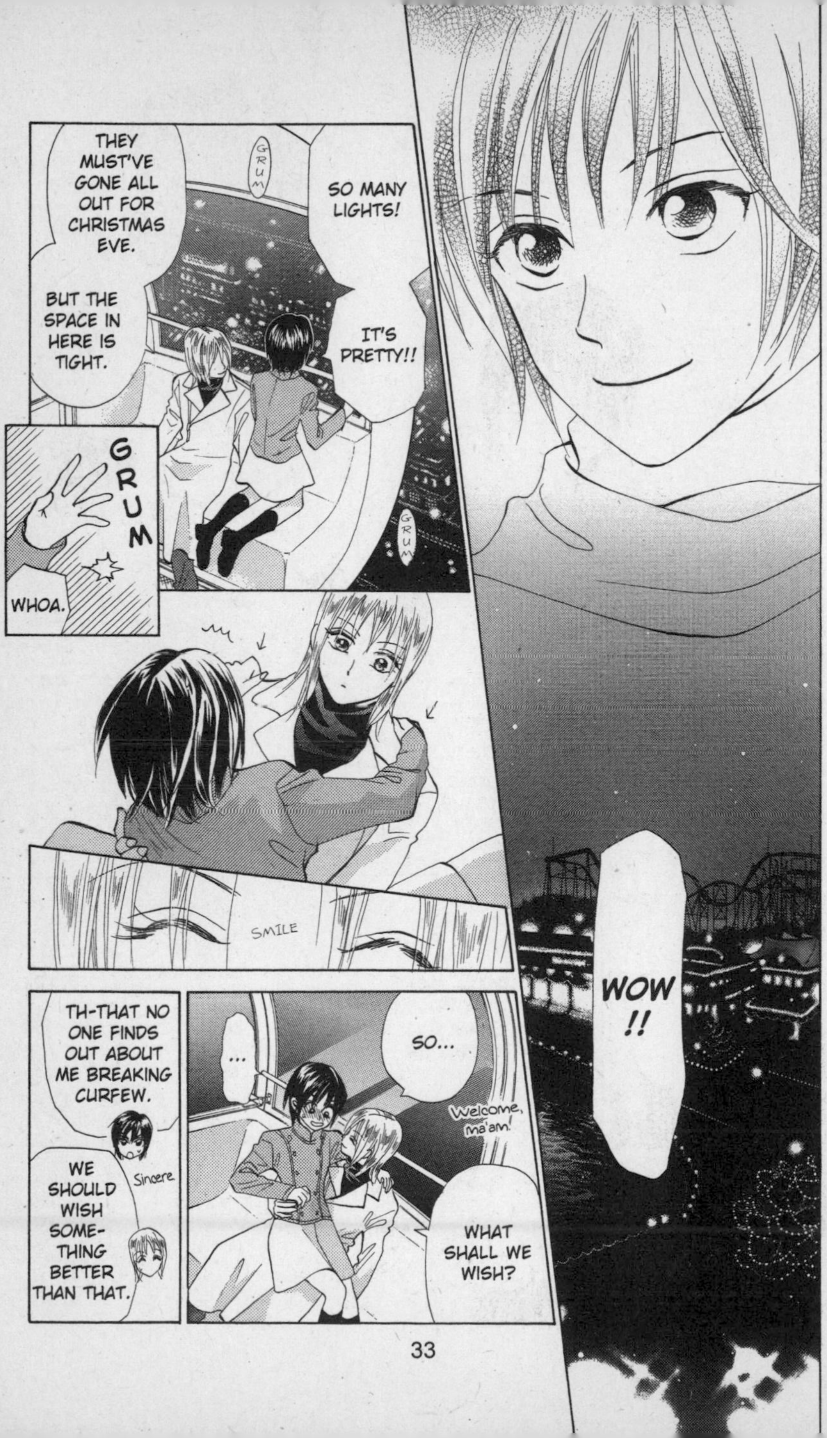
WOW !!
SO MANY LIGHTS!
IT'S PRETTY!!
GRUM
THEY MUST'VE GONE ALL OUT FOR CHRISTMAS EVE.
BUT THE SPACE IN HERE IS TIGHT.
GRUM
GRUM
WHOA.
SMILE
SO...
...
Welcome, Ma'am!
WHAT SHALL WE WISH?
TH-THAT NO ONE FINDS OUT ABOUT ME BREAKING CURFEW.
Sincere
WE SHOULD WISH SOME-THING BETTER THAN THAT.

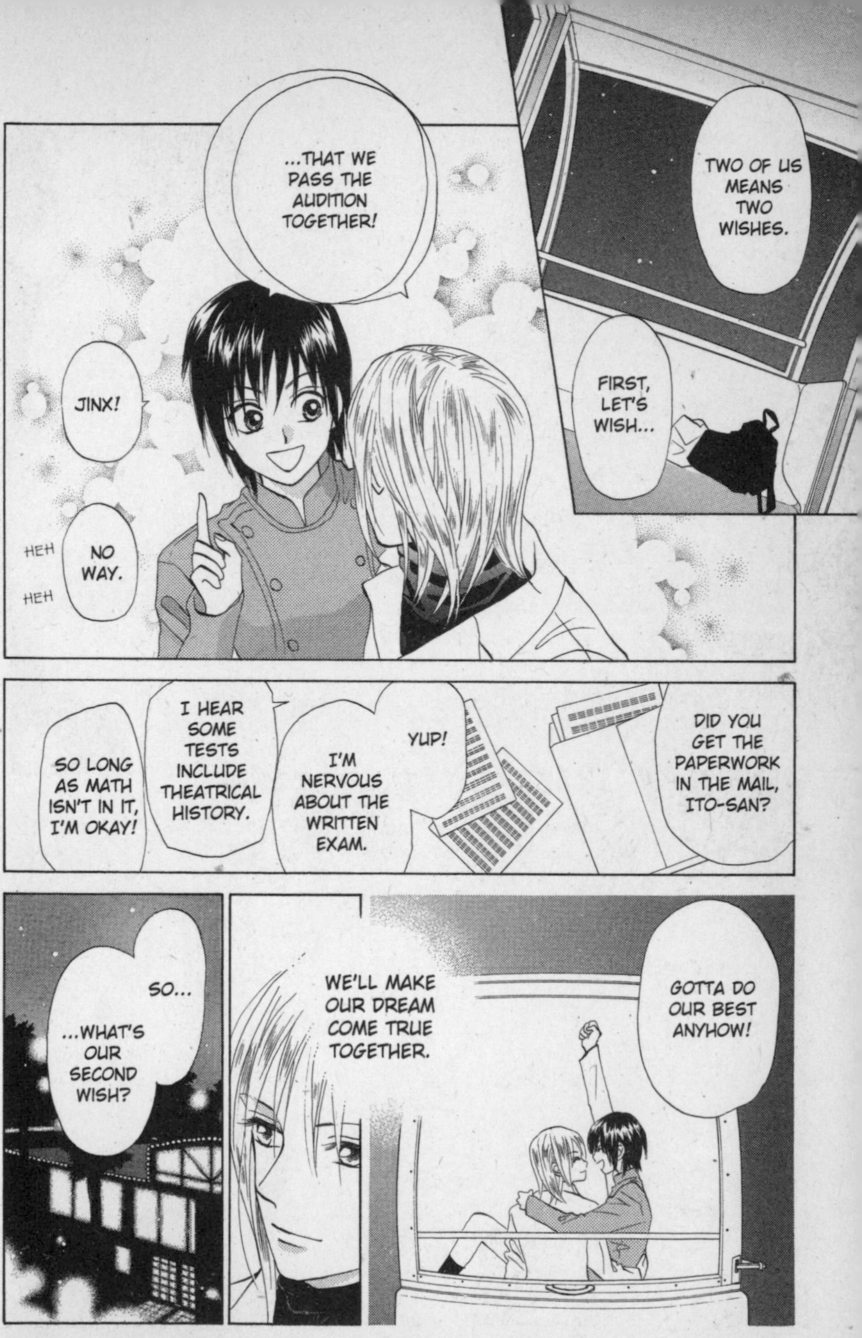
TWO OF US MEANS TWO WISHES.
FIRST, LET'S WISH...
...THAT WE PASS THE AUDITION TOGETHER!
JINX!
HEH HEH
NO WAY.
DID YOU GET THE PAPERWORK IN THE MAIL, ITO-SAN?
YUP!
I'M NERVOUS ABOUT THE WRITTEN EXAM.
I HEAR SOME TESTS INCLUDE THEATRICAL HISTORY.
SO LONG AS MATH ISN'T IN IT, I'M OKAY!
GOTTA DO OUR BEST ANYHOW!
WE'LL MAKE OUR DREAM COME TRUE TOGETHER.
SO...
...WHAT'S OUR SECOND WISH?

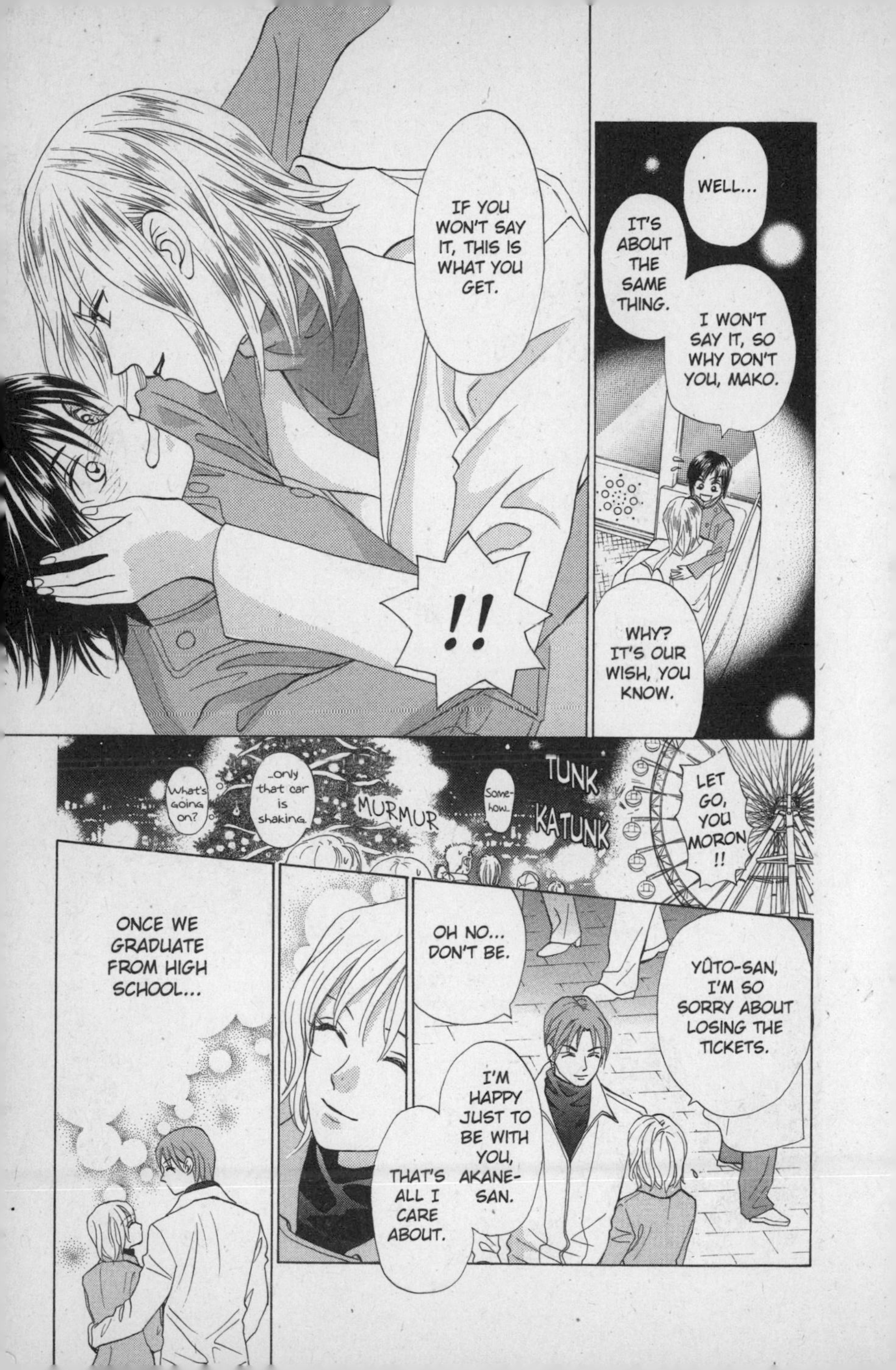

WELL...
IT'S ABOUT THE SAME THING.
I WON'T SAY IT, SO WHY DON'T YOU, MAKO.
WHY? IT'S OUR WISH, YOU KNOW.
IF YOU WON'T SAY IT, THIS IS WHAT YOU GET.
!!
LET GO, YOU MORON !!
TUNK
KATUNK
Somehow...
MURMUR
...only that car is shaking.
What's going on?
YÛTO-SAN, I'M SO SORRY ABOUT LOSING THE TICKETS.
OH NO... DON'T BE.
I'M HAPPY JUST TO BE WITH YOU, AKANE-SAN.
THAT'S ALL I CARE ABOUT.
ONCE WE GRADUATE FROM HIGH SCHOOL...

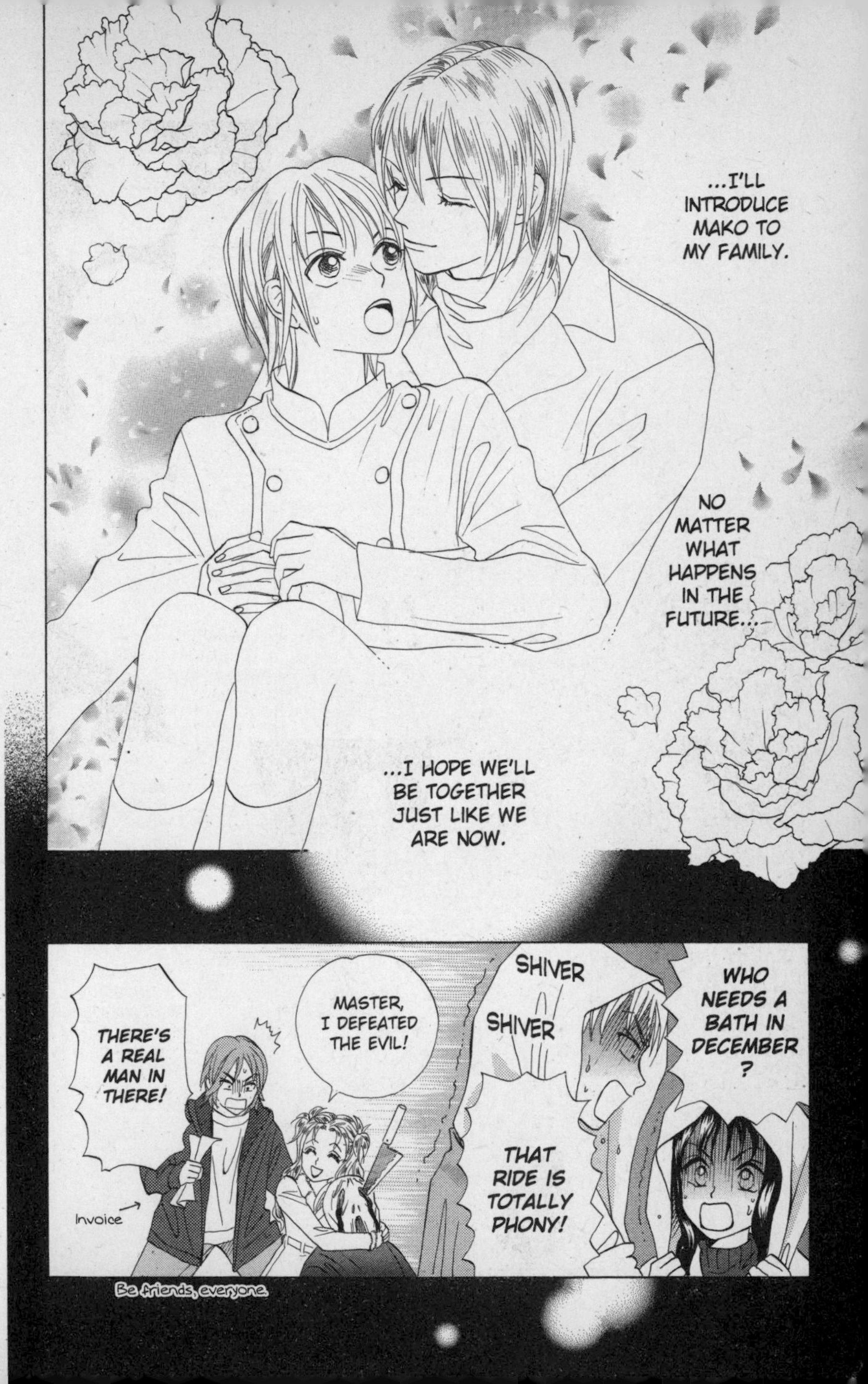
...I'LL INTRODUCE MAKO TO MY FAMILY.
NO MATTER WHAT HAPPENS IN THE FUTURE...
...I HOPE WE'LL BE TOGETHER JUST LIKE WE ARE NOW.
WHO NEEDS A BATH IN DECEMBER?
SHIVER
SHIVER
THAT RIDE IS TOTALLY PHONY!
MASTER, I DEFEATED THE EVIL!
THERE'S A REAL MAN IN THERE!
Invoice
Be friends, everyone.

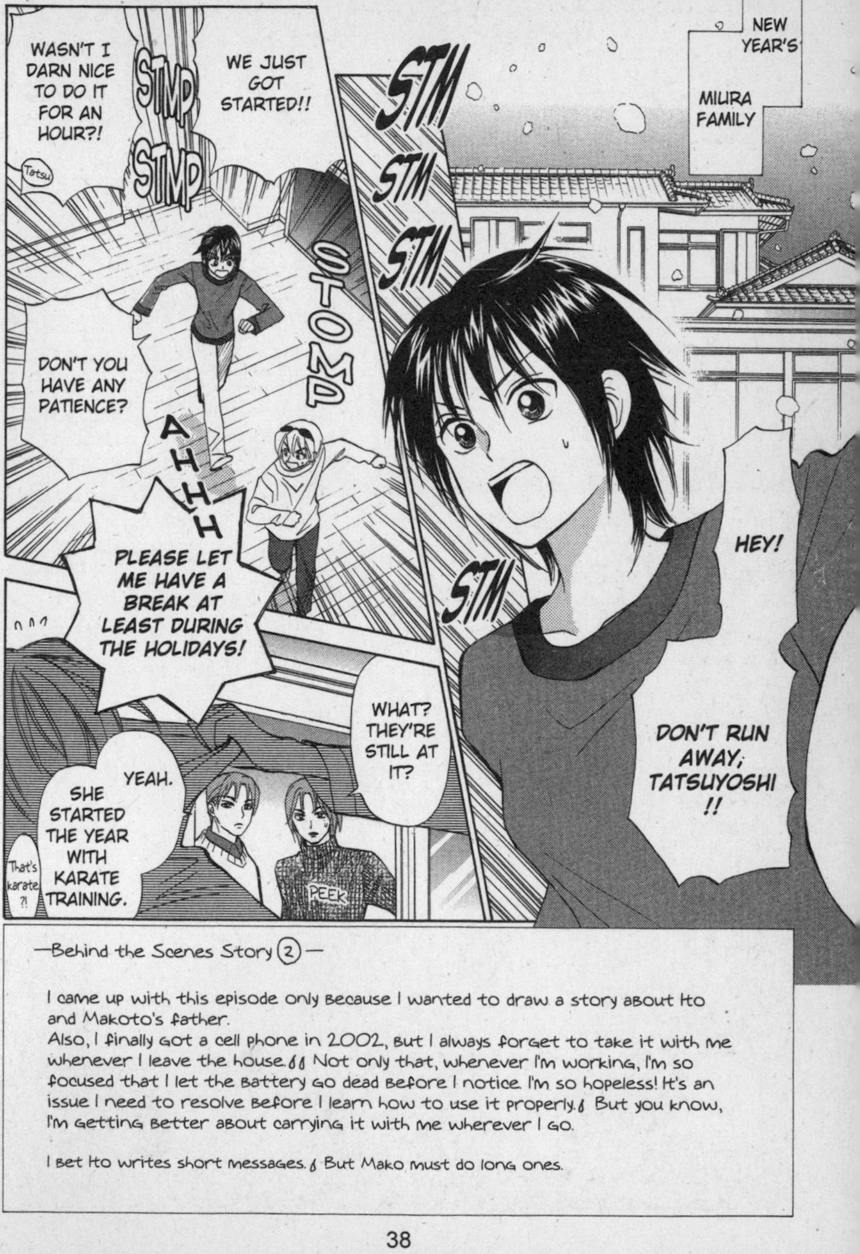
NEW YEAR'S
MIURA FAMILY
STM
STM
STM
HEY!
DON'T RUN AWAY; TATSUYOSHI!!
STM
WE JUST GOT STARTED!!
STMP
STMP
WASN'T I DARN NICE TO DO IT FOR AN HOUR?!
Tatsu
STOMP
DON'T YOU HAVE ANY PATIENCE?
AHHHH
PLEASE LET ME HAVE A BREAK AT LEAST DURING THE HOLIDAYS!
WHAT? THEY'RE STILL AT IT?
YEAH.
SHE STARTED THE YEAR WITH KARATE TRAINING.
That's karate?!
PEEK

—Behind the Scenes Story ②—

I came up with this episode only because I wanted to draw a story about Ito and Makoto's father.
Also, I finally got a cell phone in 2002, but I always forget to take it with me whenever I leave the house. Not only that, whenever I'm working, I'm so focused that I let the battery go dead before I notice. I'm so hopeless! It's an issue I need to resolve before I learn how to use it properly. But you know, I'm getting better about carrying it with me wherever I go.

I bet Ito writes short messages. But Mako must do long ones.

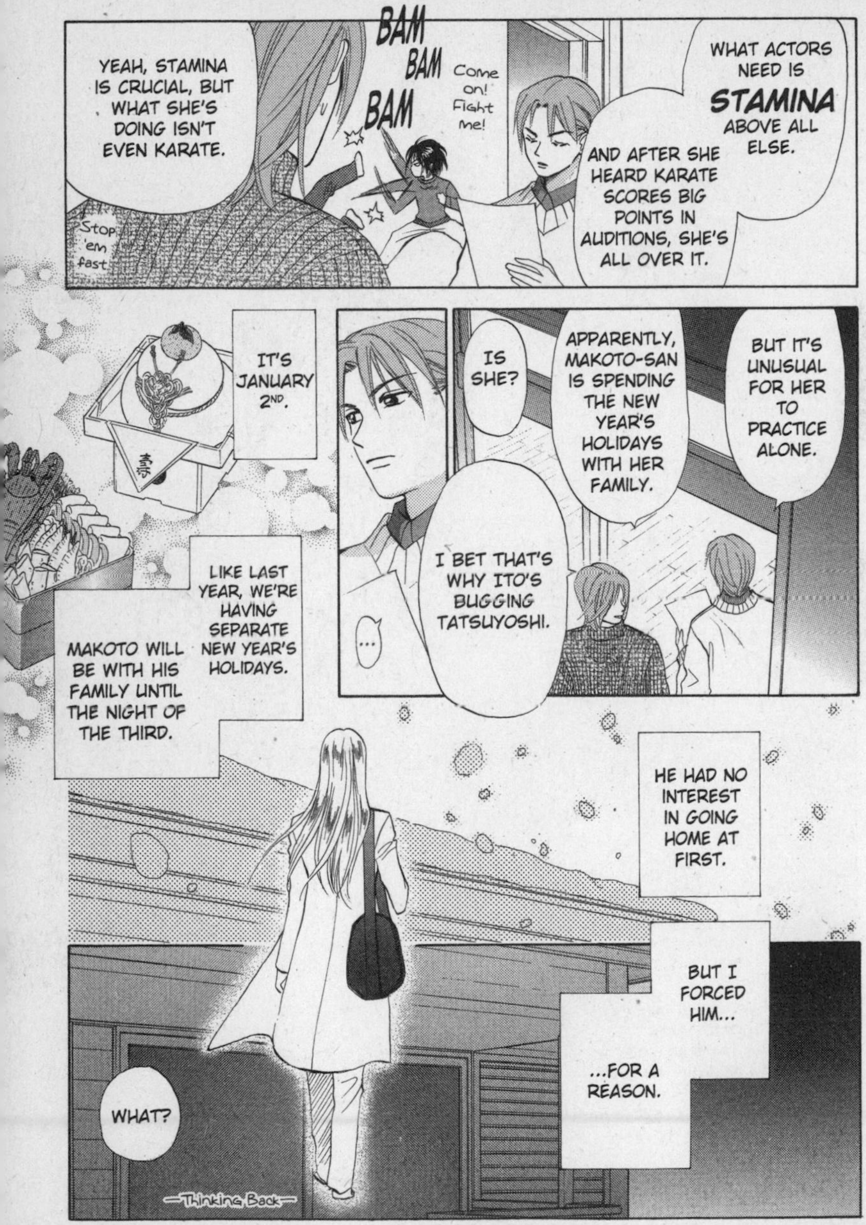
WHAT ACTORS NEED IS STAMINA ABOVE ALL ELSE.
AND AFTER SHE HEARD KARATE SCORES BIG POINTS IN AUDITIONS, SHE'S ALL OVER IT.
Come on! Fight me!
BAM BAM BAM
YEAH, STAMINA IS CRUCIAL, BUT WHAT SHE'S DOING ISN'T EVEN KARATE.
Stop 'em fast
BUT IT'S UNUSUAL FOR HER TO PRACTICE ALONE.
APPARENTLY, MAKOTO-SAN IS SPENDING THE NEW YEAR'S HOLIDAYS WITH HER FAMILY.
IS SHE?
I BET THAT'S WHY ITO'S BUGGING TATSUYOSHI.
...
IT'S JANUARY 2ND.
LIKE LAST YEAR, WE'RE HAVING SEPARATE NEW YEAR'S HOLIDAYS.
MAKOTO WILL BE WITH HIS FAMILY UNTIL THE NIGHT OF THE THIRD.
HE HAD NO INTEREST IN GOING HOME AT FIRST.
BUT I FORCED HIM...
...FOR A REASON.
WHAT?
—Thinking Back—

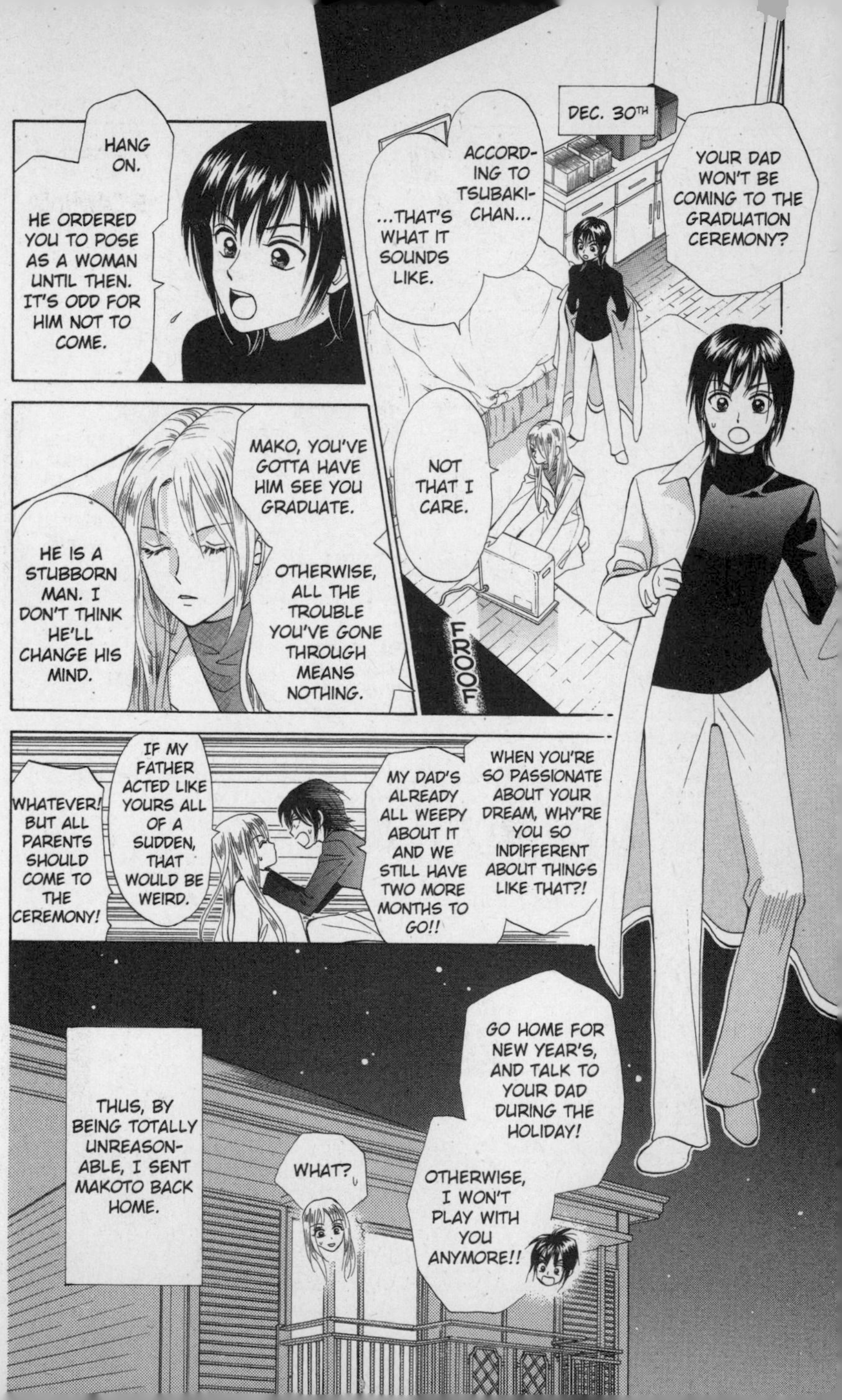

DEC. 30TH
YOUR DAD WON'T BE COMING TO THE GRADUATION CEREMONY?
ACCORD-ING TO TSUBAKI-CHAN...
...THAT'S WHAT IT SOUNDS LIKE.
NOT THAT I CARE.
FROOF
HANG ON.
HE ORDERED YOU TO POSE AS A WOMAN UNTIL THEN. IT'S ODD FOR HIM NOT TO COME.
MAKO, YOU'VE GOTTA HAVE HIM SEE YOU GRADUATE.
OTHERWISE, ALL THE TROUBLE YOU'VE GONE THROUGH MEANS NOTHING.
HE IS A STUBBORN MAN. I DON'T THINK HE'LL CHANGE HIS MIND.
WHEN YOU'RE SO PASSIONATE ABOUT YOUR DREAM, WHY'RE YOU SO INDIFFERENT ABOUT THINGS LIKE THAT?!
MY DAD'S ALREADY ALL WEEPY ABOUT IT AND WE STILL HAVE TWO MORE MONTHS TO GO!!
IF MY FATHER ACTED LIKE YOURS ALL OF A SUDDEN, THAT WOULD BE WEIRD.
WHATEVER! BUT ALL PARENTS SHOULD COME TO THE CEREMONY!
GO HOME FOR NEW YEAR'S, AND TALK TO YOUR DAD DURING THE HOLIDAY!
OTHERWISE, I WON'T PLAY WITH YOU ANYMORE!!
WHAT?
THUS, BY BEING TOTALLY UNREASON-ABLE, I SENT MAKOTO BACK HOME.

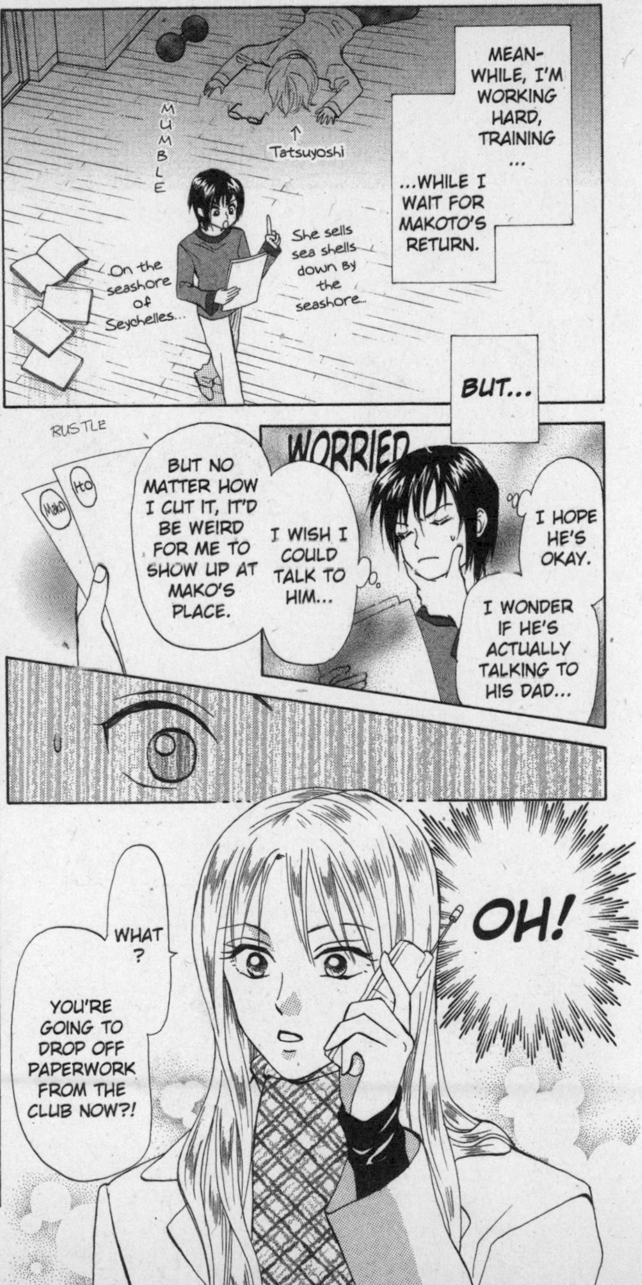
MEAN-WHILE, I'M WORKING HARD, TRAINING ...
...WHILE I WAIT FOR MAKOTO'S RETURN.
Tatsuyoshi
MUMBLE
She sells sea shells down by the seashore...
On the seashore of Seychelles...
BUT...
WORRIED
I HOPE HE'S OKAY.
I WONDER IF HE'S ACTUALLY TALKING TO HIS DAD...
I WISH I COULD TALK TO HIM...
BUT NO MATTER HOW I CUT IT, IT'D BE WEIRD FOR ME TO SHOW UP AT MAKO'S PLACE.
RUSTLE
Ito
Mako
OH!
WHAT?
YOU'RE GOING TO DROP OFF PAPERWORK FROM THE CLUB NOW?!

QUESTION CORNER

● I read your comments in the magazine that you made a mistake while coloring the Romeo-Juliet splash page for volume 12 and that you had to glue a piece of paper on top to correct it. Will you tell us which part it was?

Ⓔ Tons of readers asked the same question. Everyone, you do pay attention to every detail, don't you?! If you look at it in color, I'm sure you can tell, but in black and white, it's impossible.

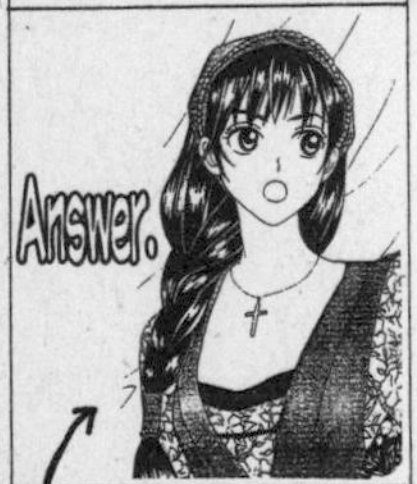
Answer.

I painted her right arm behind her hair in the same red used next to it. I glued a piece of paper in a hurry and drew in the flower pattern.

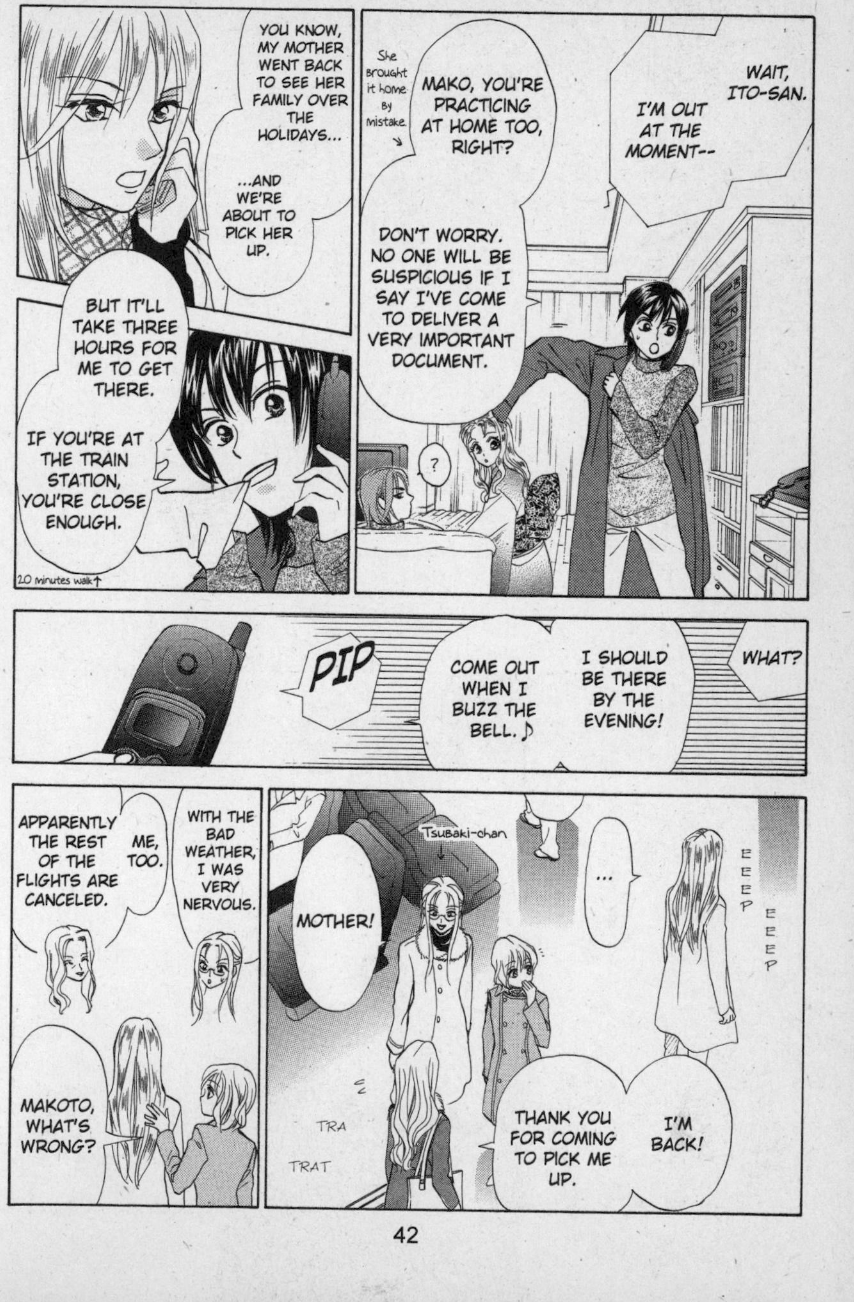
WAIT, ITO-SAN.
I'M OUT AT THE MOMENT--
MAKO, YOU'RE PRACTICING AT HOME TOO, RIGHT?
She brought it home by mistake.
DON'T WORRY. NO ONE WILL BE SUSPICIOUS IF I SAY I'VE COME TO DELIVER A VERY IMPORTANT DOCUMENT.
?
YOU KNOW, MY MOTHER WENT BACK TO SEE HER FAMILY OVER THE HOLIDAYS...
...AND WE'RE ABOUT TO PICK HER UP.
BUT IT'LL TAKE THREE HOURS FOR ME TO GET THERE.
IF YOU'RE AT THE TRAIN STATION, YOU'RE CLOSE ENOUGH.
20 minutes walk↑
WHAT?
I SHOULD BE THERE BY THE EVENING!
COME OUT WHEN I BUZZ THE BELL.♪
PIP
EEEP EEEP
...
I'M BACK!
THANK YOU FOR COMING TO PICK ME UP.
Tsubaki-chan
MOTHER!
TRA TRAT
WITH THE BAD WEATHER, I WAS VERY NERVOUS.
ME, TOO.
APPARENTLY THE REST OF THE FLIGHTS ARE CANCELED.
MAKOTO, WHAT'S WRONG?

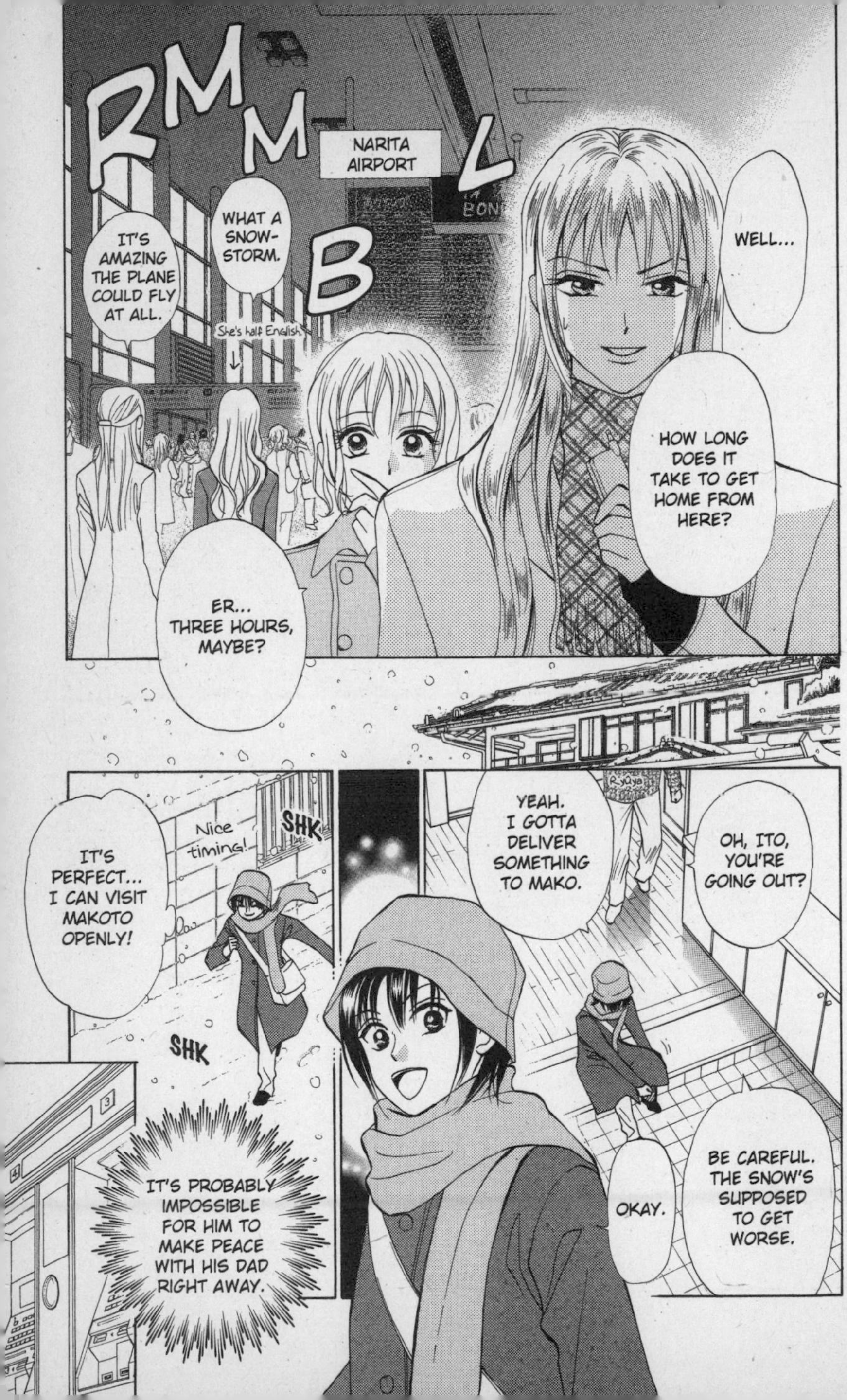
RMMBL
NARITA AIRPORT
WHAT A SNOW-STORM.
IT'S AMAZING THE PLANE COULD FLY AT ALL.
She's half English
WELL...
HOW LONG DOES IT TAKE TO GET HOME FROM HERE?
ER... THREE HOURS, MAYBE?
OH, ITO, YOU'RE GOING OUT?
YEAH. I GOTTA DELIVER SOMETHING TO MAKO.
BE CAREFUL. THE SNOW'S SUPPOSED TO GET WORSE.
OKAY.
SHK
Nice timing!
IT'S PERFECT... I CAN VISIT MAKOTO OPENLY!
SHK
IT'S PROBABLY IMPOSSIBLE FOR HIM TO MAKE PEACE WITH HIS DAD RIGHT AWAY.

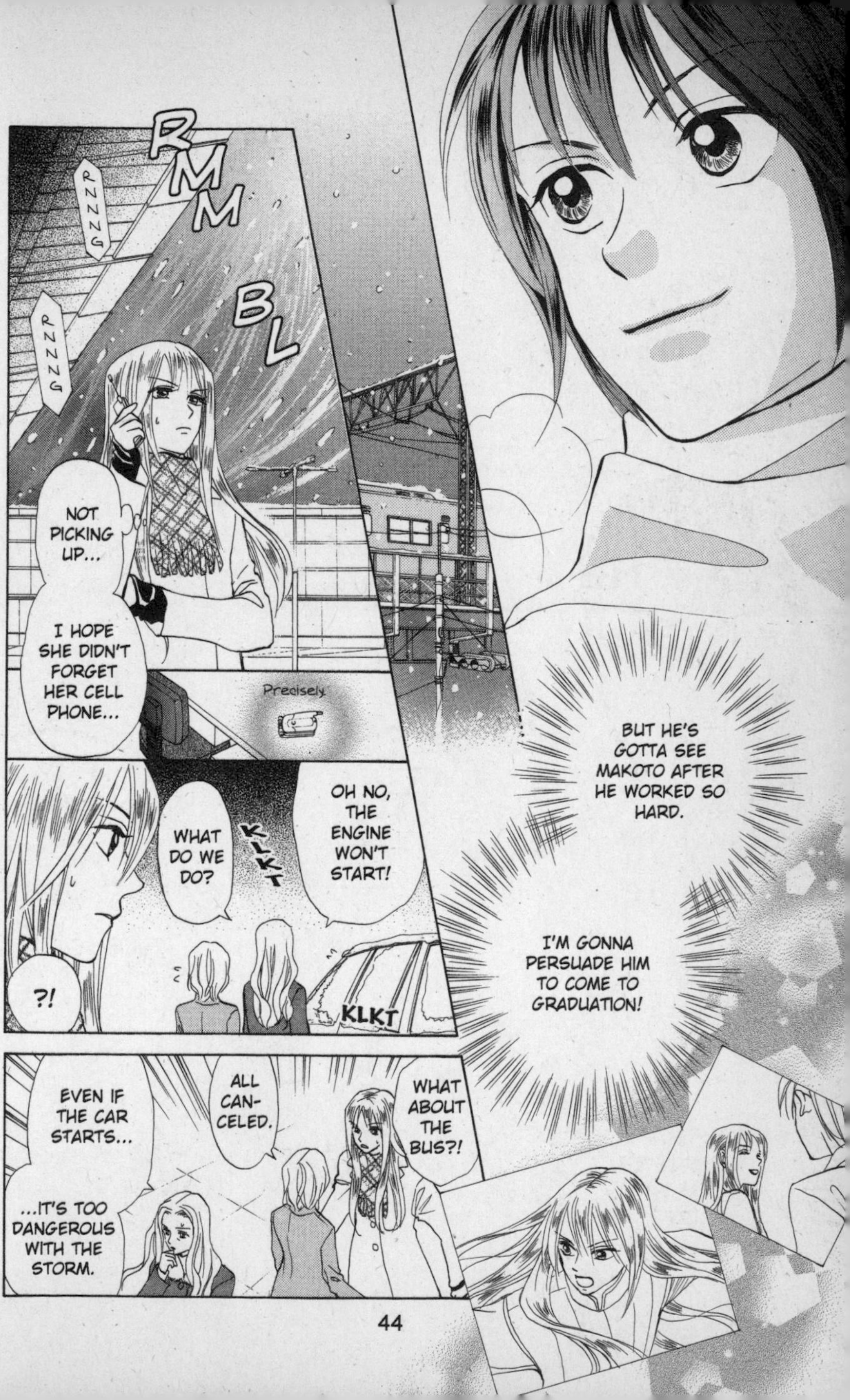
BUT HE'S GOTTA SEE MAKOTO AFTER HE WORKED SO HARD.
I'M GONNA PERSUADE HIM TO COME TO GRADUATION!
RMMBL
RNNNG
RNNNG
NOT PICKING UP...
I HOPE SHE DIDN'T FORGET HER CELL PHONE...
Precisely.
OH NO, THE ENGINE WON'T START!
KLKT
WHAT DO WE DO?
?!
KLKT
WHAT ABOUT THE BUS?!
ALL CAN-CELED.
EVEN IF THE CAR STARTS...
...IT'S TOO DANGEROUS WITH THE STORM.

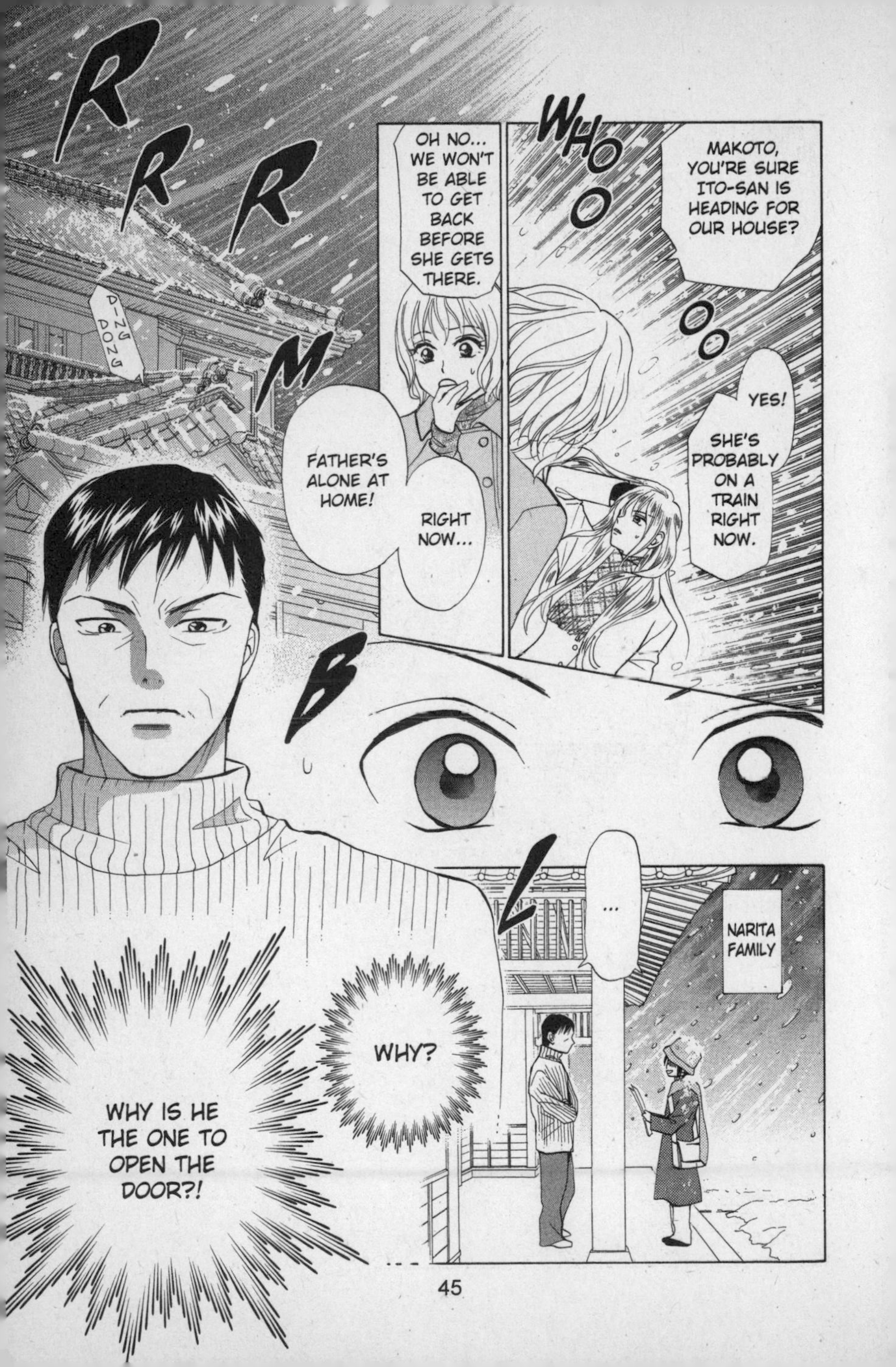

WHOOOOO
MAKOTO, YOU'RE SURE ITO-SAN IS HEADING FOR OUR HOUSE?
YES!
SHE'S PROBABLY ON A TRAIN RIGHT NOW.
OH NO... WE WON'T BE ABLE TO GET BACK BEFORE SHE GETS THERE.
FATHER'S ALONE AT HOME!
RIGHT NOW...
BL
RRRRRM
DING DONG
...
NARITA FAMILY
WHY?
WHY IS HE THE ONE TO OPEN THE DOOR?!

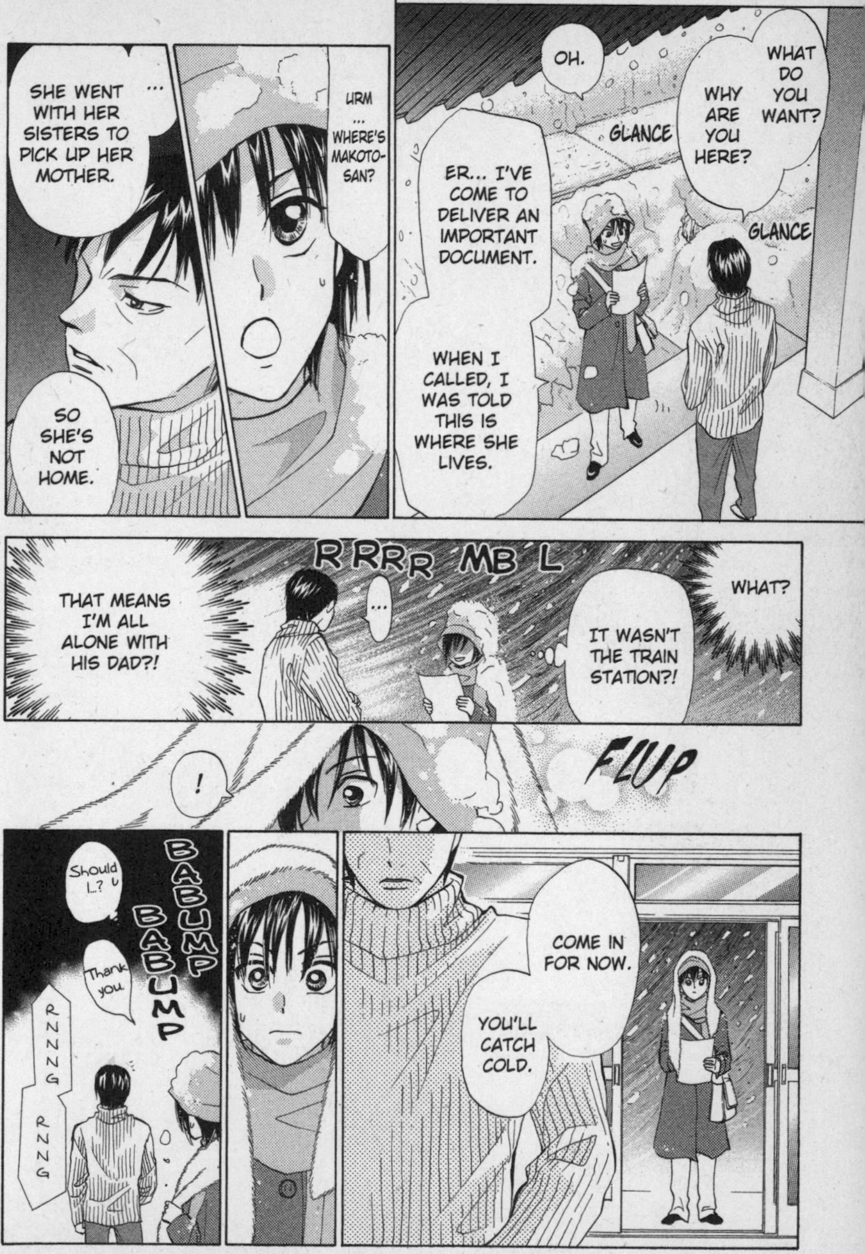
WHAT DO YOU WANT?
WHY ARE YOU HERE?
OH.
GLANCE
GLANCE
ER... I'VE COME TO DELIVER AN IMPORTANT DOCUMENT.
WHEN I CALLED, I WAS TOLD THIS IS WHERE SHE LIVES.
URM ... WHERE'S MAKOTO-SAN?
...
SHE WENT WITH HER SISTERS TO PICK UP HER MOTHER.
SO SHE'S NOT HOME.
WHAT?
IT WASN'T THE TRAIN STATION?!
RRRR MB L
...
THAT MEANS I'M ALL ALONE WITH HIS DAD?!
FLUP
!
COME IN FOR NOW.
YOU'LL CATCH COLD.
BABUMP
BABUMP
Should I..?
Thank you.
RNNNG
RNNG

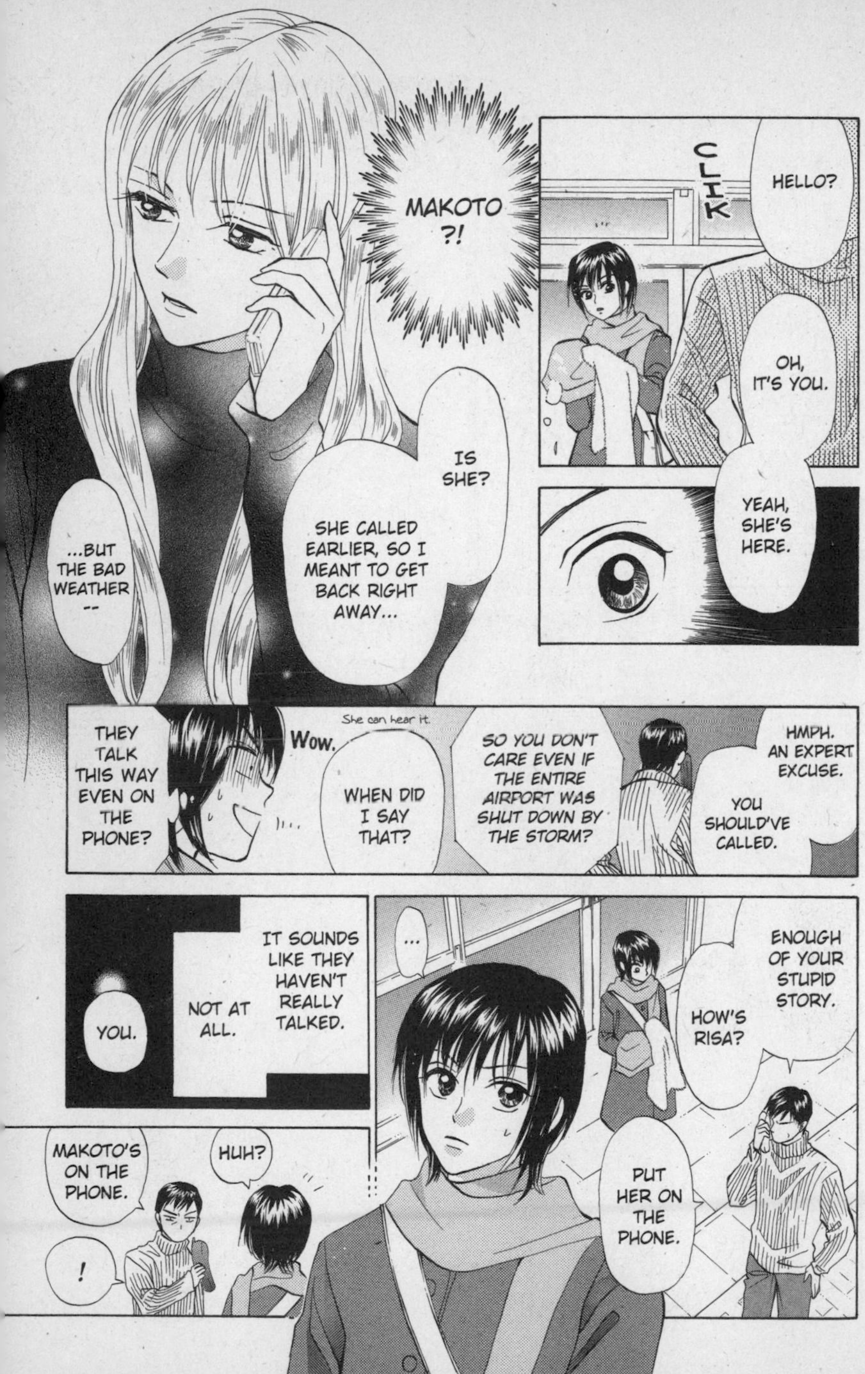
CLIK
HELLO?
OH, IT'S YOU.
YEAH, SHE'S HERE.
MAKOTO ?!
IS SHE?
SHE CALLED EARLIER, SO I MEANT TO GET BACK RIGHT AWAY...
...BUT THE BAD WEATHER --
HMPH. AN EXPERT EXCUSE.
YOU SHOULD'VE CALLED.
SO YOU DON'T CARE EVEN IF THE ENTIRE AIRPORT WAS SHUT DOWN BY THE STORM?
WHEN DID I SAY THAT?
She can hear it.
Wow.
THEY TALK THIS WAY EVEN ON THE PHONE?
ENOUGH OF YOUR STUPID STORY.
HOW'S RISA?
...
PUT HER ON THE PHONE.
IT SOUNDS LIKE THEY HAVEN'T REALLY TALKED.
NOT AT ALL.
YOU.
HUH?
MAKOTO'S ON THE PHONE.
!

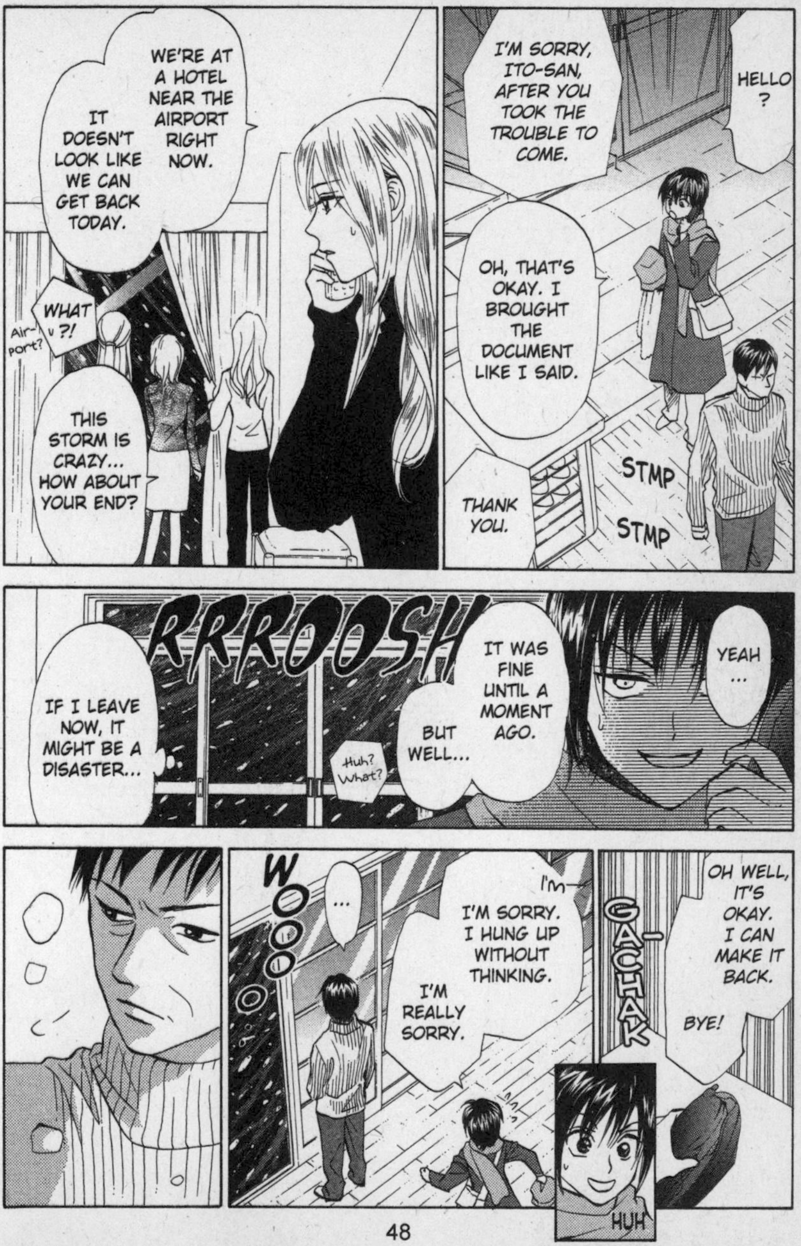
HELLO ?
I'M SORRY, ITO-SAN, AFTER YOU TOOK THE TROUBLE TO COME.
OH, THAT'S OKAY. I BROUGHT THE DOCUMENT LIKE I SAID.
THANK YOU.
STMP
STMP
WE'RE AT A HOTEL NEAR THE AIRPORT RIGHT NOW.
IT DOESN'T LOOK LIKE WE CAN GET BACK TODAY.
WHAT ?!
Air-port?
THIS STORM IS CRAZY... HOW ABOUT YOUR END?
YEAH ...
IT WAS FINE UNTIL A MOMENT AGO.
BUT WELL...
Huh? What?
RRROOSH
IF I LEAVE NOW, IT MIGHT BE A DISASTER...
OH WELL, IT'S OKAY. I CAN MAKE IT BACK.
BYE!
GACHAK
HUH
I'm—
I'M SORRY. I HUNG UP WITHOUT THINKING.
I'M REALLY SORRY.
...
WOOO

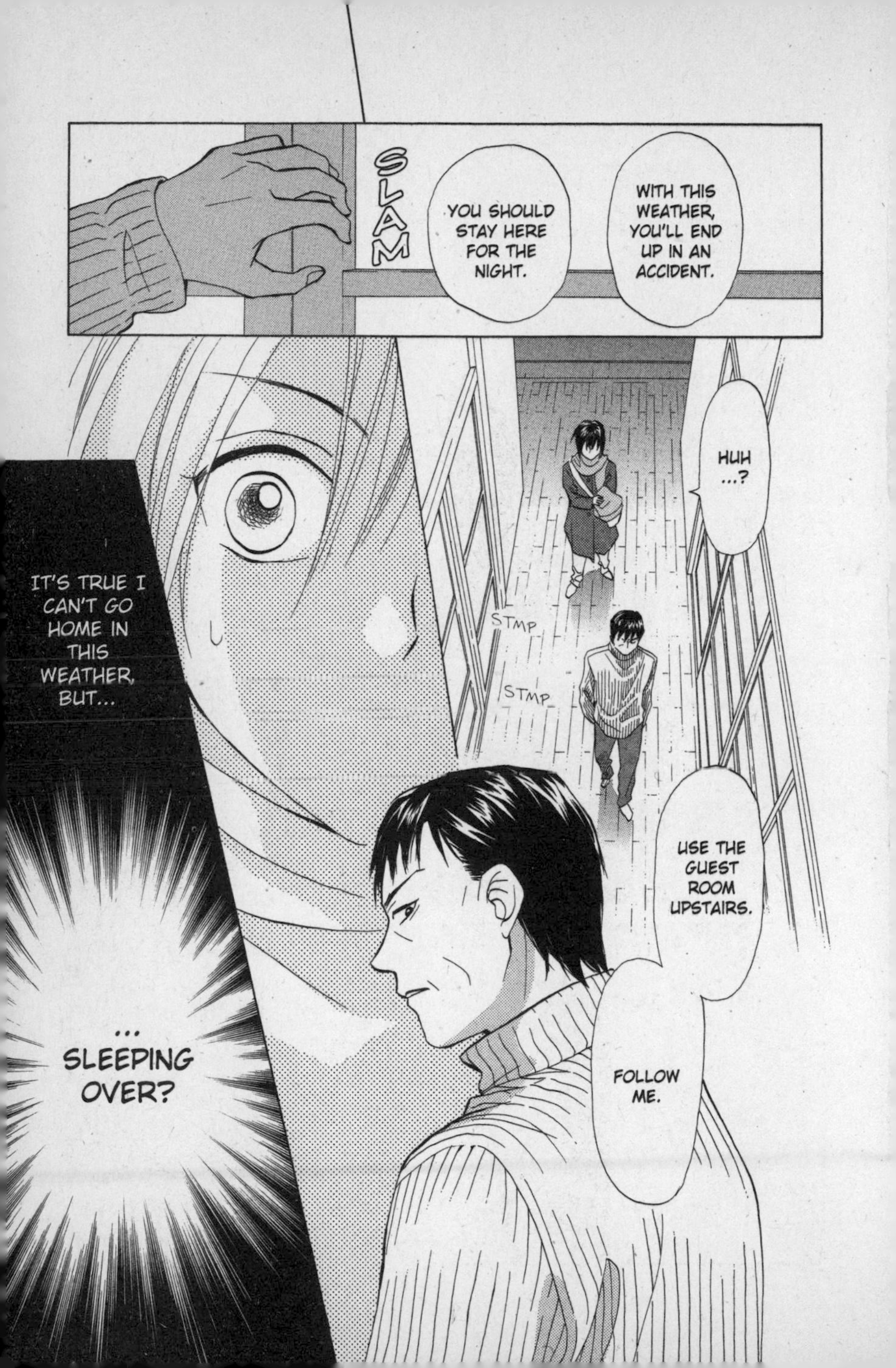
WITH THIS WEATHER, YOU'LL END UP IN AN ACCIDENT.
YOU SHOULD STAY HERE FOR THE NIGHT.
SLAM
HUH ...?
STMP
STMP
USE THE GUEST ROOM UPSTAIRS.
FOLLOW ME.
IT'S TRUE I CAN'T GO HOME IN THIS WEATHER, BUT...
... SLEEPING OVER?

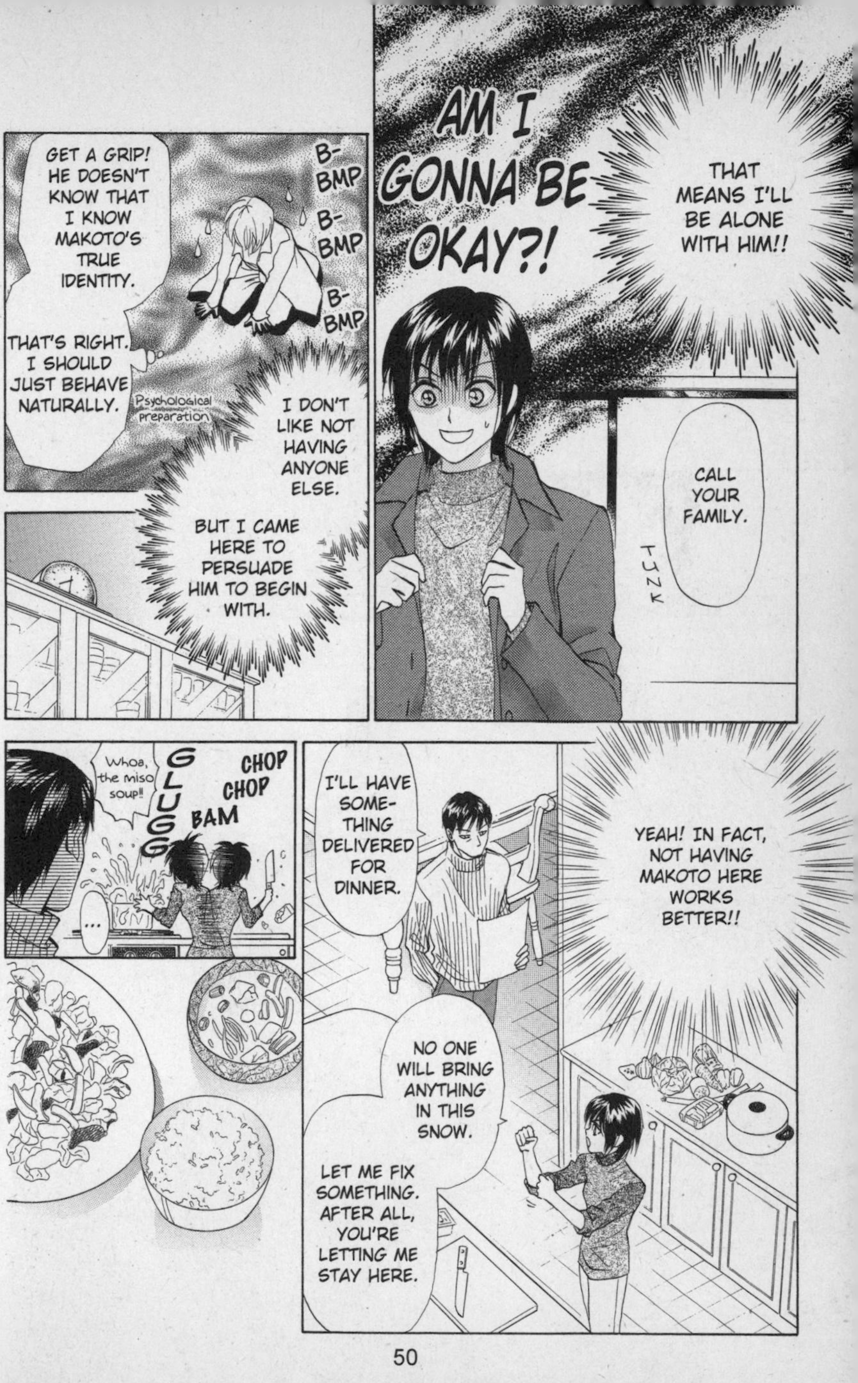
CALL YOUR FAMILY.
TUNK
THAT MEANS I'LL BE ALONE WITH HIM!!
AM I GONNA BE OKAY?!
B-BMP B-BMP B-BMP
GET A GRIP! HE DOESN'T KNOW THAT I KNOW MAKOTO'S TRUE IDENTITY.
THAT'S RIGHT. I SHOULD JUST BEHAVE NATURALLY.
Psychological preparation
I DON'T LIKE NOT HAVING ANYONE ELSE.
BUT I CAME HERE TO PERSUADE HIM TO BEGIN WITH.
I'LL HAVE SOME-THING DELIVERED FOR DINNER.
YEAH! IN FACT, NOT HAVING MAKOTO HERE WORKS BETTER!!
NO ONE WILL BRING ANYTHING IN THIS SNOW.
LET ME FIX SOMETHING. AFTER ALL, YOU'RE LETTING ME STAY HERE.
CHOP CHOP
BAM
GLUGG
Whoa, the miso soup!!
...

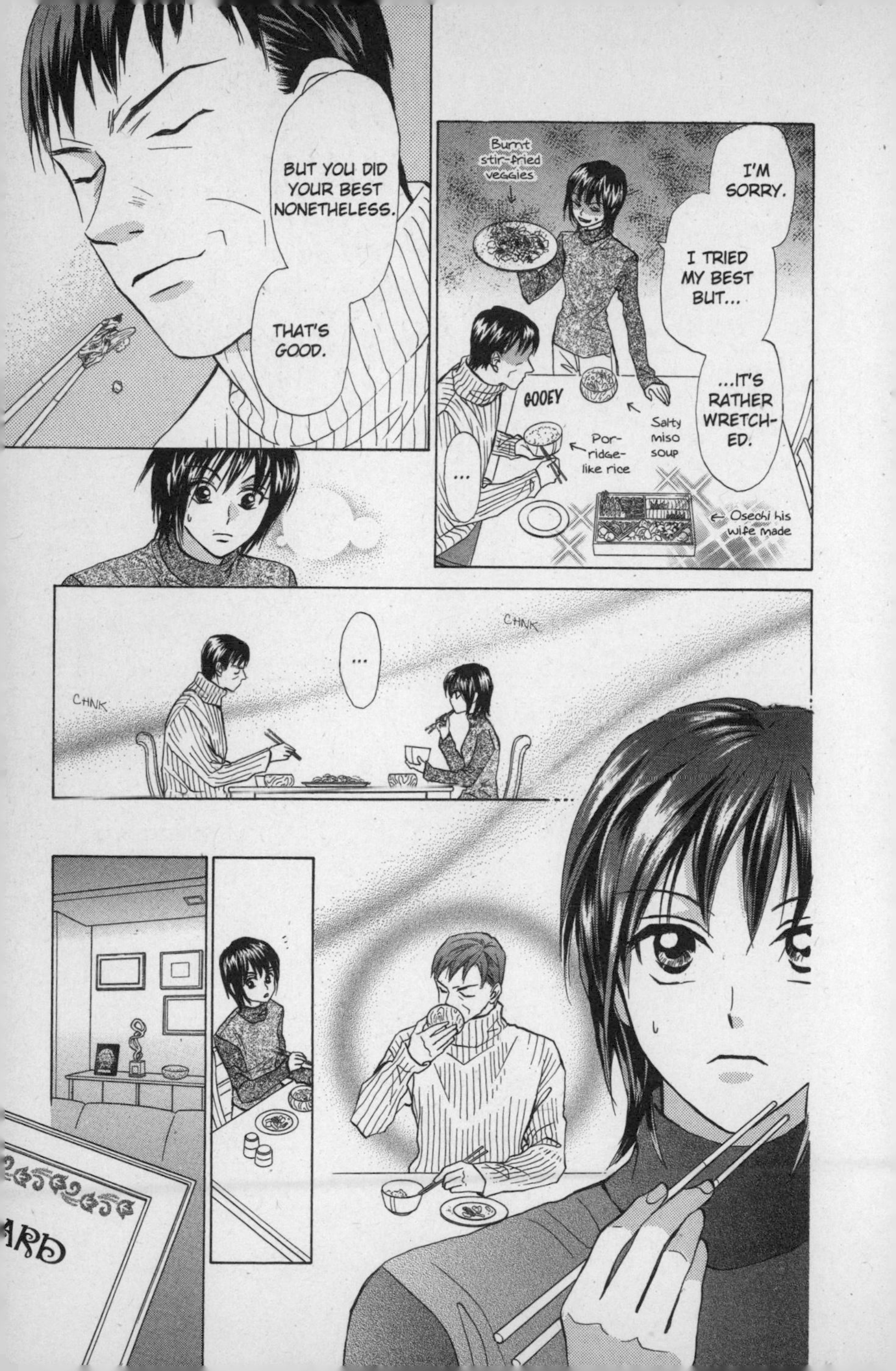

I'M SORRY.
I TRIED MY BEST BUT...
...IT'S RATHER WRETCHED.
Burnt stir-fried veggies
GOOEY
Salty miso soup
Porridge-like rice
...
Osechi his wife made
BUT YOU DID YOUR BEST NONETHELESS.
THAT'S GOOD.
CHNK
...
CHNK

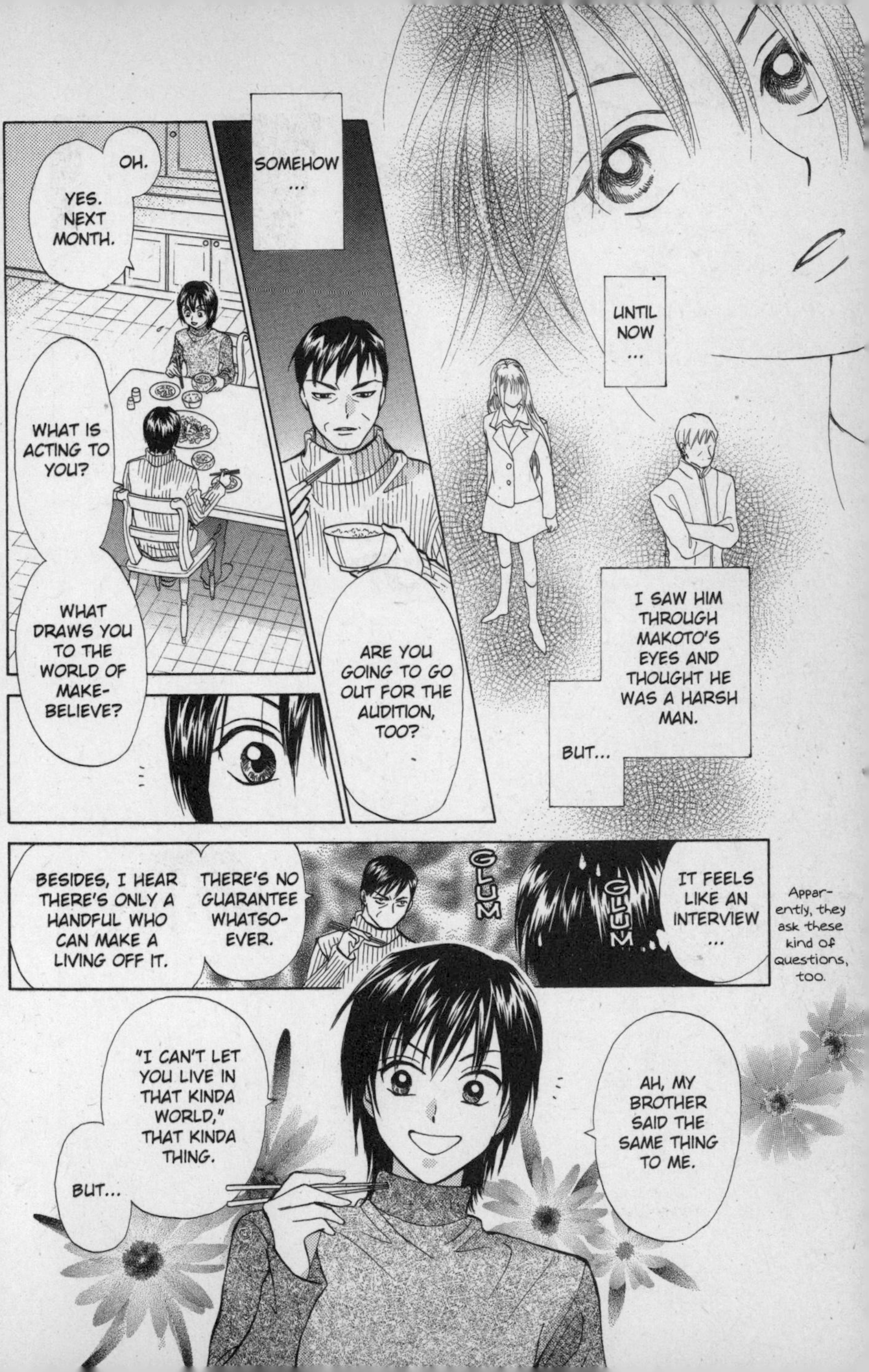
UNTIL NOW...
I SAW HIM THROUGH MAKOTO'S EYES AND THOUGHT HE WAS A HARSH MAN.
BUT...
SOMEHOW...
ARE YOU GOING TO GO OUT FOR THE AUDITION, TOO?
OH.
YES. NEXT MONTH.
WHAT IS ACTING TO YOU?
WHAT DRAWS YOU TO THE WORLD OF MAKE-BELIEVE?
Apparently, they ask these kind of questions, too.
IT FEELS LIKE AN INTERVIEW...
GLUM
GLUM
THERE'S NO GUARANTEE WHATSOEVER.
BESIDES, I HEAR THERE'S ONLY A HANDFUL WHO CAN MAKE A LIVING OFF IT.
AH, MY BROTHER SAID THE SAME THING TO ME.
"I CAN'T LET YOU LIVE IN THAT KINDA WORLD," THAT KINDA THING.
BUT...

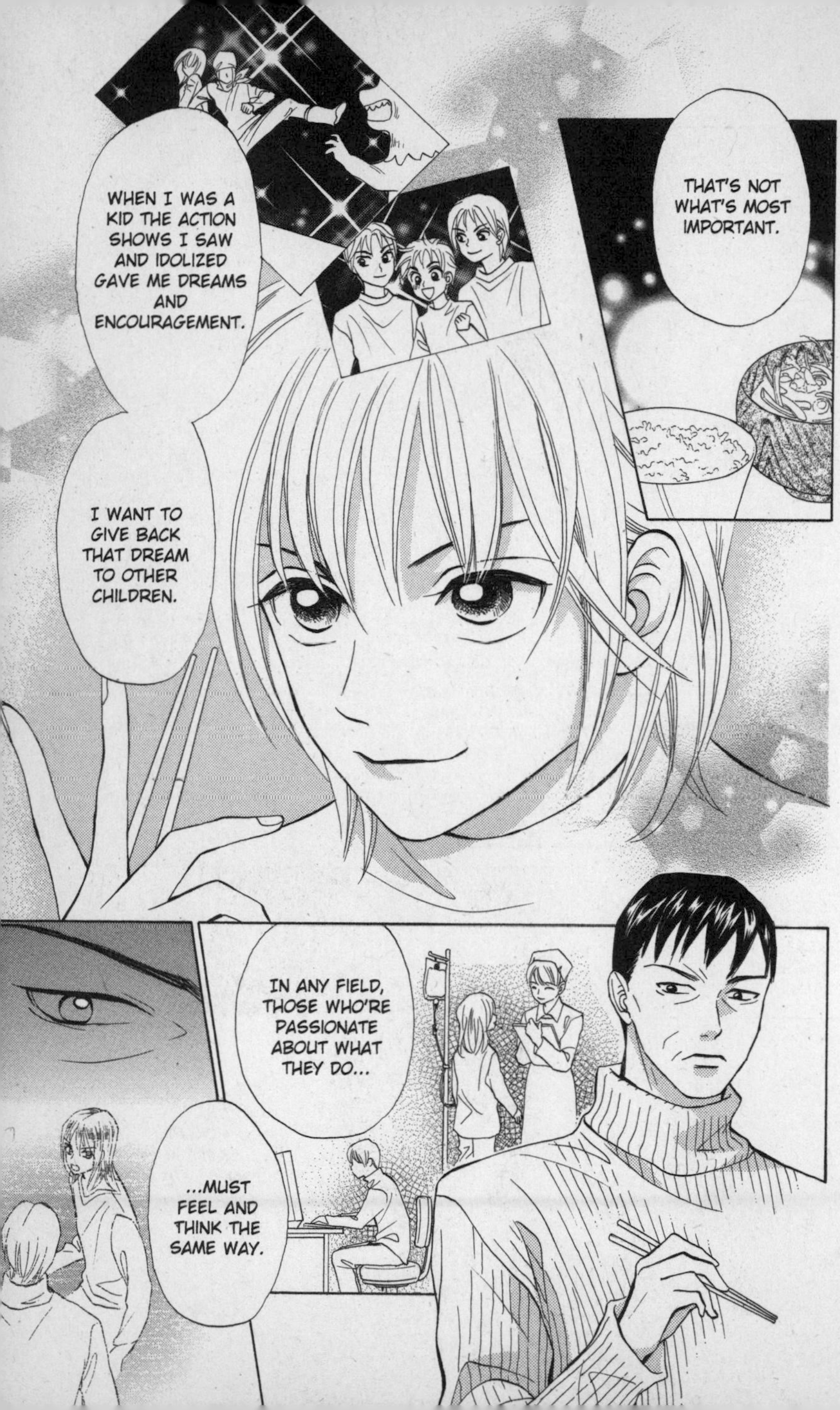
THAT'S NOT WHAT'S MOST IMPORTANT.
WHEN I WAS A KID THE ACTION SHOWS I SAW AND IDOLIZED GAVE ME DREAMS AND ENCOURAGEMENT.
I WANT TO GIVE BACK THAT DREAM TO OTHER CHILDREN.
IN ANY FIELD, THOSE WHO'RE PASSIONATE ABOUT WHAT THEY DO...
...MUST FEEL AND THINK THE SAME WAY.

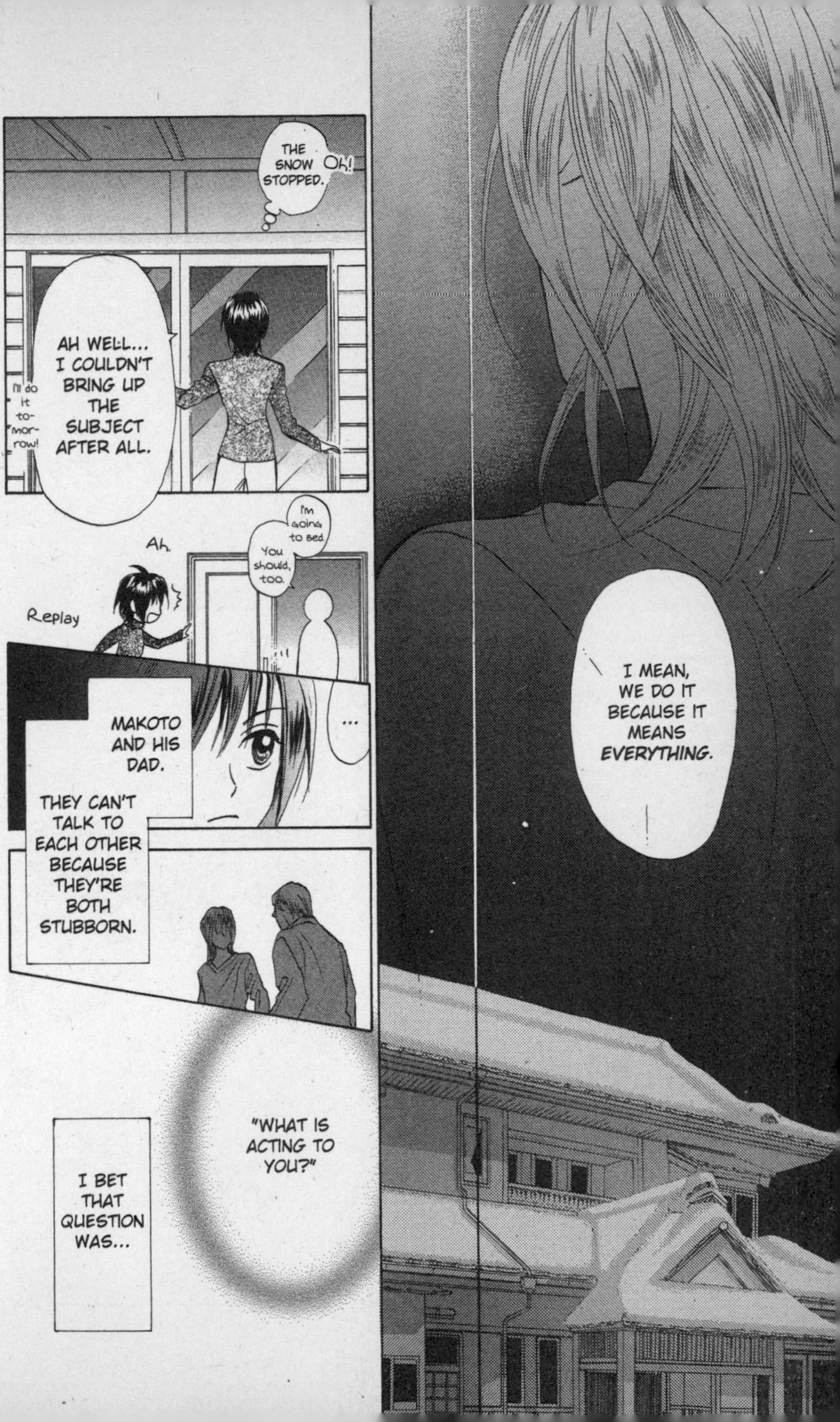
I MEAN, WE DO IT BECAUSE IT MEANS EVERYTHING.
Oh!
THE SNOW STOPPED.
AH WELL... I COULDN'T BRING UP THE SUBJECT AFTER ALL.
I'll do it to-morrow!
I'm going to bed.
You should, too.
Ah.
Replay
...
MAKOTO AND HIS DAD.
THEY CAN'T TALK TO EACH OTHER BECAUSE THEY'RE BOTH STUBBORN.
"WHAT IS ACTING TO YOU?"
I BET THAT QUESTION WAS...

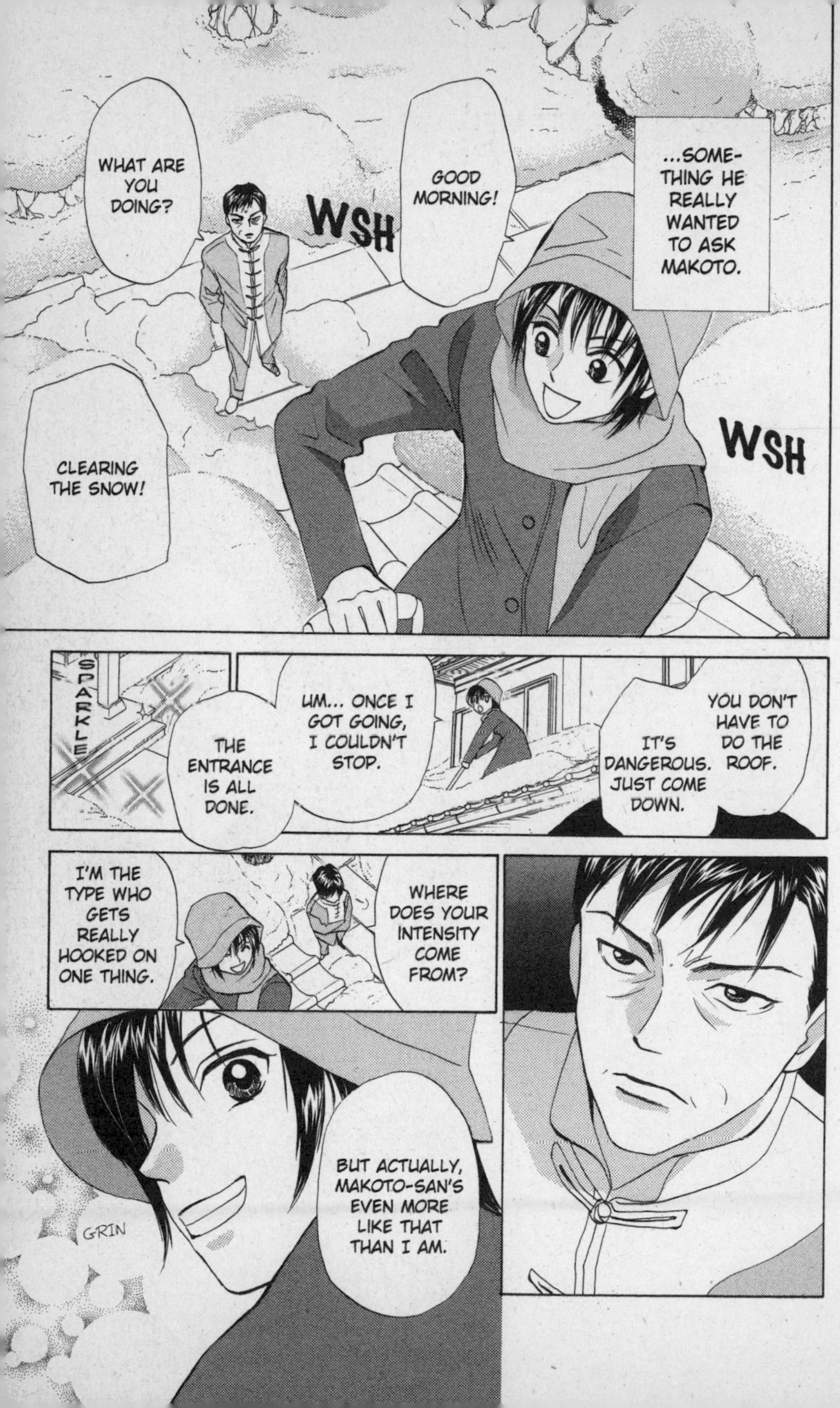
...SOME-THING HE REALLY WANTED TO ASK MAKOTO.
WSH
GOOD MORNING!
WSH
WHAT ARE YOU DOING?
CLEARING THE SNOW!
YOU DON'T HAVE TO DO THE ROOF.
IT'S DANGEROUS. JUST COME DOWN.
UM... ONCE I GOT GOING, I COULDN'T STOP.
THE ENTRANCE IS ALL DONE.
SPARKLE
WHERE DOES YOUR INTENSITY COME FROM?
I'M THE TYPE WHO GETS REALLY HOOKED ON ONE THING.
BUT ACTUALLY, MAKOTO-SAN'S EVEN MORE LIKE THAT THAN I AM.
GRIN

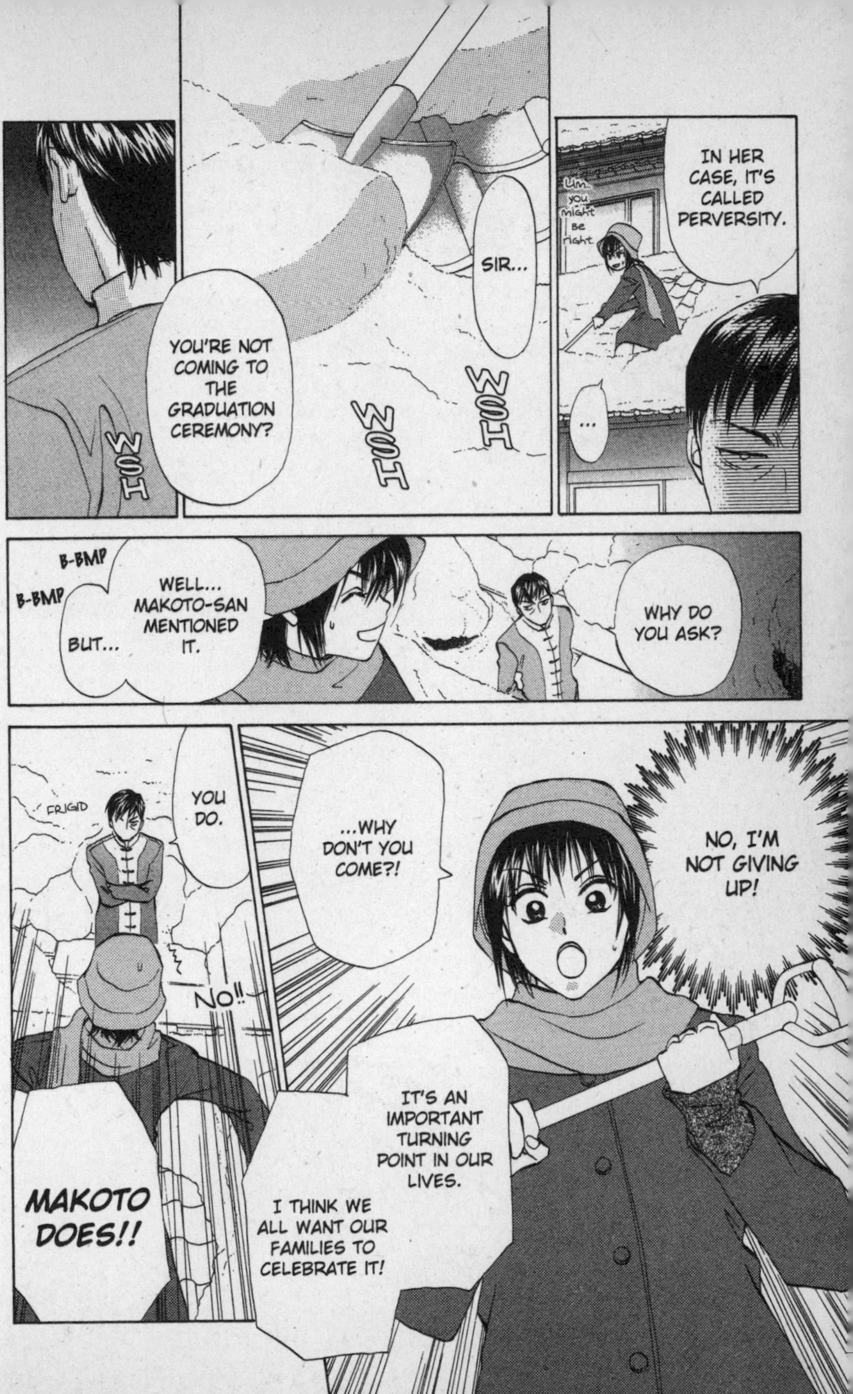
IN HER CASE, IT'S CALLED PERVERSITY.
Um... you might be right
...
SIR...
WSH
WSH
YOU'RE NOT COMING TO THE GRADUATION CEREMONY?
WSH
WHY DO YOU ASK?
WELL... MAKOTO-SAN MENTIONED IT.
BUT...
B-BMP
B-BMP
NO, I'M NOT GIVING UP!
...WHY DON'T YOU COME?!
IT'S AN IMPORTANT TURNING POINT IN OUR LIVES.
I THINK WE ALL WANT OUR FAMILIES TO CELEBRATE IT!
YOU DO.
FRIGID
NO!!
MAKOTO DOES!!

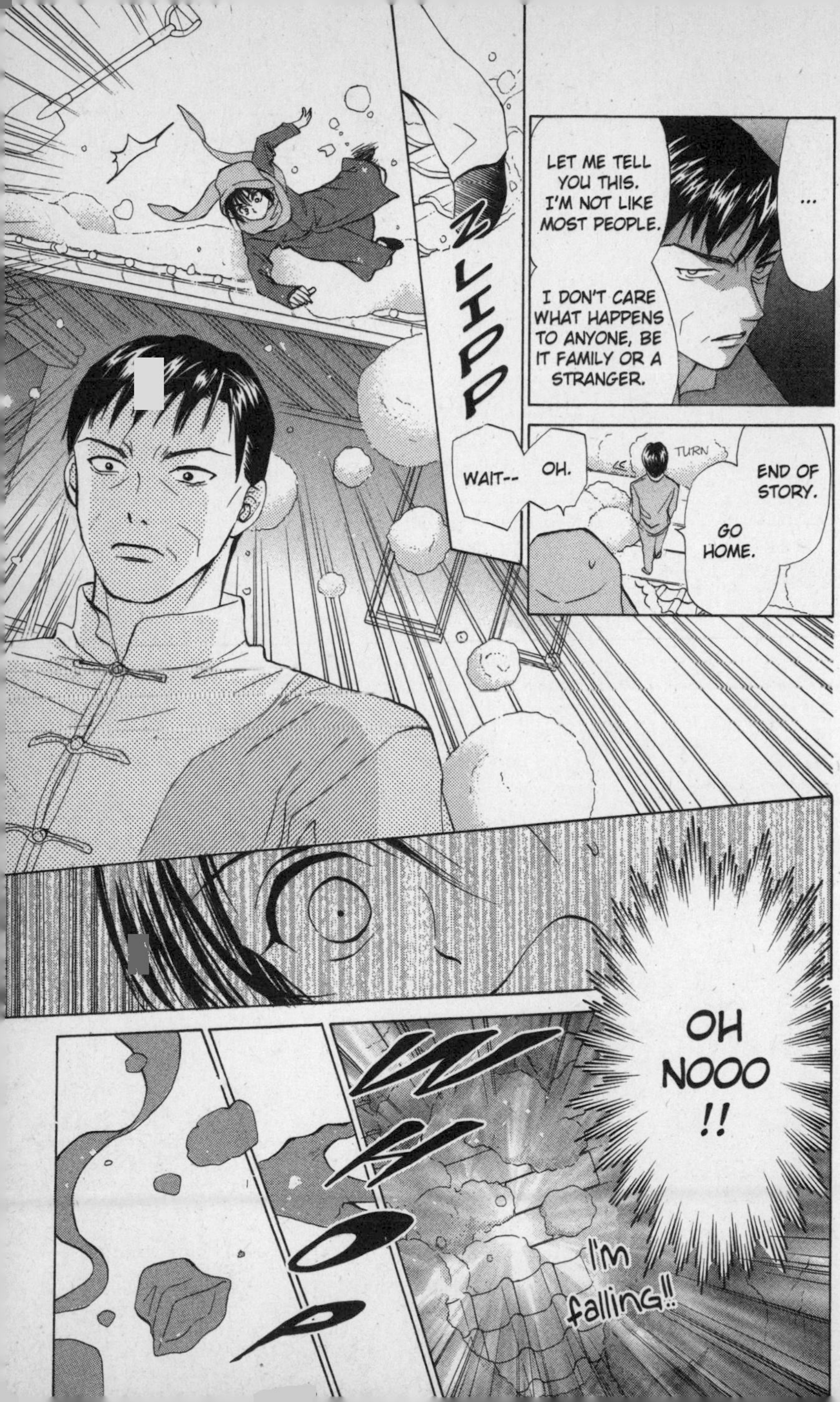
...
LET ME TELL YOU THIS. I'M NOT LIKE MOST PEOPLE.
I DON'T CARE WHAT HAPPENS TO ANYONE, BE IT FAMILY OR A STRANGER.
END OF STORY.
GO HOME.
TURN
OH.
WAIT--
ZLIPP
OH NOOO !!
WHOOP
I'm falling!!

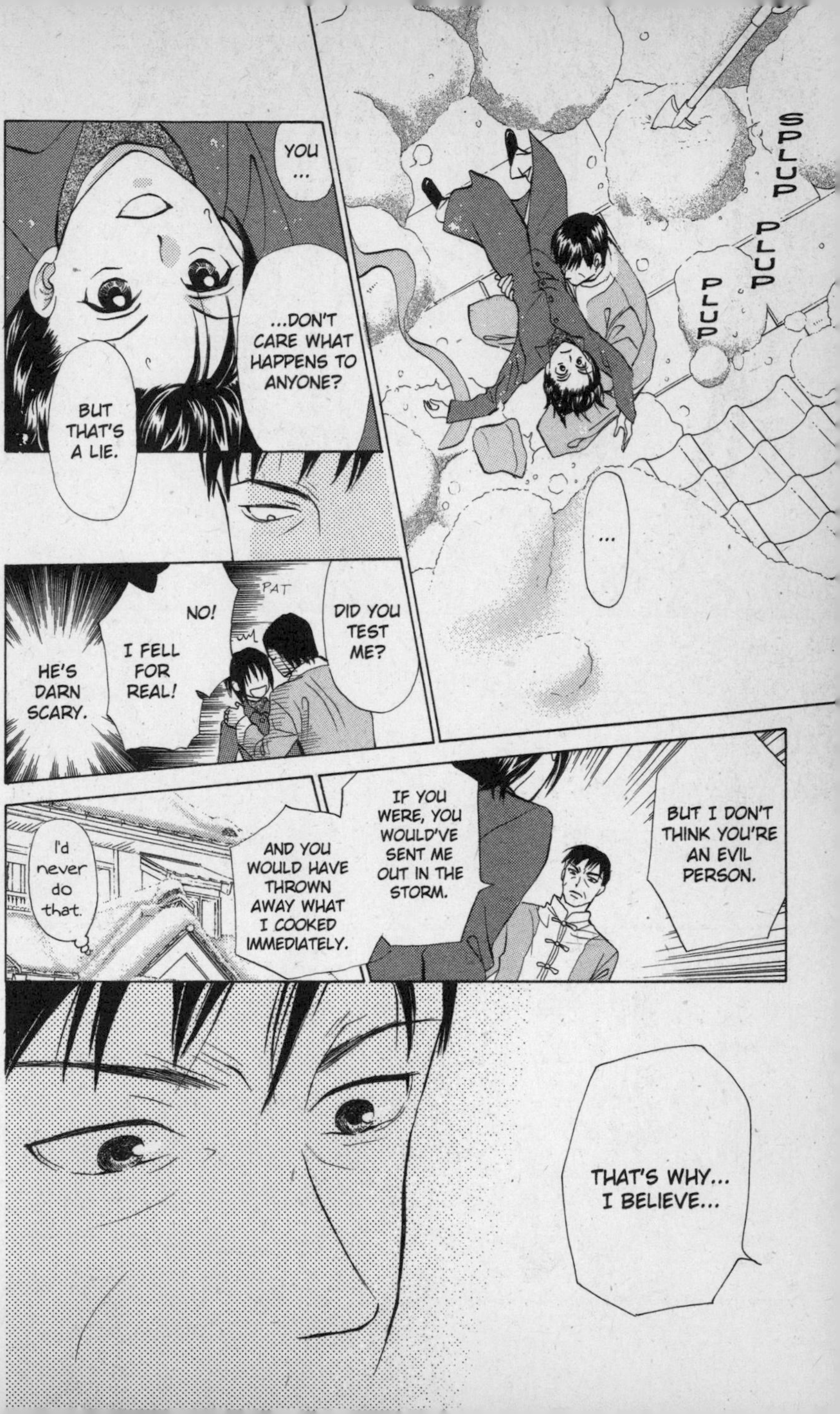
SPLUP
PLUP
PLUP
...
YOU ...
...DON'T CARE WHAT HAPPENS TO ANYONE?
BUT THAT'S A LIE.
DID YOU TEST ME?
PAT
NO!
I FELL FOR REAL!
HE'S DARN SCARY.
BUT I DON'T THINK YOU'RE AN EVIL PERSON.
IF YOU WERE, YOU WOULD'VE SENT ME OUT IN THE STORM.
AND YOU WOULD HAVE THROWN AWAY WHAT I COOKED IMMEDIATELY.
I'd never do that.
THAT'S WHY... I BELIEVE...

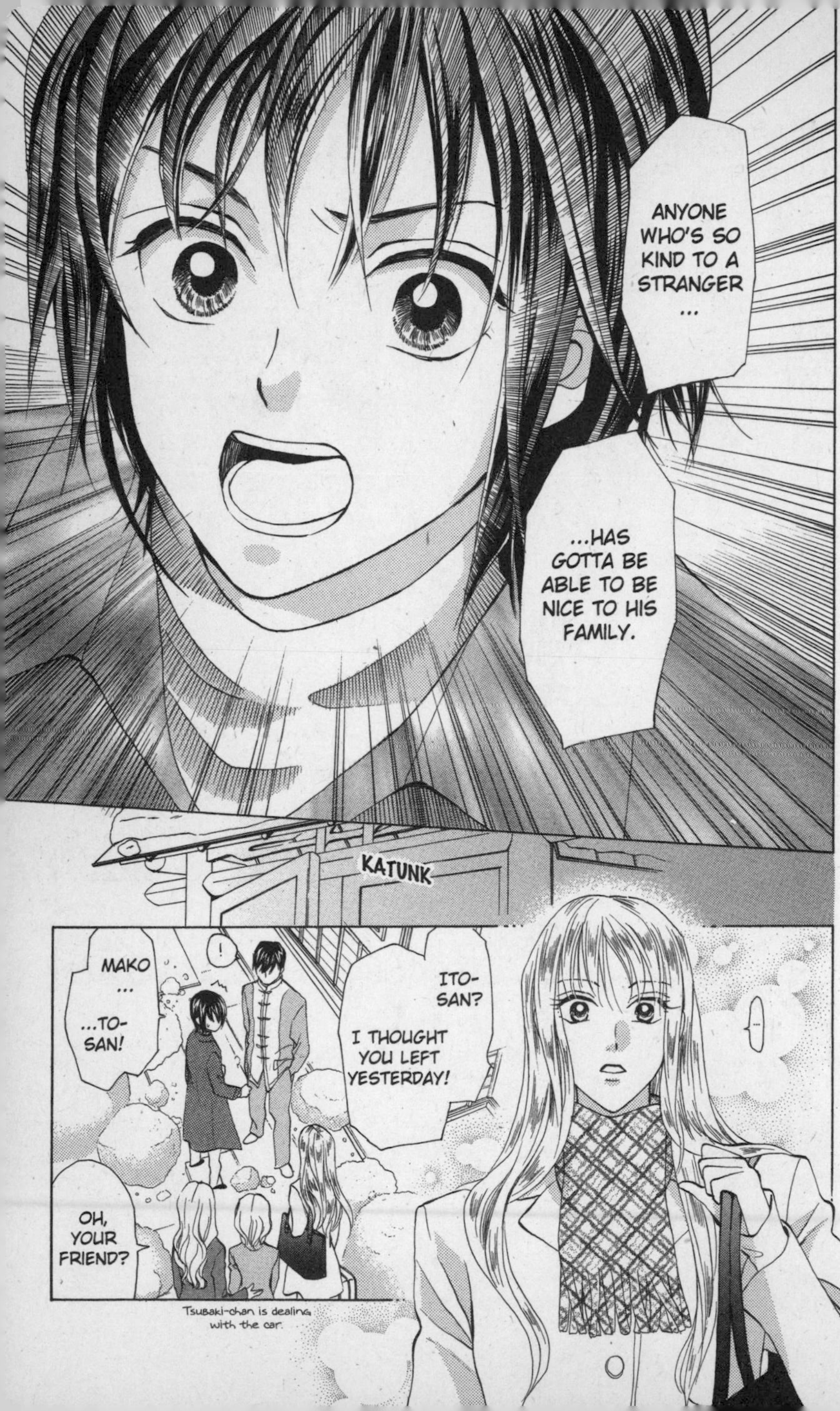
ANYONE WHO'S SO KIND TO A STRANGER ...
...HAS GOTTA BE ABLE TO BE NICE TO HIS FAMILY.
KATUNK
...
ITO-SAN?
I THOUGHT YOU LEFT YESTERDAY!
!
MAKO ...
...TO-SAN!
OH, YOUR FRIEND?
Tsubaki-chan is dealing with the car.

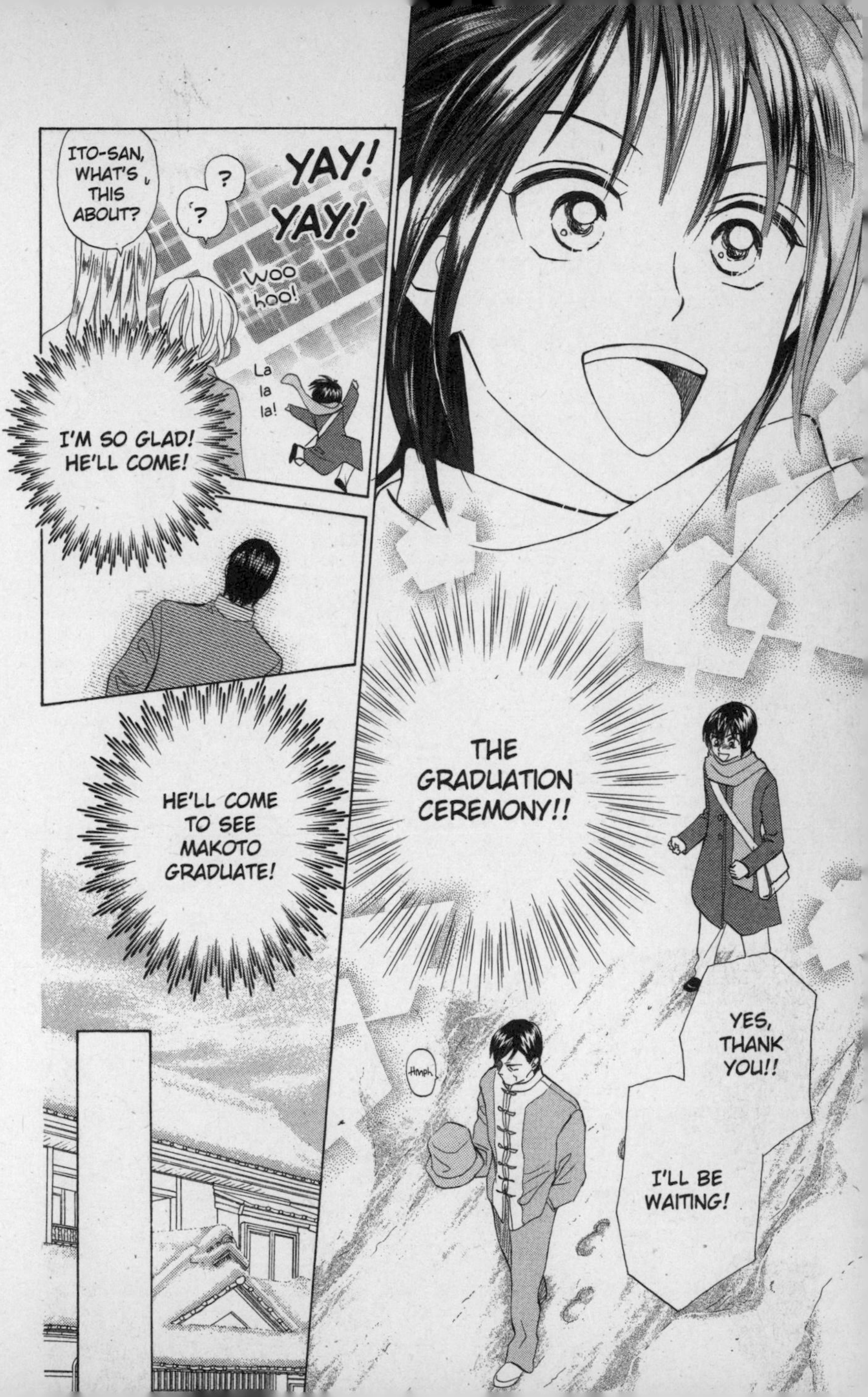
THE GRADUATION CEREMONY!!
YES, THANK YOU!!
I'LL BE WAITING!
Hmph
YAY! YAY!
?
?
ITO-SAN, WHAT'S THIS ABOUT?
Woo hoo!
La la la!
I'M SO GLAD! HE'LL COME!
HE'LL COME TO SEE MAKOTO GRADUATE!

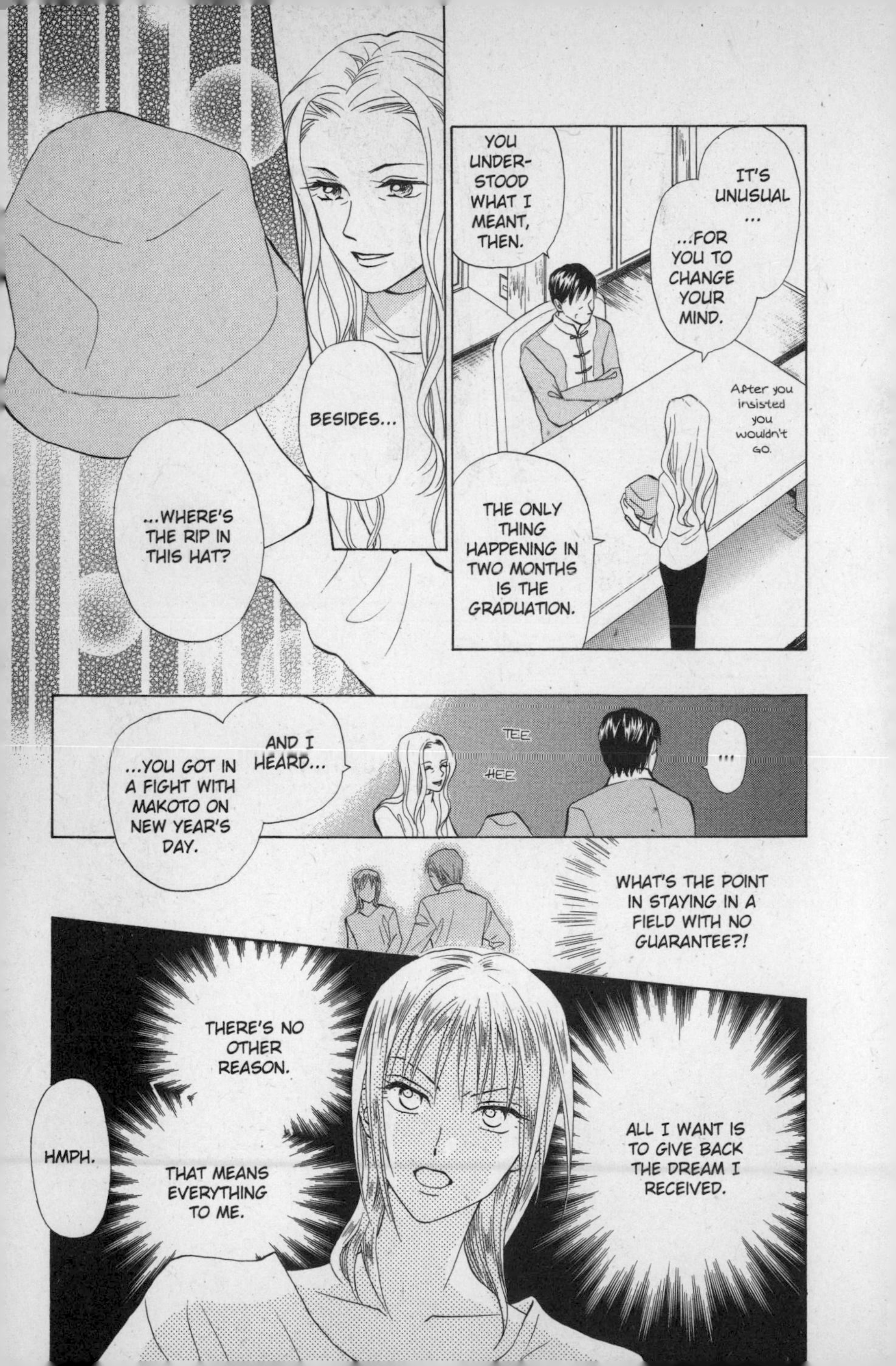
IT'S UNUSUAL...
...FOR YOU TO CHANGE YOUR MIND.
After you insisted you wouldn't go.
YOU UNDERSTOOD WHAT I MEANT, THEN.
THE ONLY THING HAPPENING IN TWO MONTHS IS THE GRADUATION.
BESIDES...
...WHERE'S THE RIP IN THIS HAT?
...
TEE HEE
AND I HEARD...
...YOU GOT IN A FIGHT WITH MAKOTO ON NEW YEAR'S DAY.
WHAT'S THE POINT IN STAYING IN A FIELD WITH NO GUARANTEE?!
ALL I WANT IS TO GIVE BACK THE DREAM I RECEIVED.
THERE'S NO OTHER REASON.
THAT MEANS EVERYTHING TO ME.
HMPH.

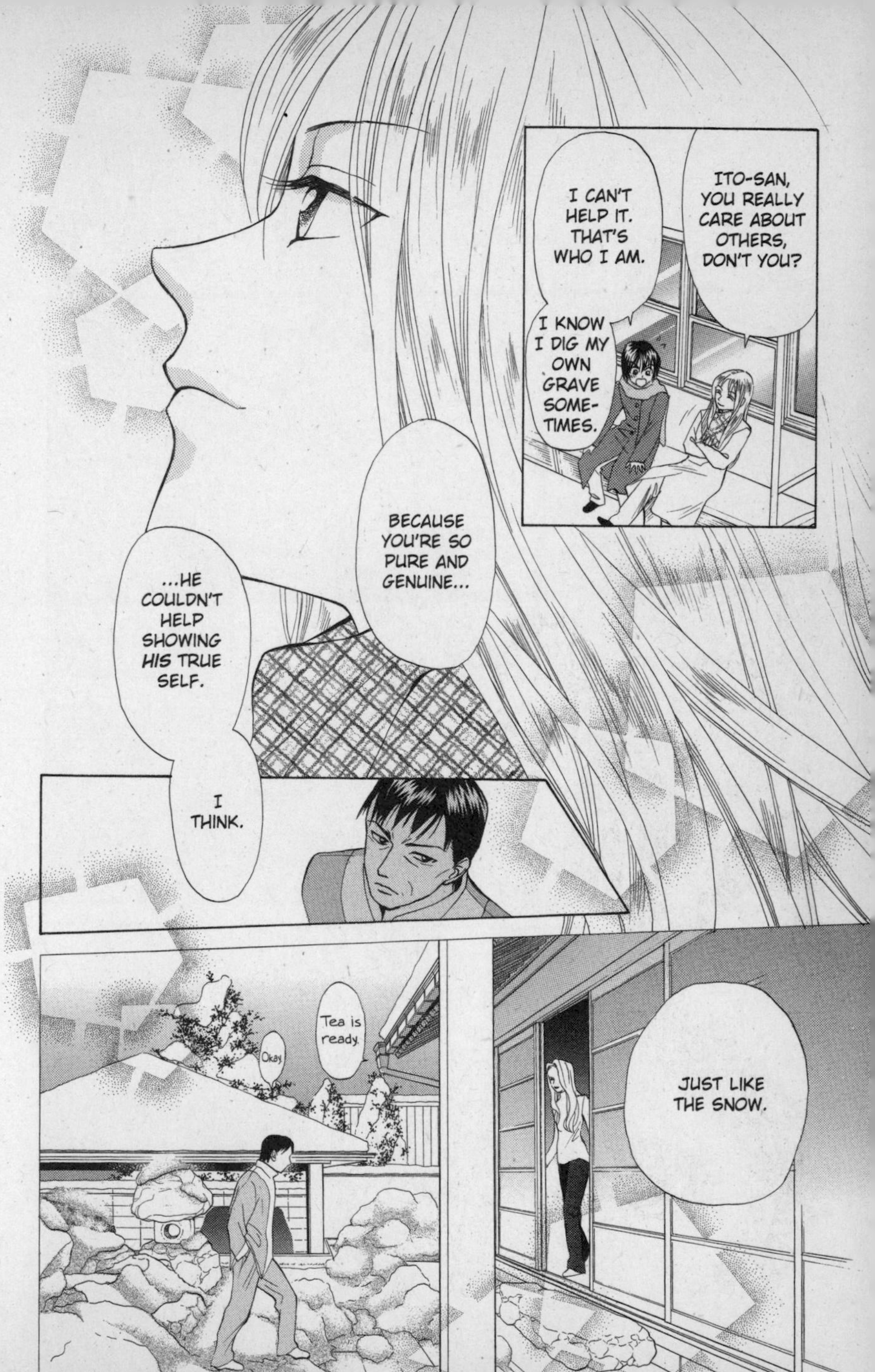
ITO-SAN, YOU REALLY CARE ABOUT OTHERS, DON'T YOU?
I CAN'T HELP IT. THAT'S WHO I AM.
I KNOW I DIG MY OWN GRAVE SOME-TIMES.
BECAUSE YOU'RE SO PURE AND GENUINE...
...HE COULDN'T HELP SHOWING HIS TRUE SELF.
I THINK.
JUST LIKE THE SNOW.
Tea is ready.
Okay.

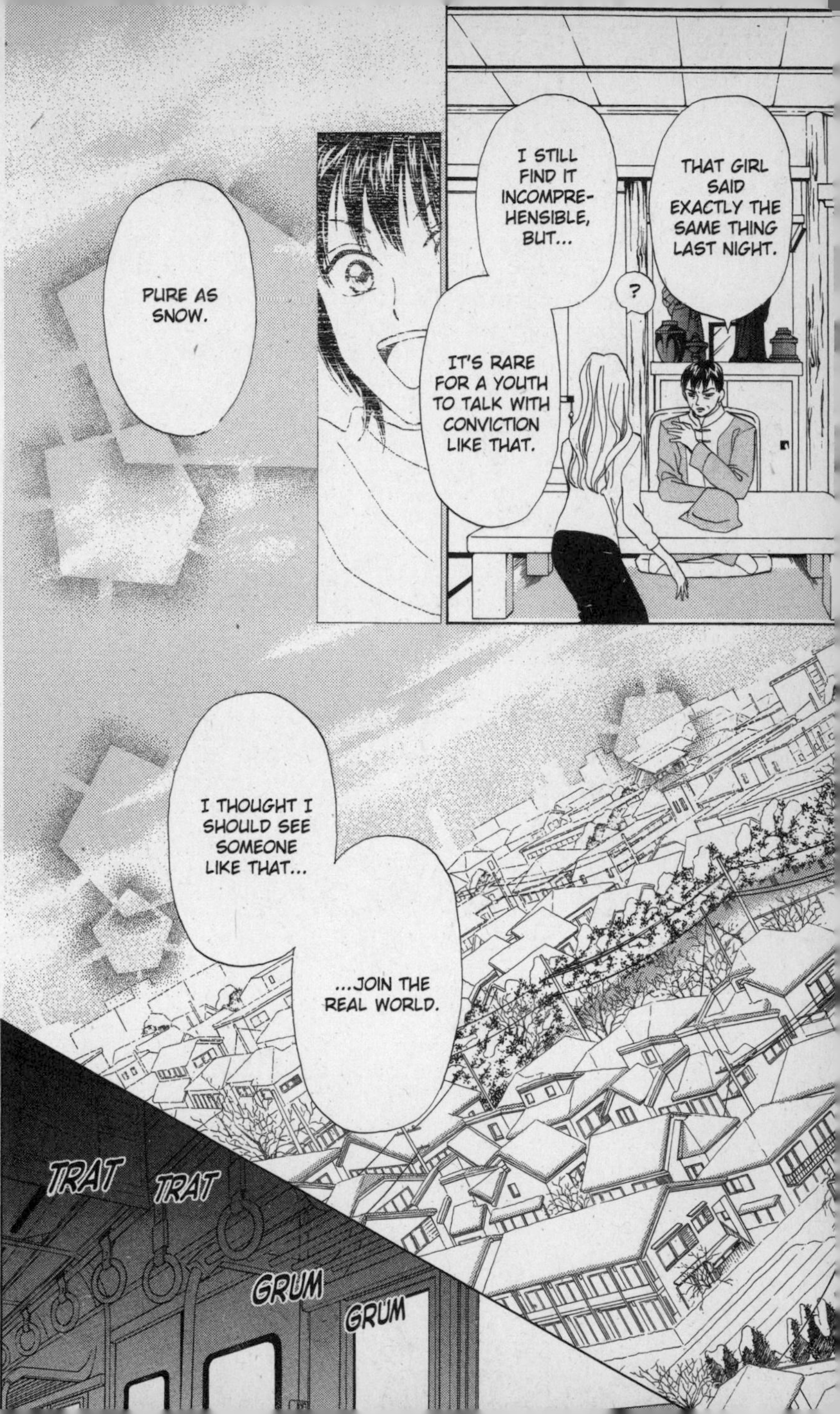
THAT GIRL SAID EXACTLY THE SAME THING LAST NIGHT.
?
I STILL FIND IT INCOMPRE-HENSIBLE, BUT...
IT'S RARE FOR A YOUTH TO TALK WITH CONVICTION LIKE THAT.
PURE AS SNOW.
I THOUGHT I SHOULD SEE SOMEONE LIKE THAT...
...JOIN THE REAL WORLD.
TRAT TRAT
GRUM GRUM

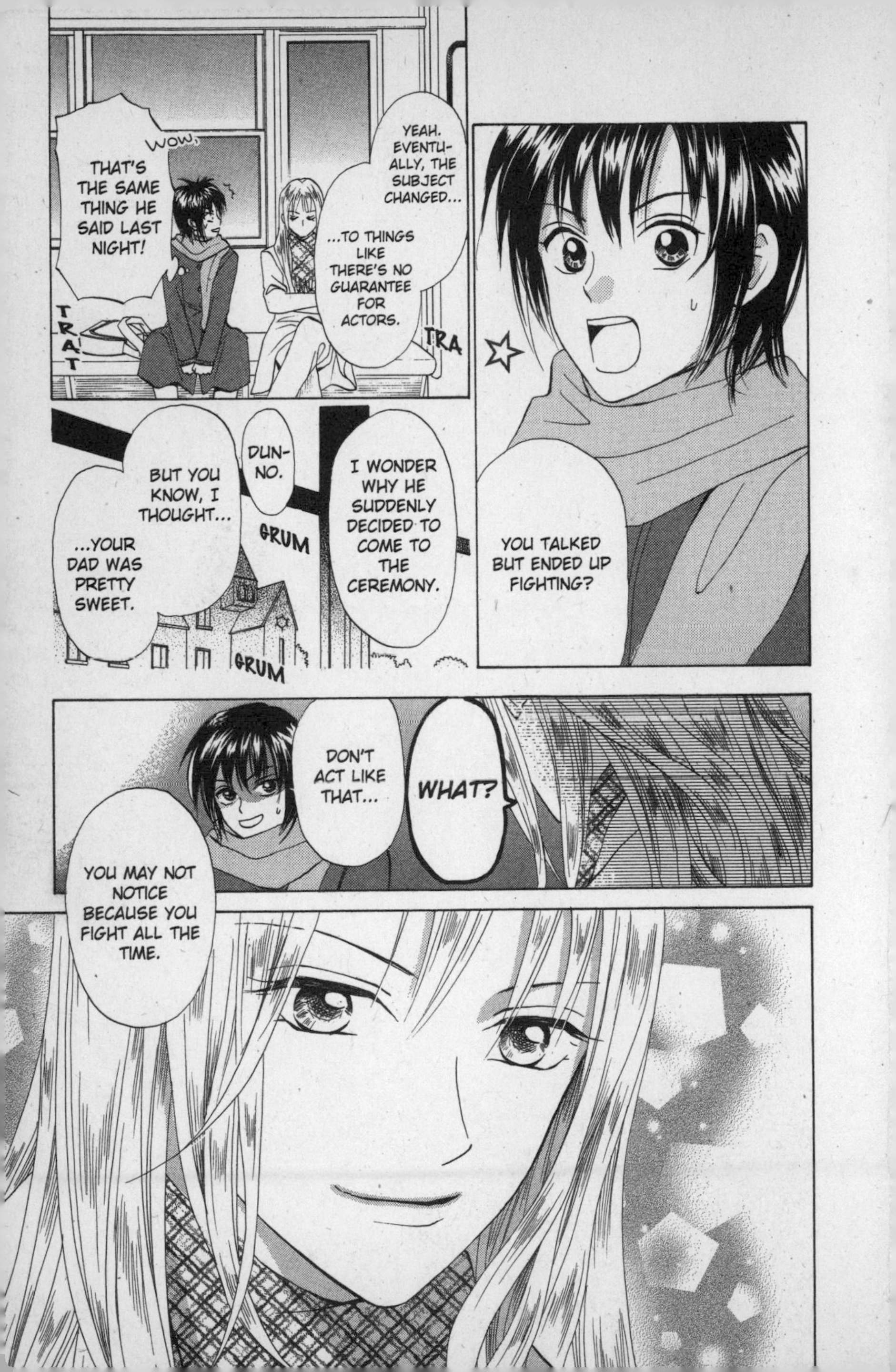
YOU TALKED BUT ENDED UP FIGHTING?
YEAH. EVENTU-ALLY, THE SUBJECT CHANGED...
...TO THINGS LIKE THERE'S NO GUARANTEE FOR ACTORS.
TRA
WOW,
THAT'S THE SAME THING HE SAID LAST NIGHT!
TRAT
I WONDER WHY HE SUDDENLY DECIDED TO COME TO THE CEREMONY.
DUN-NO.
GRUM
BUT YOU KNOW, I THOUGHT...
...YOUR DAD WAS PRETTY SWEET.
GRUM
WHAT?
DON'T ACT LIKE THAT...
YOU MAY NOT NOTICE BECAUSE YOU FIGHT ALL THE TIME.

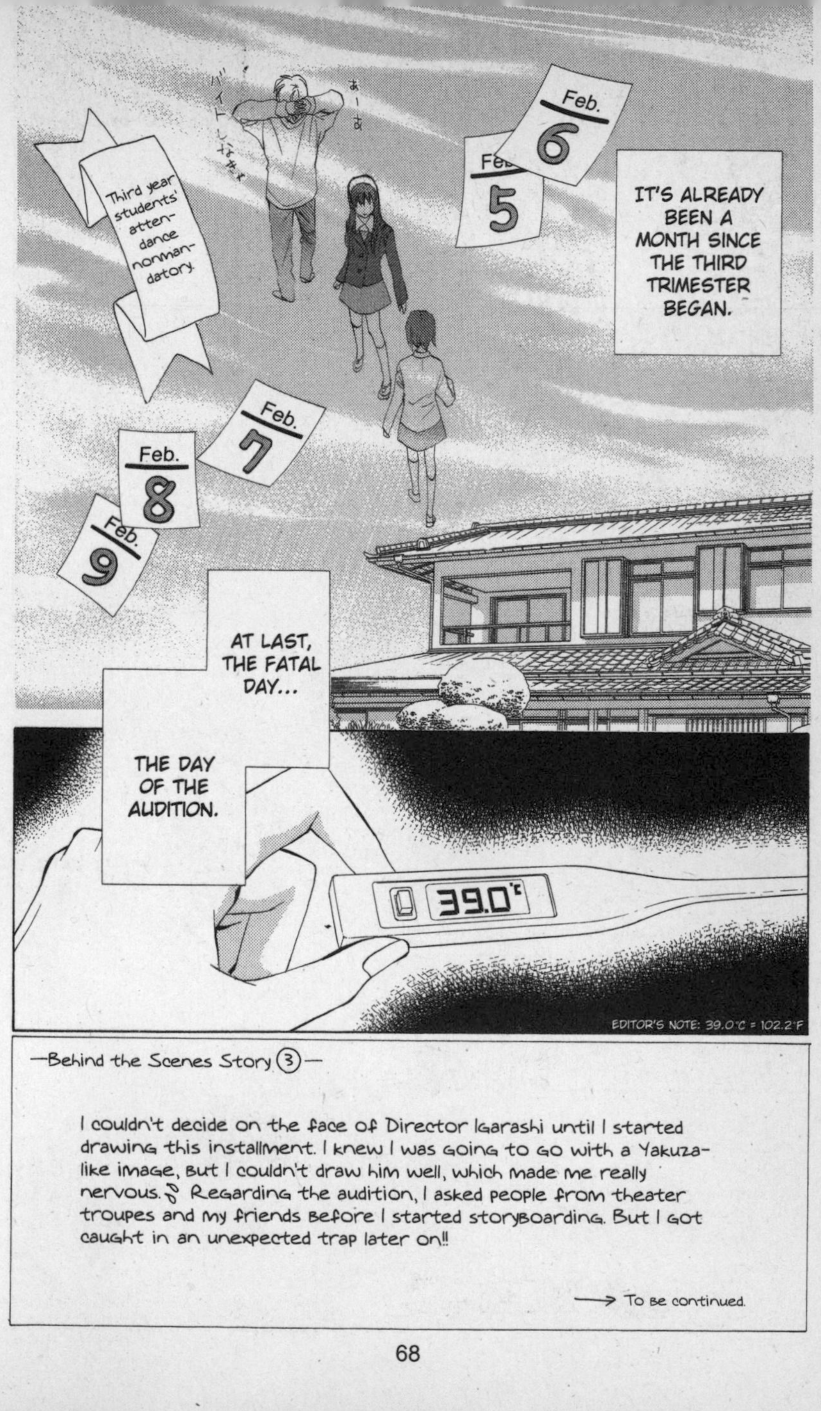
IT'S ALREADY BEEN A MONTH SINCE THE THIRD TRIMESTER BEGAN.
Feb. 6
Feb. 5
あーあ
バイトしなきゃ
Third year students' atten-dance nonman-datory.
Feb. 7
Feb. 8
Feb. 9
AT LAST, THE FATAL DAY...
THE DAY OF THE AUDITION.
39.0°c
EDITOR'S NOTE: 39.0°C = 102.2°F

—Behind the Scenes Story ③—

I couldn't decide on the face of Director Igarashi until I started drawing this installment. I knew I was going to go with a Yakuza-like image, but I couldn't draw him well, which made me really nervous. Regarding the audition, I asked people from theater troupes and my friends before I started storyboarding. But I got caught in an unexpected trap later on!!

→ To be continued.

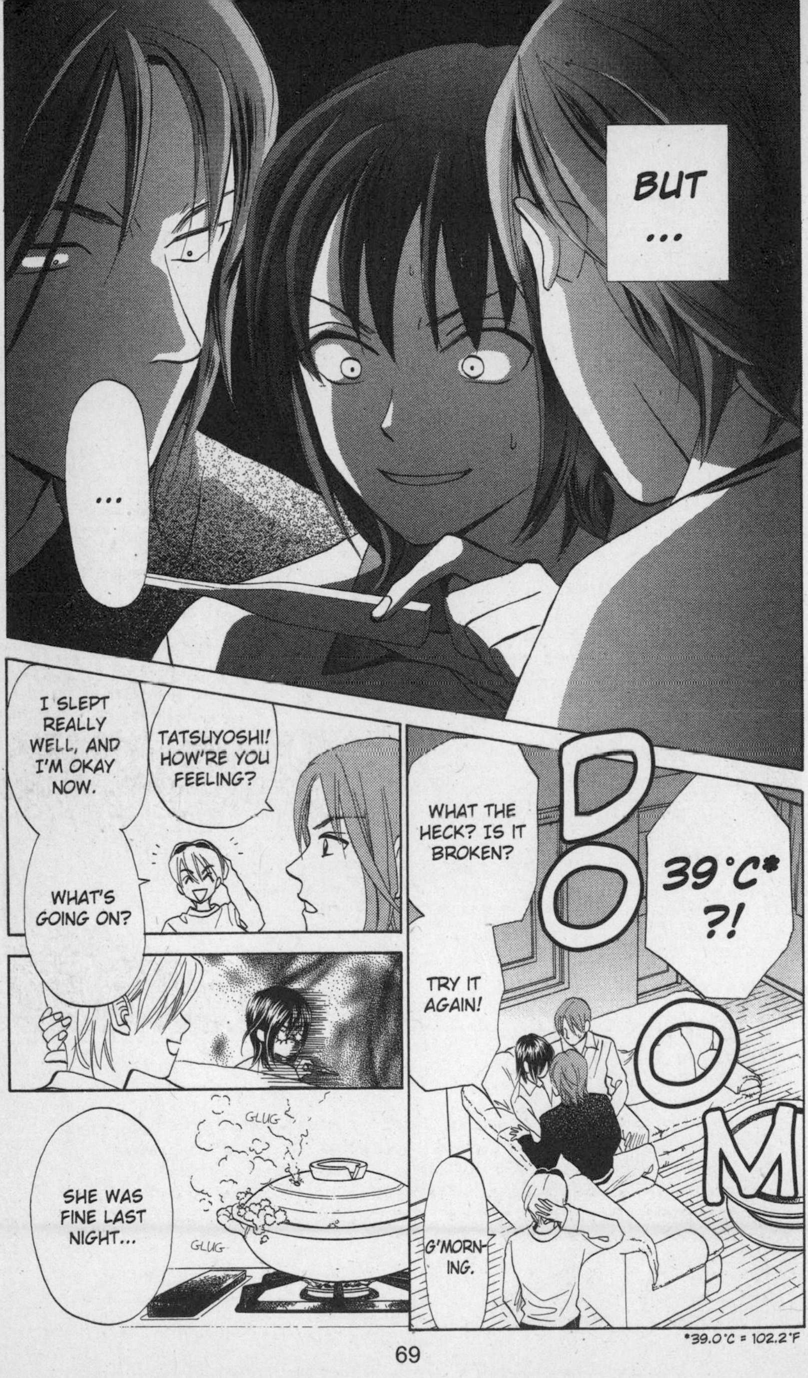
BUT ...
...
39°C* ?!
DOOM
WHAT THE HECK? IS IT BROKEN?
TRY IT AGAIN!
G'MORNING.
TATSUYOSHI! HOW'RE YOU FEELING?
I SLEPT REALLY WELL, AND I'M OKAY NOW.
WHAT'S GOING ON?
GLUG
GLUG
SHE WAS FINE LAST NIGHT...

*39.0°C = 102.2°F

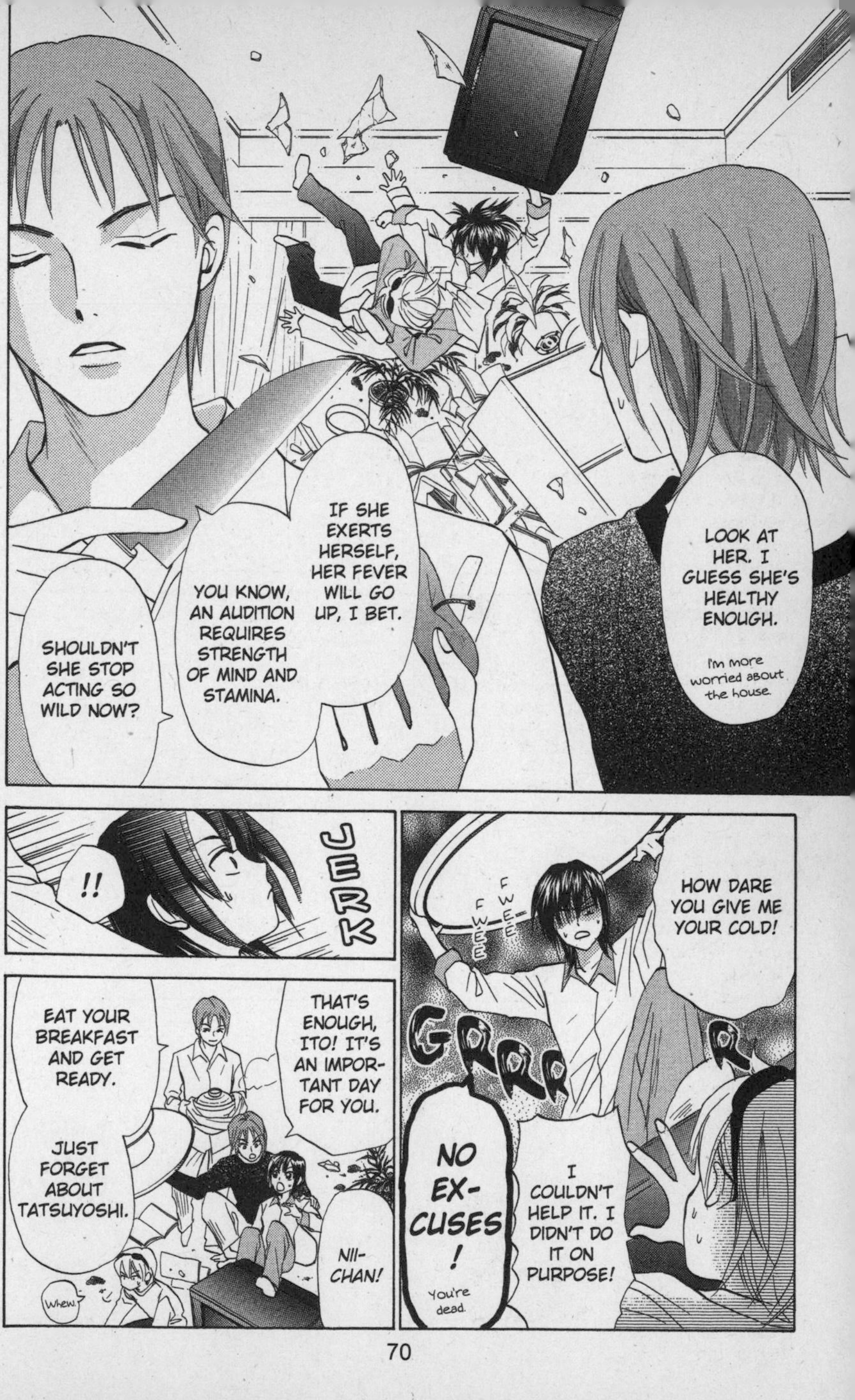
LOOK AT HER. I GUESS SHE'S HEALTHY ENOUGH.
I'm more worried about the house.
IF SHE EXERTS HERSELF, HER FEVER WILL GO UP, I BET.
YOU KNOW, AN AUDITION REQUIRES STRENGTH OF MIND AND STAMINA.
SHOULDN'T SHE STOP ACTING SO WILD NOW?
HOW DARE YOU GIVE ME YOUR COLD!
FWEE FWEE
GRRRR
I COULDN'T HELP IT. I DIDN'T DO IT ON PURPOSE!
NO EX-CUSES!
You're dead.
JERK
!!
THAT'S ENOUGH, ITO! IT'S AN IMPOR-TANT DAY FOR YOU.
EAT YOUR BREAKFAST AND GET READY.
JUST FORGET ABOUT TATSUYOSHI.
NII-CHAN!
Whew.

WE'LL TAKE CARE OF HIM. HE'S HALF DEAD ALREADY.
HEY!!
Why?!
REST ASSURED. EVEN THIS WILL BECOME A GOOD MEMORY SOMEDAY.
YEAH, YOU'LL LAUGH ABOUT IT...
I'M YELLED AT EVERY DAY! WHEN WILL THAT EVER BE A GOOD MEMORY?
STM
STM
AAHHHHH
CAN'T BE HELPED.
He infected someone he shouldn't have.
URGH, MY HEAD HURTS.
THROB
THROB
BY THE WAY, ITO, WEREN'T YOU GOING TO HEAD OUT AT 8:30?
HUH? YEAH?
9:00 A.M.

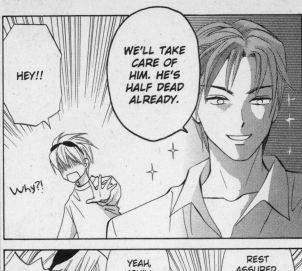

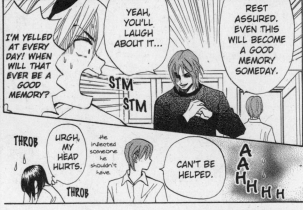

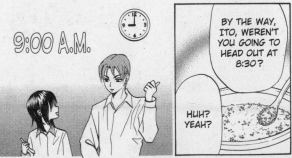

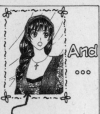

And ...

There were a considerable number of readers who thought I painted this red on Ito's skin right next to it. Of course, some readers got it right, too—although not so many. The red on the dress sure looks a bit blurred and dirty.

I remember I had no time to correct it...

Not only that, the splash page was done in the shortest time ever. It usually takes three to five days, but I finished it in 16 hours, including the time it took to do the rough sketch—and that was after I pulled all-nighters for two nights in a row. You know... I just had no time at all.

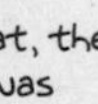

It would be nice if I could do the splash page after a break. (Laugh)

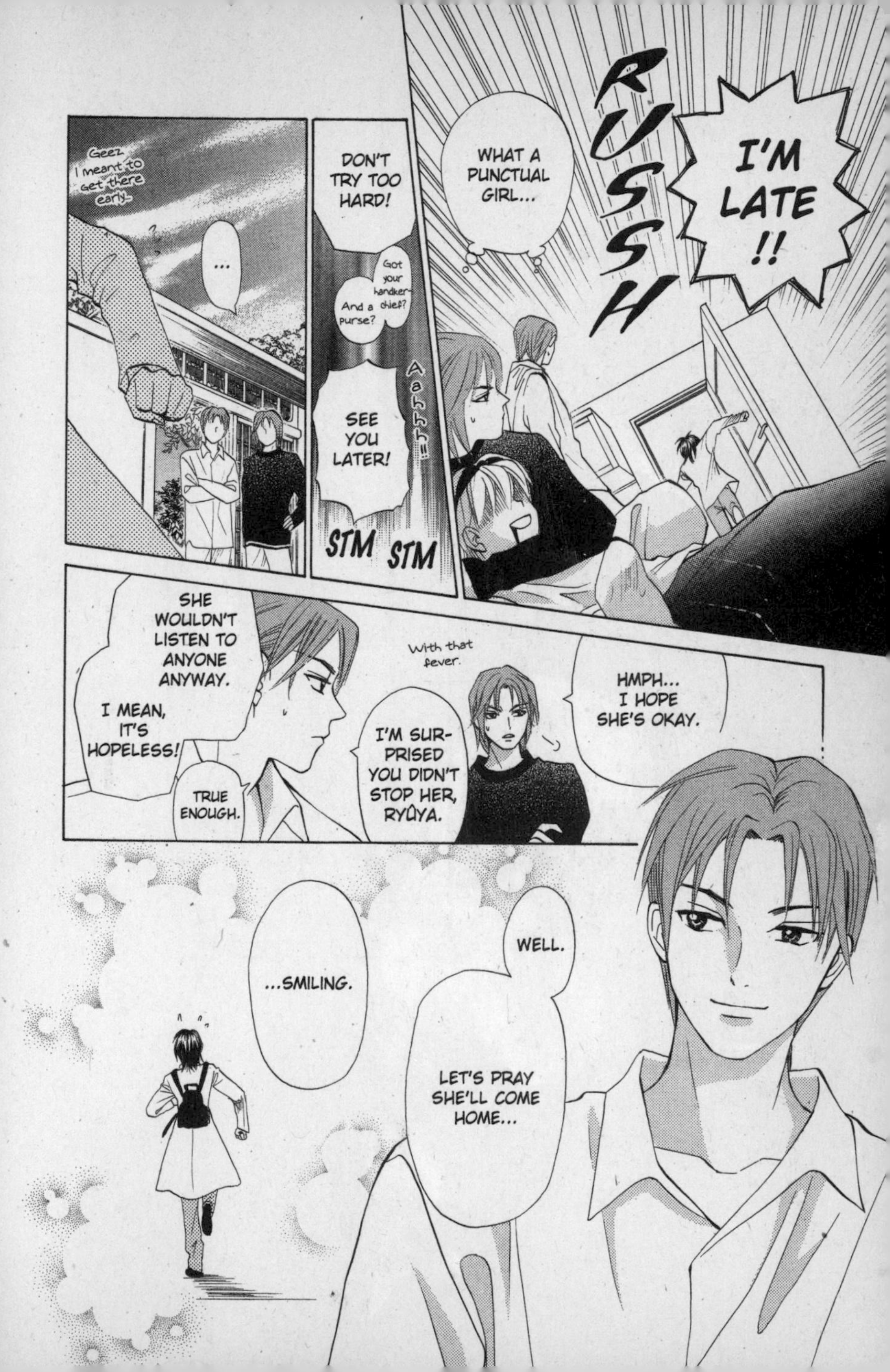
I'M LATE !!
RUSH
WHAT A PUNCTUAL GIRL...
DON'T TRY TOO HARD!
Got your handker-chief?
And a purse?
SEE YOU LATER!
Aahhh!!
STM STM
Geez I meant to get there early...
...
HMPH... I HOPE SHE'S OKAY.
With that fever.
I'M SUR-PRISED YOU DIDN'T STOP HER, RYÛYA.
SHE WOULDN'T LISTEN TO ANYONE ANYWAY.
I MEAN, IT'S HOPELESS!
TRUE ENOUGH.
WELL.
LET'S PRAY SHE'LL COME HOME...
...SMILING.

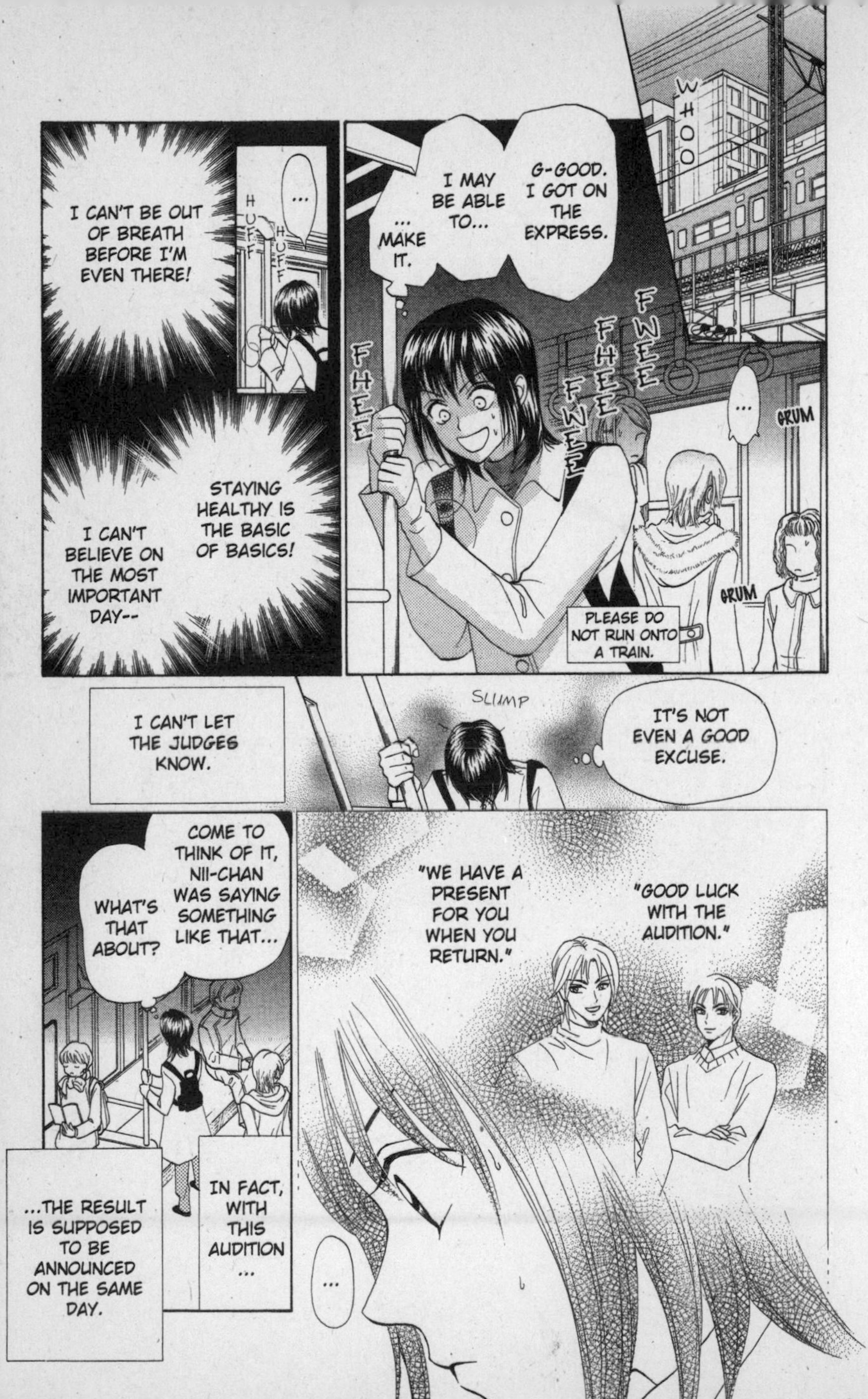
WHOO
G-GOOD. I GOT ON THE EXPRESS.
I MAY BE ABLE TO...
... MAKE IT.
FWEE
FHEE
FWEE
FHEE
...
GRUM
GRUM
PLEASE DO NOT RUN ONTO A TRAIN.
...
HUFF
HUFF
I CAN'T BE OUT OF BREATH BEFORE I'M EVEN THERE!
STAYING HEALTHY IS THE BASIC OF BASICS!
I CAN'T BELIEVE ON THE MOST IMPORTANT DAY--
IT'S NOT EVEN A GOOD EXCUSE.
SLUMP
I CAN'T LET THE JUDGES KNOW.
"GOOD LUCK WITH THE AUDITION."
"WE HAVE A PRESENT FOR YOU WHEN YOU RETURN."
...
COME TO THINK OF IT, NII-CHAN WAS SAYING SOMETHING LIKE THAT...
WHAT'S THAT ABOUT?
IN FACT, WITH THIS AUDITION ...
...THE RESULT IS SUPPOSED TO BE ANNOUNCED ON THE SAME DAY.

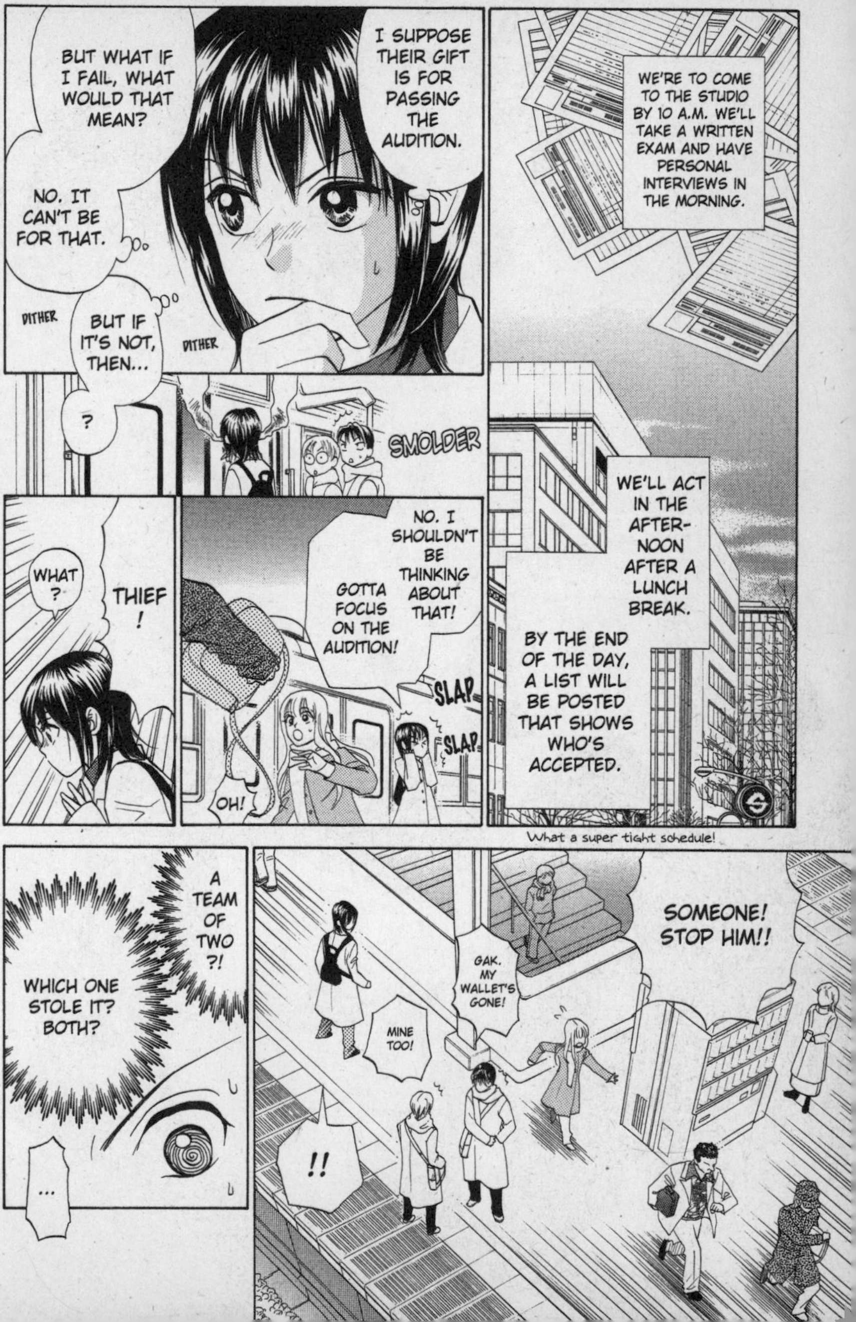
WE'RE TO COME TO THE STUDIO BY 10 A.M. WE'LL TAKE A WRITTEN EXAM AND HAVE PERSONAL INTERVIEWS IN THE MORNING.
WE'LL ACT IN THE AFTER-NOON AFTER A LUNCH BREAK.
BY THE END OF THE DAY, A LIST WILL BE POSTED THAT SHOWS WHO'S ACCEPTED.
I SUPPOSE THEIR GIFT IS FOR PASSING THE AUDITION.
BUT WHAT IF I FAIL, WHAT WOULD THAT MEAN?
NO. IT CAN'T BE FOR THAT.
DITHER
BUT IF IT'S NOT, THEN...
DITHER
SMOLDER
?
NO. I SHOULDN'T BE THINKING ABOUT THAT!
GOTTA FOCUS ON THE AUDITION!
SLAP
SLAP
OH!
THIEF!
WHAT?
What a super tight schedule!
SOMEONE! STOP HIM!!
GAK. MY WALLET'S GONE!
MINE TOO!
!!
A TEAM OF TWO?!
WHICH ONE STOLE IT? BOTH?
...

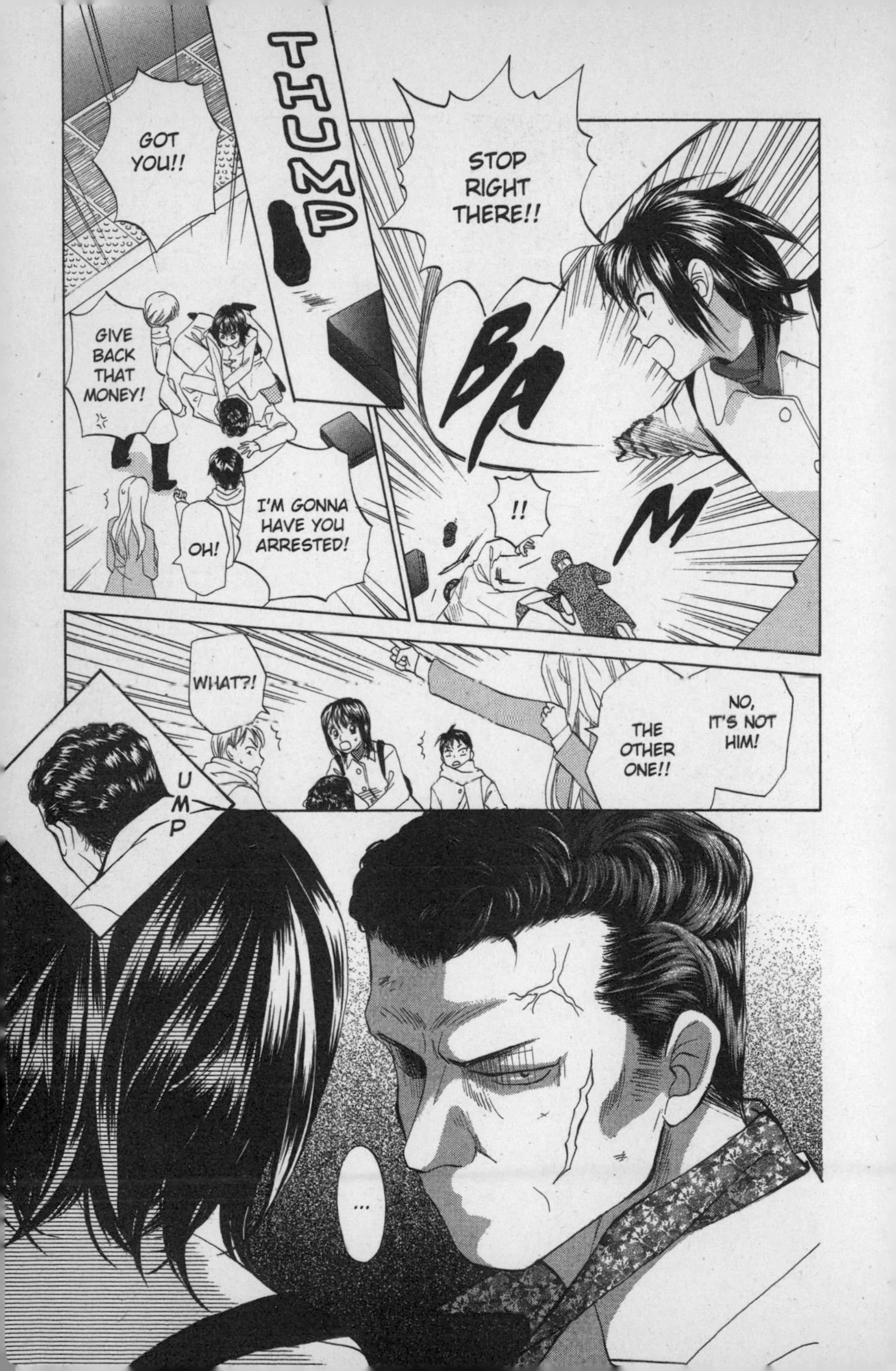
STOP RIGHT THERE!!
BAM
!!
THUMP
GOT YOU!!
GIVE BACK THAT MONEY!
I'M GONNA HAVE YOU ARRESTED!
OH!
NO, IT'S NOT HIM!
THE OTHER ONE!!
WHAT?!
UMP
...

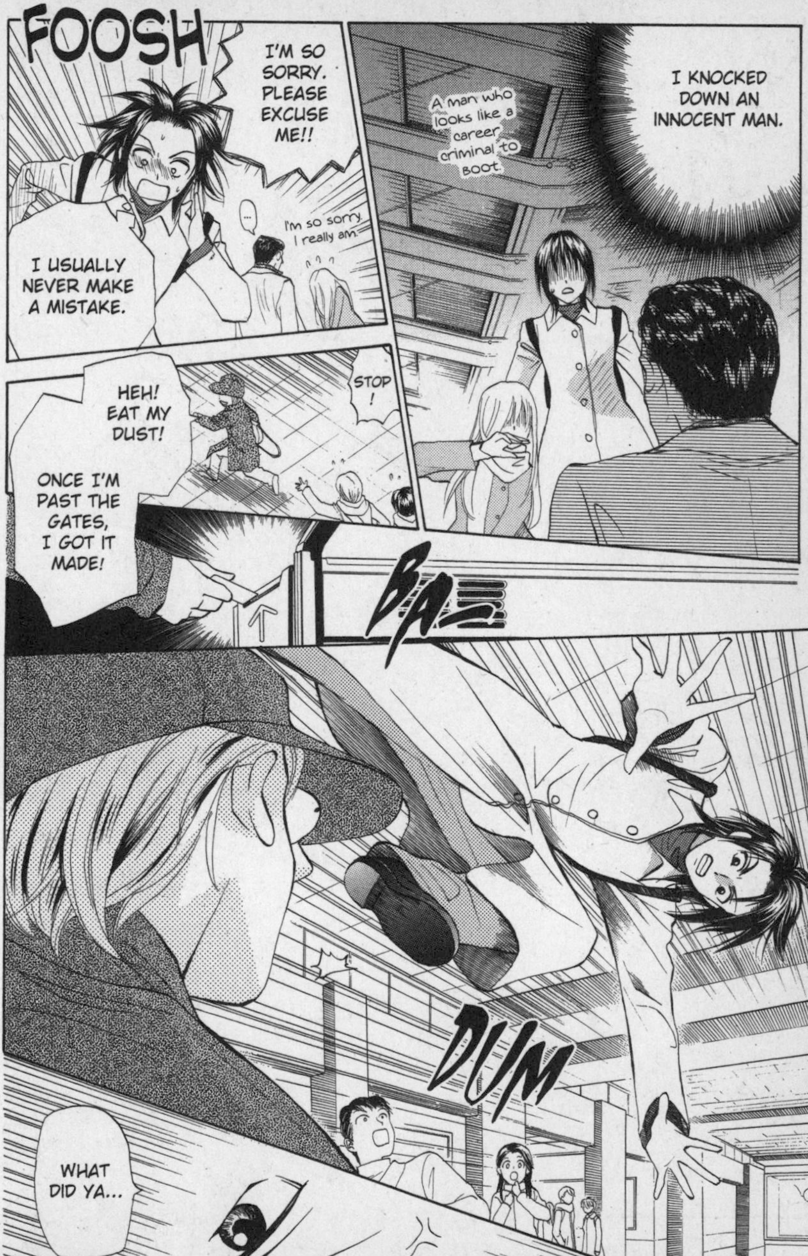
I KNOCKED DOWN AN INNOCENT MAN.
A man who looks like a career criminal to boot.
FOOSH
I'M SO SORRY. PLEASE EXCUSE ME!!
...
I'm so sorry. I really am.
I USUALLY NEVER MAKE A MISTAKE.
STOP!
HEH! EAT MY DUST!
ONCE I'M PAST THE GATES, I GOT IT MADE!
BA
DUM
WHAT DID YA...

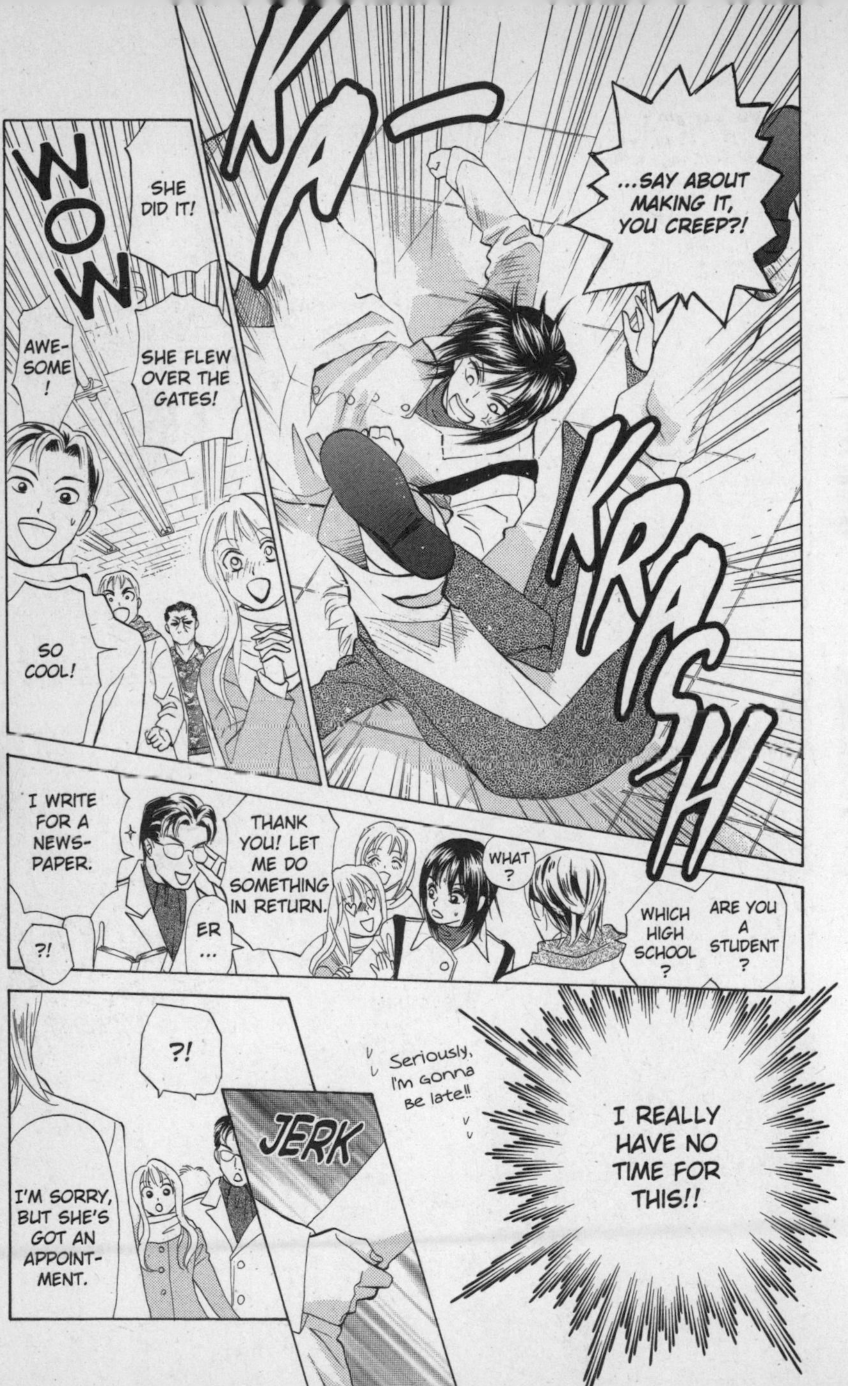
KA-
...SAY ABOUT MAKING IT, YOU CREEP?!
KRASH
WOW
SHE DID IT!
SHE FLEW OVER THE GATES!
AWE-SOME!
SO COOL!
ARE YOU A STUDENT?
WHICH HIGH SCHOOL?
WHAT?
THANK YOU! LET ME DO SOMETHING IN RETURN.
ER...
I WRITE FOR A NEWS-PAPER.
?!
I REALLY HAVE NO TIME FOR THIS!!
Seriously, I'm gonna be late!!
JERK
?!
I'M SORRY, BUT SHE'S GOT AN APPOINT-MENT.

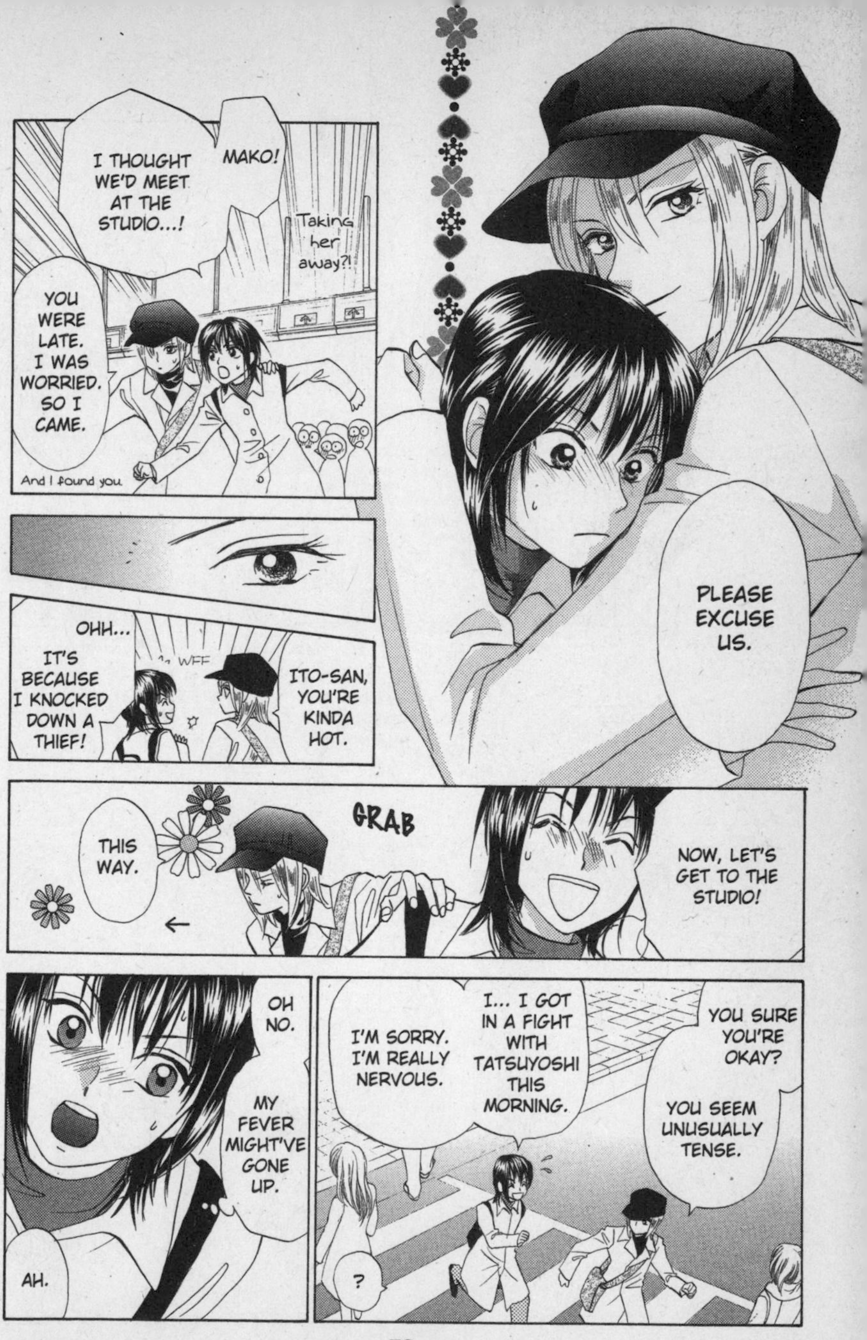

PLEASE EXCUSE US.
MAKO!
Taking her away?!
I THOUGHT WE'D MEET AT THE STUDIO...!
YOU WERE LATE. I WAS WORRIED. SO I CAME.
And I found you.
ITO-SAN, YOU'RE KINDA HOT.
OHH...
IT'S BECAUSE I KNOCKED DOWN A THIEF!
NOW, LET'S GET TO THE STUDIO!
GRAB
THIS WAY.
YOU SURE YOU'RE OKAY?
YOU SEEM UNUSUALLY TENSE.
I... I GOT IN A FIGHT WITH TATSUYOSHI THIS MORNING.
I'M SORRY. I'M REALLY NERVOUS.
?
OH NO.
MY FEVER MIGHT'VE GONE UP.
AH.

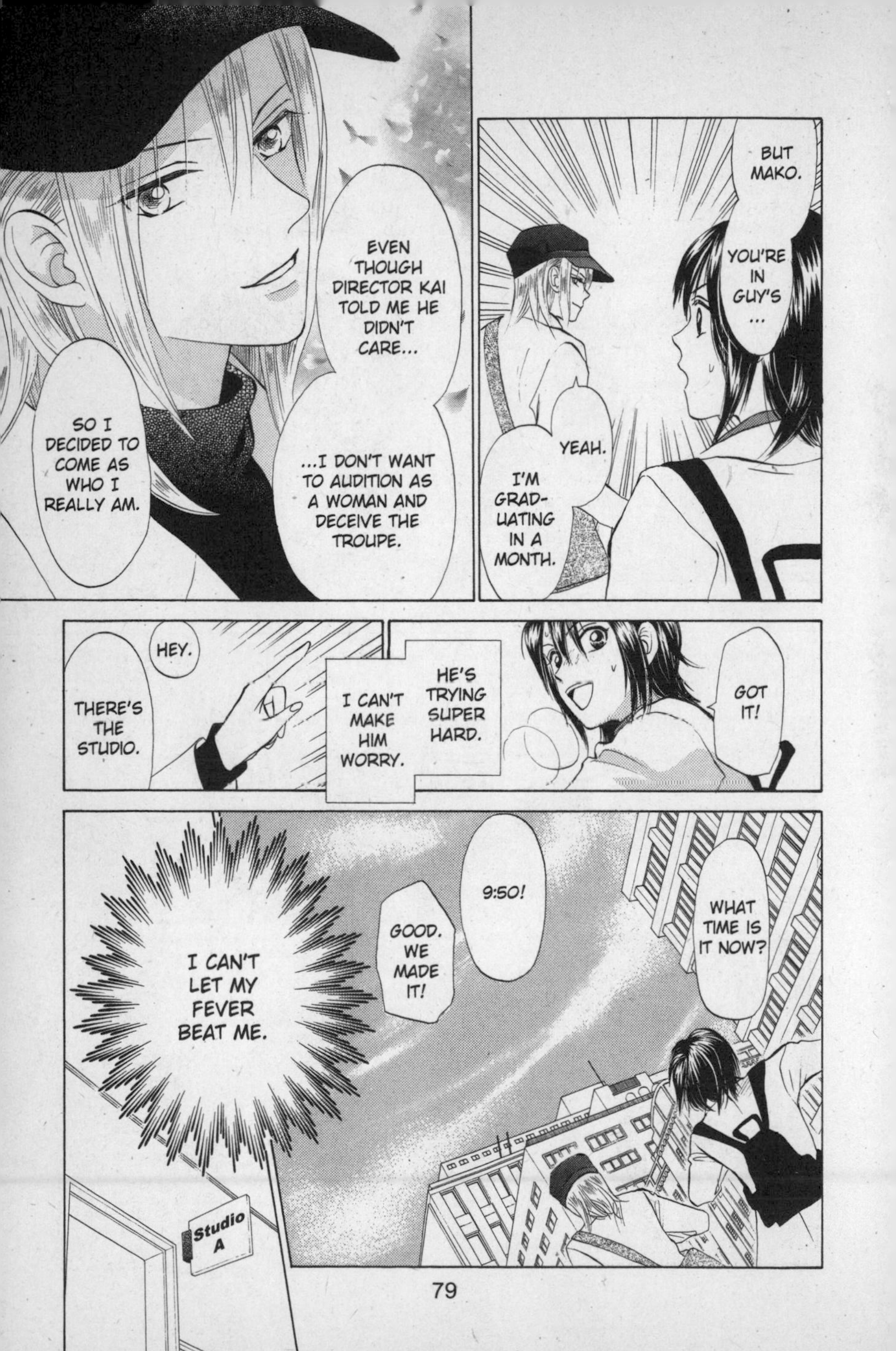
BUT MAKO.
YOU'RE IN GUY'S ...
YEAH.
I'M GRAD-UATING IN A MONTH.
EVEN THOUGH DIRECTOR KAI TOLD ME HE DIDN'T CARE...
...I DON'T WANT TO AUDITION AS A WOMAN AND DECEIVE THE TROUPE.
SO I DECIDED TO COME AS WHO I REALLY AM.
GOT IT!
HE'S TRYING SUPER HARD.
I CAN'T MAKE HIM WORRY.
HEY.
THERE'S THE STUDIO.
WHAT TIME IS IT NOW?
9:50!
GOOD. WE MADE IT!
I CAN'T LET MY FEVER BEAT ME.
Studio A

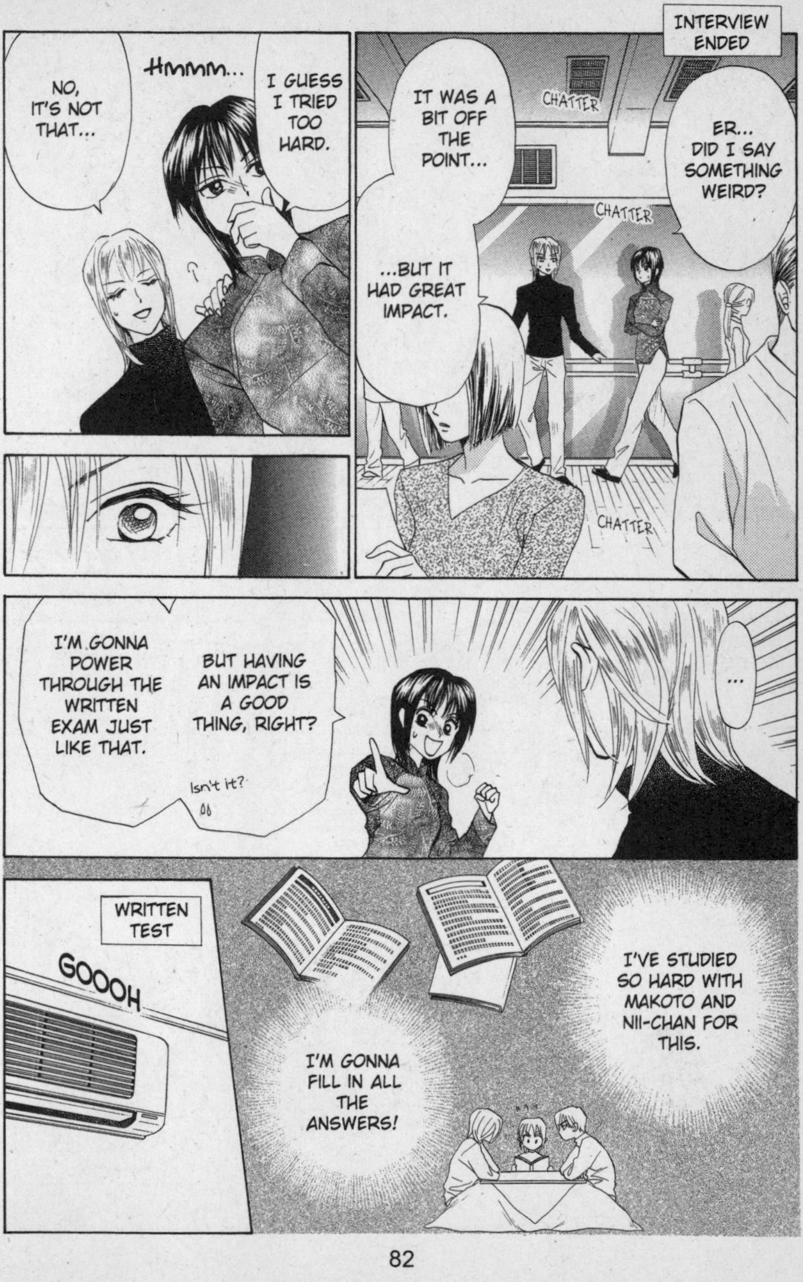
INTERVIEW ENDED
ER... DID I SAY SOMETHING WEIRD?
CHATTER
IT WAS A BIT OFF THE POINT...
CHATTER
...BUT IT HAD GREAT IMPACT.
CHATTER
I GUESS I TRIED TOO HARD.
Hmmm...
NO, IT'S NOT THAT...
...
BUT HAVING AN IMPACT IS A GOOD THING, RIGHT?
Isn't it?
I'M GONNA POWER THROUGH THE WRITTEN EXAM JUST LIKE THAT.
WRITTEN TEST
GOOOH
I'VE STUDIED SO HARD WITH MAKOTO AND NII-CHAN FOR THIS.
I'M GONNA FILL IN ALL THE ANSWERS!

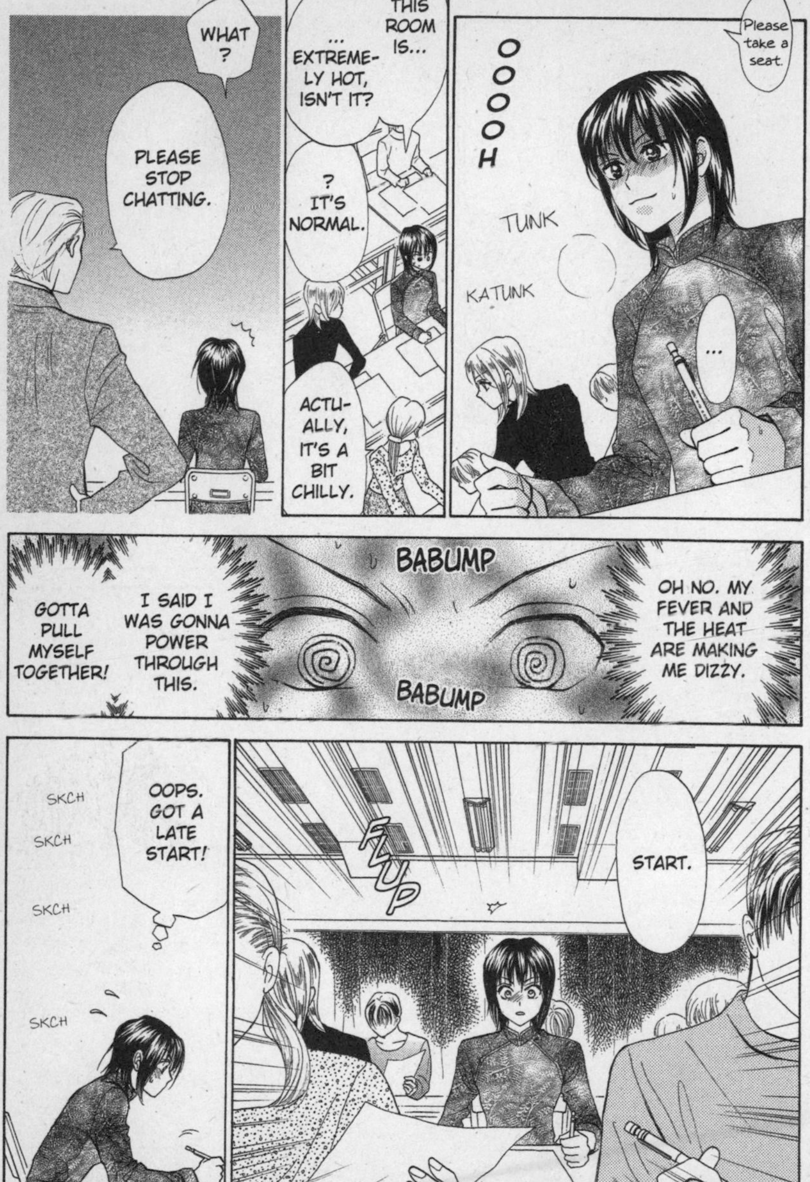

Please take a seat.
OOOOOH
TUNK
KATUNK
...
THIS ROOM IS...
... EXTREME-LY HOT, ISN'T IT?
? IT'S NORMAL.
ACTU-ALLY, IT'S A BIT CHILLY.
WHAT?
PLEASE STOP CHATTING.
OH NO. MY FEVER AND THE HEAT ARE MAKING ME DIZZY.
BABUMP
BABUMP
I SAID I WAS GONNA POWER THROUGH THIS.
GOTTA PULL MYSELF TOGETHER!
START.
FLUP
OOPS. GOT A LATE START!
SKCH
SKCH
SKCH
SKCH

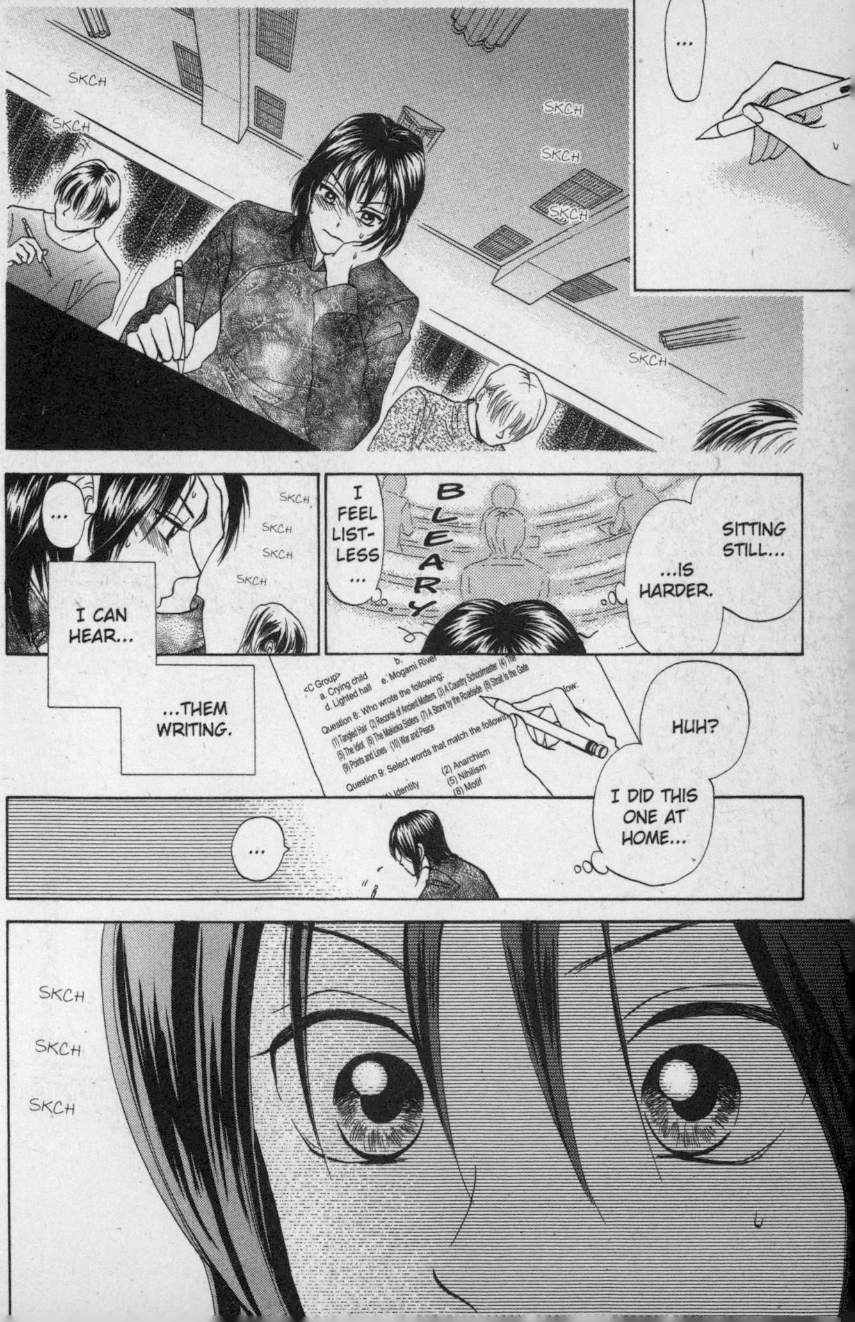
...
SKCH
SKCH
SKCH
SKCH
SKCH
SKCH
SITTING STILL...
...IS HARDER.
I FEEL LISTLESS...
BLEARY
...
SKCH
SKCH
SKCH
SKCH
I CAN HEAR...
...THEM WRITING.
HUH?
I DID THIS ONE AT HOME...
<C Group>
a. Crying child
d. Lighted hall
e. Mogami River
Question 8: Who wrote the following:
(1) Tangled Hair (2) Records of Ancient Matters (3) A Country Schoolmaster
(5) The Idiot (6) The Makioka Sisters (7) A Stone by the Roadside (8) Strait Is the Gate
(9) Points and Lines (10) War and Peace
Question 9: Select words that match the followi
(2) Anarchism
(5) Nihilism
(8) Motif
...
SKCH
SKCH
SKCH

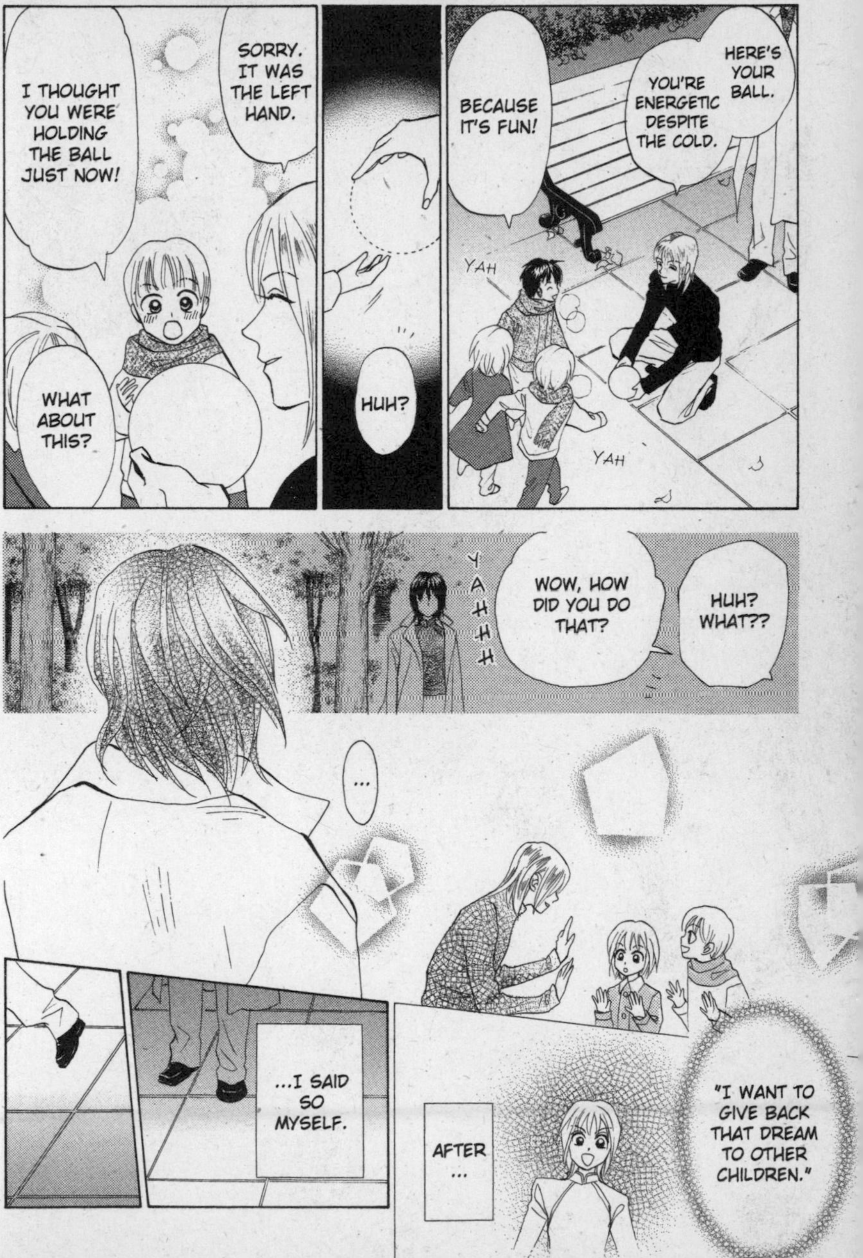
HERE'S YOUR BALL.
YOU'RE ENERGETIC DESPITE THE COLD.
BECAUSE IT'S FUN!
YAH
YAH
HUH?
SORRY. IT WAS THE LEFT HAND.
I THOUGHT YOU WERE HOLDING THE BALL JUST NOW!
WHAT ABOUT THIS?
HUH? WHAT??
WOW, HOW DID YOU DO THAT?
YAHHH
...
"I WANT TO GIVE BACK THAT DREAM TO OTHER CHILDREN."
AFTER ...
...I SAID SO MYSELF.

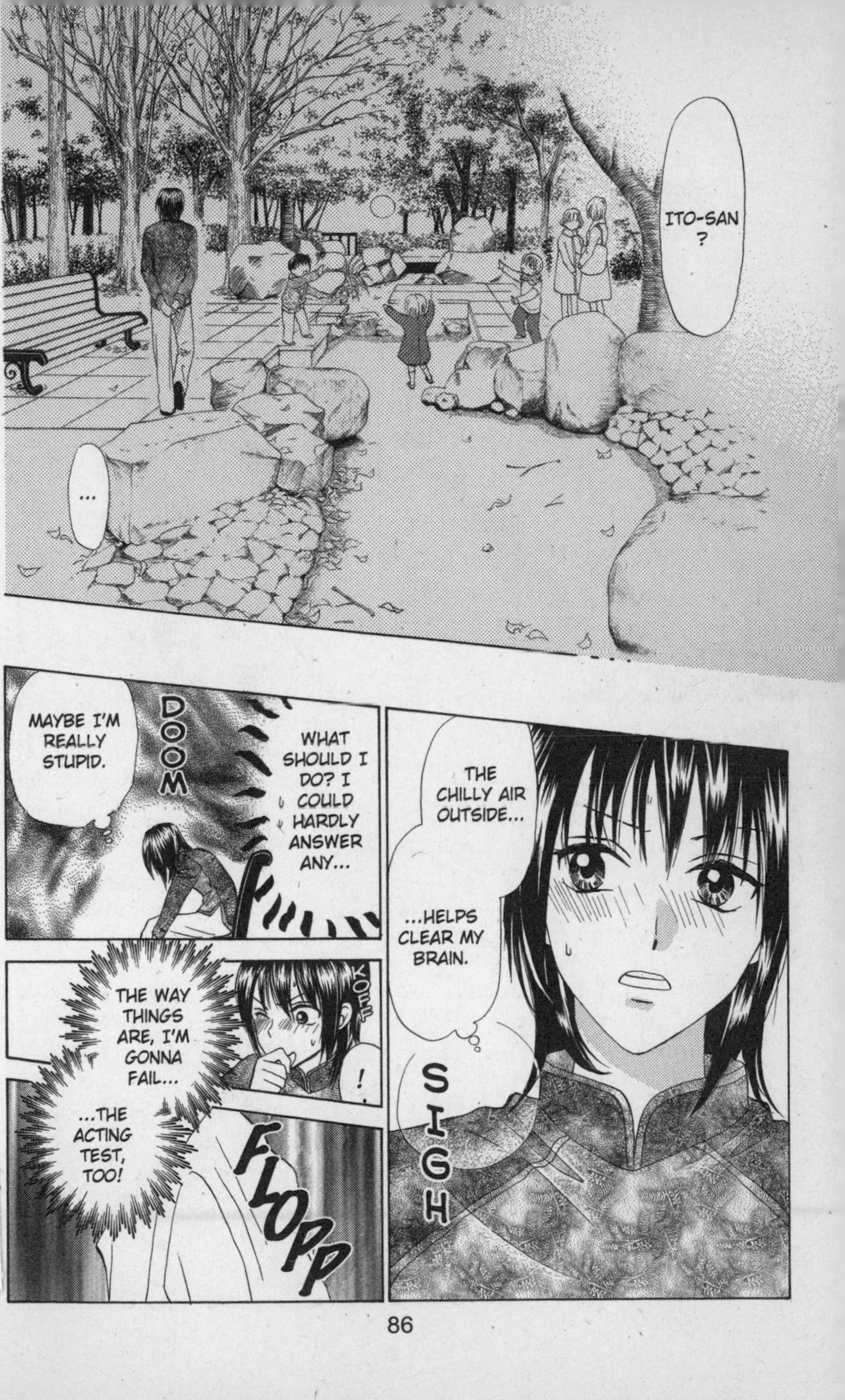
ITO-SAN ?
...
THE CHILLY AIR OUTSIDE...
...HELPS CLEAR MY BRAIN.
SIGH
WHAT SHOULD I DO? I COULD HARDLY ANSWER ANY...
DOOM
MAYBE I'M REALLY STUPID.
KOFF
!
THE WAY THINGS ARE, I'M GONNA FAIL...
...THE ACTING TEST, TOO!
FLOPP

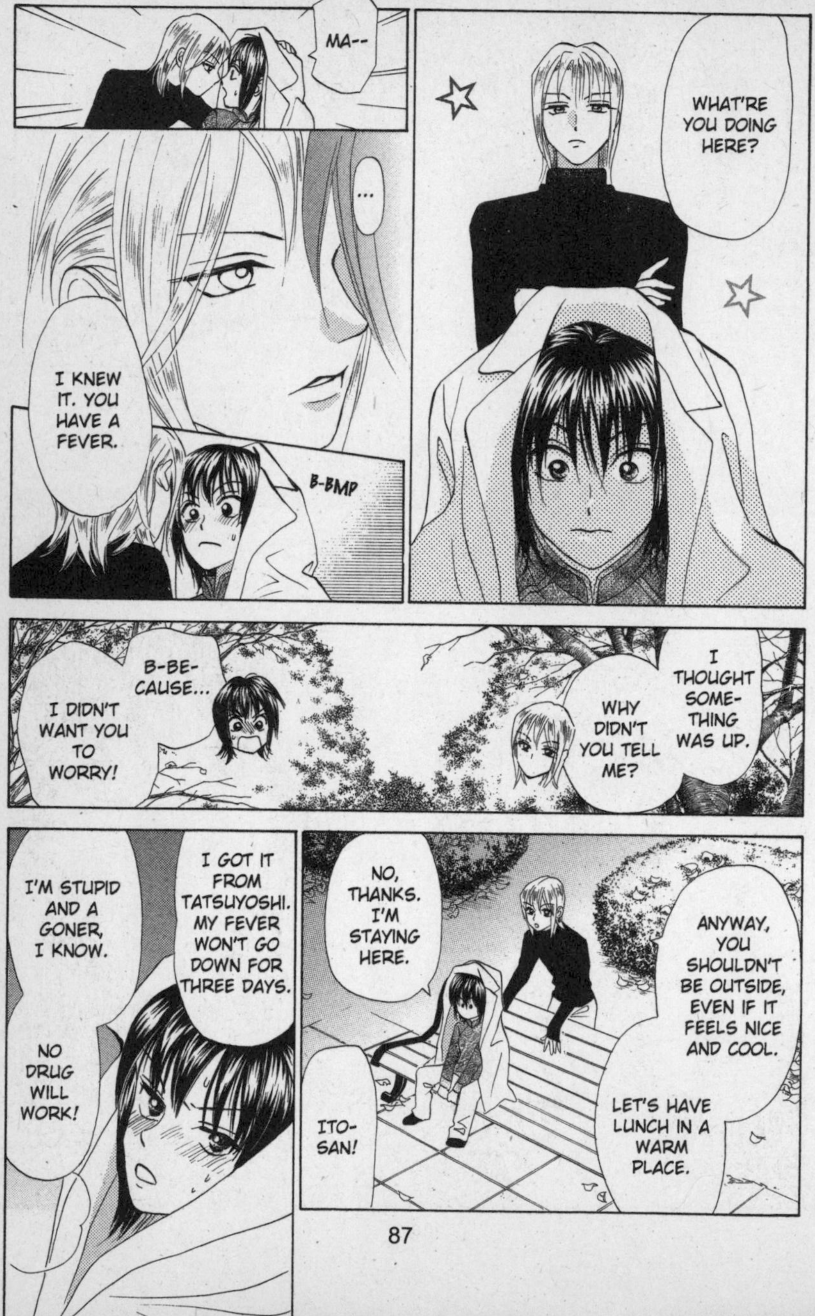
WHAT'RE YOU DOING HERE?
MA--
...
I KNEW IT. YOU HAVE A FEVER.
B-BMP
I THOUGHT SOMETHING WAS UP.
WHY DIDN'T YOU TELL ME?
B-BE-CAUSE...
I DIDN'T WANT YOU TO WORRY!
ANYWAY, YOU SHOULDN'T BE OUTSIDE, EVEN IF IT FEELS NICE AND COOL.
LET'S HAVE LUNCH IN A WARM PLACE.
NO, THANKS. I'M STAYING HERE.
ITO-SAN!
I GOT IT FROM TATSUYOSHI. MY FEVER WON'T GO DOWN FOR THREE DAYS.
I'M STUPID AND A GONER, I KNOW.
NO DRUG WILL WORK!

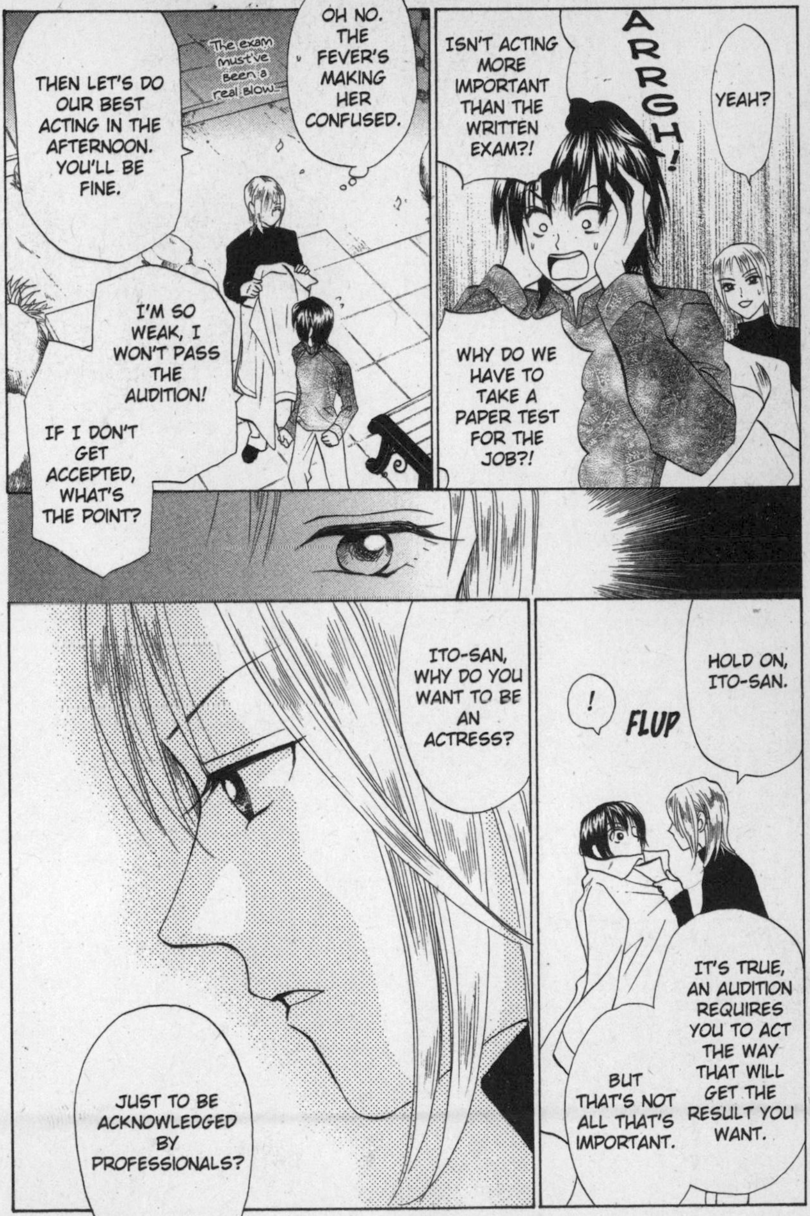

YEAH?
ARRGH!
ISN'T ACTING MORE IMPORTANT THAN THE WRITTEN EXAM?!
WHY DO WE HAVE TO TAKE A PAPER TEST FOR THE JOB?!
OH NO. THE FEVER'S MAKING HER CONFUSED.
The exam must've been a real blow...
THEN LET'S DO OUR BEST ACTING IN THE AFTERNOON. YOU'LL BE FINE.
I'M SO WEAK, I WON'T PASS THE AUDITION!
IF I DON'T GET ACCEPTED, WHAT'S THE POINT?
HOLD ON, ITO-SAN.
!
FLUP
IT'S TRUE, AN AUDITION REQUIRES YOU TO ACT THE WAY THAT WILL GET THE RESULT YOU WANT.
BUT THAT'S NOT ALL THAT'S IMPORTANT.
ITO-SAN, WHY DO YOU WANT TO BE AN ACTRESS?
JUST TO BE ACKNOWLEDGED BY PROFESSIONALS?

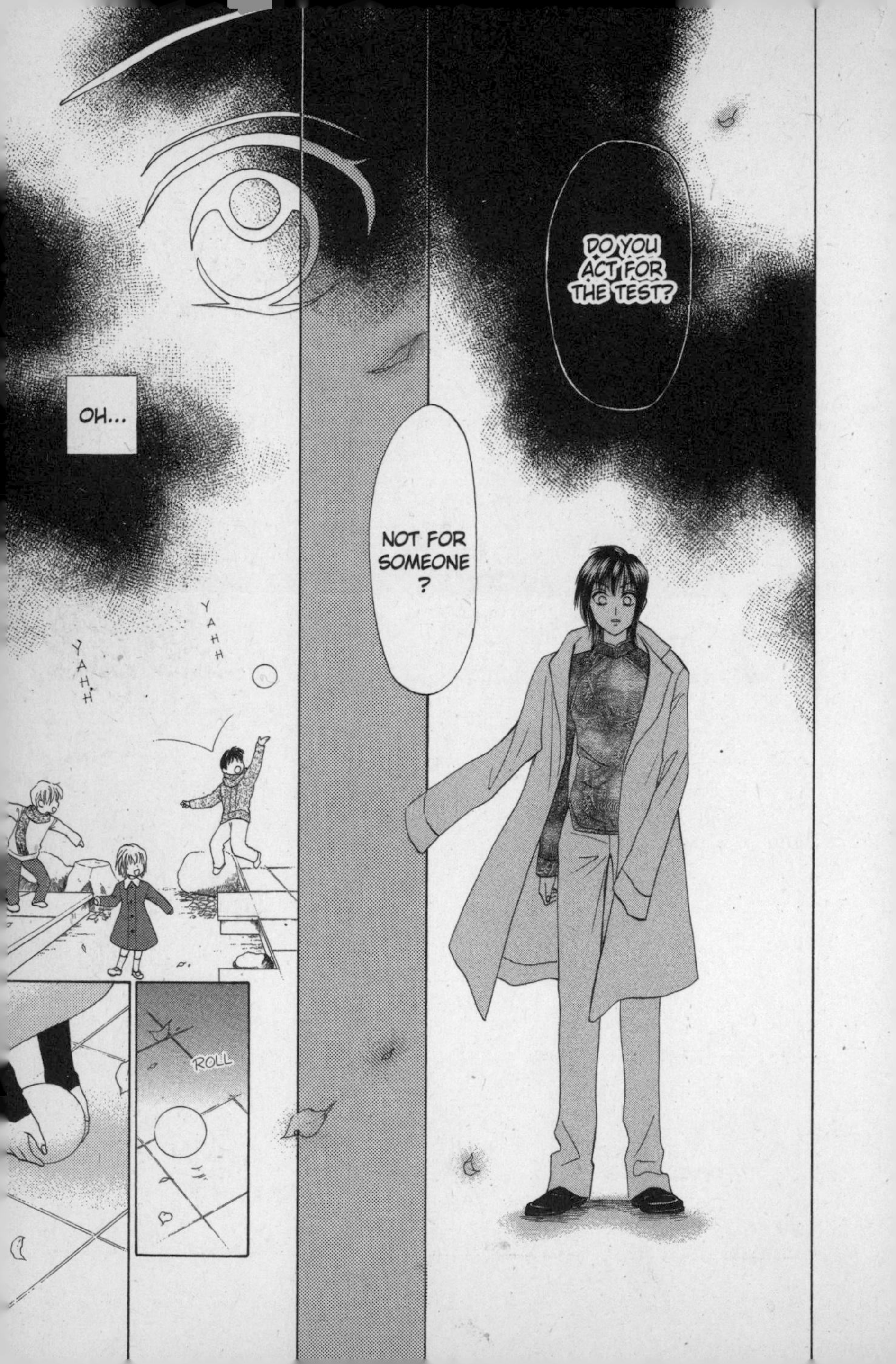
DO YOU ACT FOR THE TEST?
NOT FOR SOMEONE ?
OH...
YAHH
YAHH
ROLL

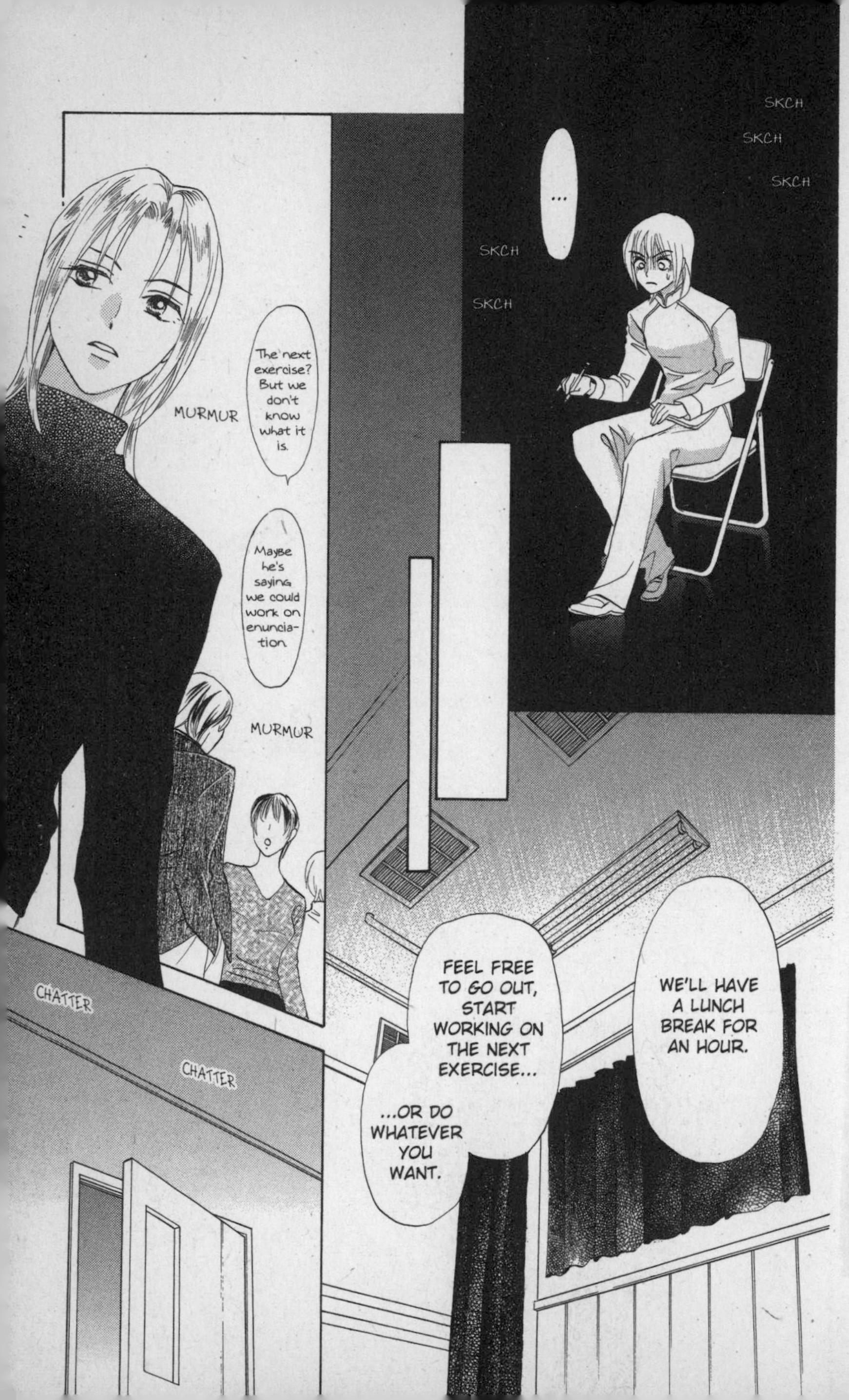
SKCH
SKCH
SKCH
...
SKCH
SKCH
WE'LL HAVE A LUNCH BREAK FOR AN HOUR.
FEEL FREE TO GO OUT, START WORKING ON THE NEXT EXERCISE...
...OR DO WHATEVER YOU WANT.
The next exercise? But we don't know what it is.
MURMUR
Maybe he's saying we could work on enuncia-tion.
MURMUR
CHATTER
CHATTER

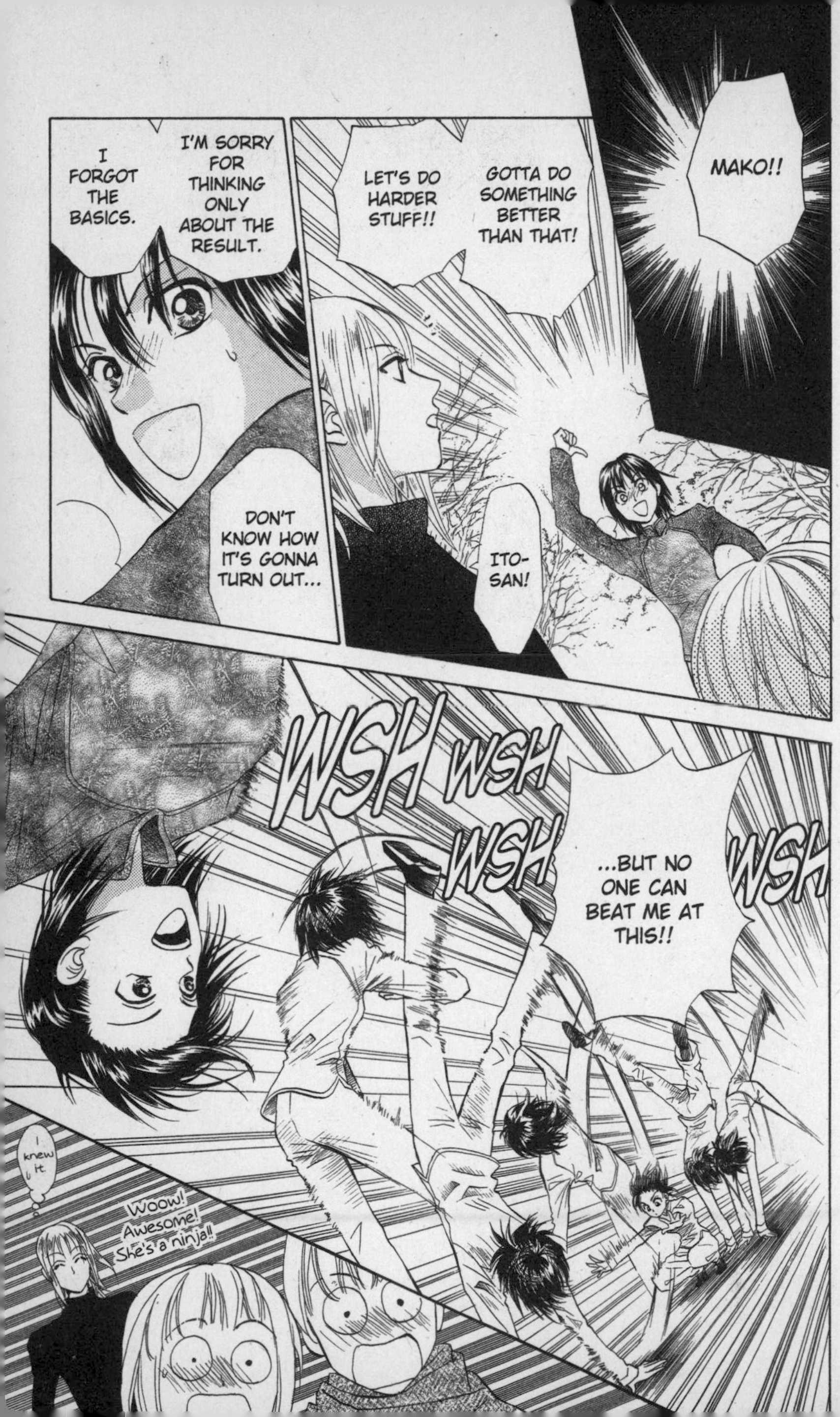
MAKO!!
GOTTA DO SOMETHING BETTER THAN THAT!
LET'S DO HARDER STUFF!!
ITO-SAN!
I'M SORRY FOR THINKING ONLY ABOUT THE RESULT.
I FORGOT THE BASICS.
DON'T KNOW HOW IT'S GONNA TURN OUT...
WSH
WSH WSH
WSH
...BUT NO ONE CAN BEAT ME AT THIS!!
Woow! Awesome! She's a ninja!!
I knew it.

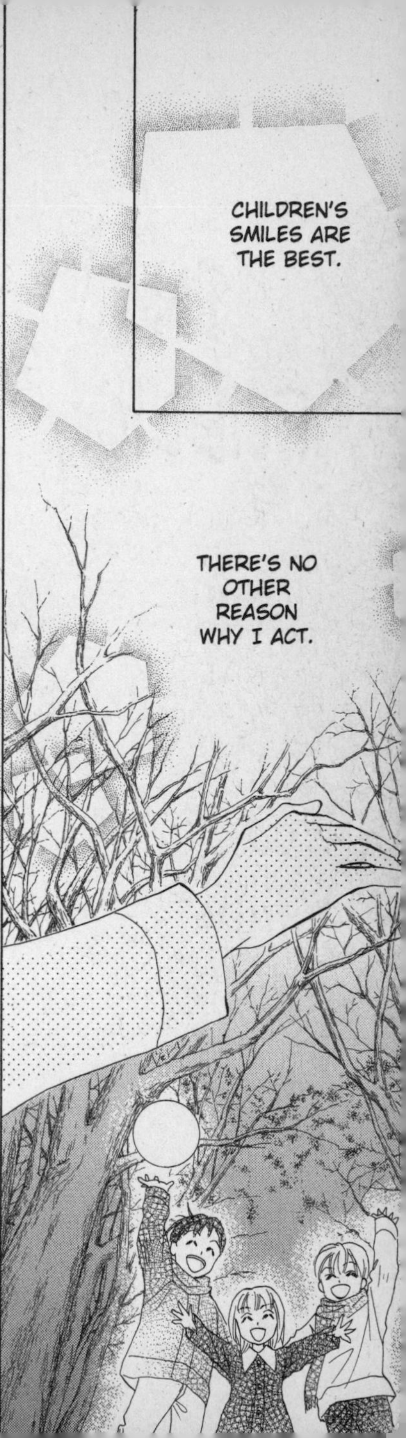
CHILDREN'S SMILES ARE THE BEST.
THERE'S NO OTHER REASON WHY I ACT.

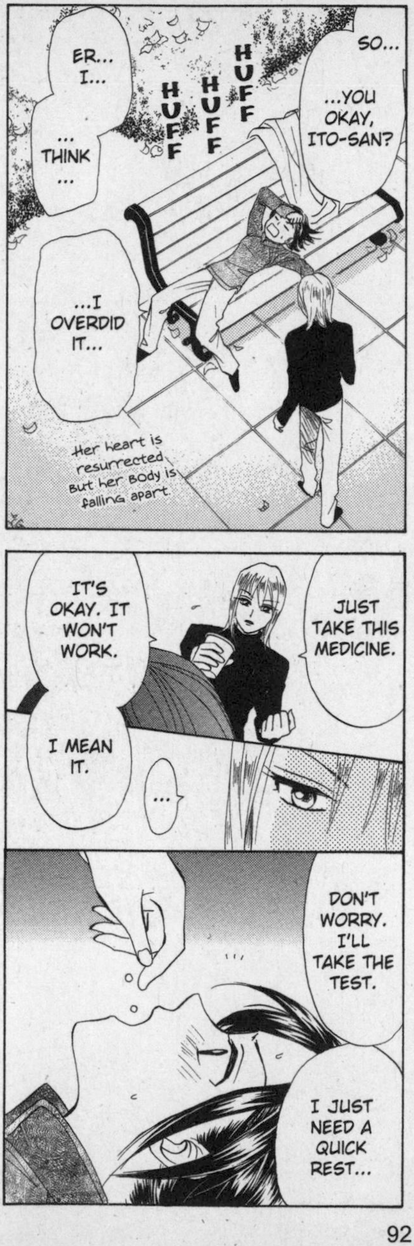
SO...
...YOU OKAY, ITO-SAN?
HUFF HUFF HUFF
ER... I...
... THINK ...
...I OVERDID IT...
Her heart is resurrected but her body is falling apart.
JUST TAKE THIS MEDICINE.
IT'S OKAY. IT WON'T WORK.
I MEAN IT.
...
DON'T WORRY. I'LL TAKE THE TEST.
I JUST NEED A QUICK REST...

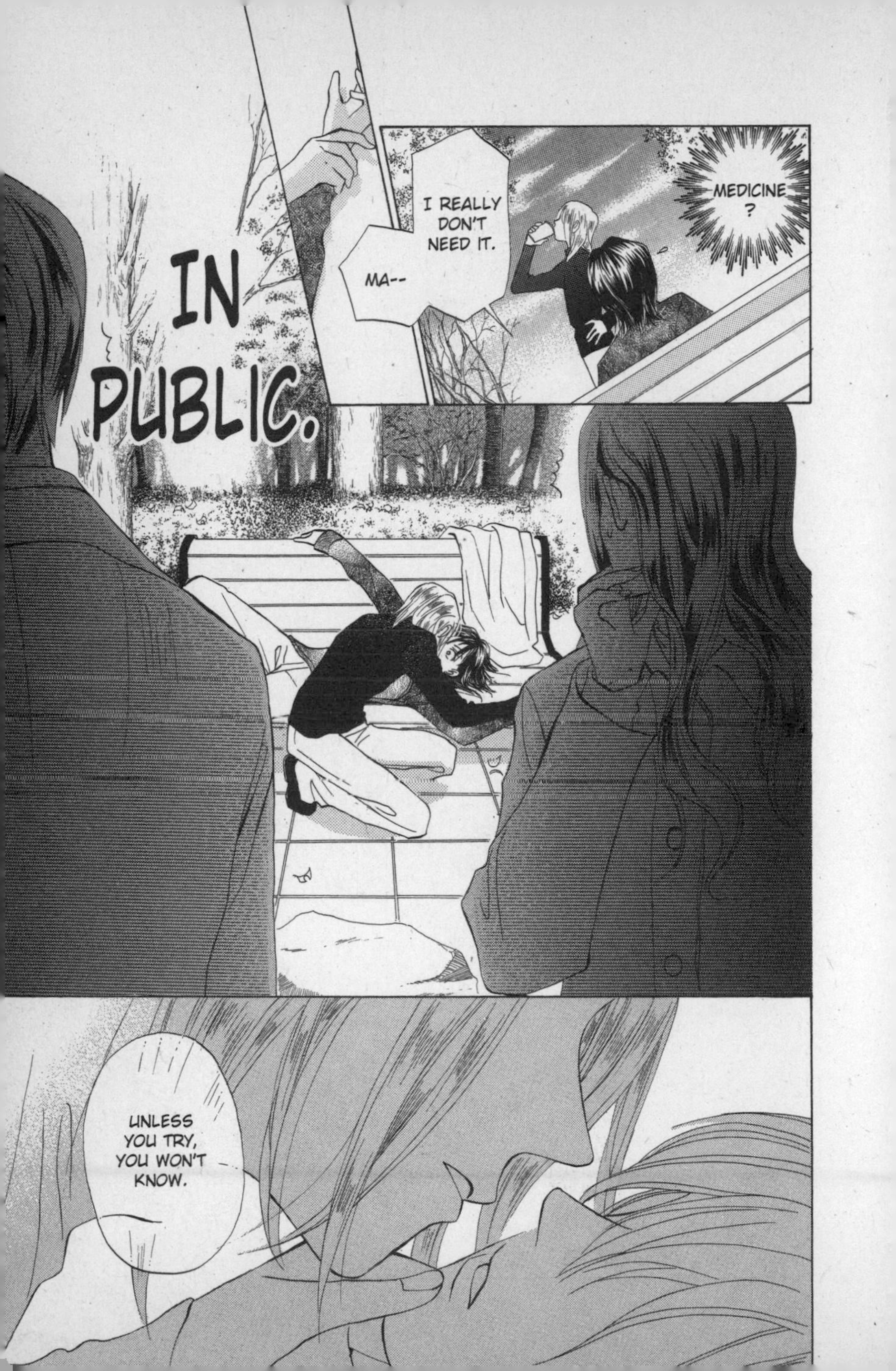
MEDICINE ?
I REALLY DON'T NEED IT.
MA--
IN PUBLIC.
UNLESS YOU TRY, YOU WON'T KNOW.

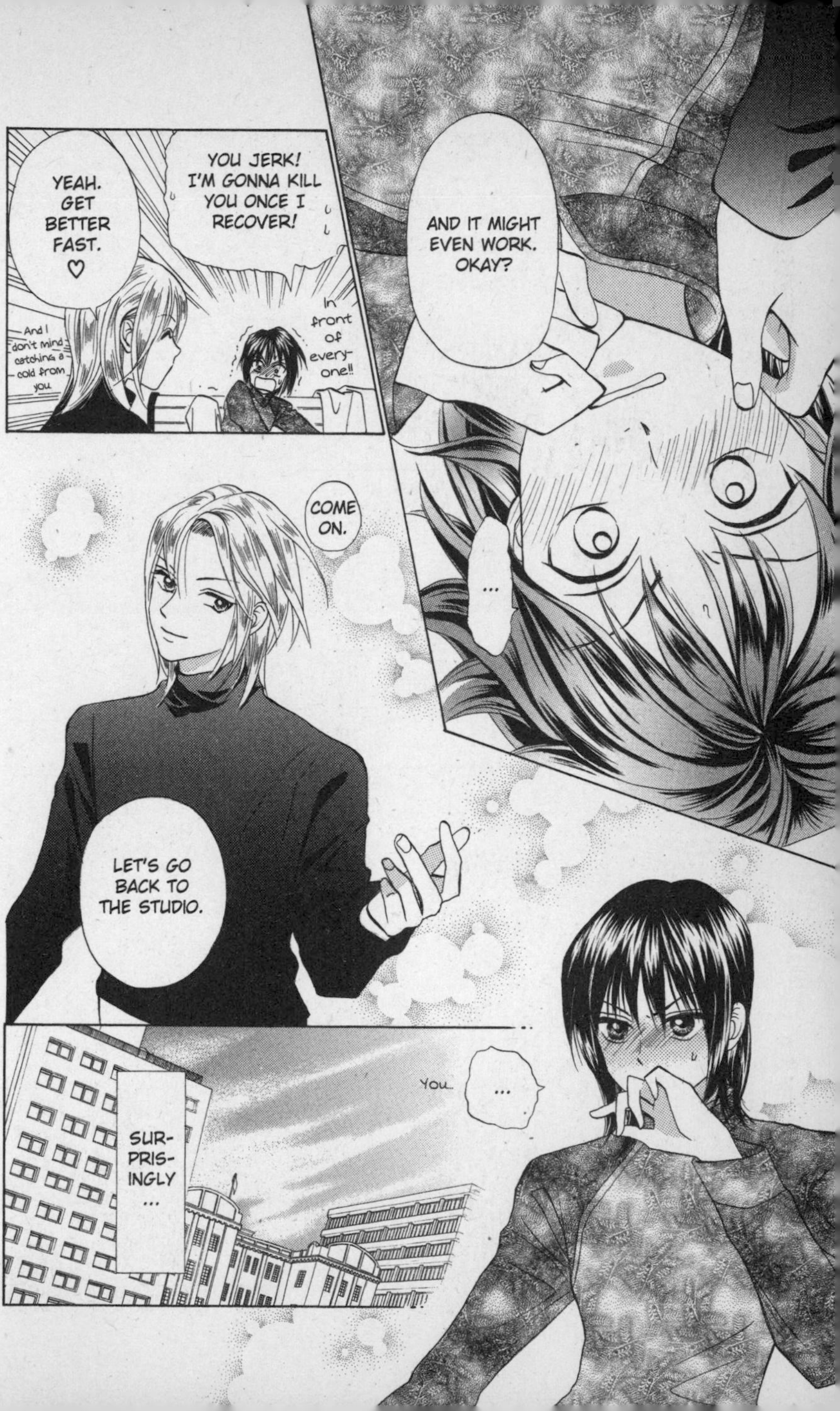
AND IT MIGHT EVEN WORK. OKAY?
...
YOU JERK! I'M GONNA KILL YOU ONCE I RECOVER!
YEAH. GET BETTER FAST. ♡
In front of everyone!!
And I don't mind catching a cold from you
You...
...
COME ON.
LET'S GO BACK TO THE STUDIO.
SURPRISINGLY ...

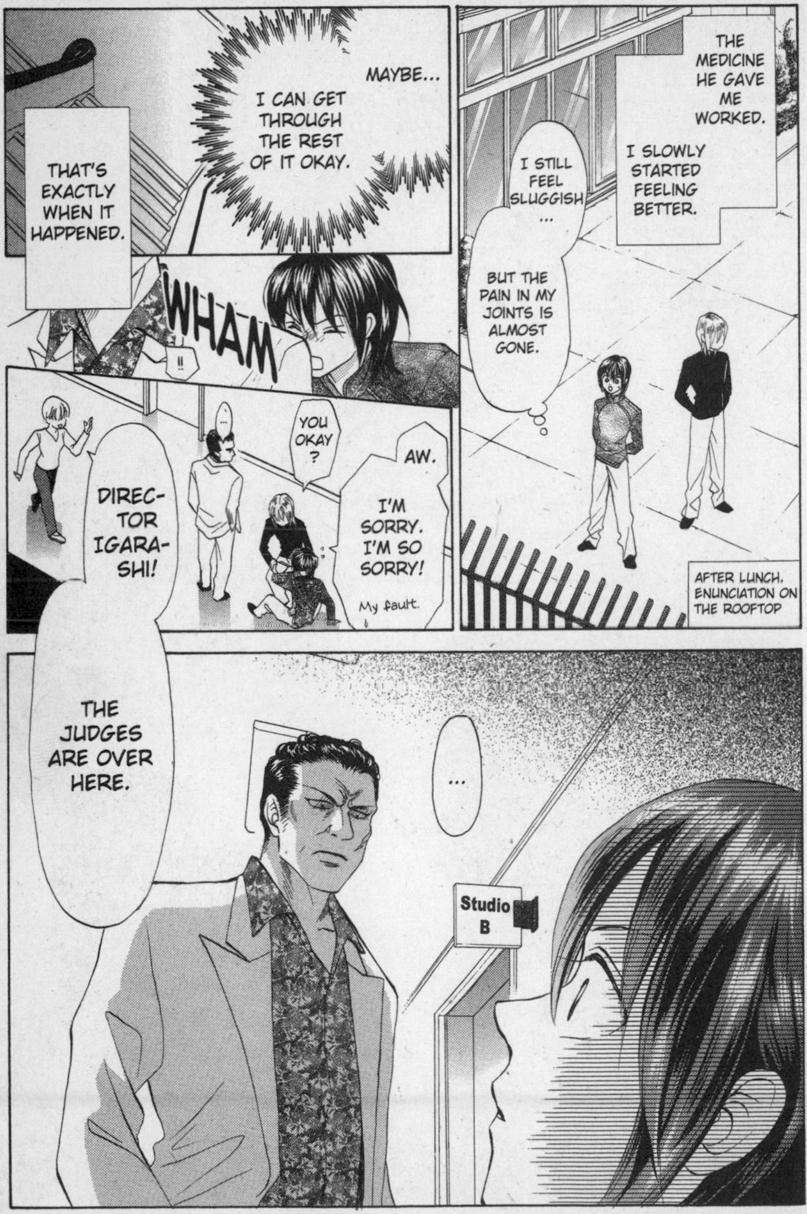
THE MEDICINE HE GAVE ME WORKED.
I SLOWLY STARTED FEELING BETTER.
I STILL FEEL SLUGGISH...
BUT THE PAIN IN MY JOINTS IS ALMOST GONE.
AFTER LUNCH, ENUNCIATION ON THE ROOFTOP
MAYBE...
I CAN GET THROUGH THE REST OF IT OKAY.
THAT'S EXACTLY WHEN IT HAPPENED.
WHAM
!!
AW.
I'M SORRY. I'M SO SORRY!
My fault.
YOU OKAY?
...
DIREC-TOR IGARA-SHI!
...
THE JUDGES ARE OVER HERE.
Studio B

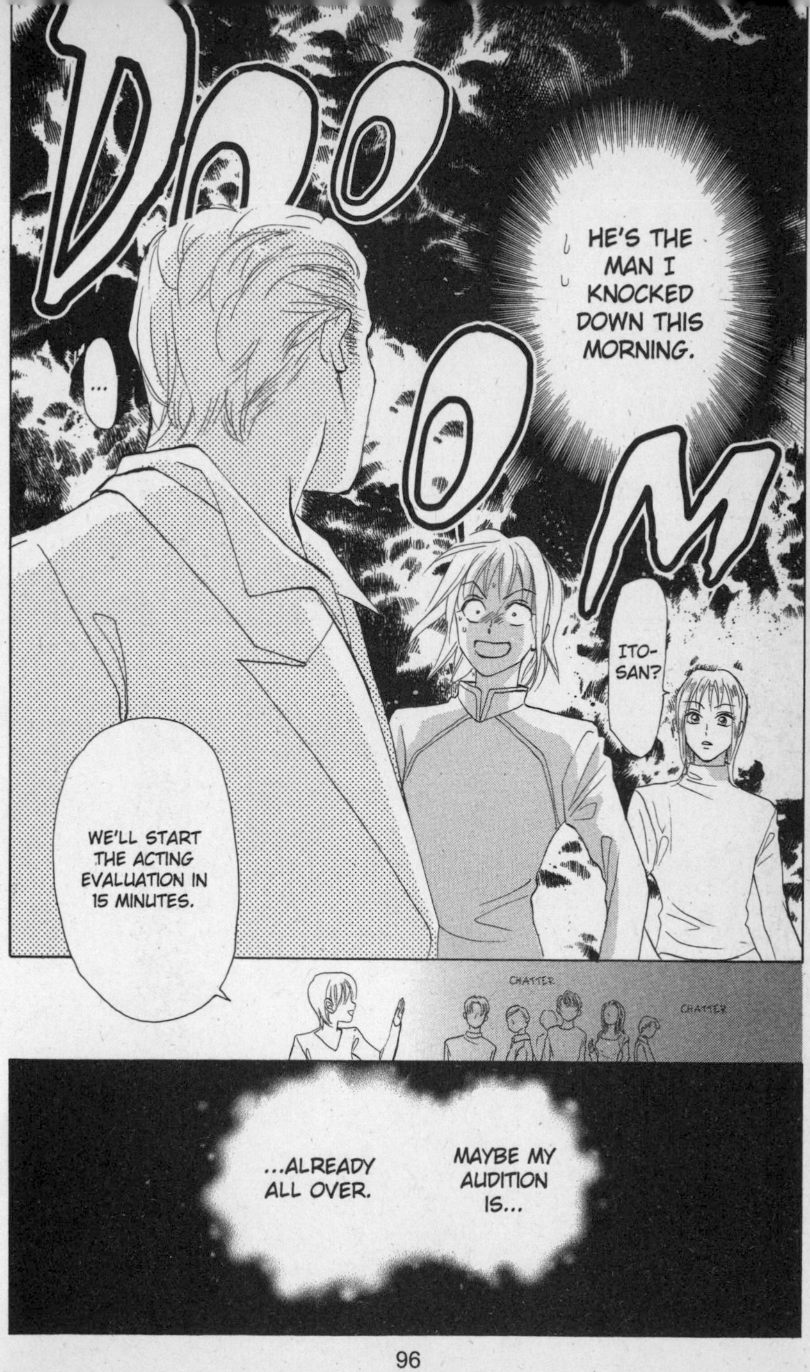
HE'S THE MAN I KNOCKED DOWN THIS MORNING.
DOOOM
ITO-SAN?
...
WE'LL START THE ACTING EVALUATION IN 15 MINUTES.
CHATTER
CHATTER
MAYBE MY AUDITION IS...
...ALREADY ALL OVER.

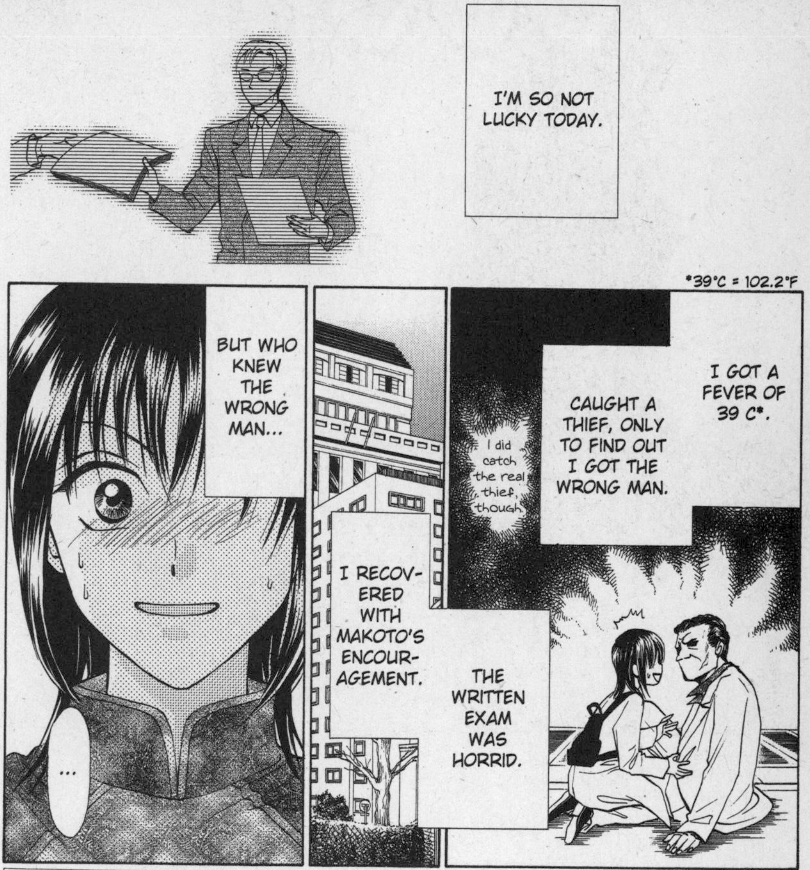
I'M SO NOT LUCKY TODAY.
*39°C = 102.2°F
I GOT A FEVER OF 39 C*.
CAUGHT A THIEF, ONLY TO FIND OUT I GOT THE WRONG MAN.
I did catch the real thief, though.
I RECOVERED WITH MAKOTO'S ENCOURAGEMENT.
THE WRITTEN EXAM WAS HORRID.
BUT WHO KNEW THE WRONG MAN...
...

—Behind the Scenes Story (4)—

A while back, someone said to me, "If you know too much, you can't draw." That's exactly what happened. Not that I researched that much, but I couldn't depart from the real world. I'd come up with an idea, and then I'd end up criticizing myself saying, "This can't be happening here." (SOB) Yes, I remember the hard times I went through... Of course, I eventually got over it. Manga is about entertaining, not being realistic.

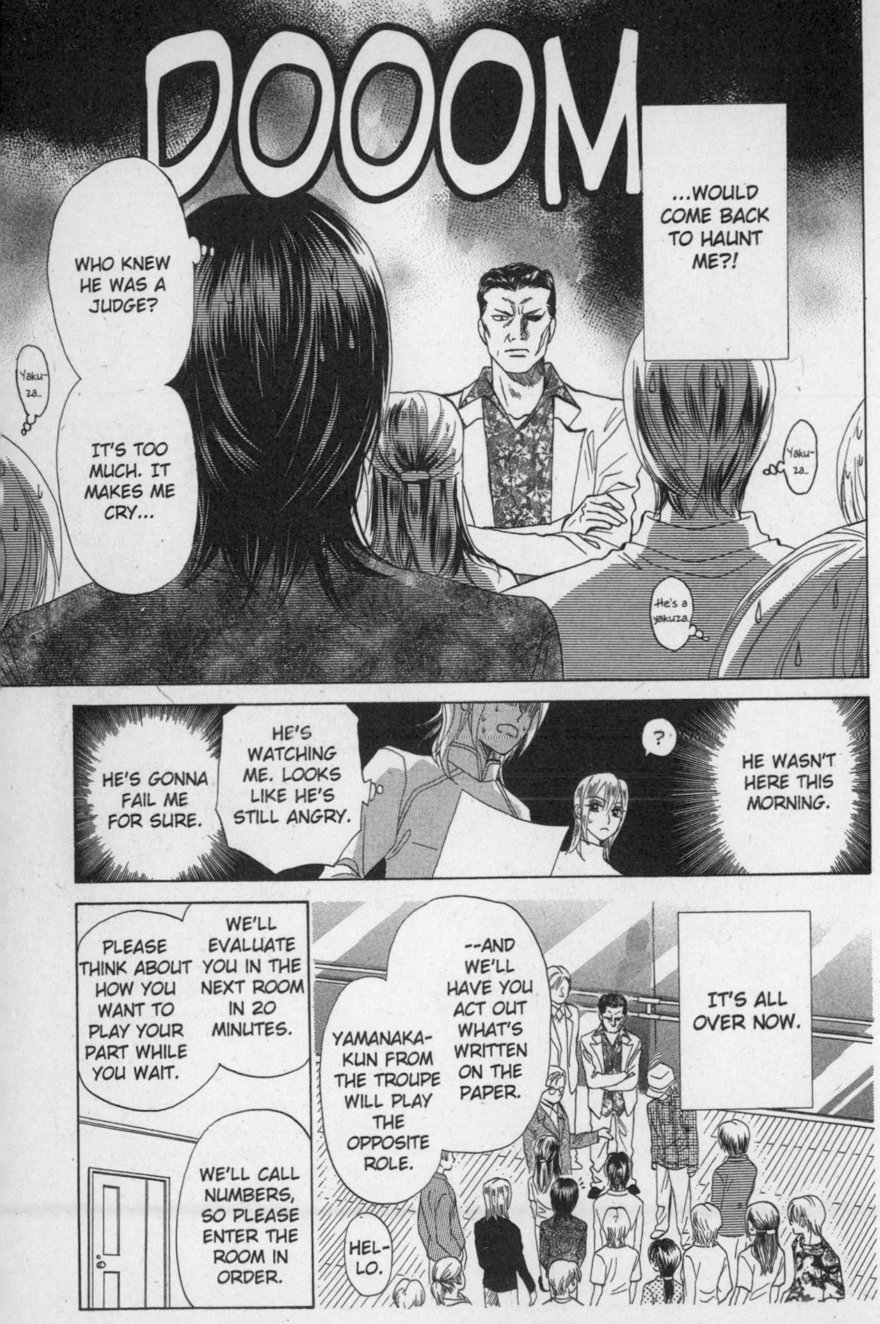
DOOOM
...WOULD COME BACK TO HAUNT ME?!
Yaku-za...
He's a yakuza.
WHO KNEW HE WAS A JUDGE?
IT'S TOO MUCH. IT MAKES ME CRY...
Yaku-za...
HE WASN'T HERE THIS MORNING.
?
HE'S WATCHING ME. LOOKS LIKE HE'S STILL ANGRY.
HE'S GONNA FAIL ME FOR SURE.
IT'S ALL OVER NOW.
--AND WE'LL HAVE YOU ACT OUT WHAT'S WRITTEN ON THE PAPER.
YAMANAKA-KUN FROM THE TROUPE WILL PLAY THE OPPOSITE ROLE.
HEL-LO.
WE'LL EVALUATE YOU IN THE NEXT ROOM IN 20 MINUTES.
PLEASE THINK ABOUT HOW YOU WANT TO PLAY YOUR PART WHILE YOU WAIT.
WE'LL CALL NUMBERS, SO PLEASE ENTER THE ROOM IN ORDER.

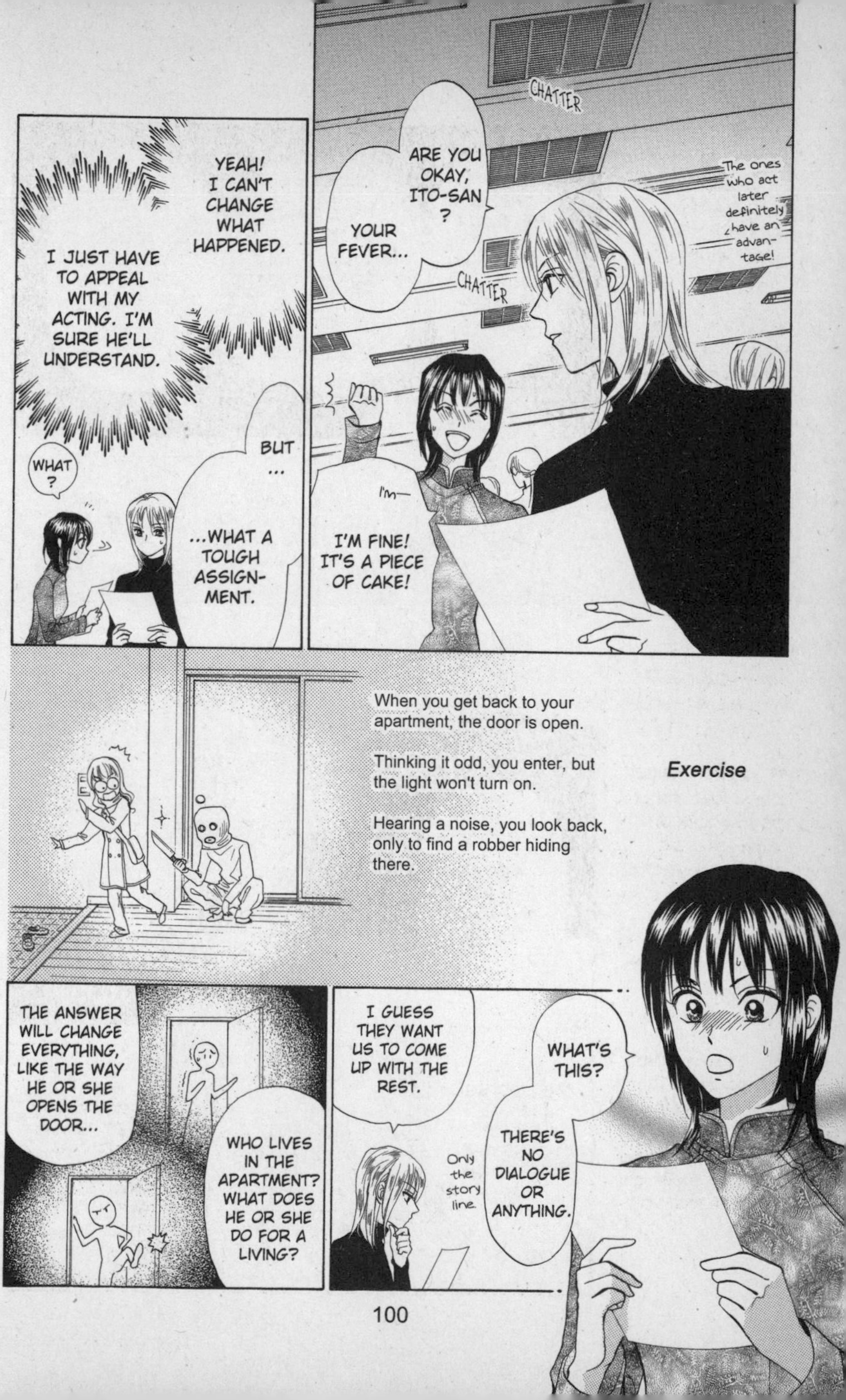
CHATTER
ARE YOU OKAY, ITO-SAN?
YOUR FEVER...
CHATTER
The ones who act later definitely have an advantage!
I'm—
I'M FINE! IT'S A PIECE OF CAKE!
YEAH! I CAN'T CHANGE WHAT HAPPENED.
I JUST HAVE TO APPEAL WITH MY ACTING. I'M SURE HE'LL UNDERSTAND.
BUT ...
...WHAT A TOUGH ASSIGNMENT.
WHAT?
Exercise
When you get back to your apartment, the door is open.
Thinking it odd, you enter, but the light won't turn on.
Hearing a noise, you look back, only to find a robber hiding there.
WHAT'S THIS?
THERE'S NO DIALOGUE OR ANYTHING.
I GUESS THEY WANT US TO COME UP WITH THE REST.
Only the story line.
THE ANSWER WILL CHANGE EVERYTHING, LIKE THE WAY HE OR SHE OPENS THE DOOR...
WHO LIVES IN THE APARTMENT? WHAT DOES HE OR SHE DO FOR A LIVING?

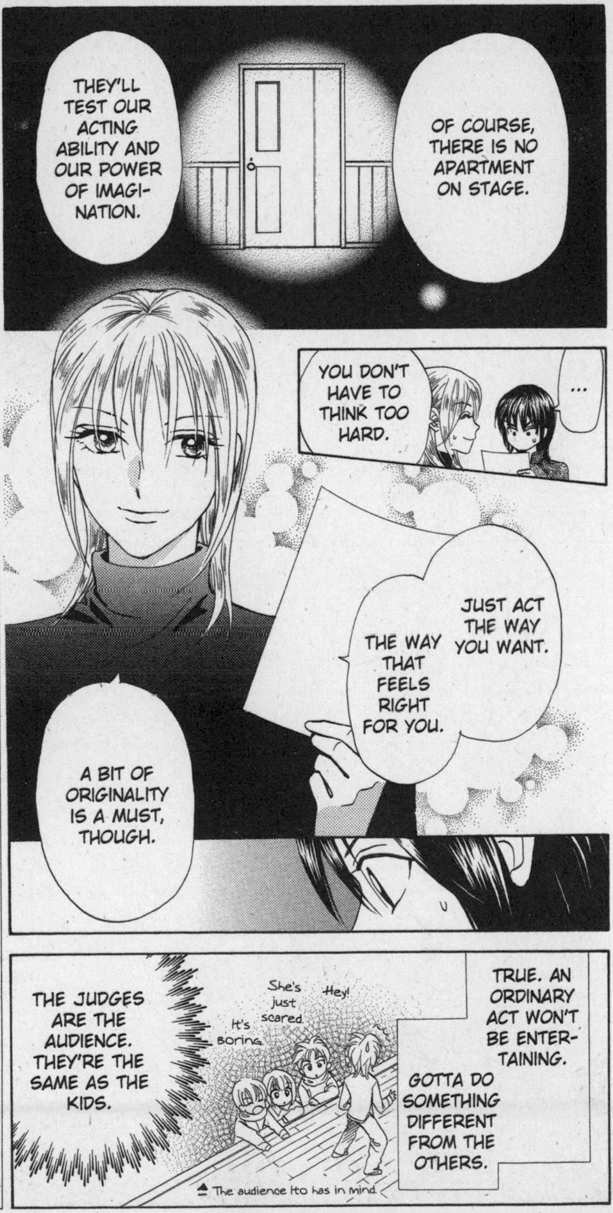
OF COURSE, THERE IS NO APARTMENT ON STAGE.
THEY'LL TEST OUR ACTING ABILITY AND OUR POWER OF IMAGI-NATION.
...
YOU DON'T HAVE TO THINK TOO HARD.
JUST ACT THE WAY YOU WANT.
THE WAY THAT FEELS RIGHT FOR YOU.
A BIT OF ORIGINALITY IS A MUST, THOUGH.
TRUE. AN ORDINARY ACT WON'T BE ENTER-TAINING.
GOTTA DO SOMETHING DIFFERENT FROM THE OTHERS.
Hey!
She's just scared.
It's boring.
THE JUDGES ARE THE AUDIENCE. THEY'RE THE SAME AS THE KIDS.
The audience Ito has in mind.

I ended up using two column spaces for a single question. Now, the next!

● Do you hold signing events only in big cities? You've got a lot of fans outside the major cities, too.

Ⓔ Y—Yeah, you're right. But that's not something I decide.

Mr. Editor! Please let me! ♥

● When I tried drawing manga, I could come up with lots of ideas in my mind, but my hand wouldn't work the way I wanted it to. Does that happen to you, too?

Ⓔ Yes, it does. Of course! That's why I'm super happy when I manage to draw the way I want, even if it's only a panel!

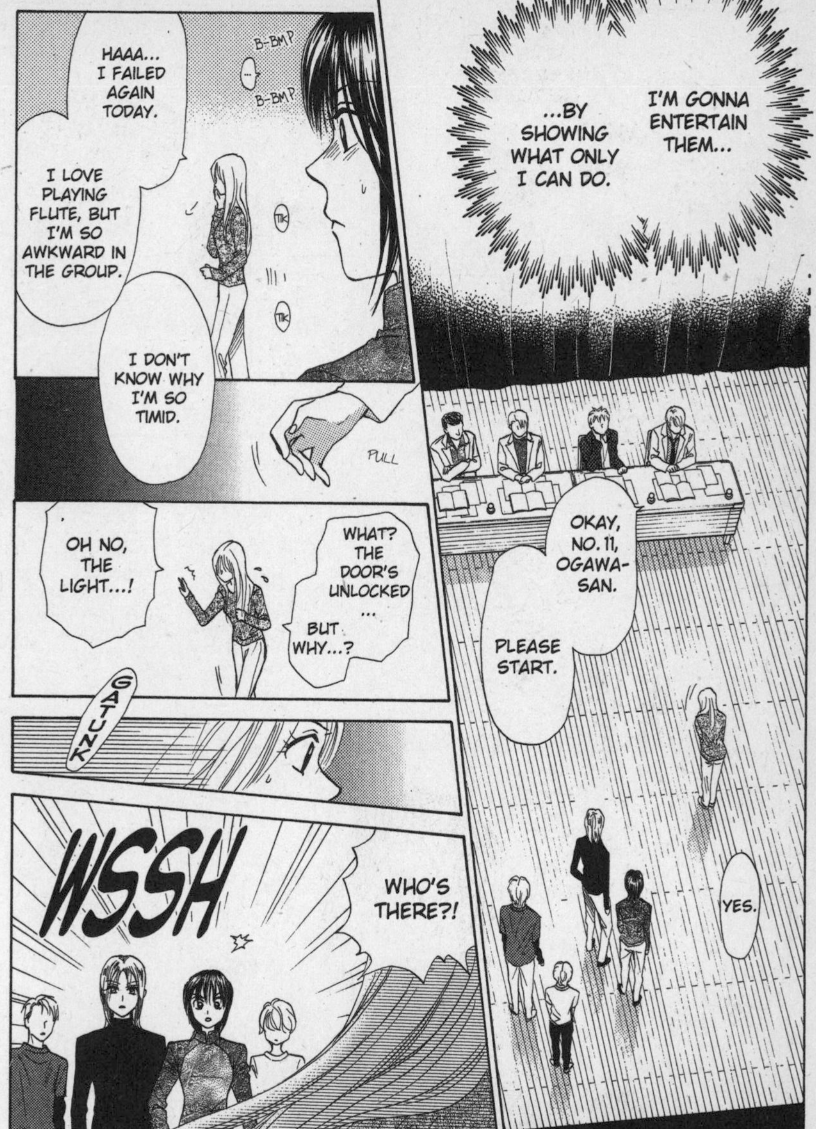
I'M GONNA ENTERTAIN THEM...
...BY SHOWING WHAT ONLY I CAN DO.
OKAY, NO. 11, OGAWA-SAN.
PLEASE START.
YES.
B-BMP
...
B-BMP
HAAA... I FAILED AGAIN TODAY.
I LOVE PLAYING FLUTE, BUT I'M SO AWKWARD IN THE GROUP.
TIK
TIK
I DON'T KNOW WHY I'M SO TIMID.
PULL
WHAT? THE DOOR'S UNLOCKED...
BUT WHY...?
OH NO, THE LIGHT...!
GATUNK
WSSH
WHO'S THERE?!

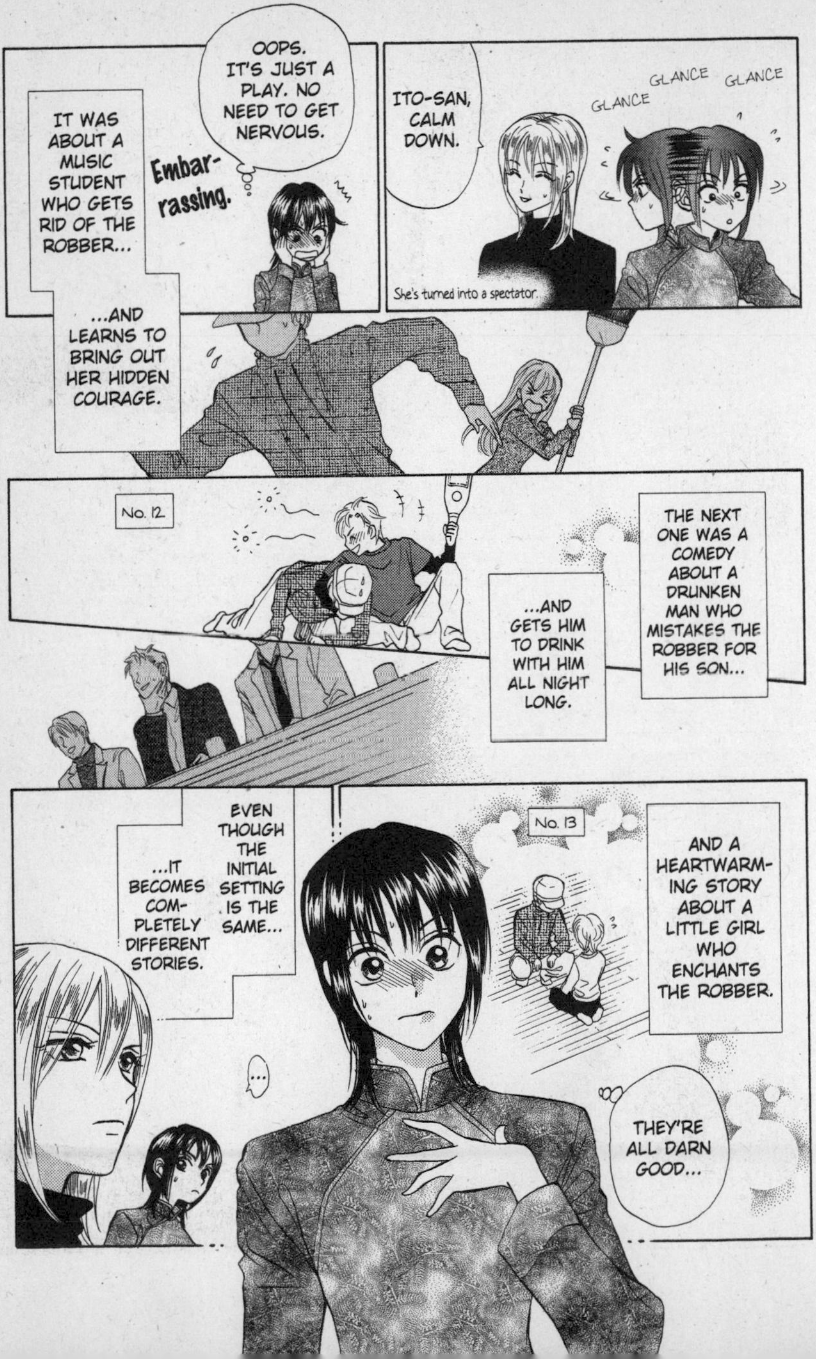
ITO-SAN, CALM DOWN.
GLANCE
GLANCE
GLANCE
She's turned into a spectator.
OOPS. IT'S JUST A PLAY. NO NEED TO GET NERVOUS.
Embarrassing.
IT WAS ABOUT A MUSIC STUDENT WHO GETS RID OF THE ROBBER...
...AND LEARNS TO BRING OUT HER HIDDEN COURAGE.
THE NEXT ONE WAS A COMEDY ABOUT A DRUNKEN MAN WHO MISTAKES THE ROBBER FOR HIS SON...
No. 12
...AND GETS HIM TO DRINK WITH HIM ALL NIGHT LONG.
AND A HEARTWARMING STORY ABOUT A LITTLE GIRL WHO ENCHANTS THE ROBBER.
No. 13
THEY'RE ALL DARN GOOD...
EVEN THOUGH THE INITIAL SETTING IS THE SAME...
...IT BECOMES COMPLETELY DIFFERENT STORIES.
...

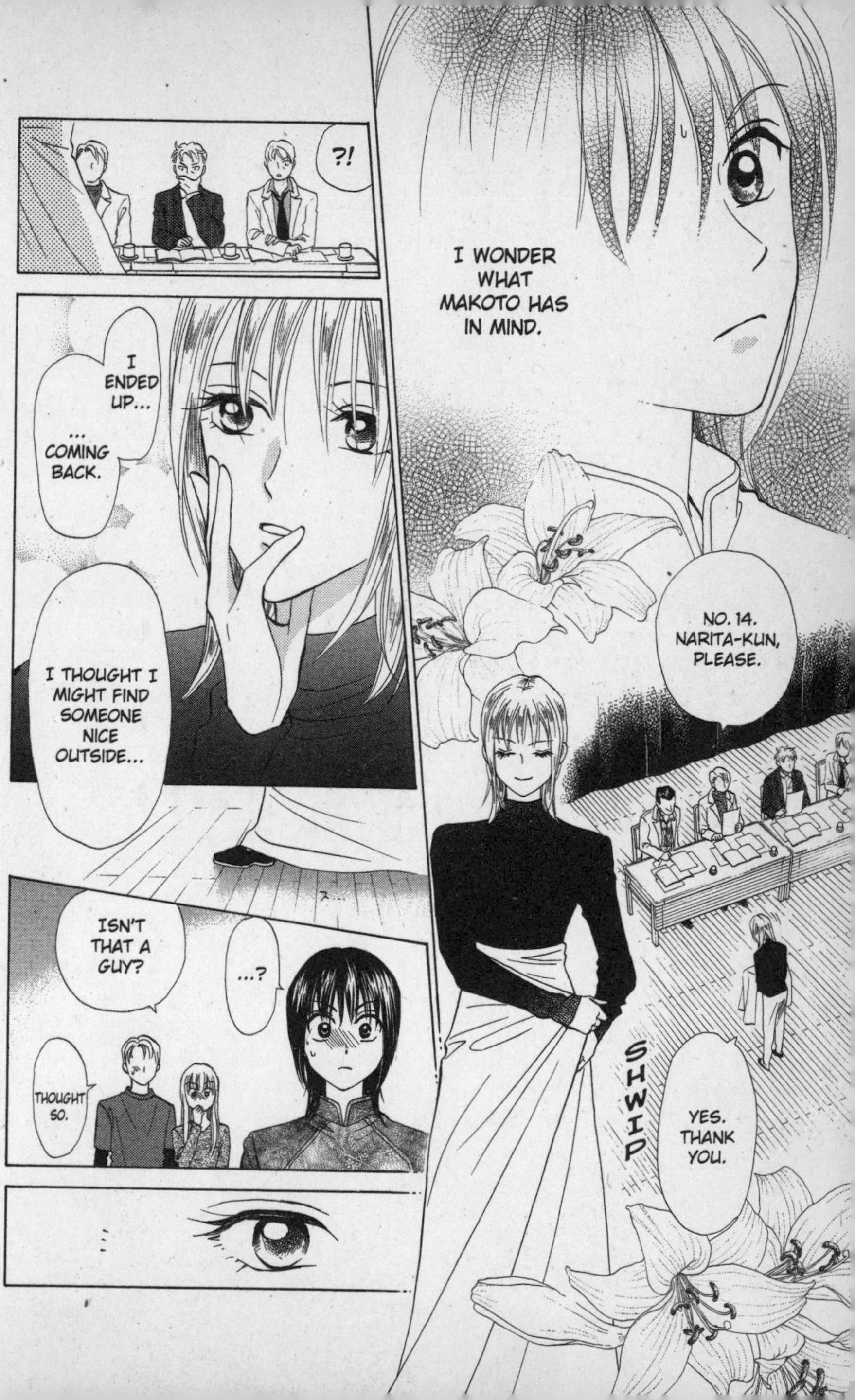
I WONDER WHAT MAKOTO HAS IN MIND.
NO. 14. NARITA-KUN, PLEASE.
SHWIP
YES. THANK YOU.
?!
I ENDED UP... ... COMING BACK.
I THOUGHT I MIGHT FIND SOMEONE NICE OUTSIDE...
...?
ISN'T THAT A GUY?
THOUGHT SO.
...

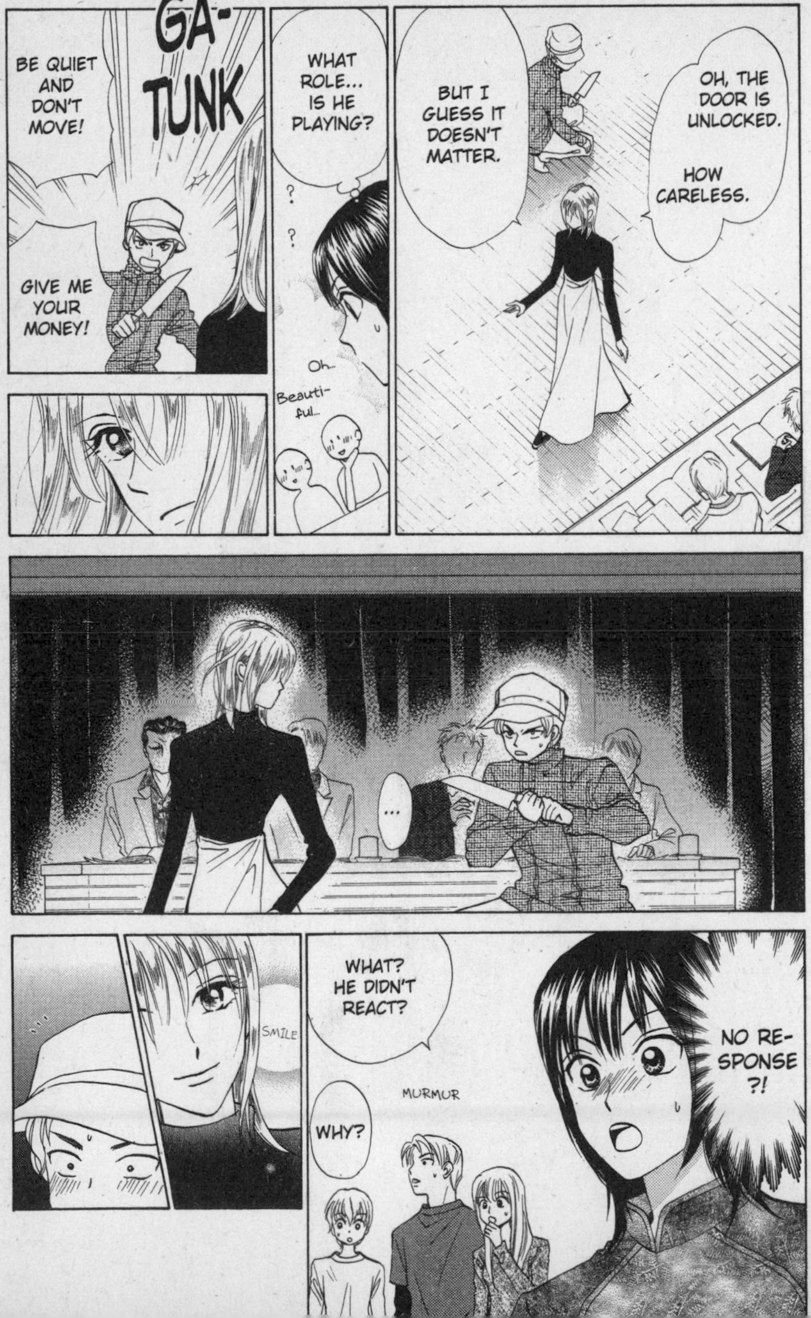
OH, THE DOOR IS UNLOCKED.
HOW CARELESS.
BUT I GUESS IT DOESN'T MATTER.
WHAT ROLE... IS HE PLAYING?
? ?
Oh... Beautiful...
GA-TUNK
BE QUIET AND DON'T MOVE!
GIVE ME YOUR MONEY!
...
NO RESPONSE?!
WHAT? HE DIDN'T REACT?
MURMUR
WHY?
SMILE

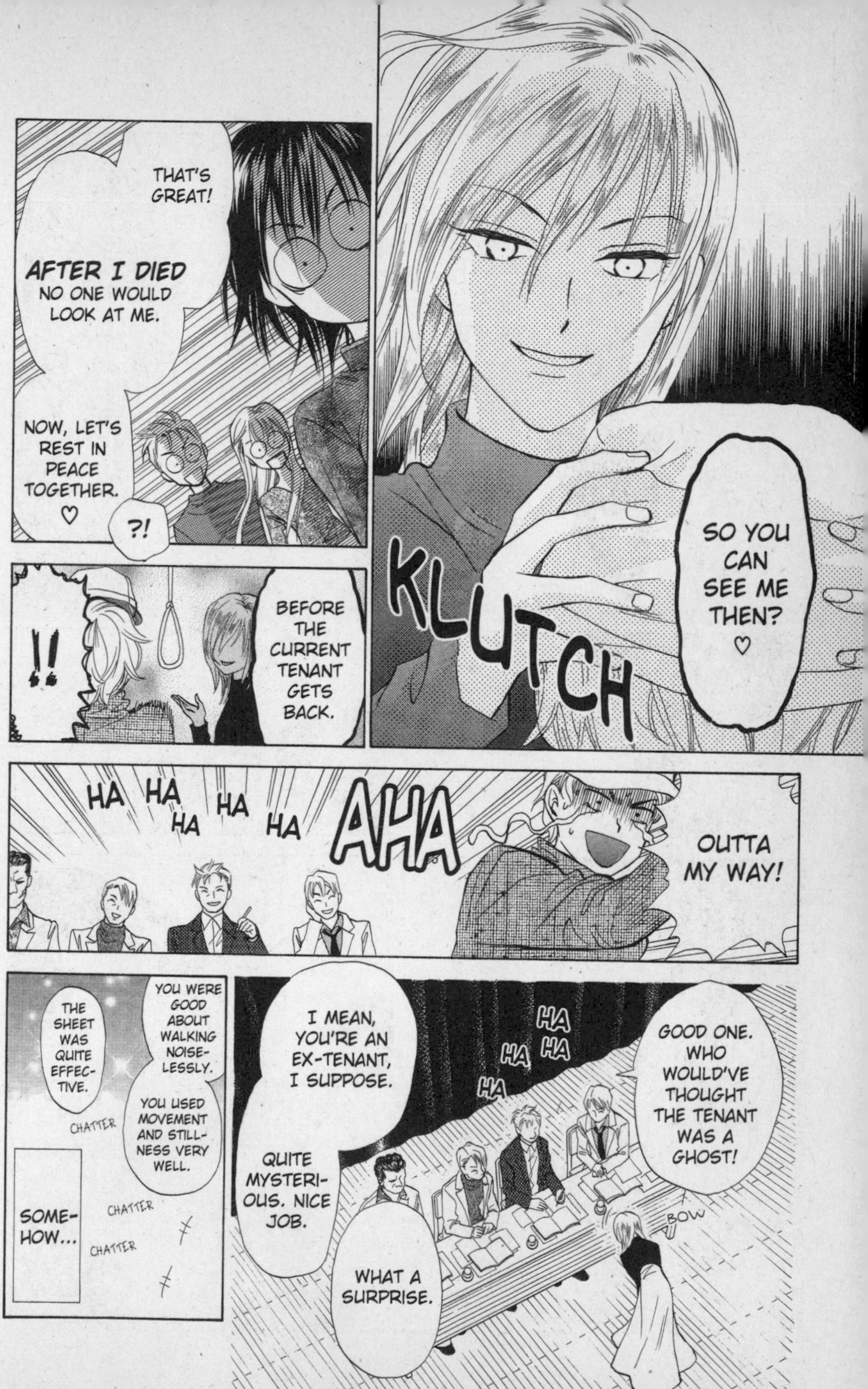
SO YOU CAN SEE ME THEN? ♡
KLUTCH
THAT'S GREAT!
AFTER I DIED NO ONE WOULD LOOK AT ME.
NOW, LET'S REST IN PEACE TOGETHER. ♡
?!
BEFORE THE CURRENT TENANT GETS BACK.
!!
OUTTA MY WAY!
AHA
HA HA HA HA HA HA
GOOD ONE. WHO WOULD'VE THOUGHT THE TENANT WAS A GHOST!
HA HA HA HA
I MEAN, YOU'RE AN EX-TENANT, I SUPPOSE.
QUITE MYSTERIOUS. NICE JOB.
WHAT A SURPRISE.
BOW
YOU WERE GOOD ABOUT WALKING NOISELESSLY.
THE SHEET WAS QUITE EFFECTIVE.
YOU USED MOVEMENT AND STILLNESS VERY WELL.
CHATTER
CHATTER
CHATTER
SOMEHOW...

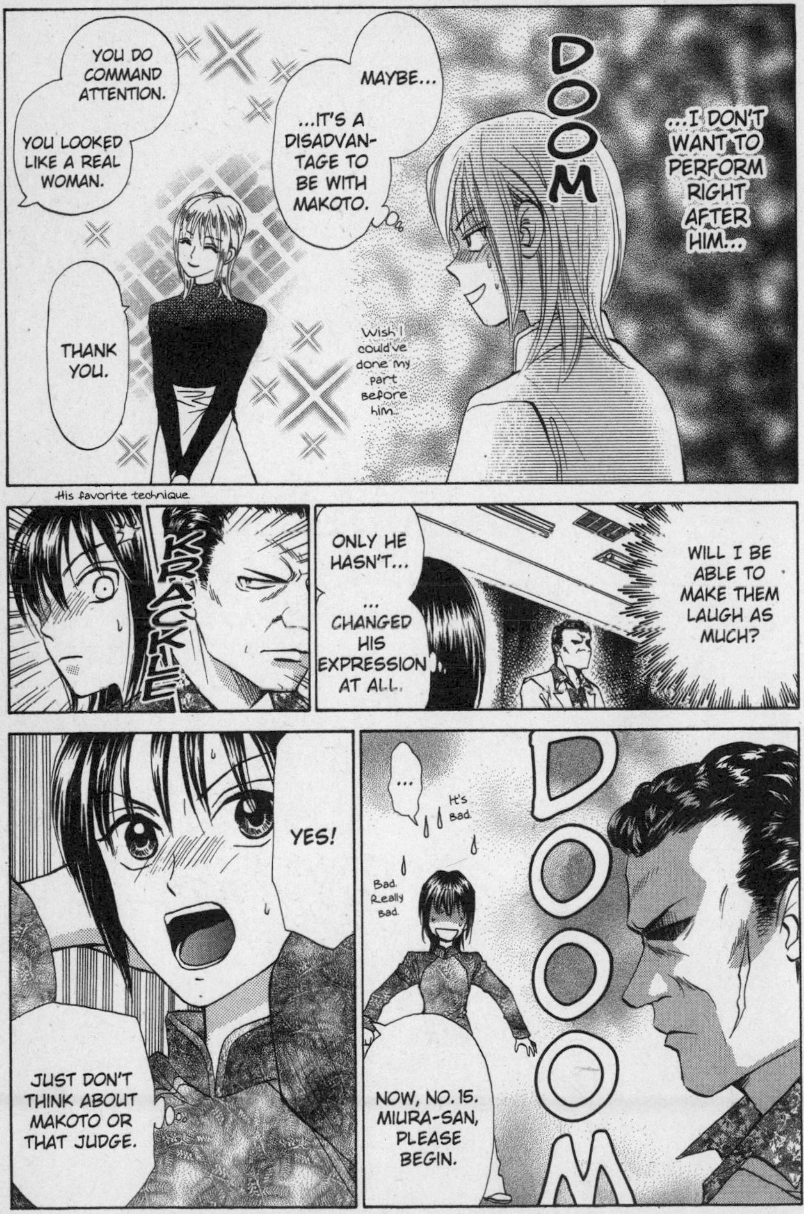
...I DON'T WANT TO PERFORM RIGHT AFTER HIM...
DOOM
MAYBE...
...IT'S A DISADVANTAGE TO BE WITH MAKOTO.
YOU DO COMMAND ATTENTION.
YOU LOOKED LIKE A REAL WOMAN.
Wish I could've done my part before him...
THANK YOU.
WILL I BE ABLE TO MAKE THEM LAUGH AS MUCH?
ONLY HE HASN'T...
... CHANGED HIS EXPRESSION AT ALL.
His favorite technique.
KRACKLE
DOOOOM
...
It's bad.
Bad. Really bad.
NOW, NO. 15. MIURA-SAN, PLEASE BEGIN.
YES!
JUST DON'T THINK ABOUT MAKOTO OR THAT JUDGE.

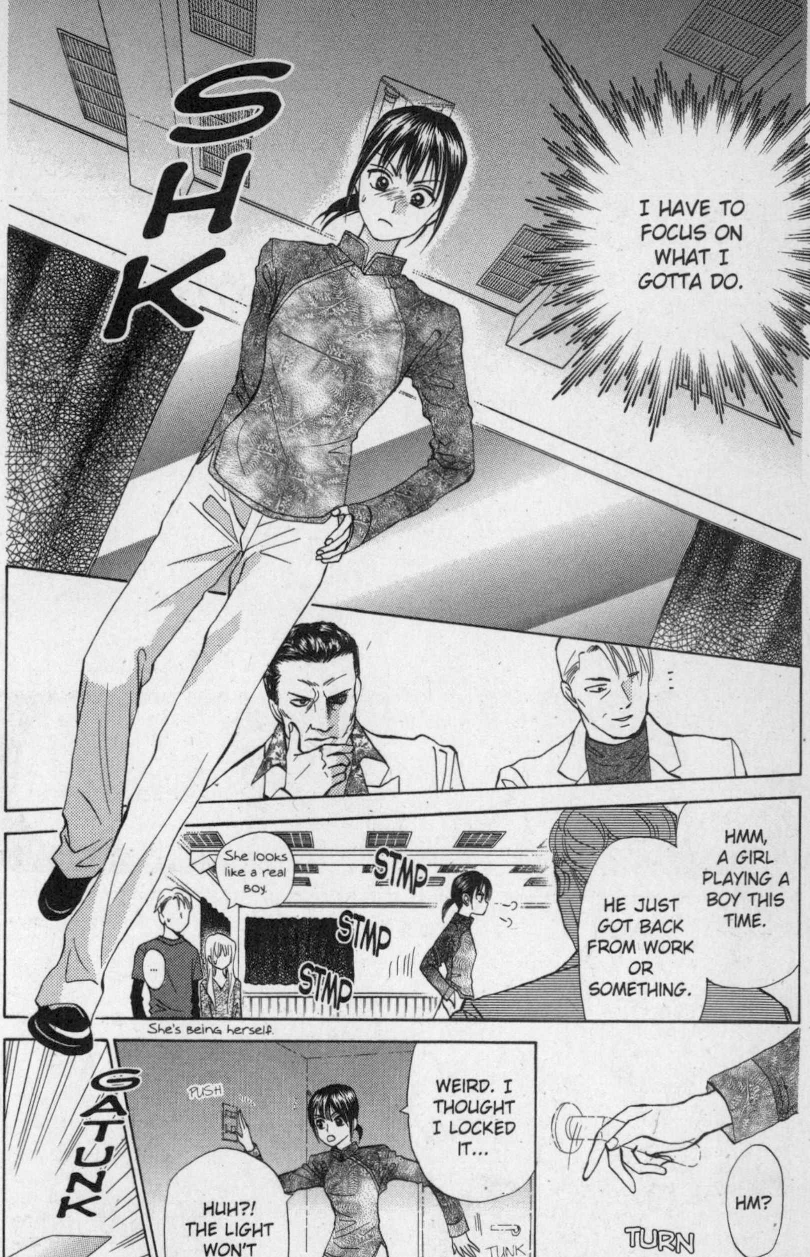
I HAVE TO FOCUS ON WHAT I GOTTA DO.
SHK
...
HMM, A GIRL PLAYING A BOY THIS TIME.
HE JUST GOT BACK FROM WORK OR SOMETHING.
STMP
STMP
STMP
She looks like a real boy.
...
She's being herself.
HM?
TURN
WEIRD. I THOUGHT I LOCKED IT...
PUSH
HUH?! THE LIGHT WON'T TURN ON...
TUNK
GATUNK

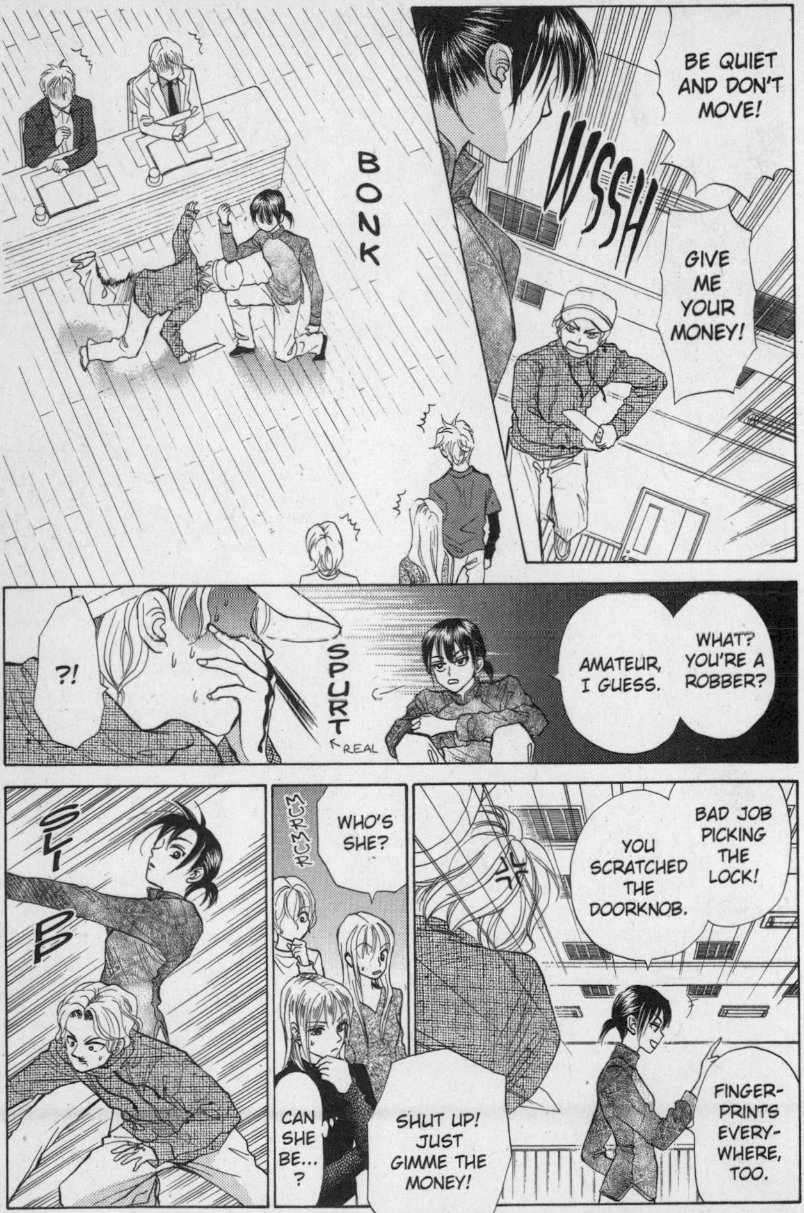
BE QUIET AND DON'T MOVE!
WSSH
GIVE ME YOUR MONEY!
BONK
WHAT? YOU'RE A ROBBER?
AMATEUR, I GUESS.
SPURT
REAL
?!
BAD JOB PICKING THE LOCK!
YOU SCRATCHED THE DOORKNOB.
FINGER-PRINTS EVERY-WHERE, TOO.
MURMUR
WHO'S SHE?
CAN SHE BE...?
SHUT UP! JUST GIMME THE MONEY!
SLIP

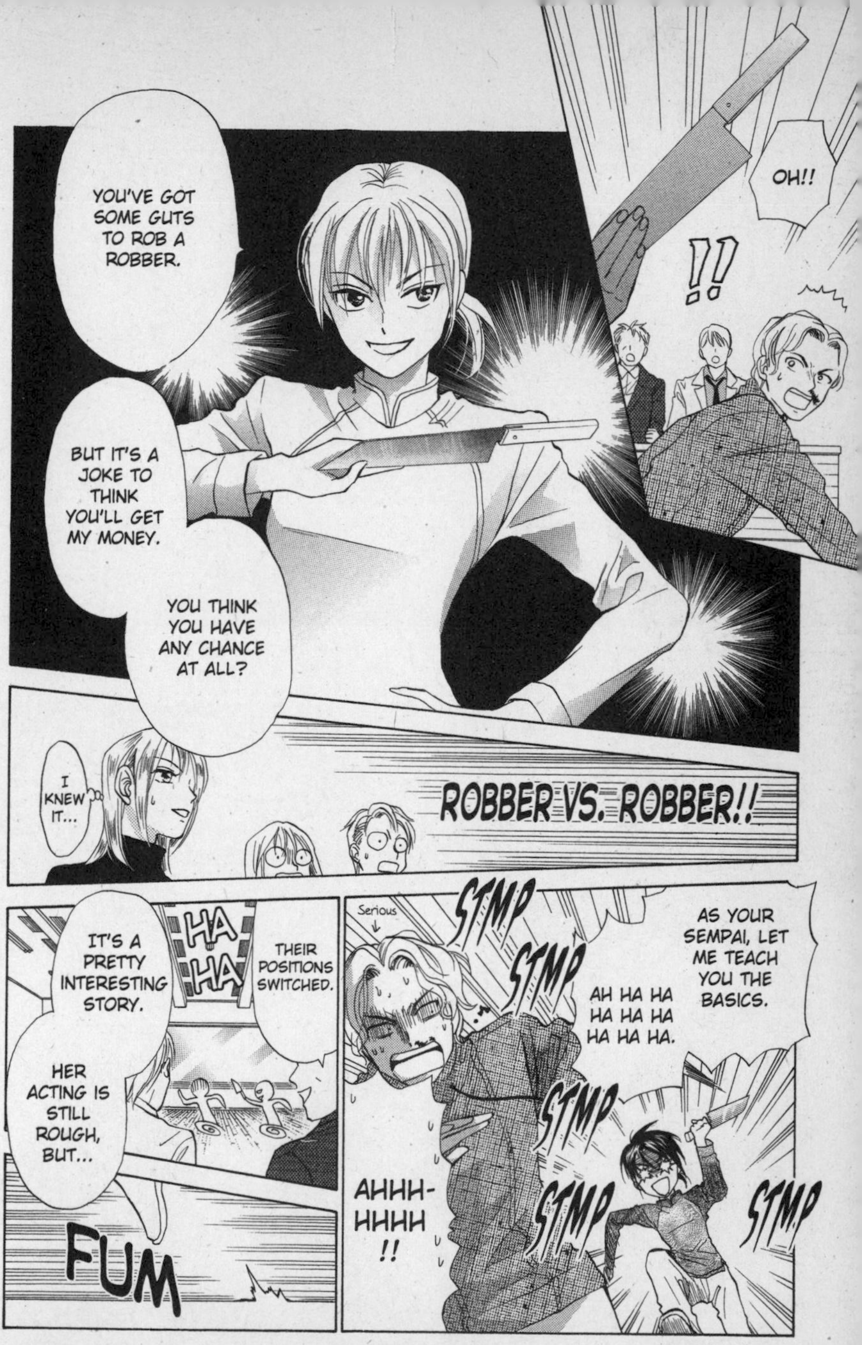
OH!!
!!
YOU'VE GOT SOME GUTS TO ROB A ROBBER.
BUT IT'S A JOKE TO THINK YOU'LL GET MY MONEY.
YOU THINK YOU HAVE ANY CHANCE AT ALL?
ROBBER VS. ROBBER!!
I KNEW IT...
AS YOUR SEMPAI, LET ME TEACH YOU THE BASICS.
STMP
STMP
AH HA HA HA HA HA HA HA HA.
Serious
STMP
STMP
STMP
AHHH-HHHH!!
THEIR POSITIONS SWITCHED.
HA HA
IT'S A PRETTY INTERESTING STORY.
HER ACTING IS STILL ROUGH, BUT...
FUM

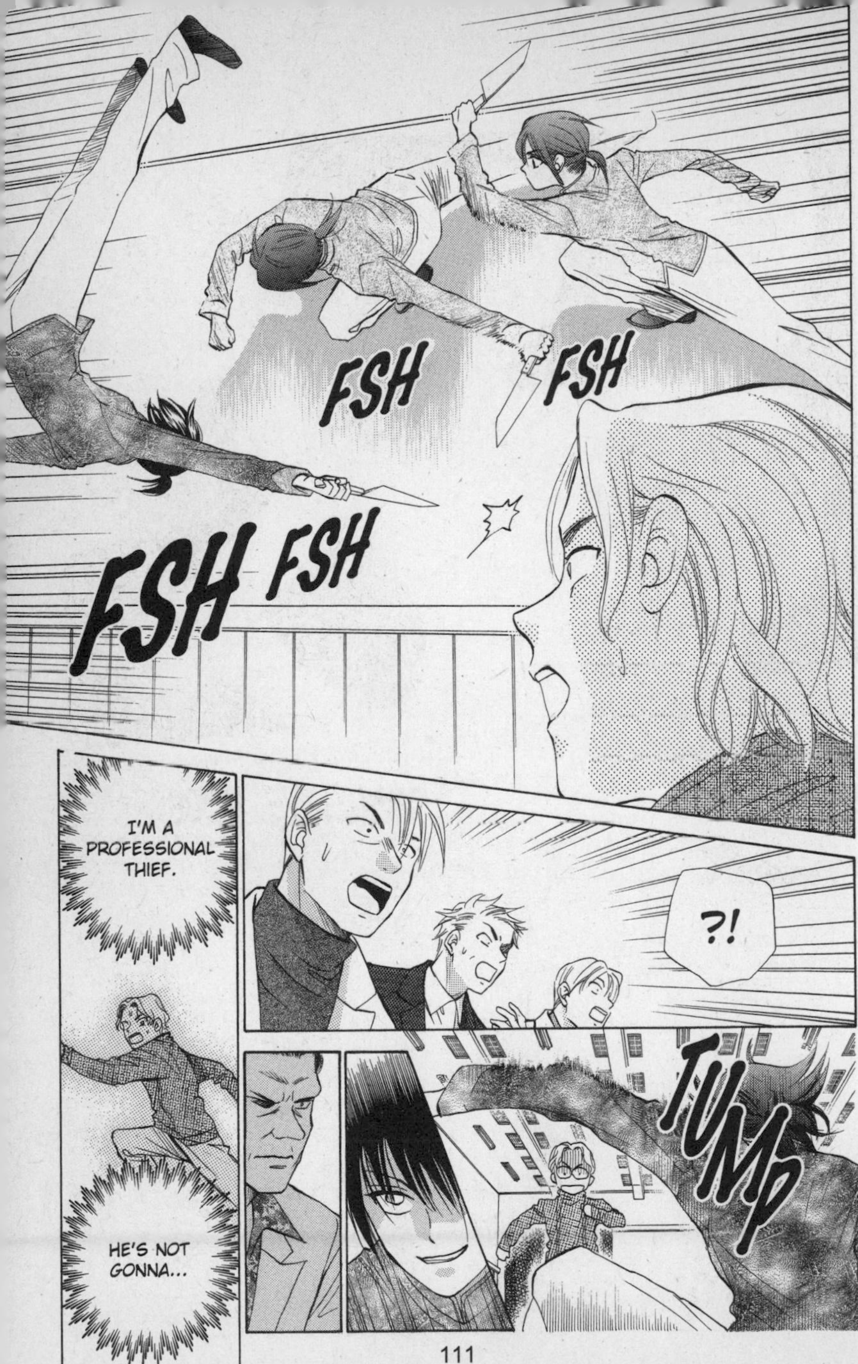
FSH
FSH
FSH
FSH
?!
TUMP
I'M A PROFESSIONAL THIEF.
HE'S NOT GONNA...

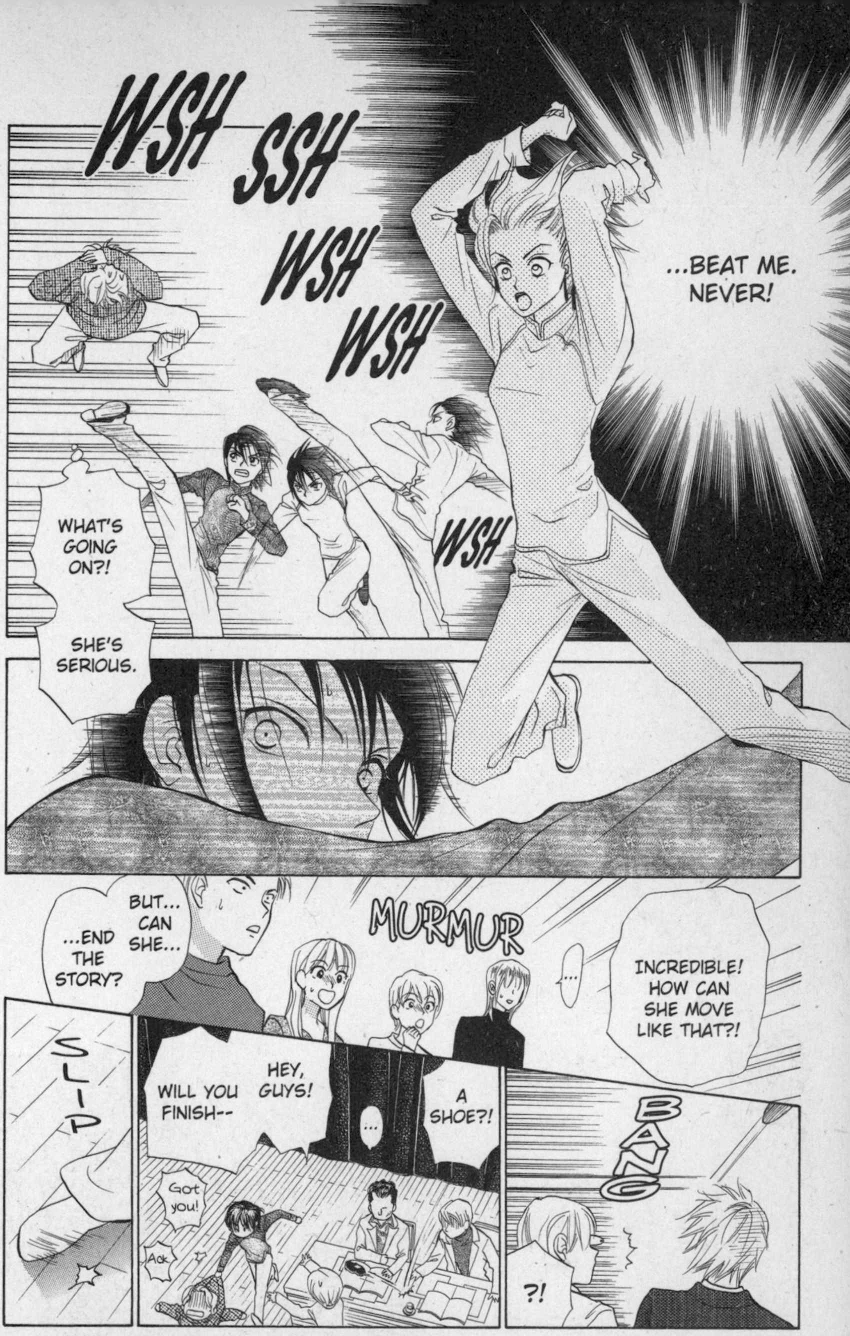
...BEAT ME. NEVER!
WSH
SSH
WSH
WSH
WSH
WHAT'S GOING ON?!
SHE'S SERIOUS.
INCREDIBLE! HOW CAN SHE MOVE LIKE THAT?!
...
MURMUR
BUT... CAN SHE...
...END THE STORY?
BANG
?!
A SHOE?!
...
HEY, GUYS!
WILL YOU FINISH--
Got you!
Ack
SLIP

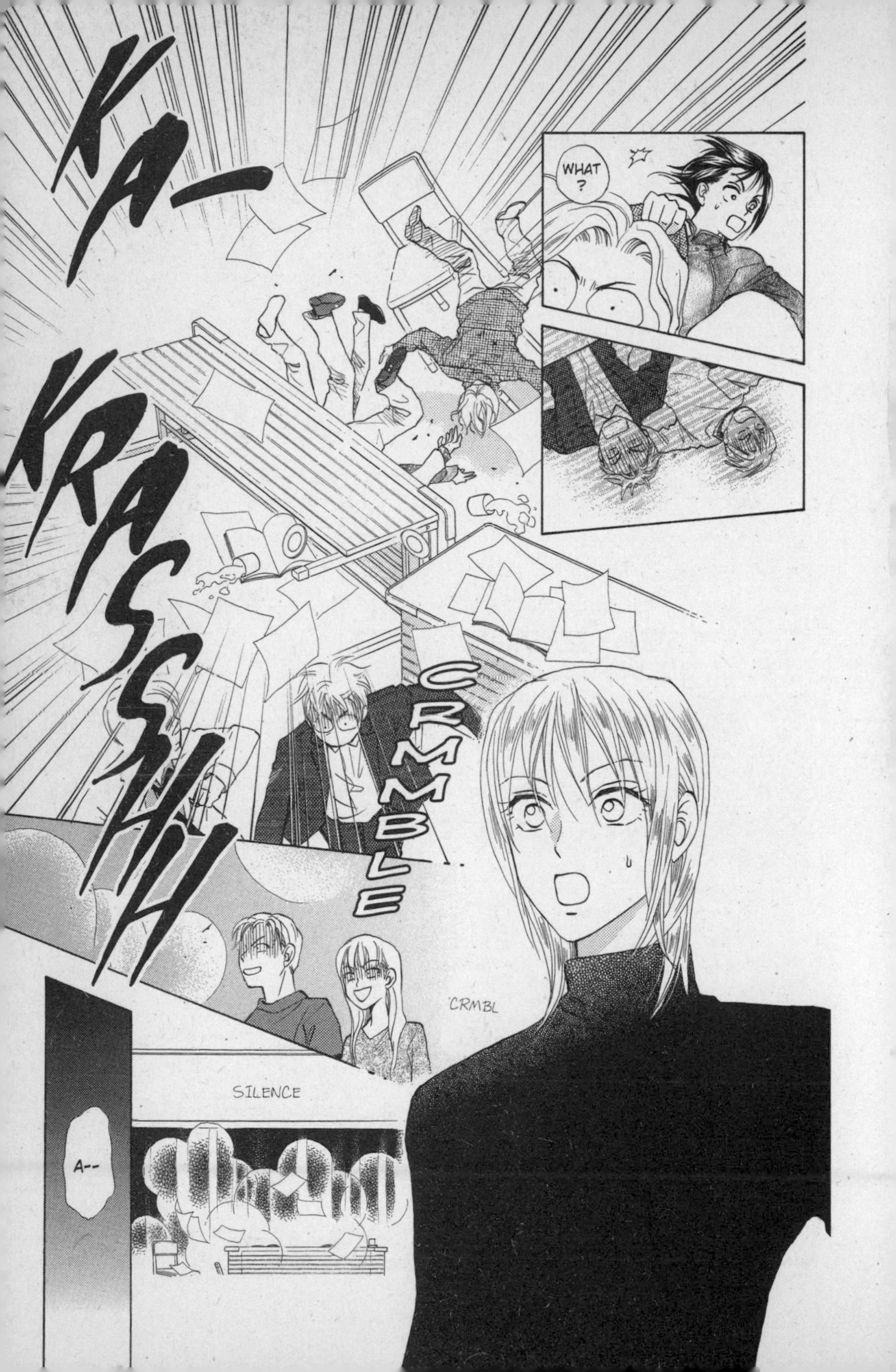
WHAT ?
KA-
KRASSHH
CRMMBLE
CRMBL
SILENCE
A--

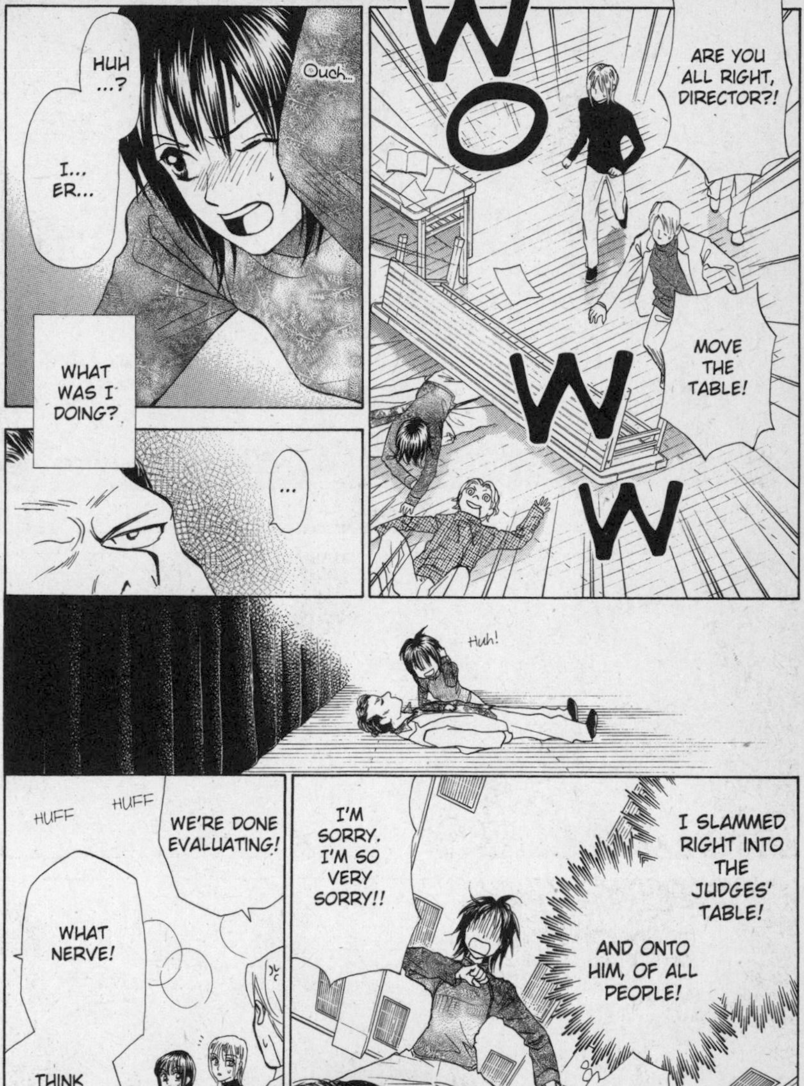
ARE YOU ALL RIGHT, DIRECTOR?!
WOW
MOVE THE TABLE!
Ouch...
HUH...?
I... ER...
WHAT WAS I DOING?
...
Huh!
I SLAMMED RIGHT INTO THE JUDGES' TABLE!
AND ONTO HIM, OF ALL PEOPLE!
I'M SORRY. I'M SO VERY SORRY!!
I MEAN...
HUFF
HUFF
WE'RE DONE EVALUATING!
WHAT NERVE!
THINK ABOUT WHAT YOU'RE DOING!

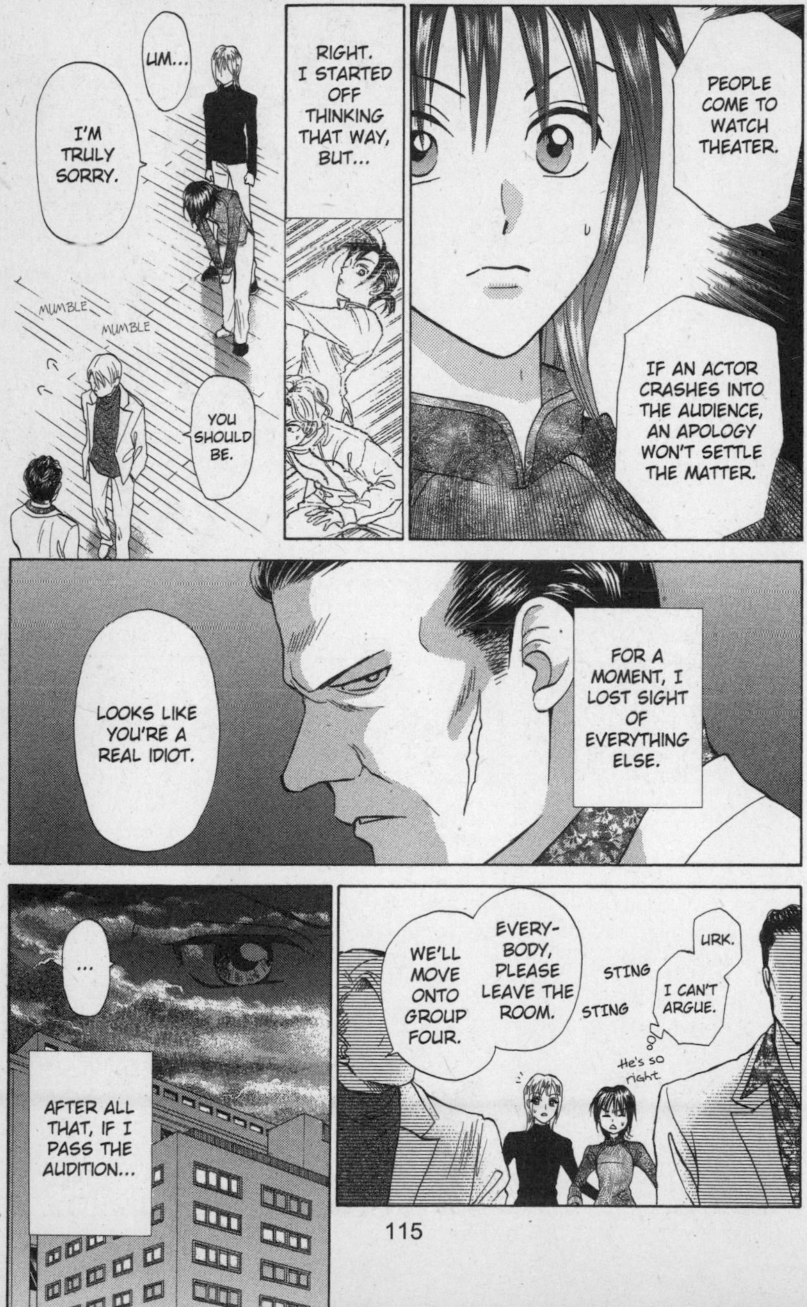
PEOPLE COME TO WATCH THEATER.
IF AN ACTOR CRASHES INTO THE AUDIENCE, AN APOLOGY WON'T SETTLE THE MATTER.
RIGHT. I STARTED OFF THINKING THAT WAY, BUT...
UM...
I'M TRULY SORRY.
MUMBLE
MUMBLE
YOU SHOULD BE.
FOR A MOMENT, I LOST SIGHT OF EVERYTHING ELSE.
LOOKS LIKE YOU'RE A REAL IDIOT.
URK.
I CAN'T ARGUE.
He's so right
STING
STING
EVERY-BODY, PLEASE LEAVE THE ROOM.
WE'LL MOVE ONTO GROUP FOUR.
...
AFTER ALL THAT, IF I PASS THE AUDITION...

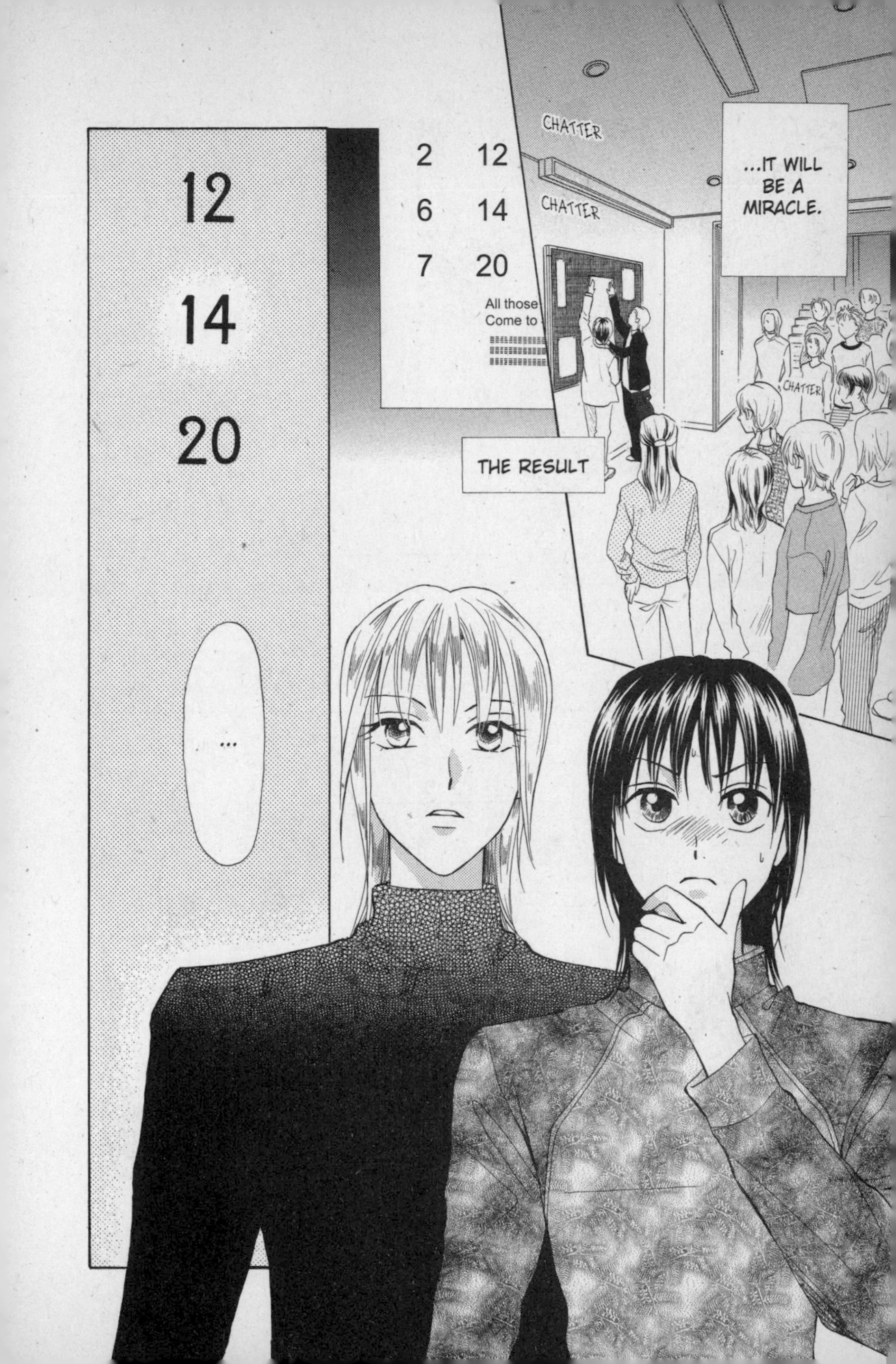
CHATTER
CHATTER
...IT WILL BE A MIRACLE.
CHATTER
THE RESULT
2 12
6 14
7 20
All those
Come to
12
14
20
...

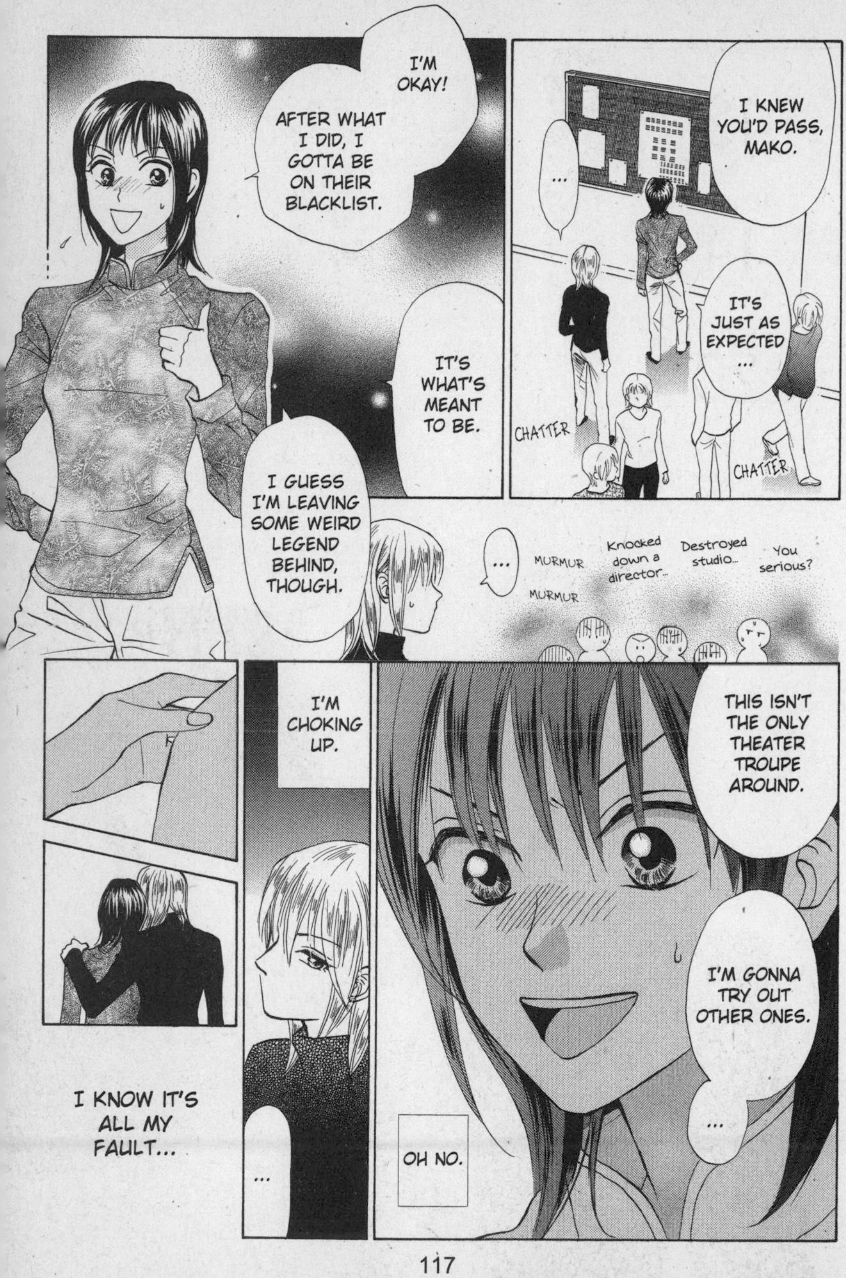

I KNEW YOU'D PASS, MAKO.
...
IT'S JUST AS EXPECTED ...
CHATTER
CHATTER
...
MURMUR
MURMUR
Knocked down a director...
Destroyed studio...
You serious?
I'M OKAY!
AFTER WHAT I DID, I GOTTA BE ON THEIR BLACKLIST.
IT'S WHAT'S MEANT TO BE.
I GUESS I'M LEAVING SOME WEIRD LEGEND BEHIND, THOUGH.
THIS ISN'T THE ONLY THEATER TROUPE AROUND.
I'M GONNA TRY OUT OTHER ONES.
...
OH NO.
I'M CHOKING UP.
...
I KNOW IT'S ALL MY FAULT...

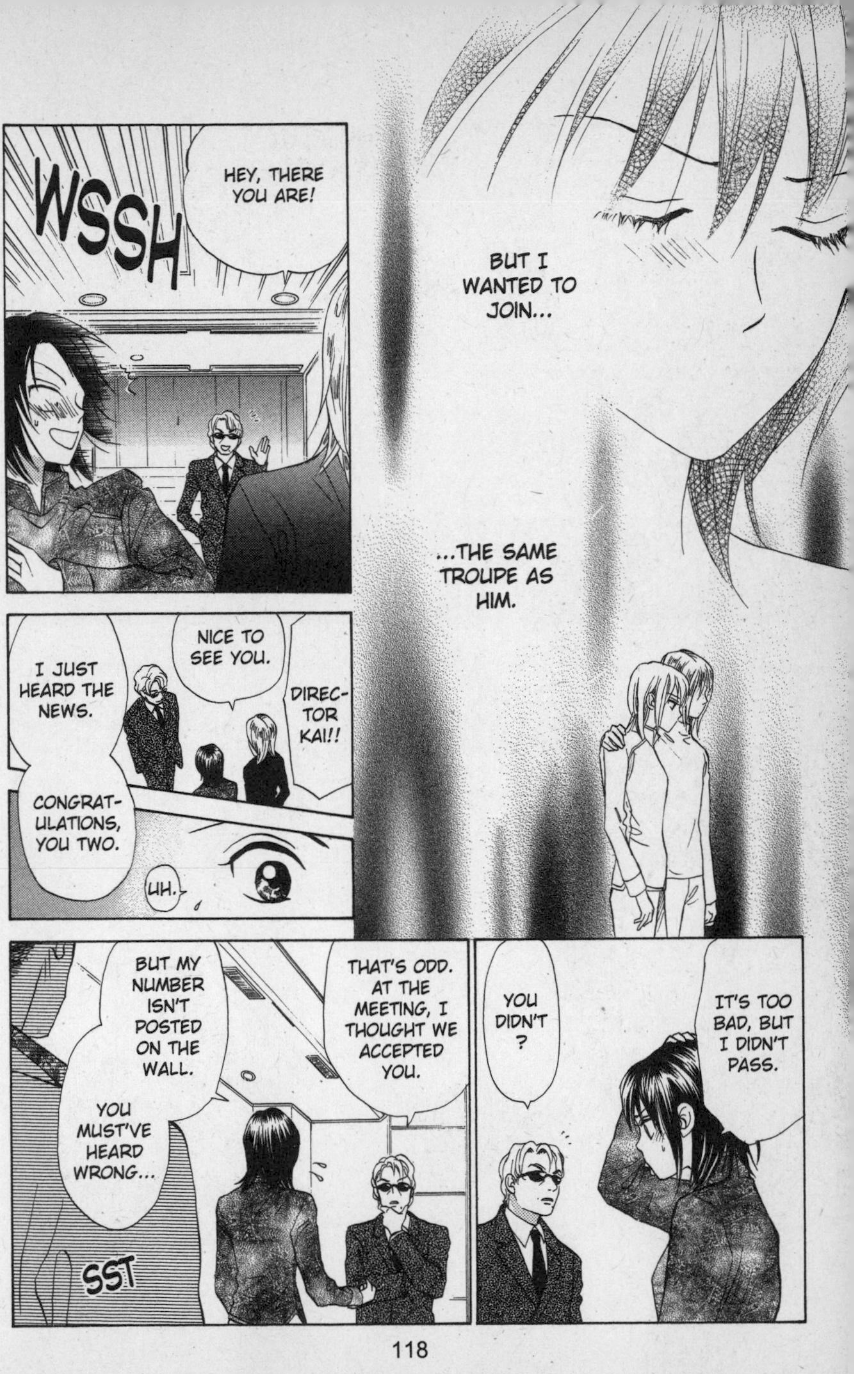
BUT I WANTED TO JOIN...
...THE SAME TROUPE AS HIM.
HEY, THERE YOU ARE!
WSSH
DIRECTOR KAI!!
NICE TO SEE YOU.
I JUST HEARD THE NEWS.
CONGRATULATIONS, YOU TWO.
UH.
IT'S TOO BAD, BUT I DIDN'T PASS.
YOU DIDN'T ?
THAT'S ODD. AT THE MEETING, I THOUGHT WE ACCEPTED YOU.
BUT MY NUMBER ISN'T POSTED ON THE WALL.
YOU MUST'VE HEARD WRONG...
SST

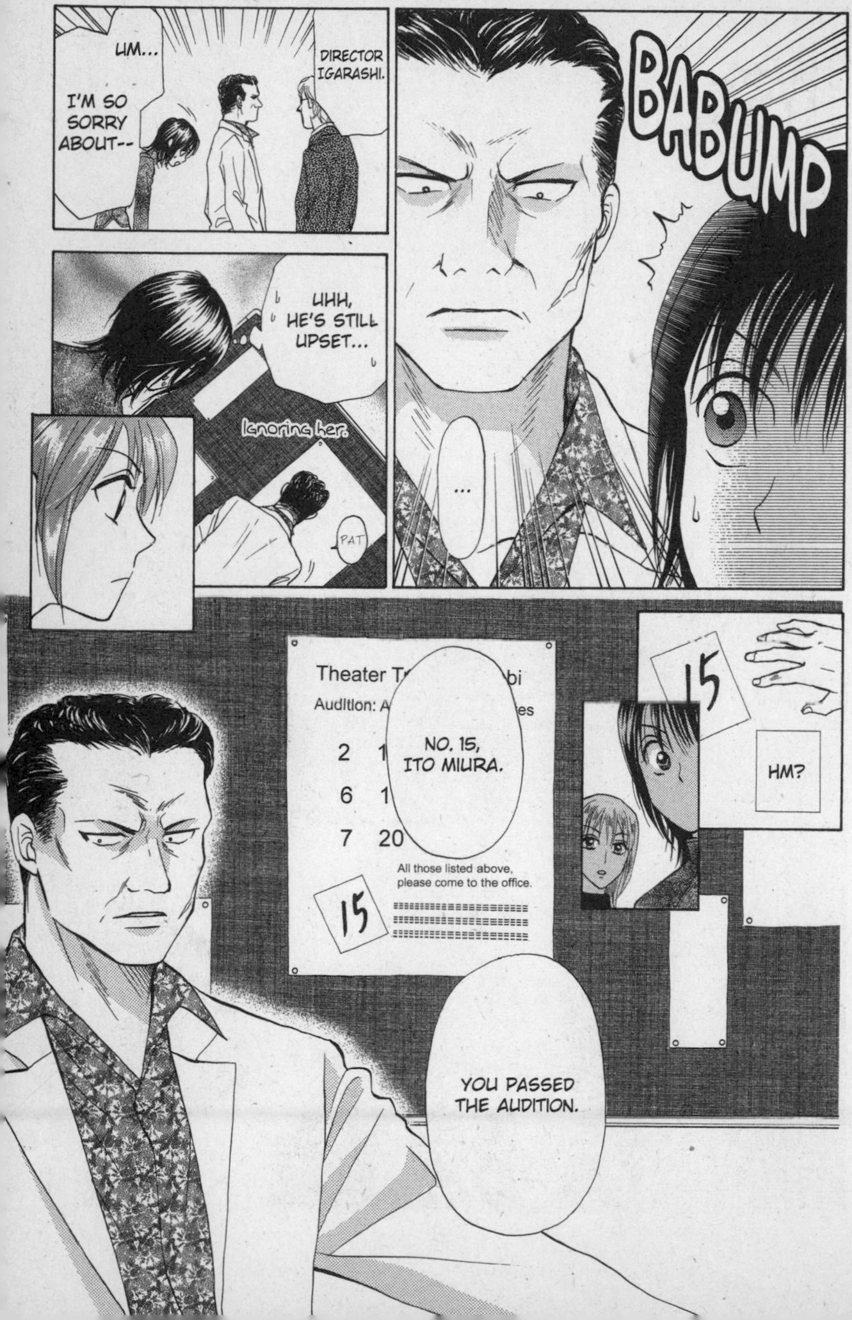

BABUMP
...
DIRECTOR IGARASHI.
UM...
I'M SO SORRY ABOUT--
UHH, HE'S STILL UPSET...
Ignoring her.
PAT
15
HM?
Theater T
Audition: A
15
NO. 15, ITO MIURA.
All those listed above, please come to the office.
YOU PASSED THE AUDITION.

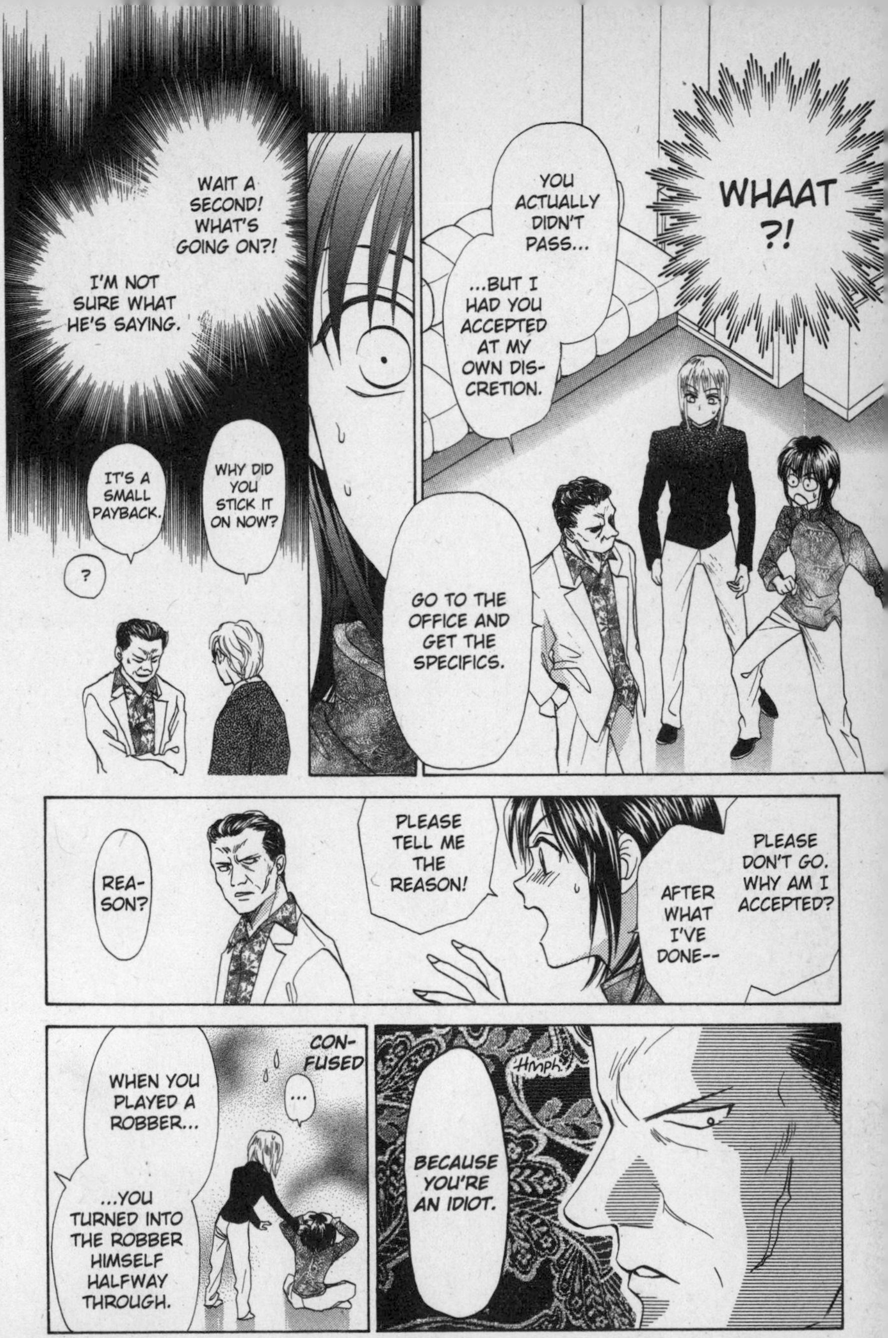
WHAAT ?!
YOU ACTUALLY DIDN'T PASS...
...BUT I HAD YOU ACCEPTED AT MY OWN DIS-CRETION.
GO TO THE OFFICE AND GET THE SPECIFICS.
WAIT A SECOND! WHAT'S GOING ON?!
I'M NOT SURE WHAT HE'S SAYING.
WHY DID YOU STICK IT ON NOW?
IT'S A SMALL PAYBACK.
?
PLEASE DON'T GO. WHY AM I ACCEPTED?
AFTER WHAT I'VE DONE--
PLEASE TELL ME THE REASON!
REA-SON?
Hmph
BECAUSE YOU'RE AN IDIOT.
CON-FUSED
...
WHEN YOU PLAYED A ROBBER...
...YOU TURNED INTO THE ROBBER HIMSELF HALFWAY THROUGH.

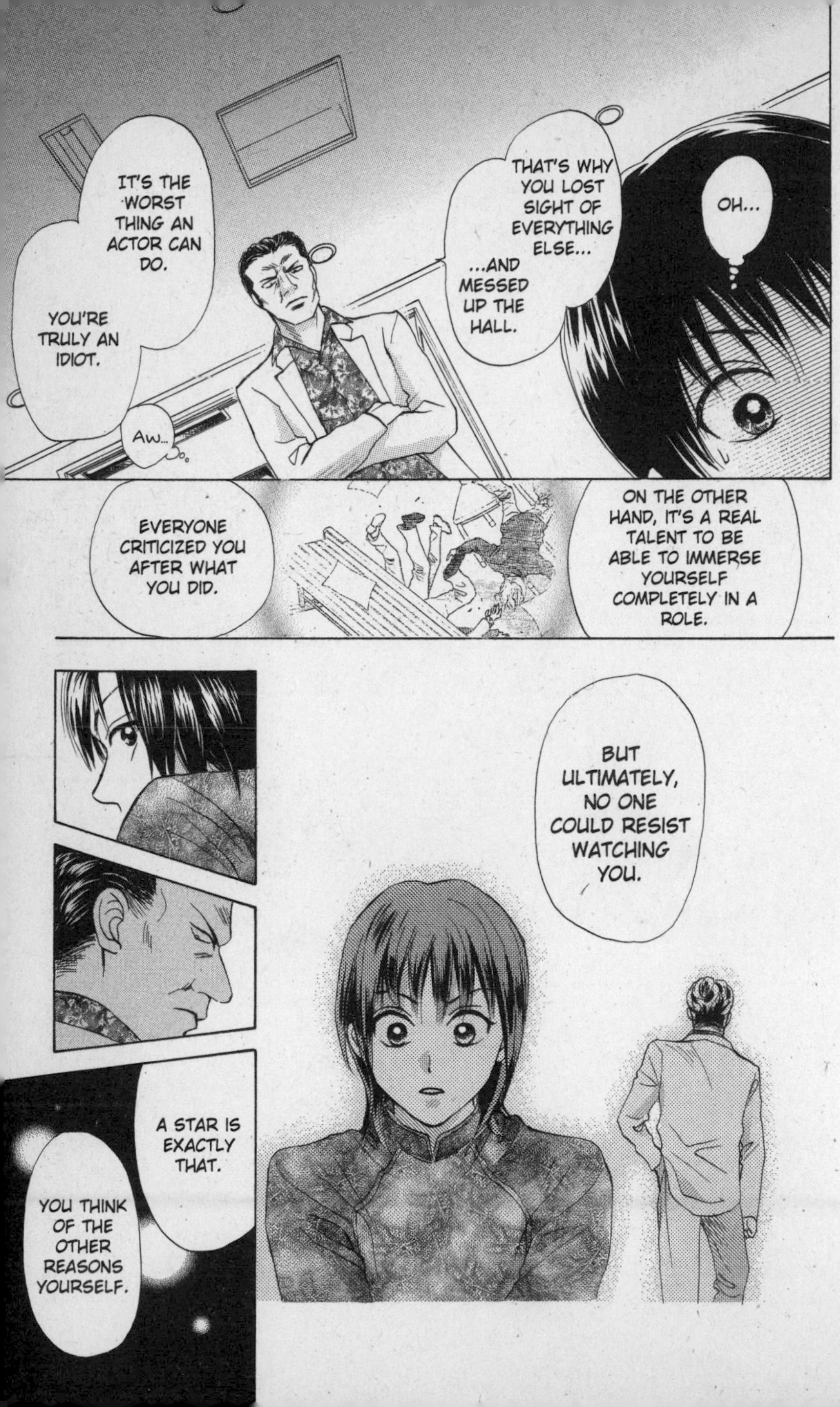
OH...
THAT'S WHY YOU LOST SIGHT OF EVERYTHING ELSE...
...AND MESSED UP THE HALL.
IT'S THE WORST THING AN ACTOR CAN DO.
YOU'RE TRULY AN IDIOT.
AW...
ON THE OTHER HAND, IT'S A REAL TALENT TO BE ABLE TO IMMERSE YOURSELF COMPLETELY IN A ROLE.
EVERYONE CRITICIZED YOU AFTER WHAT YOU DID.
BUT ULTIMATELY, NO ONE COULD RESIST WATCHING YOU.
A STAR IS EXACTLY THAT.
YOU THINK OF THE OTHER REASONS YOURSELF.

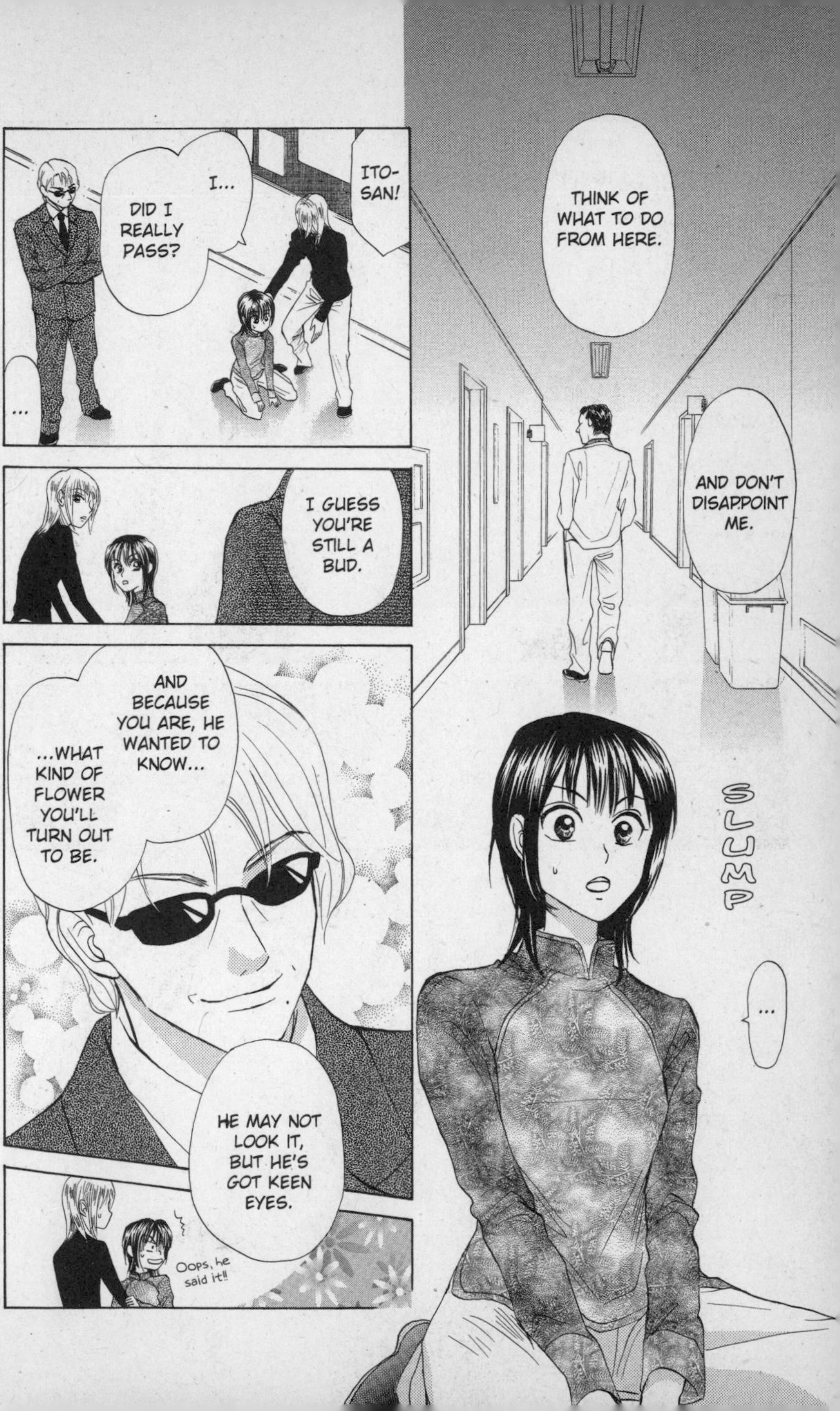
THINK OF WHAT TO DO FROM HERE.
AND DON'T DISAPPOINT ME.
SLUMP
...
ITO-SAN!
I...
DID I REALLY PASS?
...
I GUESS YOU'RE STILL A BUD.
AND BECAUSE YOU ARE, HE WANTED TO KNOW...
...WHAT KIND OF FLOWER YOU'LL TURN OUT TO BE.
HE MAY NOT LOOK IT, BUT HE'S GOT KEEN EYES.
Oops, he said it!!

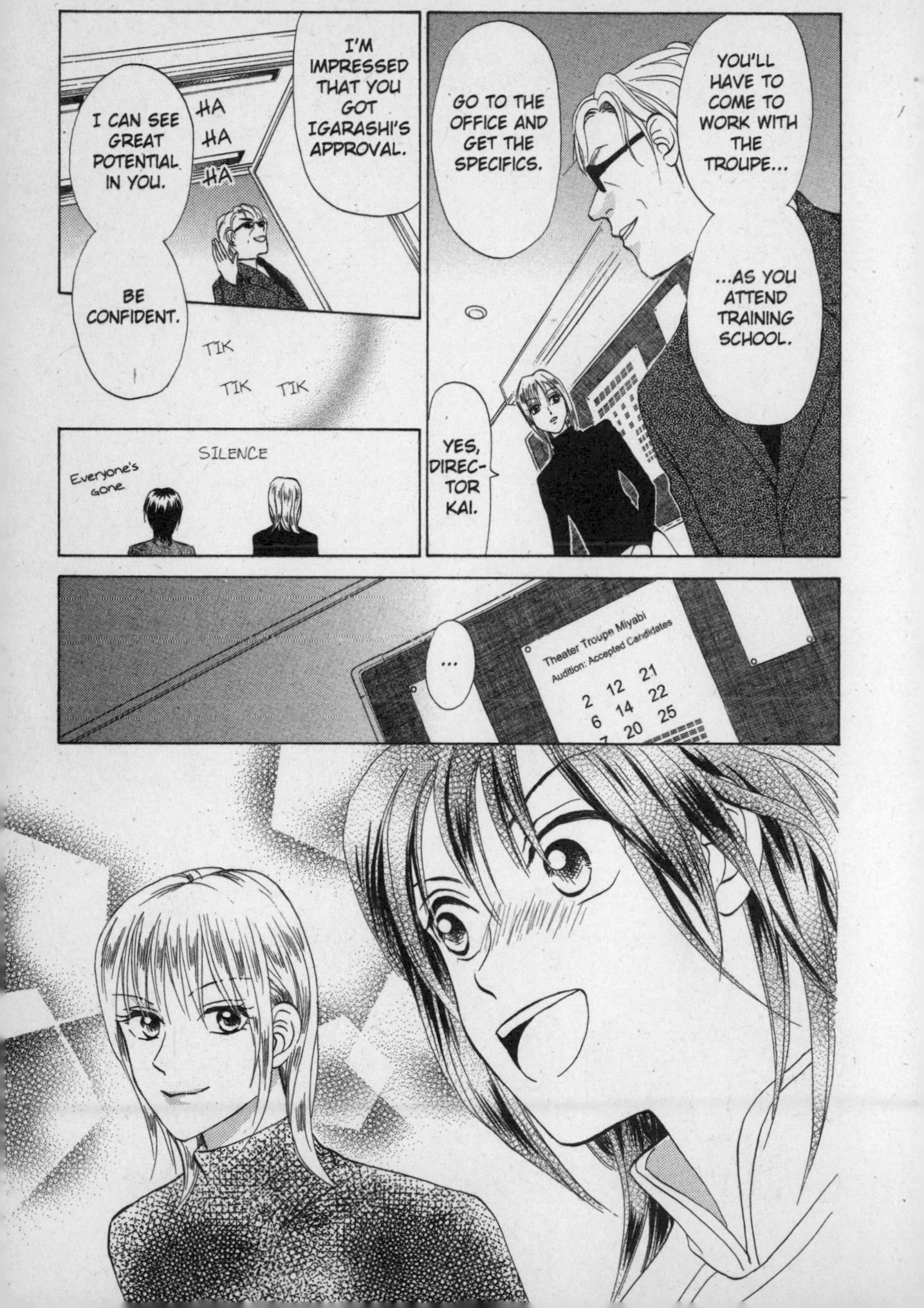

YOU'LL HAVE TO COME TO WORK WITH THE TROUPE...
...AS YOU ATTEND TRAINING SCHOOL.
GO TO THE OFFICE AND GET THE SPECIFICS.
YES, DIRECTOR KAI.
I'M IMPRESSED THAT YOU GOT IGARASHI'S APPROVAL.
HA HA HA
I CAN SEE GREAT POTENTIAL IN YOU.
BE CONFIDENT.
TIK TIK TIK
SILENCE
Everyone's gone
...
Theater Troupe Miyabi
Audition: Accepted Candidates
2 12 21
6 14 22
20 25

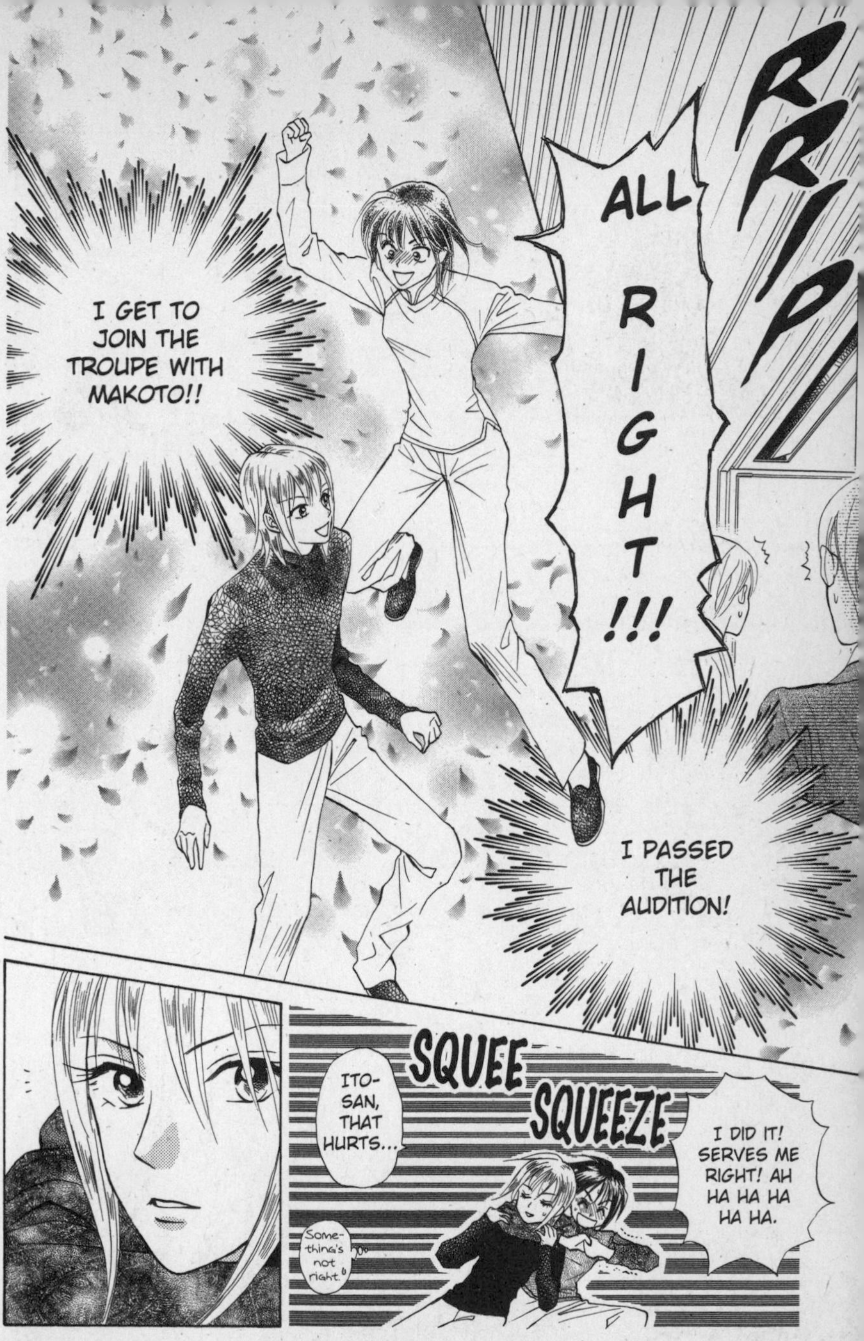
RRIP
ALL RIGHT!!!
I PASSED THE AUDITION!
I GET TO JOIN THE TROUPE WITH MAKOTO!!
SQUEE SQUEEZE
I DID IT! SERVES ME RIGHT! AH HA HA HA HA HA.
ITO-SAN, THAT HURTS...
Something's not right.

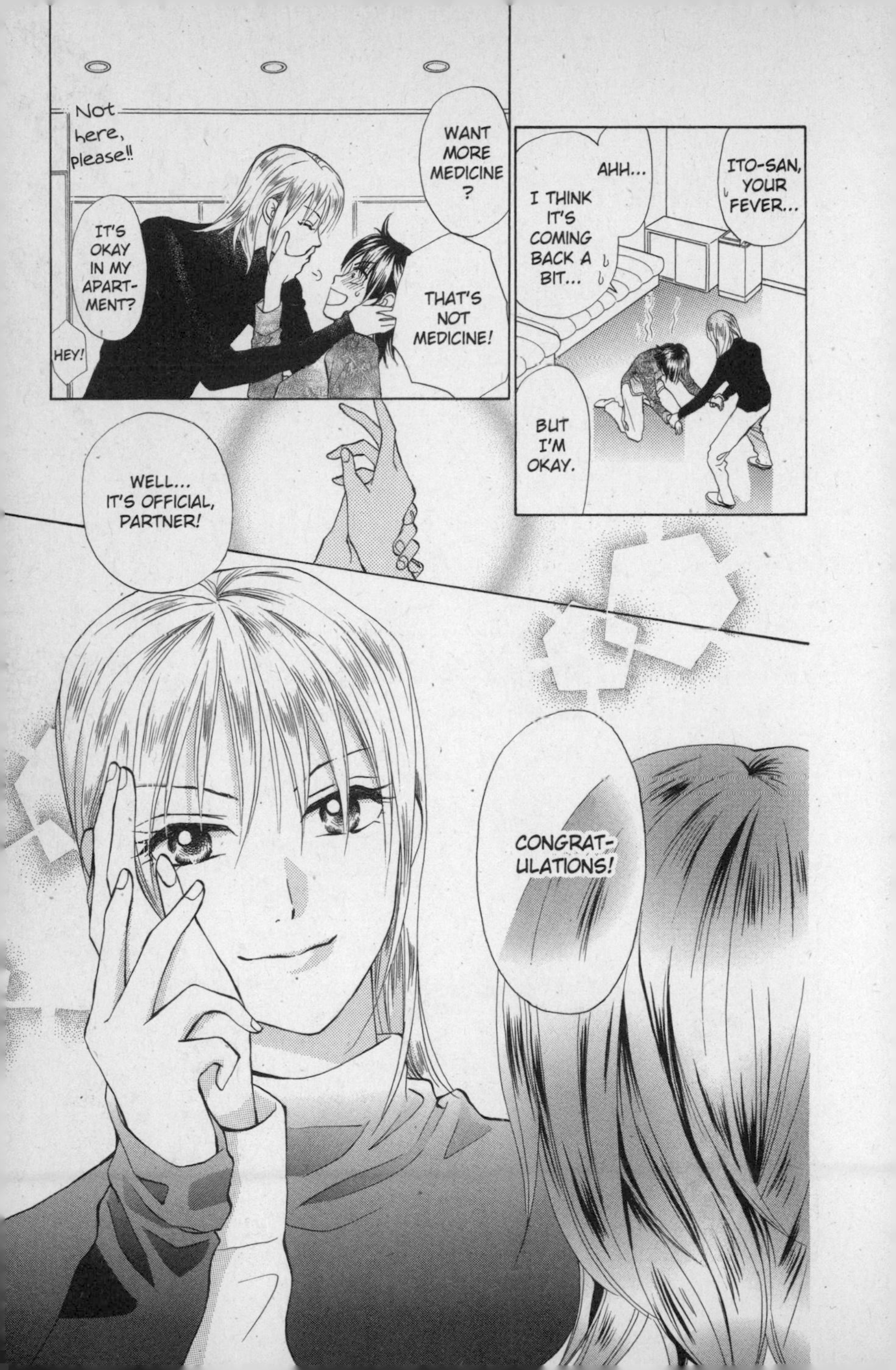
ITO-SAN, YOUR FEVER...
AHH... I THINK IT'S COMING BACK A BIT...
BUT I'M OKAY.
WANT MORE MEDICINE ?
THAT'S NOT MEDICINE!
IT'S OKAY IN MY APARTMENT?
HEY!
Not here, please!!
WELL... IT'S OFFICIAL, PARTNER!
CONGRAT-ULATIONS!

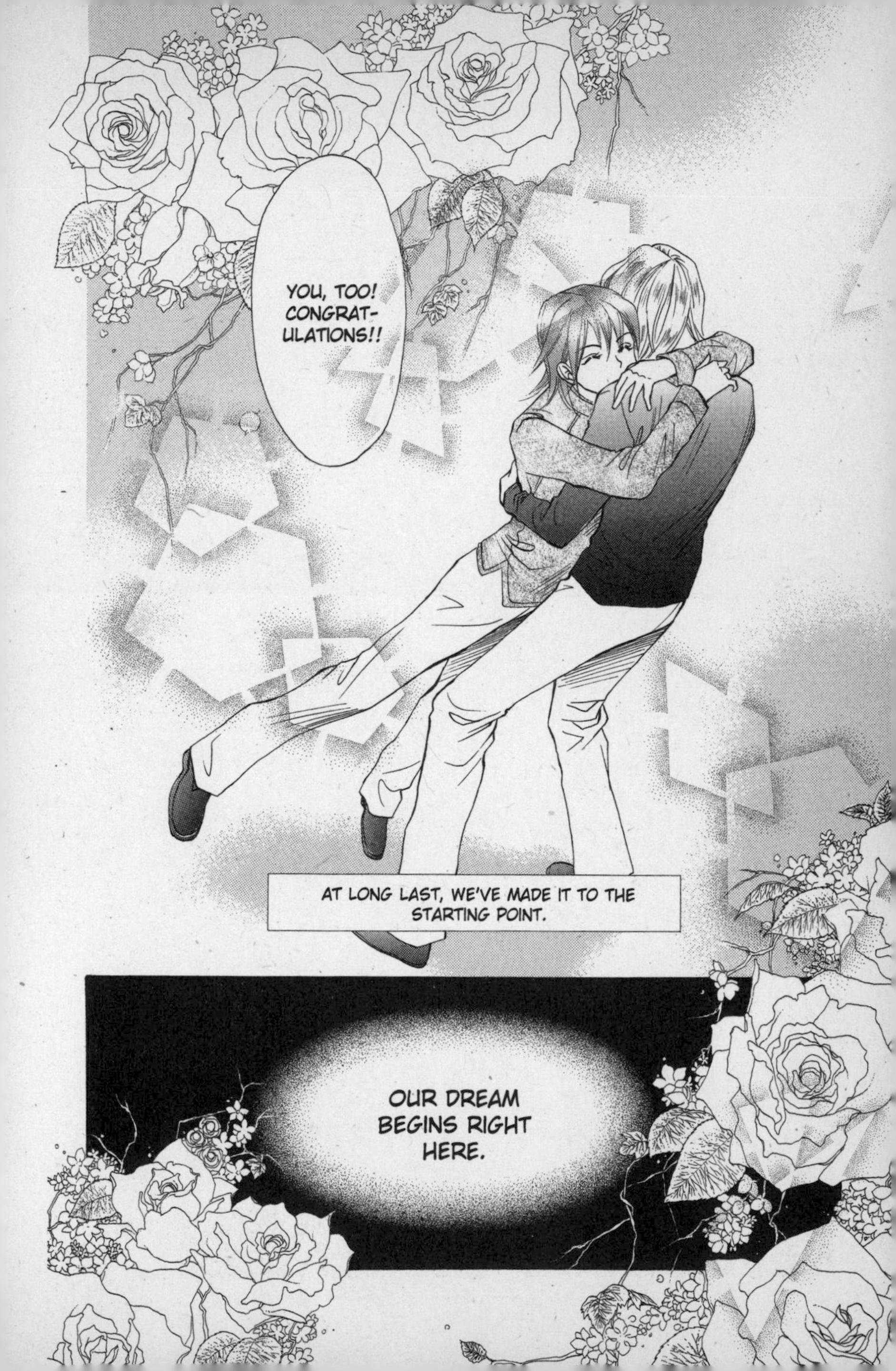
YOU, TOO! CONGRAT-ULATIONS!!
AT LONG LAST, WE'VE MADE IT TO THE STARTING POINT.
OUR DREAM BEGINS RIGHT HERE.

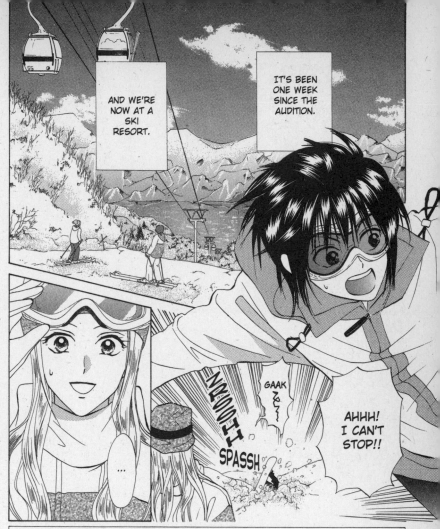

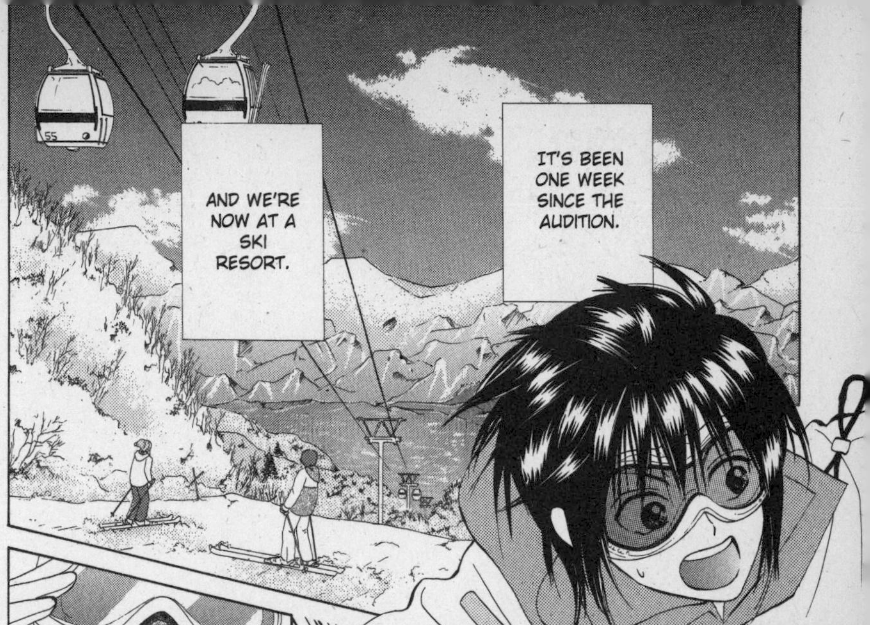
IT'S BEEN ONE WEEK SINCE THE AUDITION.
AND WE'RE NOW AT A SKI RESORT.
AHHH! I CAN'T STOP!!
GAAK
ZWOOSHH
SPASSH
...

—Behind the Scenes Story (5)—

It feels good that I finally made it this far.

It's been quite a while since I decided on using Akane's driver's license as the cause of the secret getting out. Apparently, some readers anticipated that this would happen, too. Talking about the graduation trip, I modeled it after a real hot spring inn. My sister and I went on a research trip beforehand. And yes, they did offer konyoku baths. The official name for it is "Family Bath." You can bathe as long as you want, and it's really relaxing.

Goemonburo

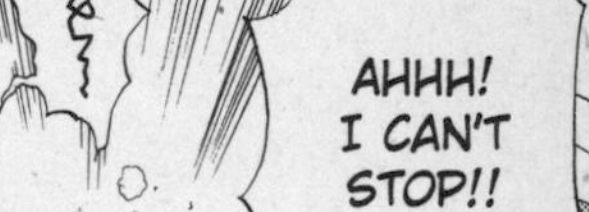
What a weird thing to rent...

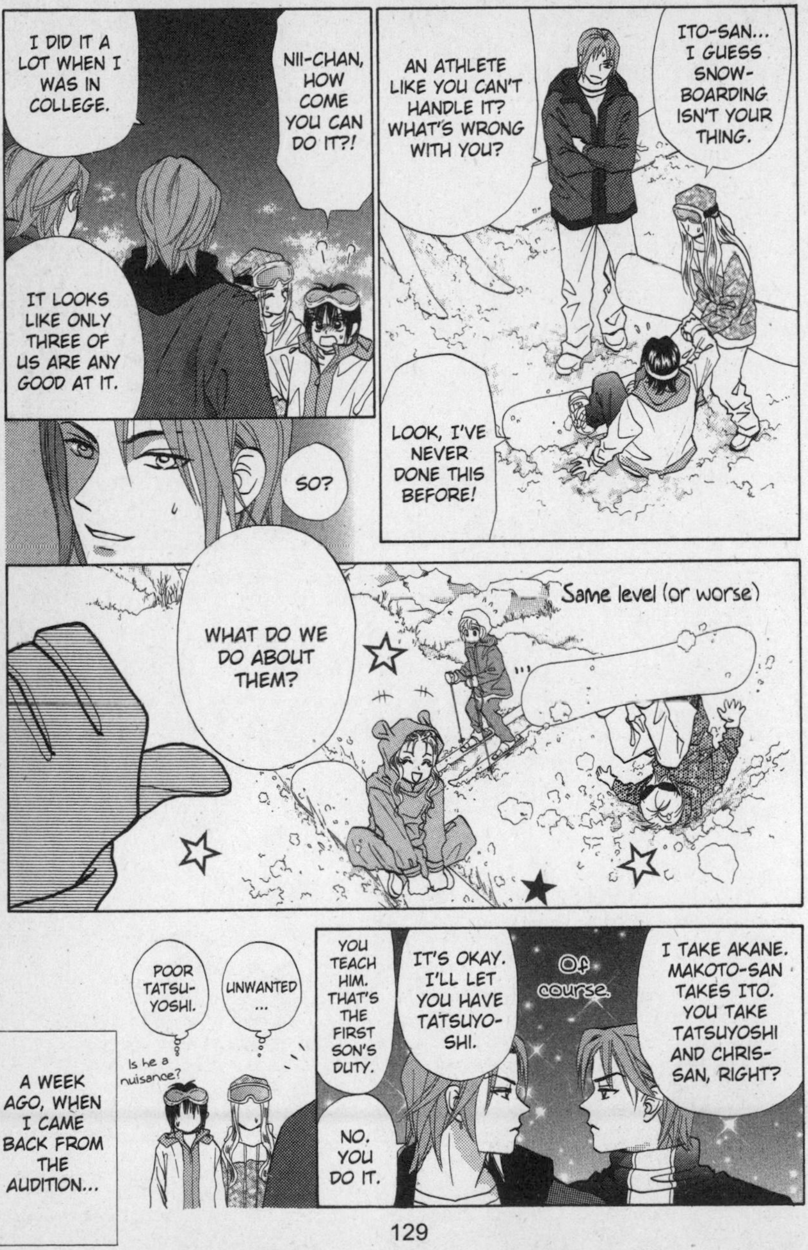
ITO-SAN... I GUESS SNOW-BOARDING ISN'T YOUR THING.
AN ATHLETE LIKE YOU CAN'T HANDLE IT? WHAT'S WRONG WITH YOU?
LOOK, I'VE NEVER DONE THIS BEFORE!
NII-CHAN, HOW COME YOU CAN DO IT?!
I DID IT A LOT WHEN I WAS IN COLLEGE.
IT LOOKS LIKE ONLY THREE OF US ARE ANY GOOD AT IT.
SO?
Same level (or worse)
WHAT DO WE DO ABOUT THEM?
I TAKE AKANE. MAKOTO-SAN TAKES ITO. YOU TAKE TATSUYOSHI AND CHRIS-SAN, RIGHT?
Of course.
IT'S OKAY. I'LL LET YOU HAVE TATSUYO-SHI.
YOU TEACH HIM. THAT'S THE FIRST SON'S DUTY.
NO. YOU DO IT.
UNWANTED ...
POOR TATSU-YOSHI.
Is he a nuisance?

A WEEK AGO, WHEN I CAME BACK FROM THE AUDITION...

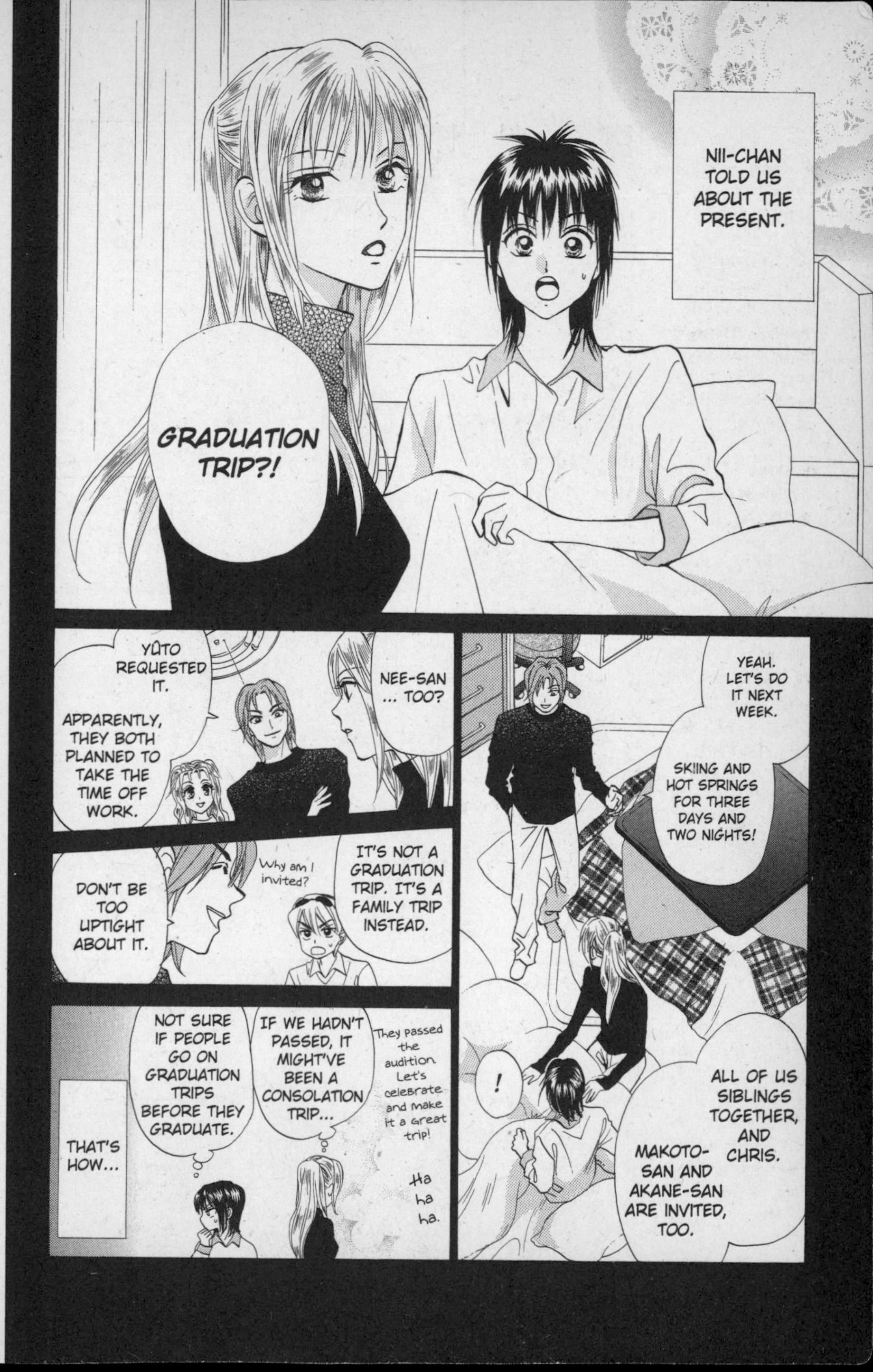
NII-CHAN TOLD US ABOUT THE PRESENT.
GRADUATION TRIP?!
YEAH. LET'S DO IT NEXT WEEK.
SKIING AND HOT SPRINGS FOR THREE DAYS AND TWO NIGHTS!
!
ALL OF US SIBLINGS TOGETHER, AND CHRIS.
MAKOTO-SAN AND AKANE-SAN ARE INVITED, TOO.
NEE-SAN ... TOO?
YÛTO REQUESTED IT.
APPARENTLY, THEY BOTH PLANNED TO TAKE THE TIME OFF WORK.
IT'S NOT A GRADUATION TRIP. IT'S A FAMILY TRIP INSTEAD.
Why am I invited?
DON'T BE TOO UPTIGHT ABOUT IT.
They passed the audition. Let's celebrate and make it a Great trip!
Ha ha ha.
IF WE HADN'T PASSED, IT MIGHT'VE BEEN A CONSOLATION TRIP...
NOT SURE IF PEOPLE GO ON GRADUATION TRIPS BEFORE THEY GRADUATE.
THAT'S HOW...

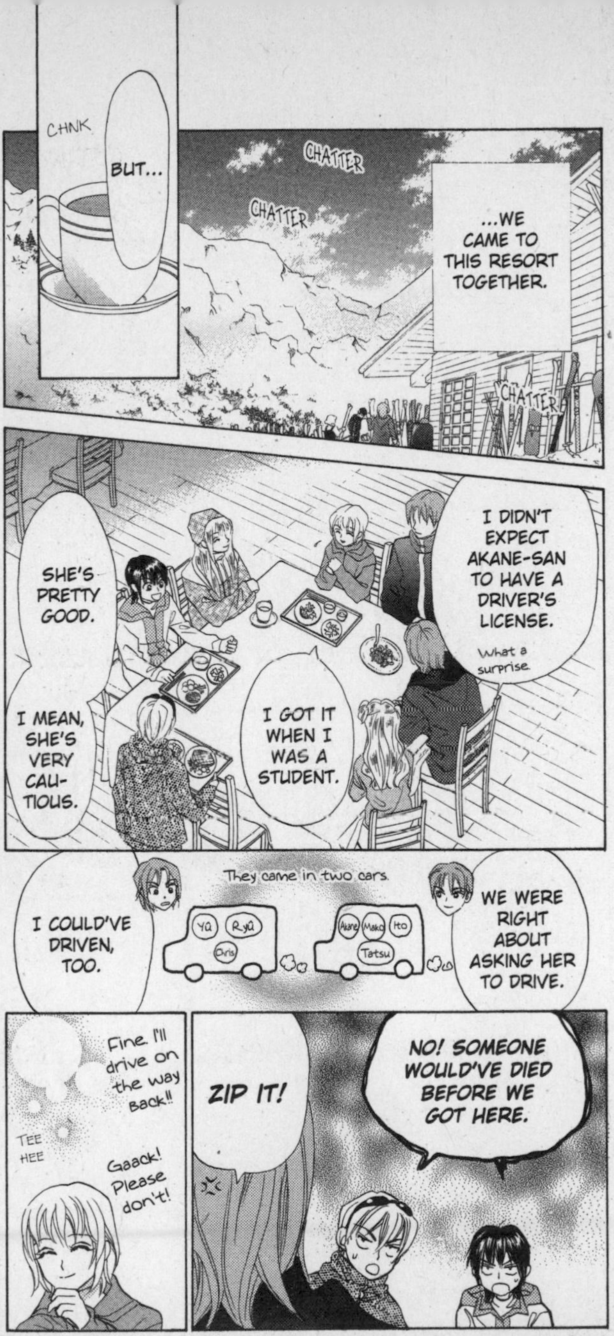
CHNK
BUT...
CHATTER
CHATTER
...WE CAME TO THIS RESORT TOGETHER.
CHATTER
I DIDN'T EXPECT AKANE-SAN TO HAVE A DRIVER'S LICENSE.
What a surprise.
I GOT IT WHEN I WAS A STUDENT.
SHE'S PRETTY GOOD.
I MEAN, SHE'S VERY CAUTIOUS.
WE WERE RIGHT ABOUT ASKING HER TO DRIVE.
They came in two cars.
Akane Mako Ito Tatsu
Yû Ryû Chris
I COULD'VE DRIVEN, TOO.
NO! SOMEONE WOULD'VE DIED BEFORE WE GOT HERE.
ZIP IT!
Fine. I'll drive on the way back!!
Gaack! Please don't!
TEE HEE

- As a manga-ka, what task do you hate most?

Ⓔ "If I must come up with an answer... not having enough time, I guess. I would love to take more time to draw!

- Have you ever thought of quitting?

Ⓔ For some reason, tons of people ask this question. I never thought of quitting. Not even once. I won't be able to continue living without manga. Not at all.

- Is Tatsuyoshi's Higashi High School a high-ranked academic school? Is it private or public?

Ⓔ Not really. It's ranked so low within the Tokyo school district, it's faster to count up from the bottom. (Laugh) Incidentally, it's a public school.

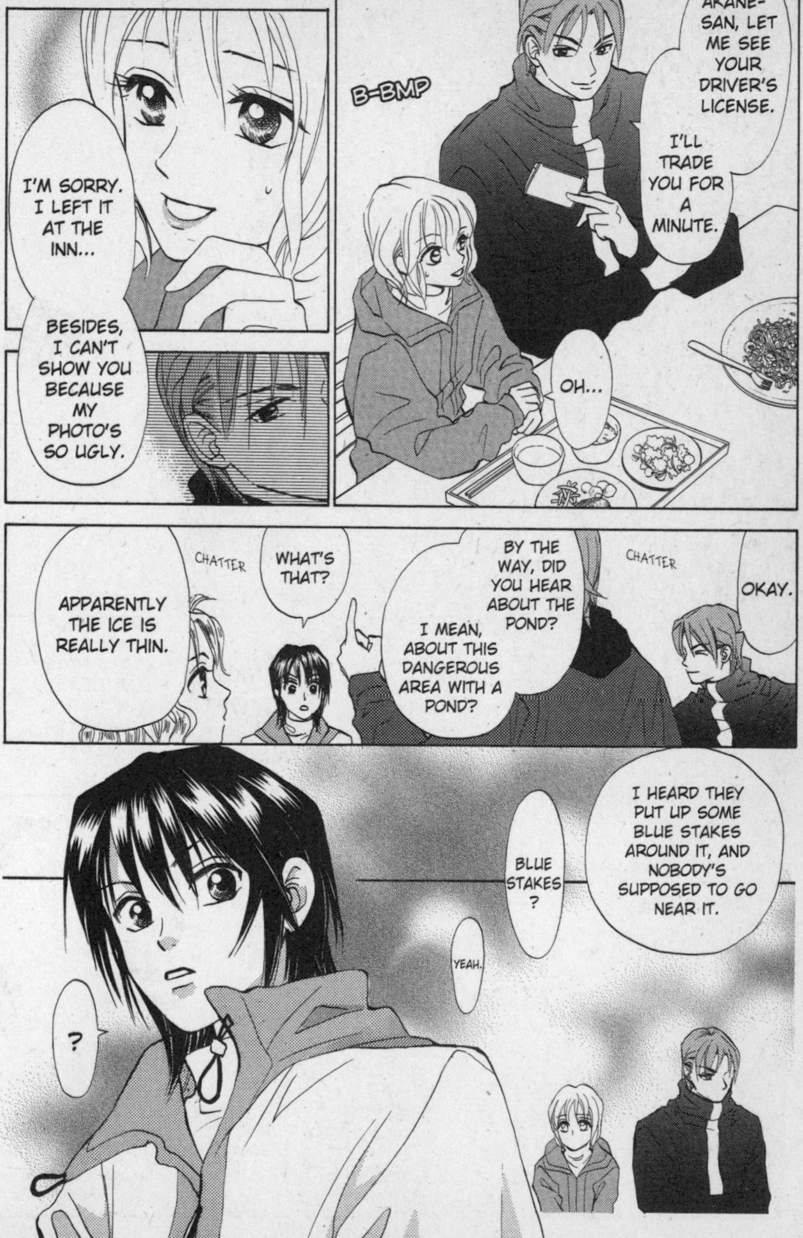
AKANE-SAN, LET ME SEE YOUR DRIVER'S LICENSE.
I'LL TRADE YOU FOR A MINUTE.
B-BMP
OH...
I'M SORRY. I LEFT IT AT THE INN...
BESIDES, I CAN'T SHOW YOU BECAUSE MY PHOTO'S SO UGLY.
OKAY.
CHATTER
BY THE WAY, DID YOU HEAR ABOUT THE POND?
I MEAN, ABOUT THIS DANGEROUS AREA WITH A POND?
WHAT'S THAT?
CHATTER
APPARENTLY THE ICE IS REALLY THIN.
I HEARD THEY PUT UP SOME BLUE STAKES AROUND IT, AND NOBODY'S SUPPOSED TO GO NEAR IT.
BLUE STAKES?
YEAH.
?

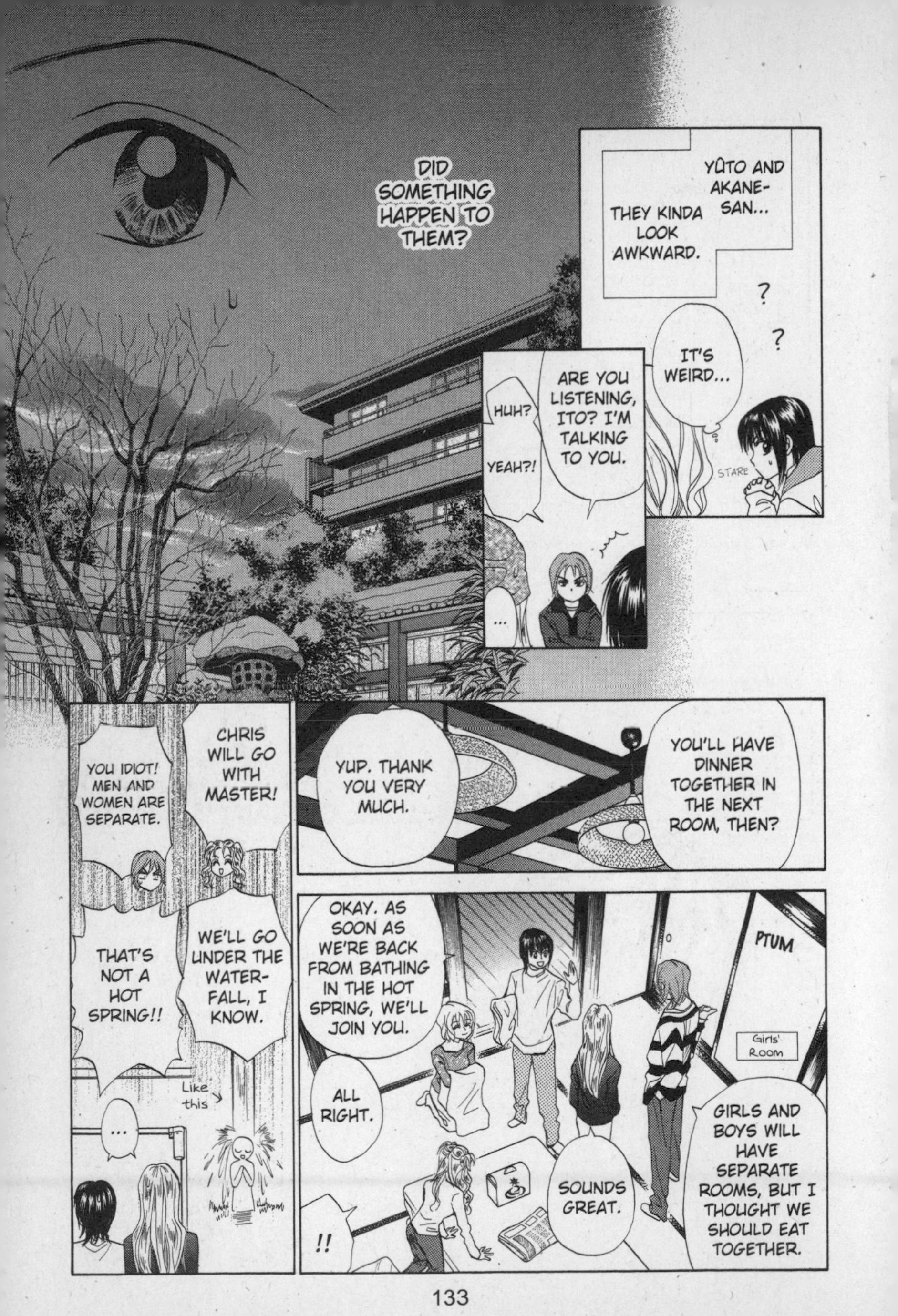
YŪTO AND AKANE-SAN...
THEY KINDA LOOK AWKWARD.
?
?
IT'S WEIRD...
STARE
ARE YOU LISTENING, ITO? I'M TALKING TO YOU.
HUH?
YEAH?!
...
DID SOMETHING HAPPEN TO THEM?
YOU'LL HAVE DINNER TOGETHER IN THE NEXT ROOM, THEN?
YUP. THANK YOU VERY MUCH.
PTUM
Girls' Room
GIRLS AND BOYS WILL HAVE SEPARATE ROOMS, BUT I THOUGHT WE SHOULD EAT TOGETHER.
SOUNDS GREAT.
OKAY. AS SOON AS WE'RE BACK FROM BATHING IN THE HOT SPRING, WE'LL JOIN YOU.
ALL RIGHT.
!!
CHRIS WILL GO WITH MASTER!
YOU IDIOT! MEN AND WOMEN ARE SEPARATE.
WE'LL GO UNDER THE WATER-FALL, I KNOW.
THAT'S NOT A HOT SPRING!!
Like this
...

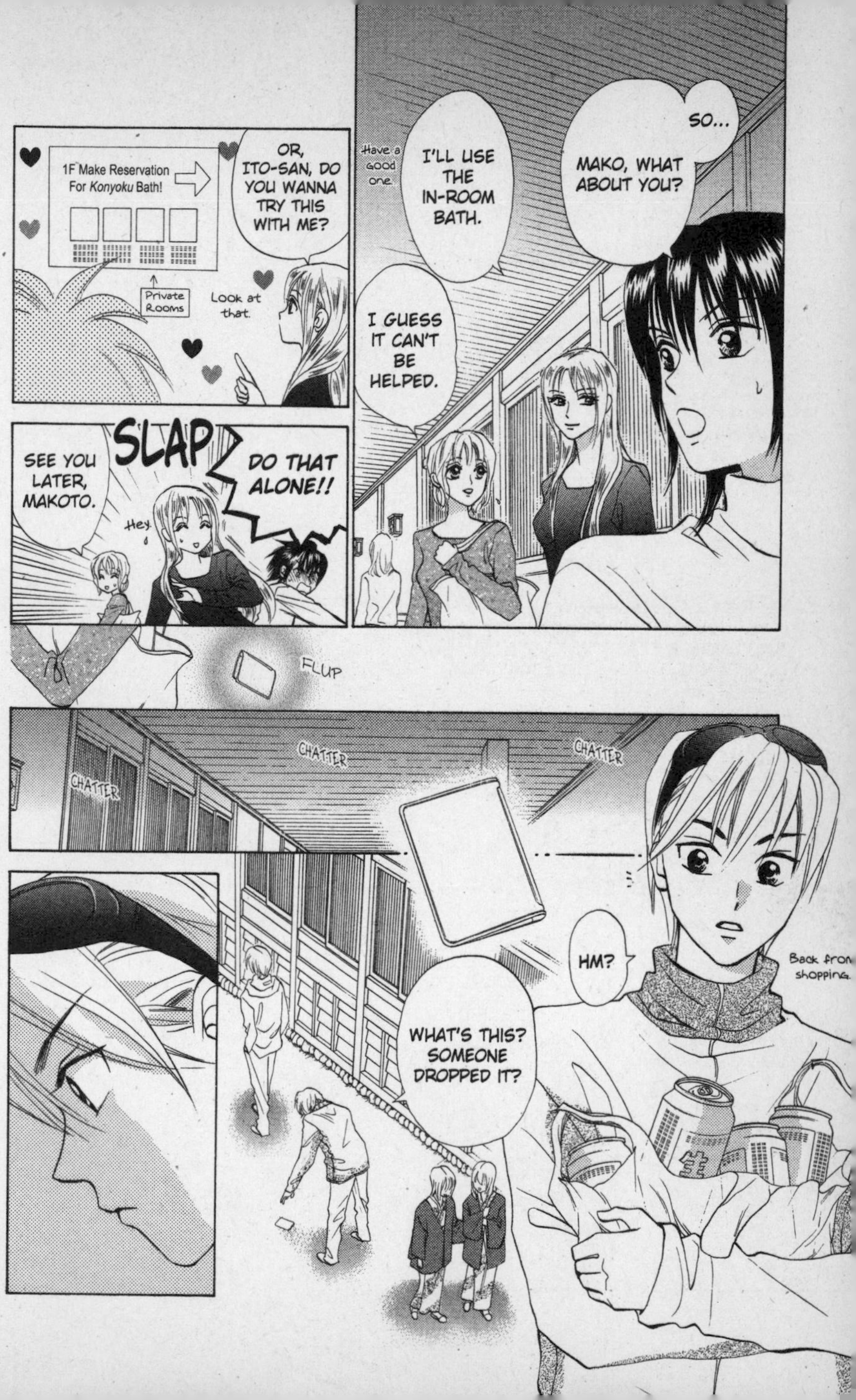
SO...
MAKO, WHAT ABOUT YOU?
I'LL USE THE IN-ROOM BATH.
Have a good one.
I GUESS IT CAN'T BE HELPED.
1F Make Reservation For Konyoku Bath!
Private Rooms
OR, ITO-SAN, DO YOU WANNA TRY THIS WITH ME?
Look at that.
DO THAT ALONE!!
SLAP
SEE YOU LATER, MAKOTO.
Hey.
FLUP
CHATTER
CHATTER
CHATTER
Back from shopping.
HM?
WHAT'S THIS? SOMEONE DROPPED IT?

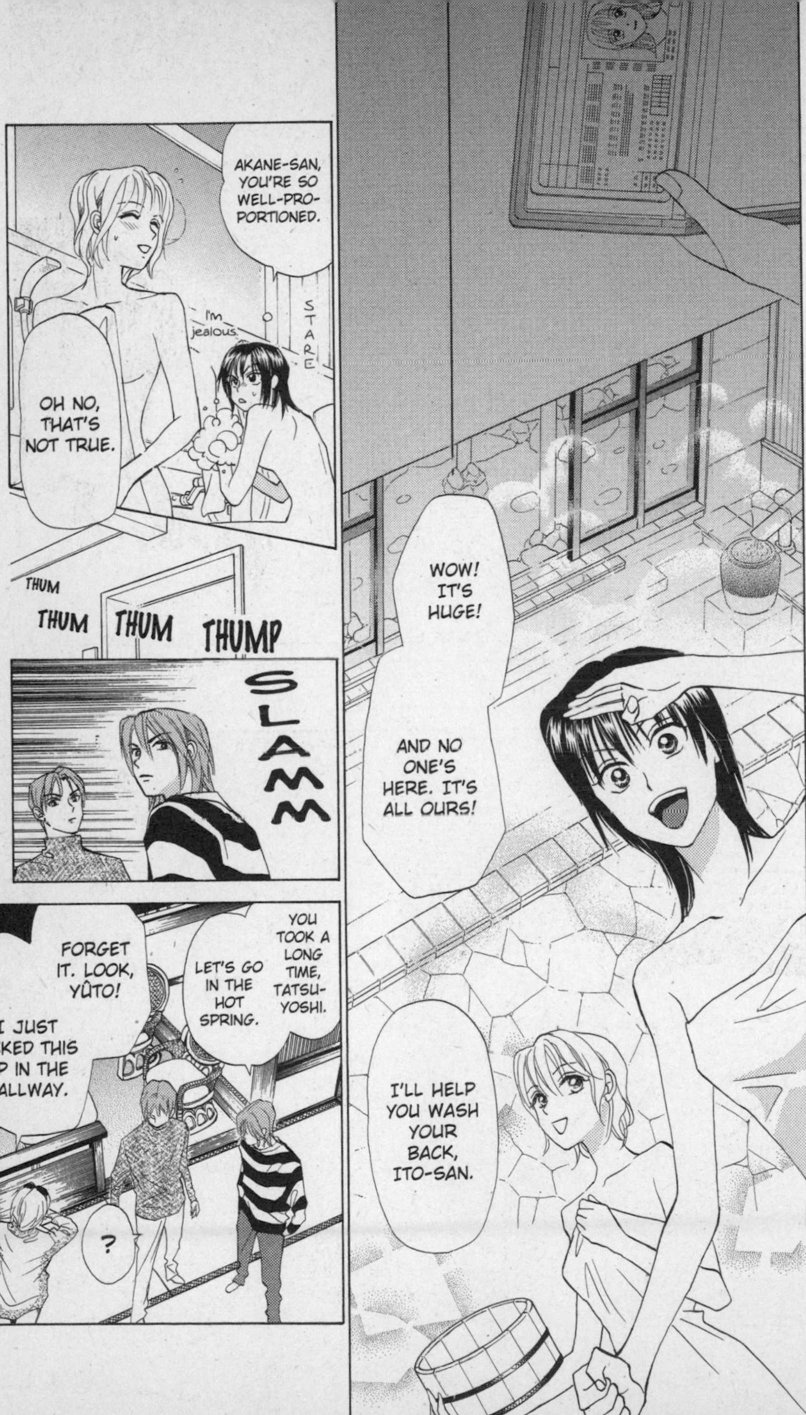
WOW! IT'S HUGE!
AND NO ONE'S HERE. IT'S ALL OURS!
I'LL HELP YOU WASH YOUR BACK, ITO-SAN.
AKANE-SAN, YOU'RE SO WELL-PROPORTIONED.
STARE
I'm jealous.
OH NO, THAT'S NOT TRUE.
THUM THUM THUM THUMP
SLAMM
YOU TOOK A LONG TIME, TATSUYOSHI.
LET'S GO IN THE HOT SPRING.
FORGET IT. LOOK, YÛTO!
I JUST PICKED THIS UP IN THE HALLWAY.
?

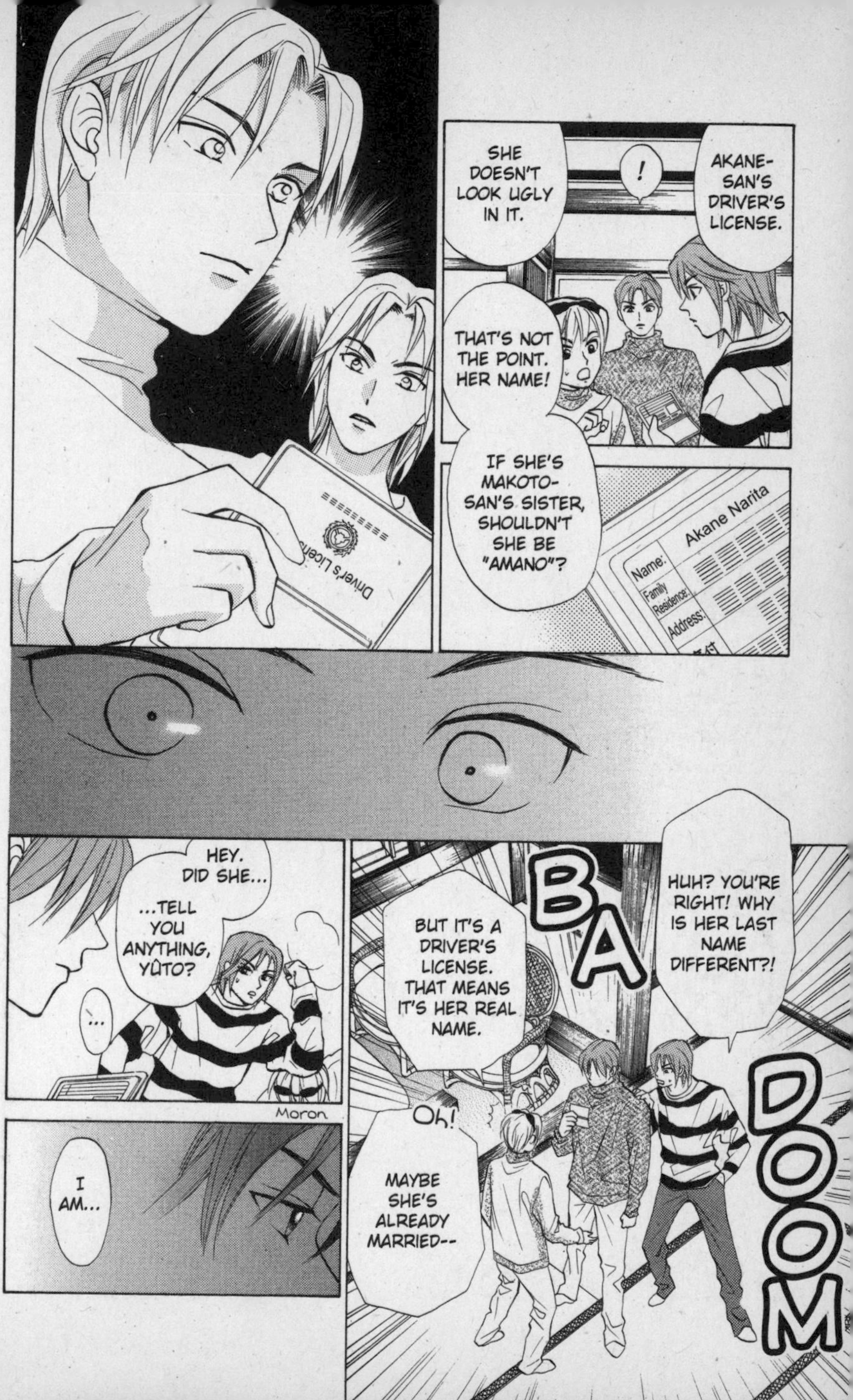

AKANE-SAN'S DRIVER'S LICENSE.
!
SHE DOESN'T LOOK UGLY IN IT.
THAT'S NOT THE POINT. HER NAME!
IF SHE'S MAKOTO-SAN'S SISTER, SHOULDN'T SHE BE "AMANO"?
Akane Narita
Name:
Family Residence:
Address:
HUH? YOU'RE RIGHT! WHY IS HER LAST NAME DIFFERENT?!
BA
DOOM
BUT IT'S A DRIVER'S LICENSE. THAT MEANS IT'S HER REAL NAME.
Oh!
MAYBE SHE'S ALREADY MARRIED--
HEY. DID SHE...
...TELL YOU ANYTHING, YÛTO?
...
Moron
I AM...

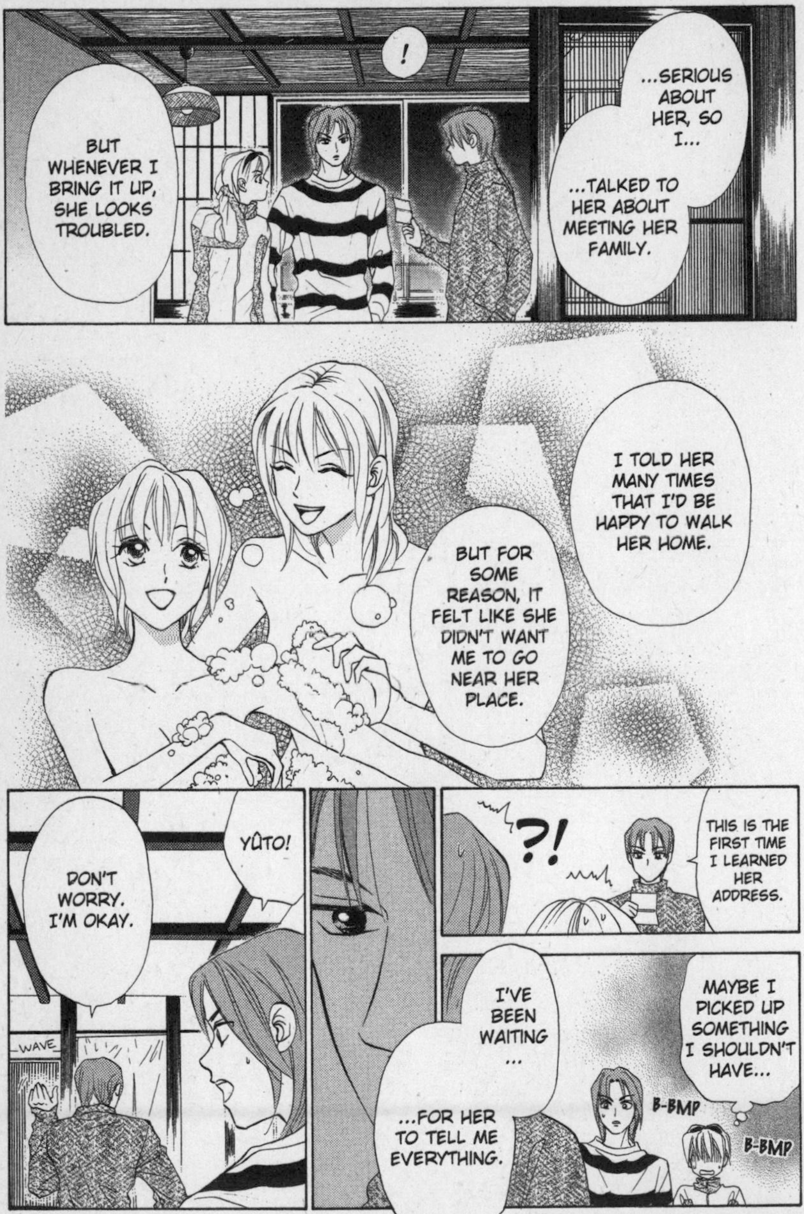
...SERIOUS ABOUT HER, SO I...
...TALKED TO HER ABOUT MEETING HER FAMILY.
!
BUT WHENEVER I BRING IT UP, SHE LOOKS TROUBLED.
I TOLD HER MANY TIMES THAT I'D BE HAPPY TO WALK HER HOME.
BUT FOR SOME REASON, IT FELT LIKE SHE DIDN'T WANT ME TO GO NEAR HER PLACE.
THIS IS THE FIRST TIME I LEARNED HER ADDRESS.
?!
MAYBE I PICKED UP SOMETHING I SHOULDN'T HAVE...
B-BMP
B-BMP
I'VE BEEN WAITING...
...FOR HER TO TELL ME EVERYTHING.
YÛTO!
DON'T WORRY. I'M OKAY.
WAVE

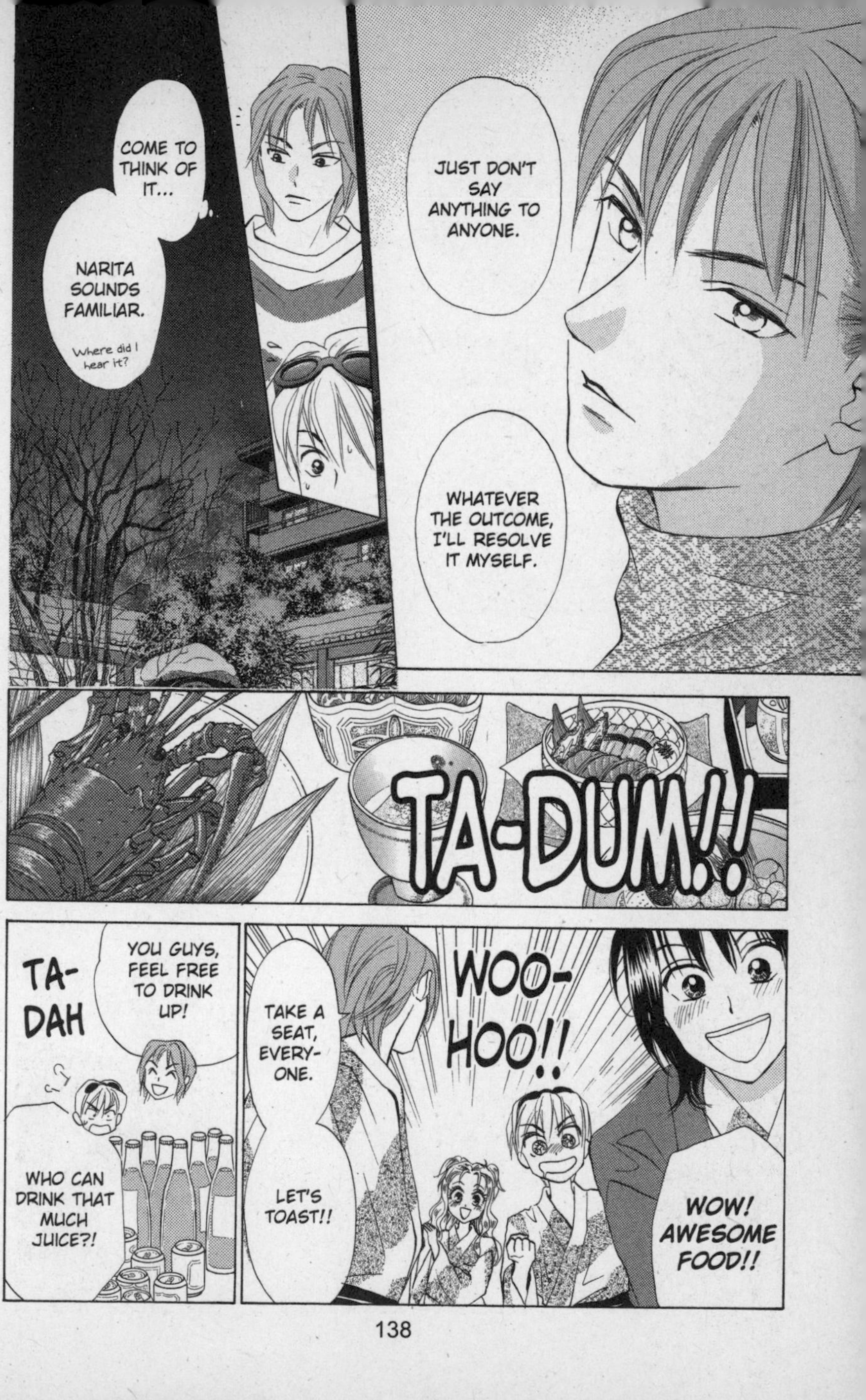
JUST DON'T SAY ANYTHING TO ANYONE.
WHATEVER THE OUTCOME, I'LL RESOLVE IT MYSELF.
COME TO THINK OF IT...
NARITA SOUNDS FAMILIAR.
Where did I hear it?
TA-DUM!!
WOO-HOO!!
WOW! AWESOME FOOD!!
TAKE A SEAT, EVERYONE.
LET'S TOAST!!
YOU GUYS, FEEL FREE TO DRINK UP!
TA-DAH
WHO CAN DRINK THAT MUCH JUICE?!

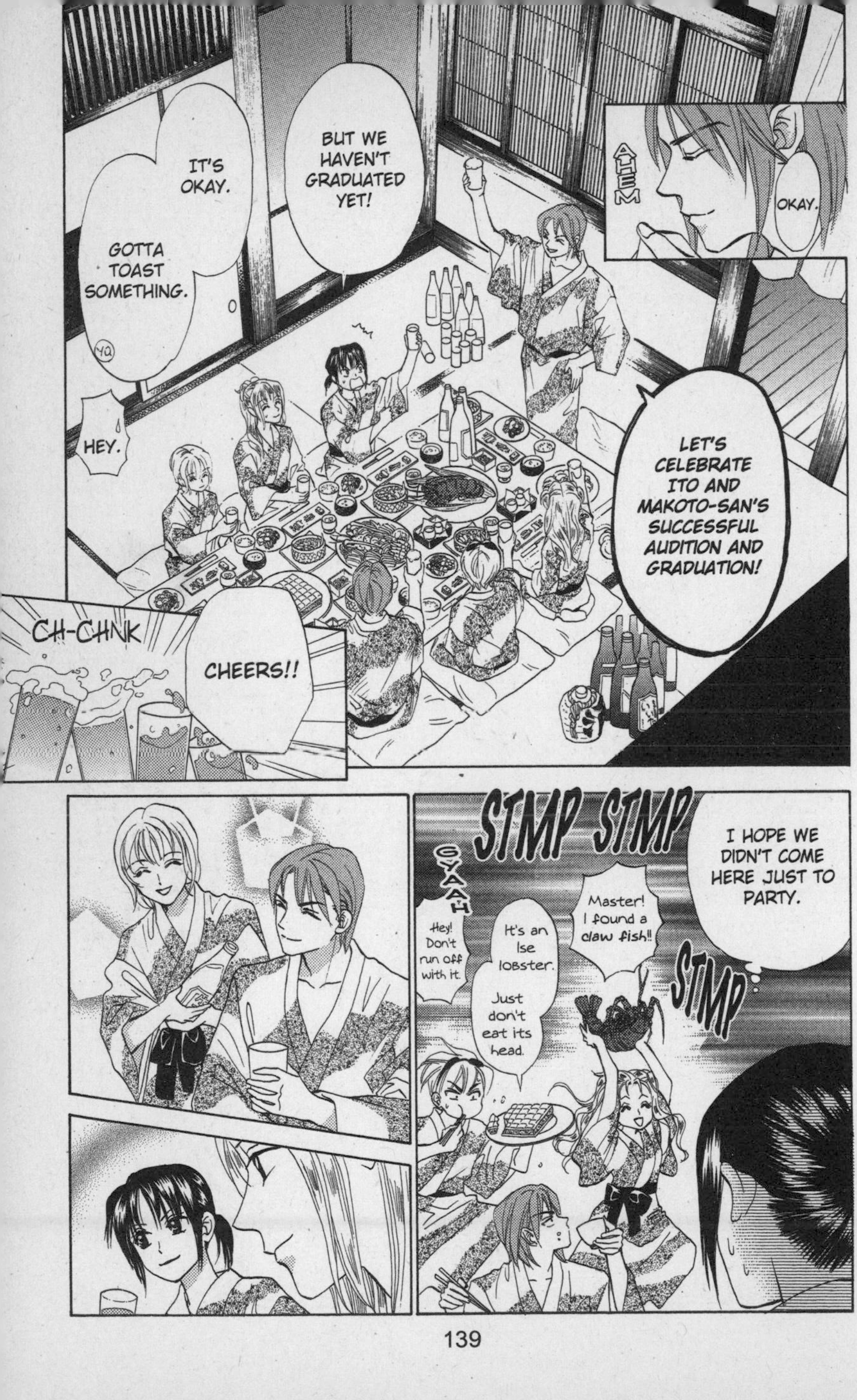
AHEM
OKAY.
LET'S CELEBRATE ITO AND MAKOTO-SAN'S SUCCESSFUL AUDITION AND GRADUATION!
BUT WE HAVEN'T GRADUATED YET!
IT'S OKAY.
GOTTA TOAST SOMETHING.
HEY.
CH-CHNK
CHEERS!!
STMP STMP
I HOPE WE DIDN'T COME HERE JUST TO PARTY.
Master! I found a claw fish!!
It's an Ise lobster.
GYAAAH
Hey! Don't run off with it.
Just don't eat its head.
STMP

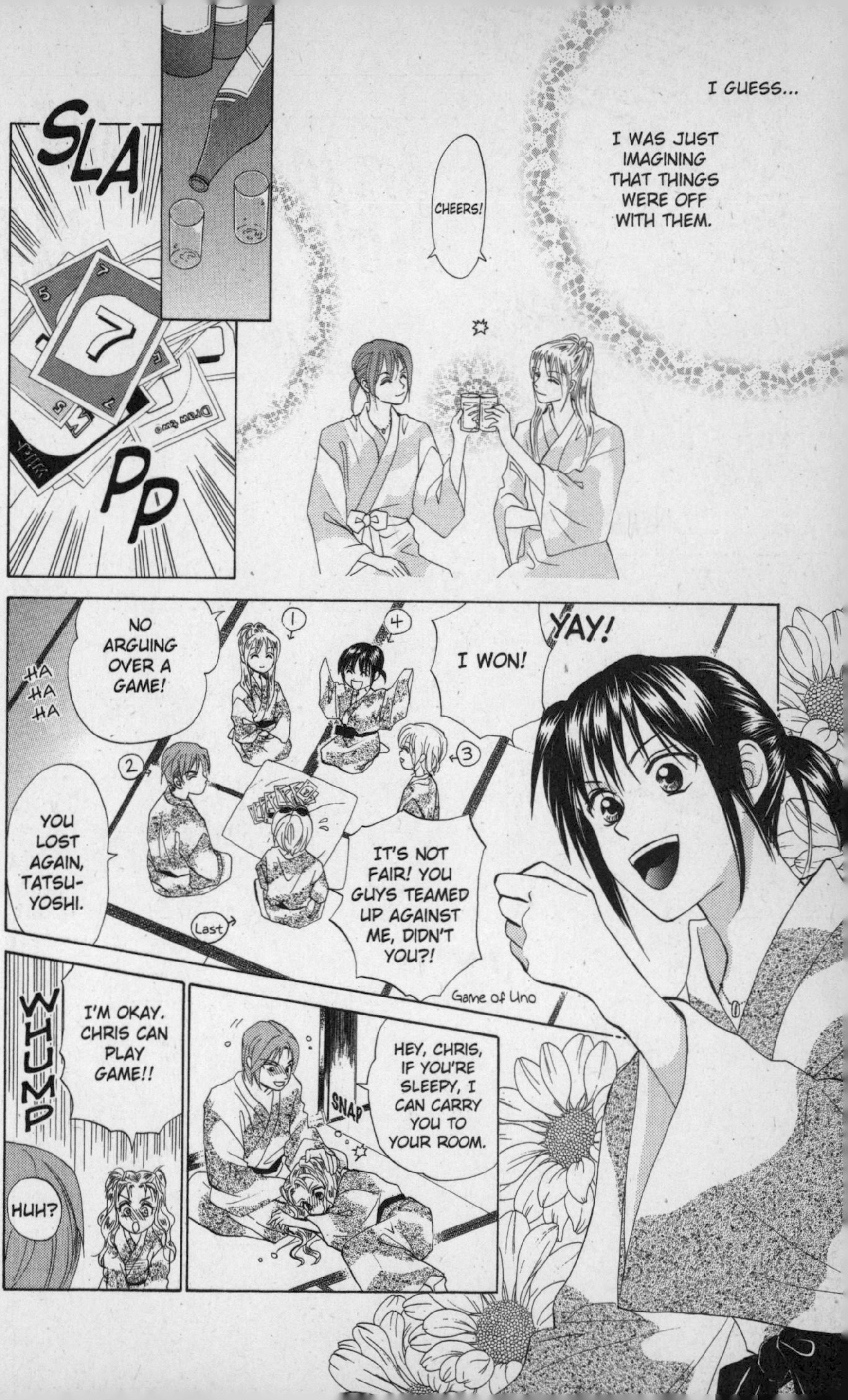
I GUESS...
I WAS JUST IMAGINING THAT THINGS WERE OFF WITH THEM.
CHEERS!
SLAPP
Draw two
YAY!
I WON!
NO ARGUING OVER A GAME!
HA HA HA
1
4
3
2
Last
IT'S NOT FAIR! YOU GUYS TEAMED UP AGAINST ME, DIDN'T YOU?!
YOU LOST AGAIN, TATSU-YOSHI.
Game of Uno
HEY, CHRIS, IF YOU'RE SLEEPY, I CAN CARRY YOU TO YOUR ROOM.
SNAP
I'M OKAY. CHRIS CAN PLAY GAME!!
WHUMP
HUH?

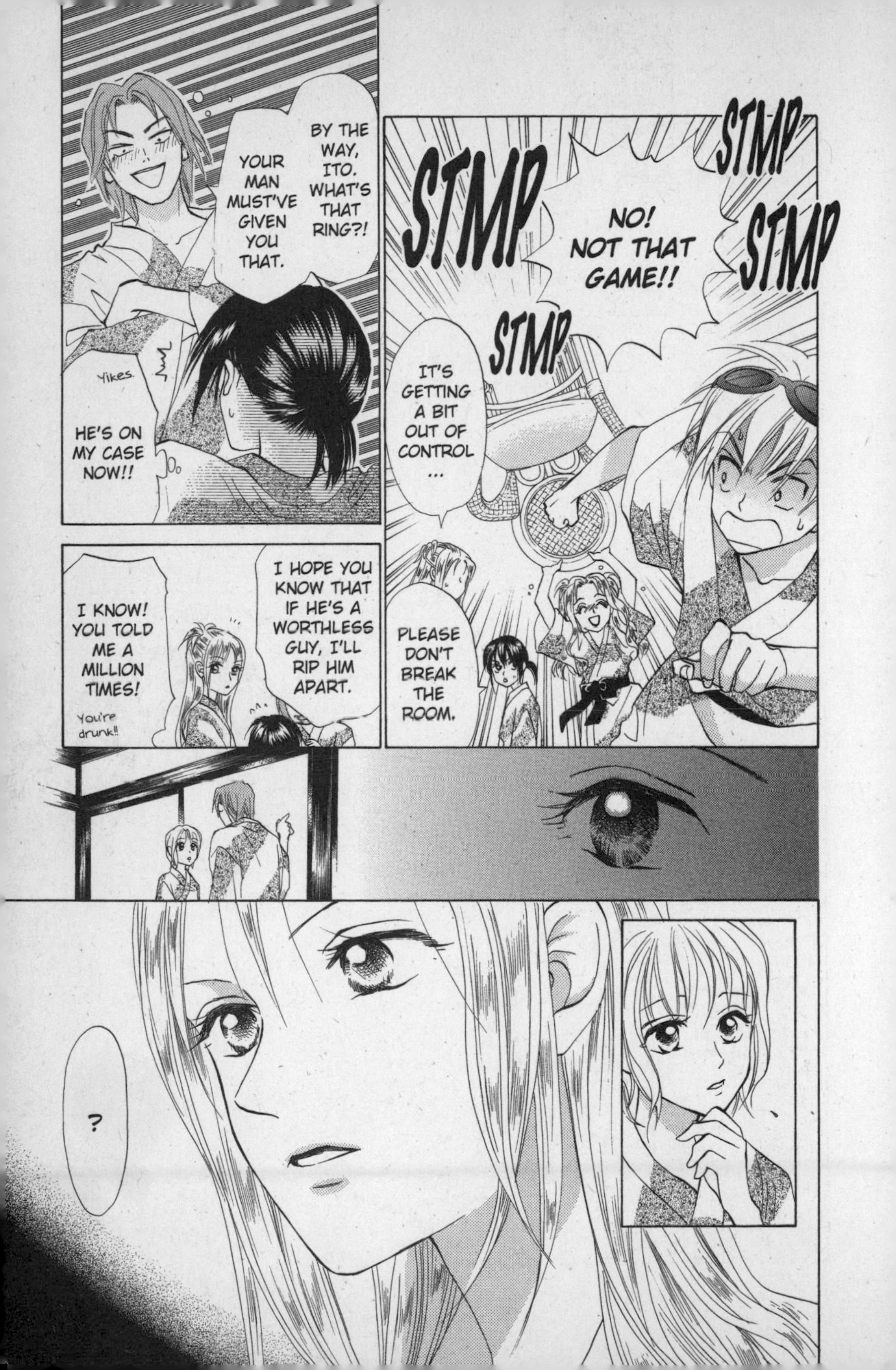
STMP
STMP
STMP
NO! NOT THAT GAME!!
STMP
IT'S GETTING A BIT OUT OF CONTROL ...
PLEASE DON'T BREAK THE ROOM.
BY THE WAY, ITO. WHAT'S THAT RING?!
YOUR MAN MUST'VE GIVEN YOU THAT.
Yikes.
HE'S ON MY CASE NOW!!
I HOPE YOU KNOW THAT IF HE'S A WORTHLESS GUY, I'LL RIP HIM APART.
I KNOW! YOU TOLD ME A MILLION TIMES!
You're drunk!!
?

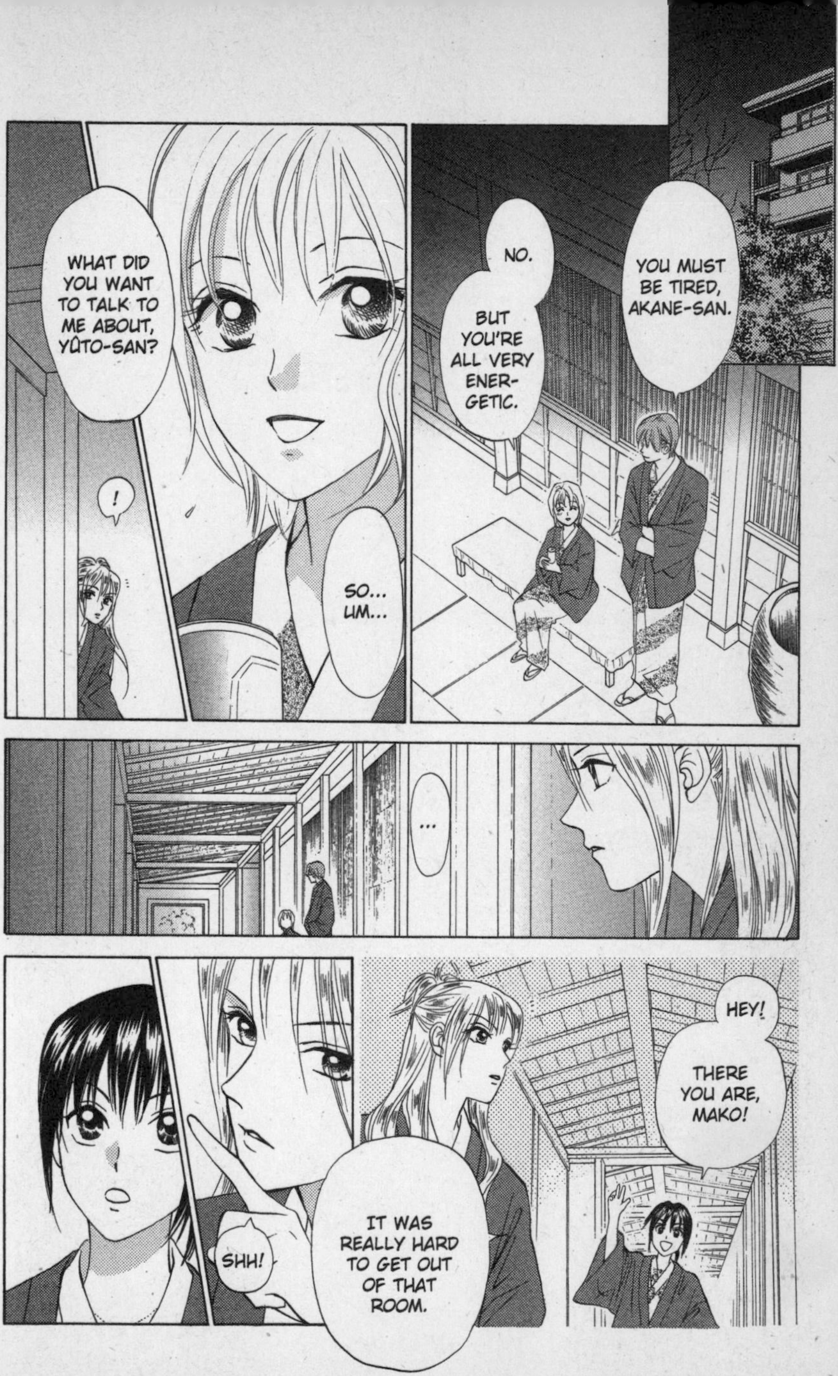
YOU MUST BE TIRED, AKANE-SAN.
NO.
BUT YOU'RE ALL VERY ENER-GETIC.
WHAT DID YOU WANT TO TALK TO ME ABOUT, YÛTO-SAN?
SO... UM...
!
...
HEY!
THERE YOU ARE, MAKO!
IT WAS REALLY HARD TO GET OUT OF THAT ROOM.
SHH!

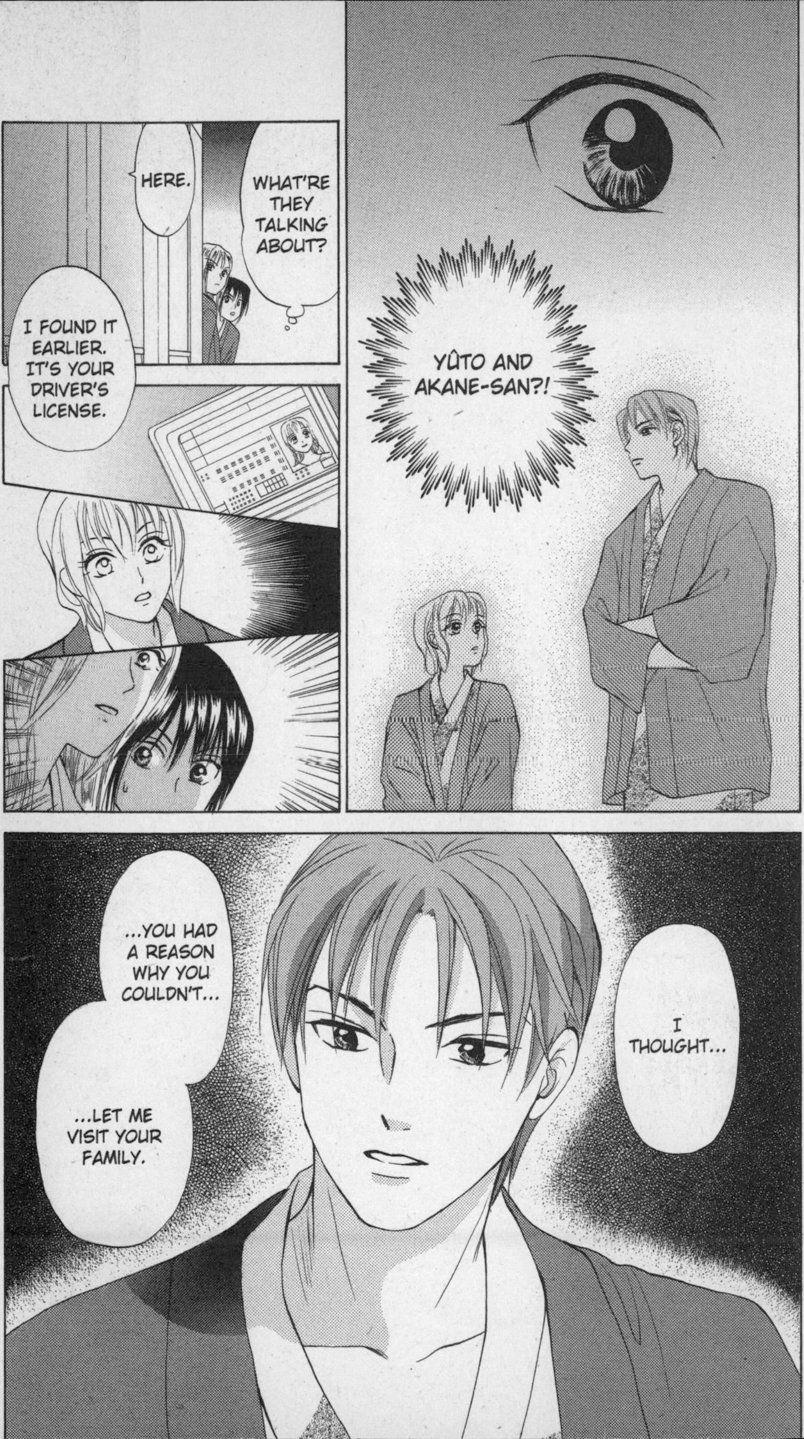
YÛTO AND AKANE-SAN?!
WHAT'RE THEY TALKING ABOUT?
HERE.
I FOUND IT EARLIER. IT'S YOUR DRIVER'S LICENSE.
I THOUGHT...
...YOU HAD A REASON WHY YOU COULDN'T...
...LET ME VISIT YOUR FAMILY.

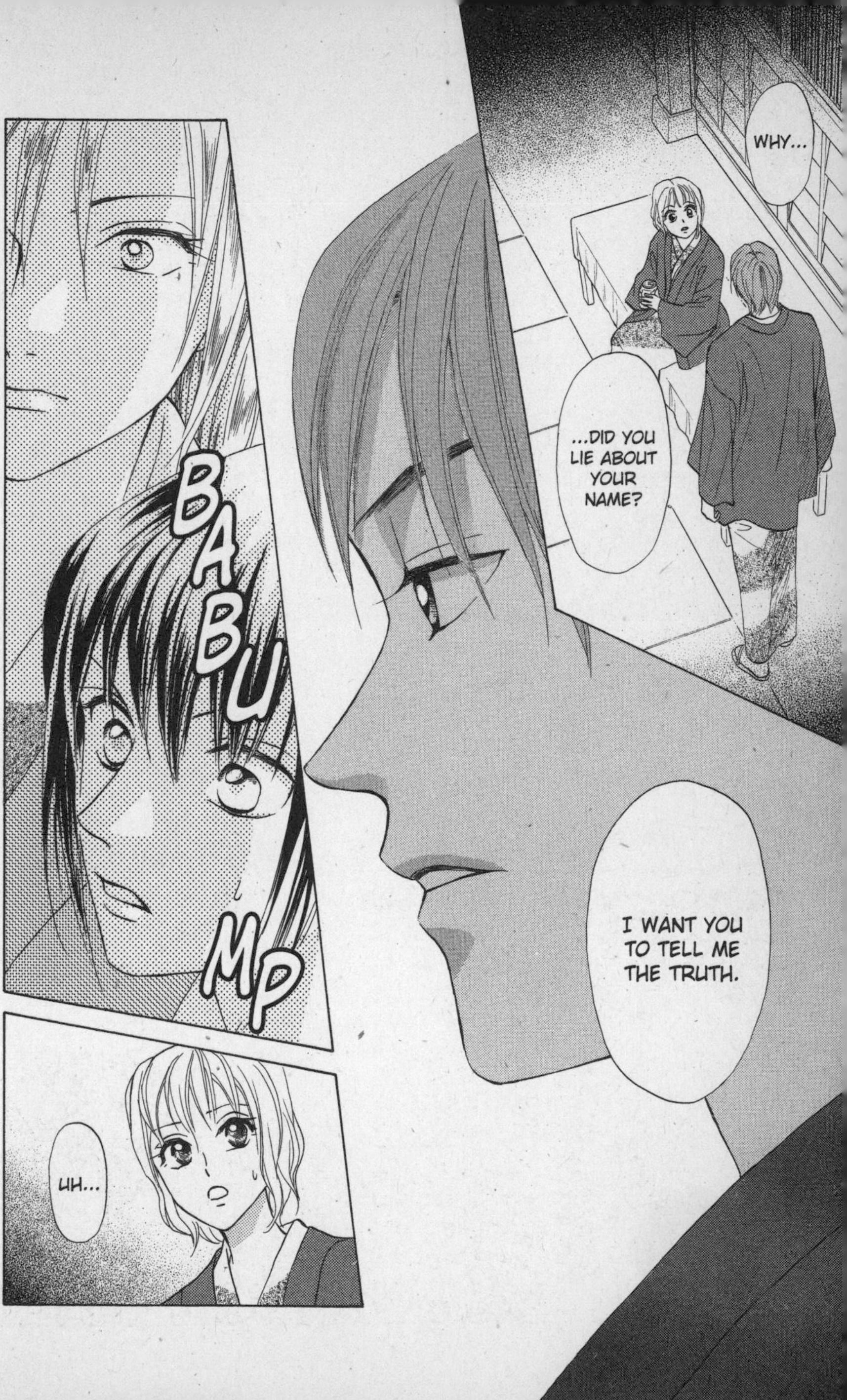
WHY...
...DID YOU LIE ABOUT YOUR NAME?
I WANT YOU TO TELL ME THE TRUTH.
BABUMP
UH...

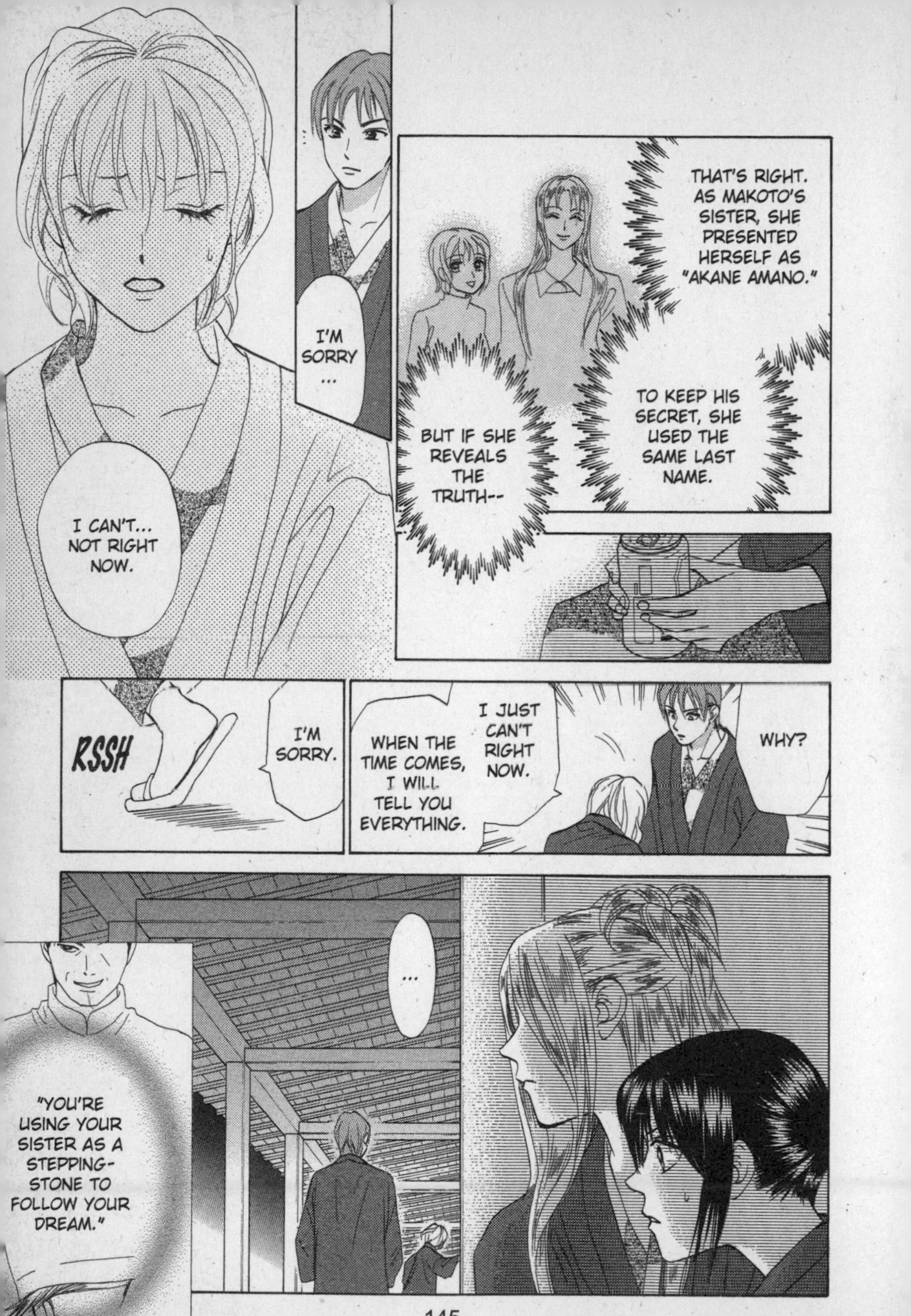
I'M SORRY ...
THAT'S RIGHT. AS MAKOTO'S SISTER, SHE PRESENTED HERSELF AS "AKANE AMANO."
TO KEEP HIS SECRET, SHE USED THE SAME LAST NAME.
BUT IF SHE REVEALS THE TRUTH--
I CAN'T... NOT RIGHT NOW.
WHY?
I JUST CAN'T RIGHT NOW.
WHEN THE TIME COMES, I WILL TELL YOU EVERYTHING.
I'M SORRY.
RSSH
...
"YOU'RE USING YOUR SISTER AS A STEPPING-STONE TO FOLLOW YOUR DREAM."

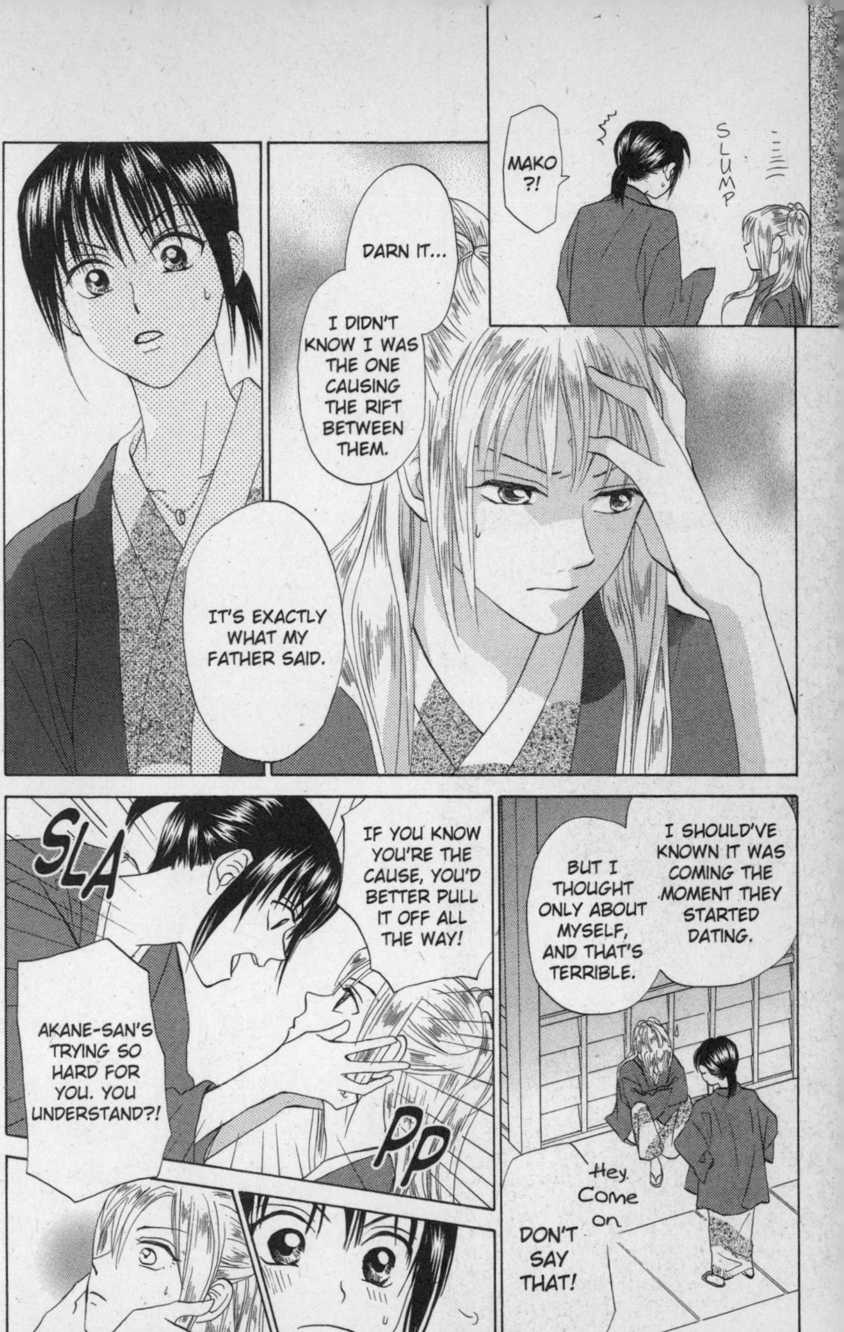
MAKO ?!
SLUMP
DARN IT...
I DIDN'T KNOW I WAS THE ONE CAUSING THE RIFT BETWEEN THEM.
IT'S EXACTLY WHAT MY FATHER SAID.
I SHOULD'VE KNOWN IT WAS COMING THE MOMENT THEY STARTED DATING.
BUT I THOUGHT ONLY ABOUT MYSELF, AND THAT'S TERRIBLE.
Hey. Come on.
DON'T SAY THAT!
IF YOU KNOW YOU'RE THE CAUSE, YOU'D BETTER PULL IT OFF ALL THE WAY!
SLA
AKANE-SAN'S TRYING SO HARD FOR YOU. YOU UNDERSTAND?!
PP

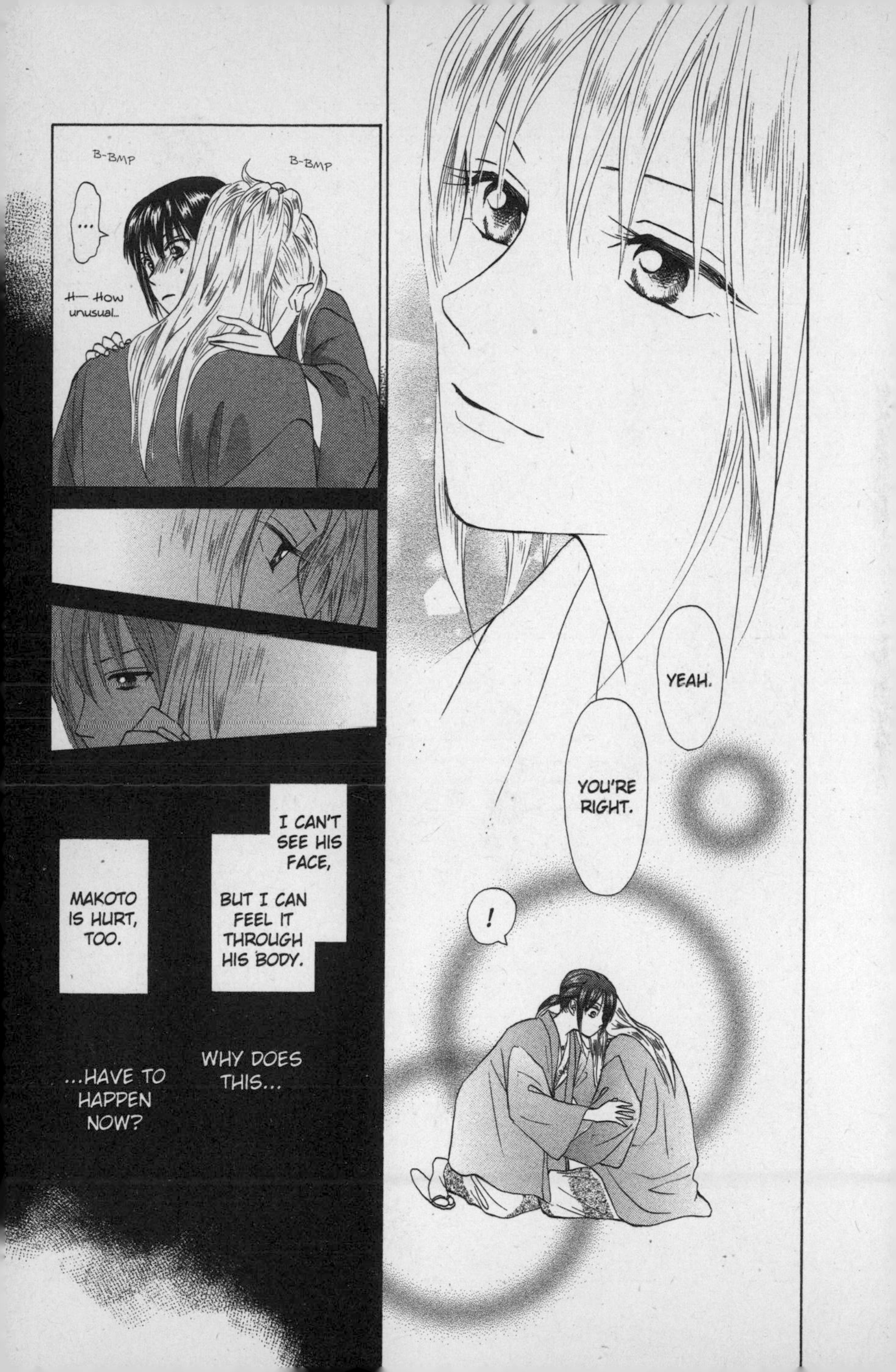
YEAH.
YOU'RE RIGHT.
!
B-BMP
B-BMP
...
H— How unusual...
I CAN'T SEE HIS FACE,
BUT I CAN FEEL IT THROUGH HIS BODY.
MAKOTO IS HURT, TOO.
WHY DOES THIS...
...HAVE TO HAPPEN NOW?

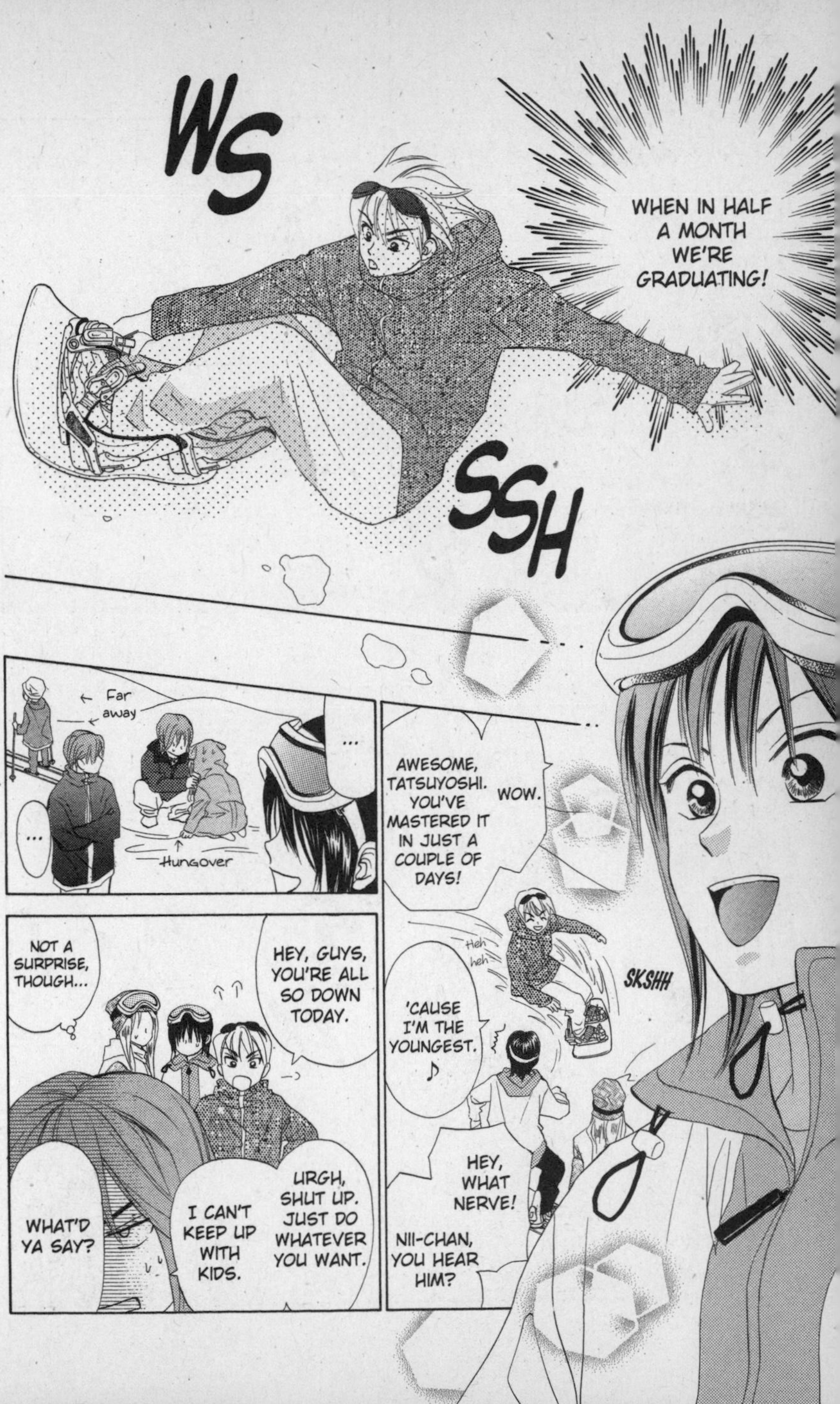
WHEN IN HALF A MONTH WE'RE GRADUATING!
WS
SSH
AWESOME, TATSUYOSHI. YOU'VE MASTERED IT IN JUST A COUPLE OF DAYS!
WOW.
SKSHH
Heh heh
'CAUSE I'M THE YOUNGEST. ♪
HEY, WHAT NERVE!
NII-CHAN, YOU HEAR HIM?
...
← Far away
Hungover
...
...
HEY, GUYS, YOU'RE ALL SO DOWN TODAY.
NOT A SURPRISE, THOUGH...
URGH, SHUT UP. JUST DO WHATEVER YOU WANT.
I CAN'T KEEP UP WITH KIDS.
WHAT'D YA SAY?

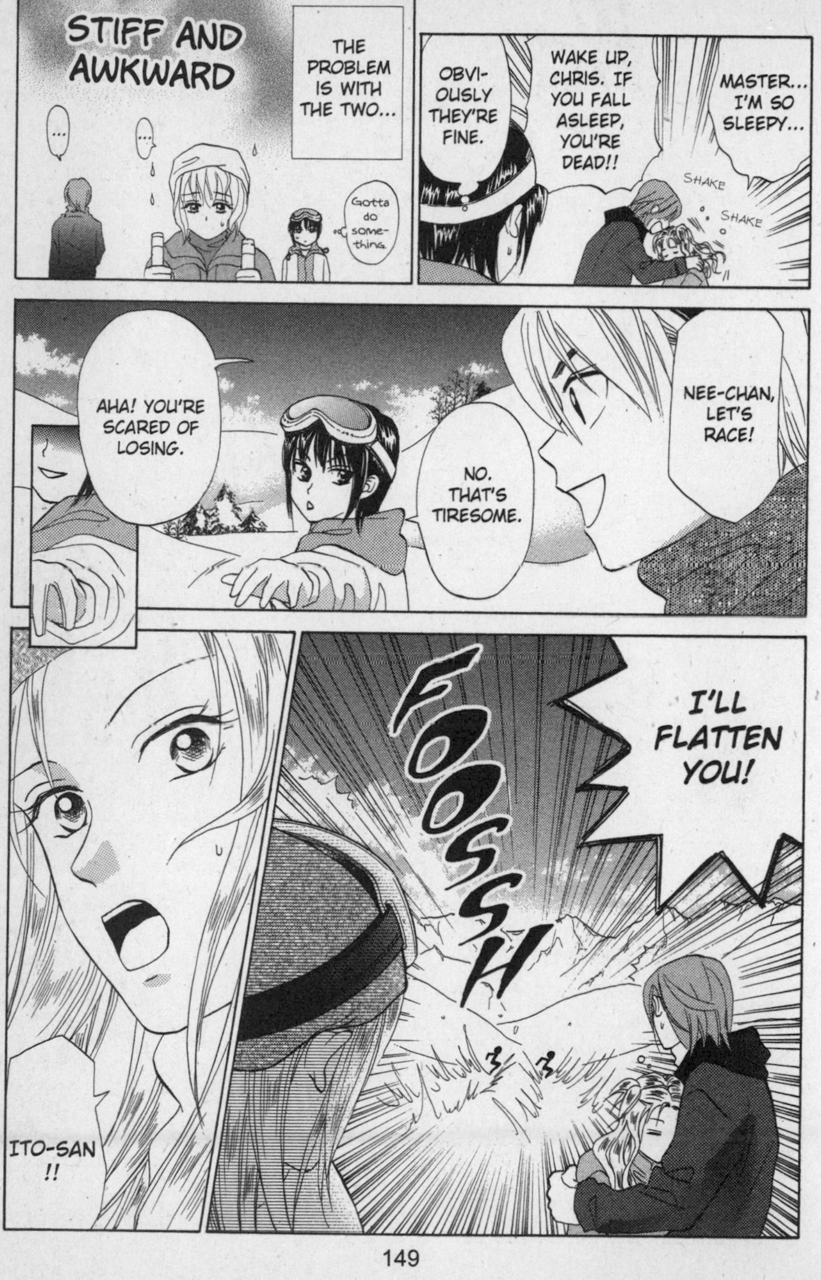
MASTER... I'M SO SLEEPY...
WAKE UP, CHRIS. IF YOU FALL ASLEEP, YOU'RE DEAD!!
OBVIOUSLY THEY'RE FINE.
SHAKE
SHAKE
THE PROBLEM IS WITH THE TWO...
STIFF AND AWKWARD
...
...
Gotta do something.
NEE-CHAN, LET'S RACE!
NO. THAT'S TIRESOME.
AHA! YOU'RE SCARED OF LOSING.
I'LL FLATTEN YOU!
FOOSSH
ITO-SAN!!

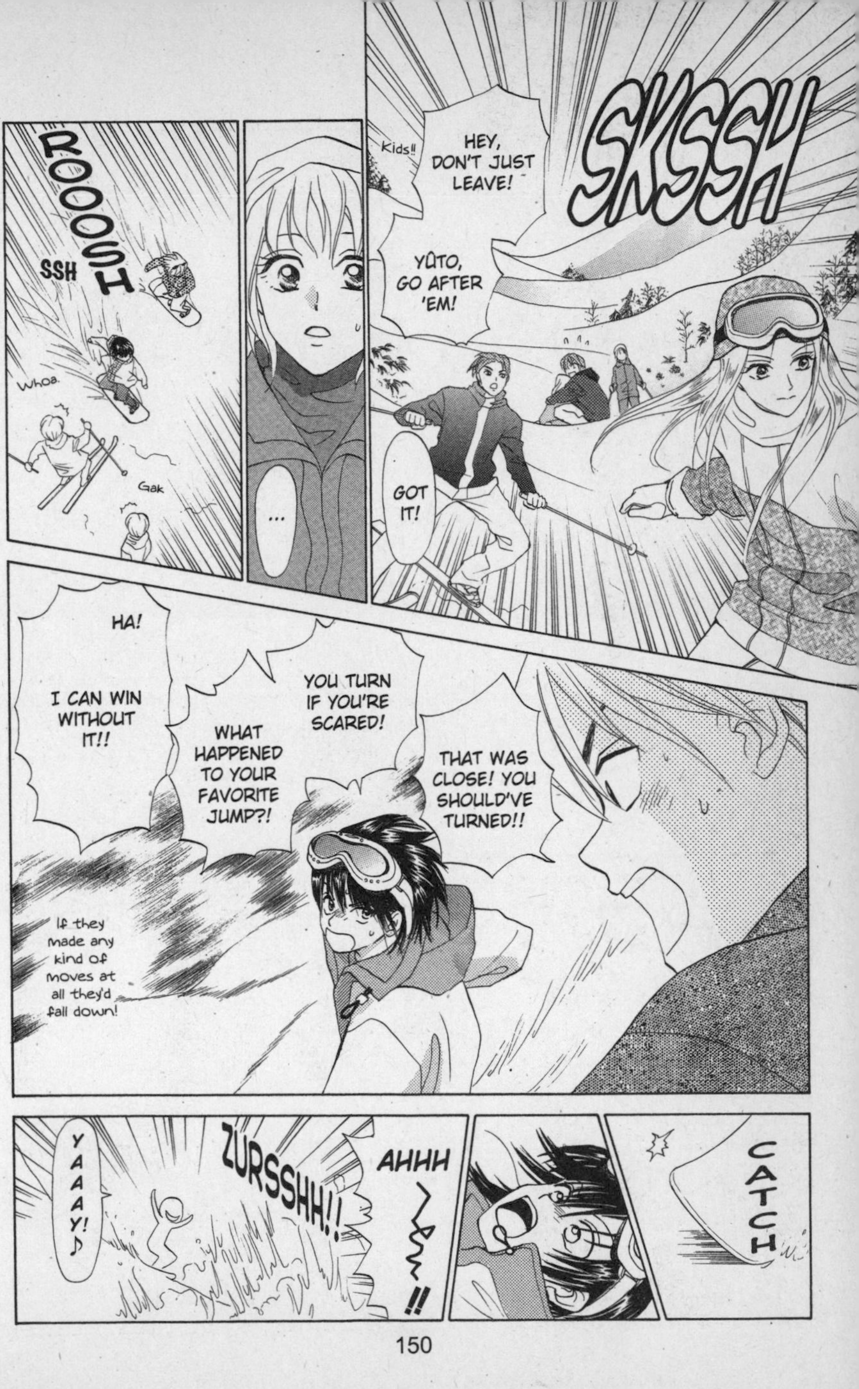

SKSSH
Kids!!
HEY, DON'T JUST LEAVE!
YÛTO, GO AFTER 'EM!
GOT IT!
...
ROOOSH
SSH
Whoa.
Gak
THAT WAS CLOSE! YOU SHOULD'VE TURNED!!
YOU TURN IF YOU'RE SCARED!
WHAT HAPPENED TO YOUR FAVORITE JUMP?!
HA!
I CAN WIN WITHOUT IT!!
If they made any kind of moves at all they'd fall down!
CATCH
AHHH
ZÜRSSHH!!
YAAAY!♪

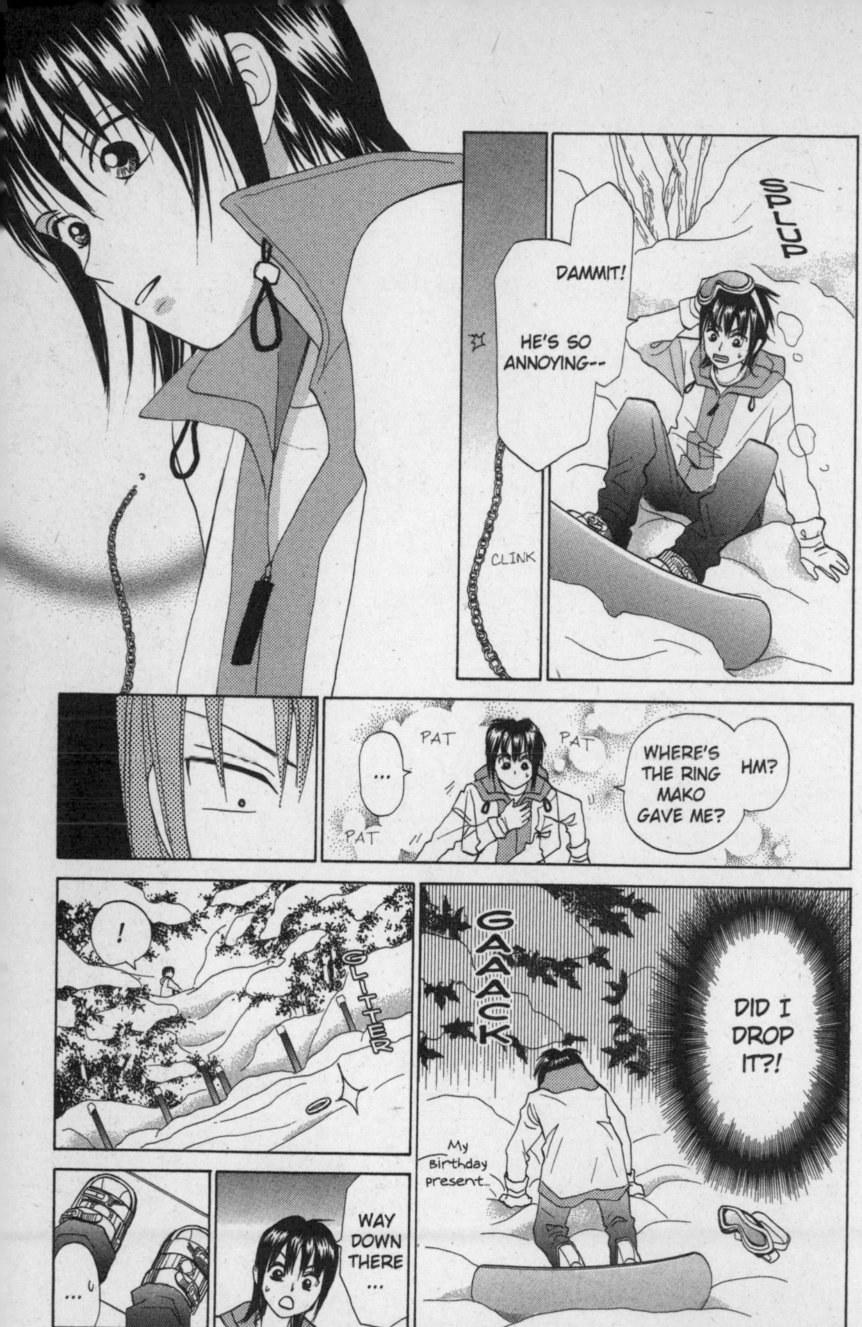
SPLUP
DAMMIT!
HE'S SO ANNOYING--
CLINK
HM?
WHERE'S THE RING MAKO GAVE ME?
PAT
PAT
...
PAT
DID I DROP IT?!
GAAACK
My Birthday present...
!
GLITTER
WAY DOWN THERE ...
...

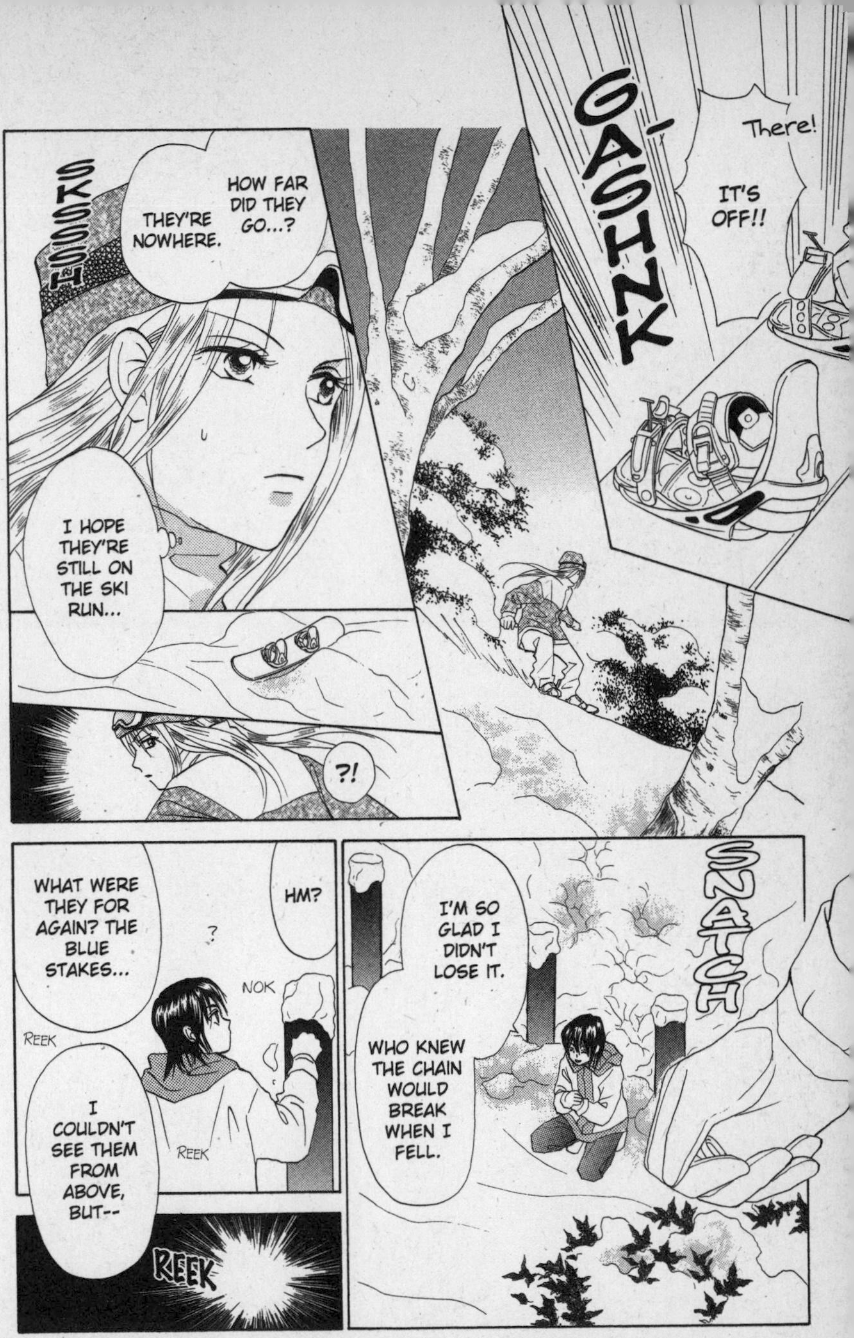
There!
IT'S OFF!!
GA-SHNK
SKSSSH
HOW FAR DID THEY GO...?
THEY'RE NOWHERE.
I HOPE THEY'RE STILL ON THE SKI RUN...
?!
SNATCH
I'M SO GLAD I DIDN'T LOSE IT.
WHO KNEW THE CHAIN WOULD BREAK WHEN I FELL.
HM?
WHAT WERE THEY FOR AGAIN? THE BLUE STAKES...
?
NOK
REEK
REEK
I COULDN'T SEE THEM FROM ABOVE, BUT--
REEK

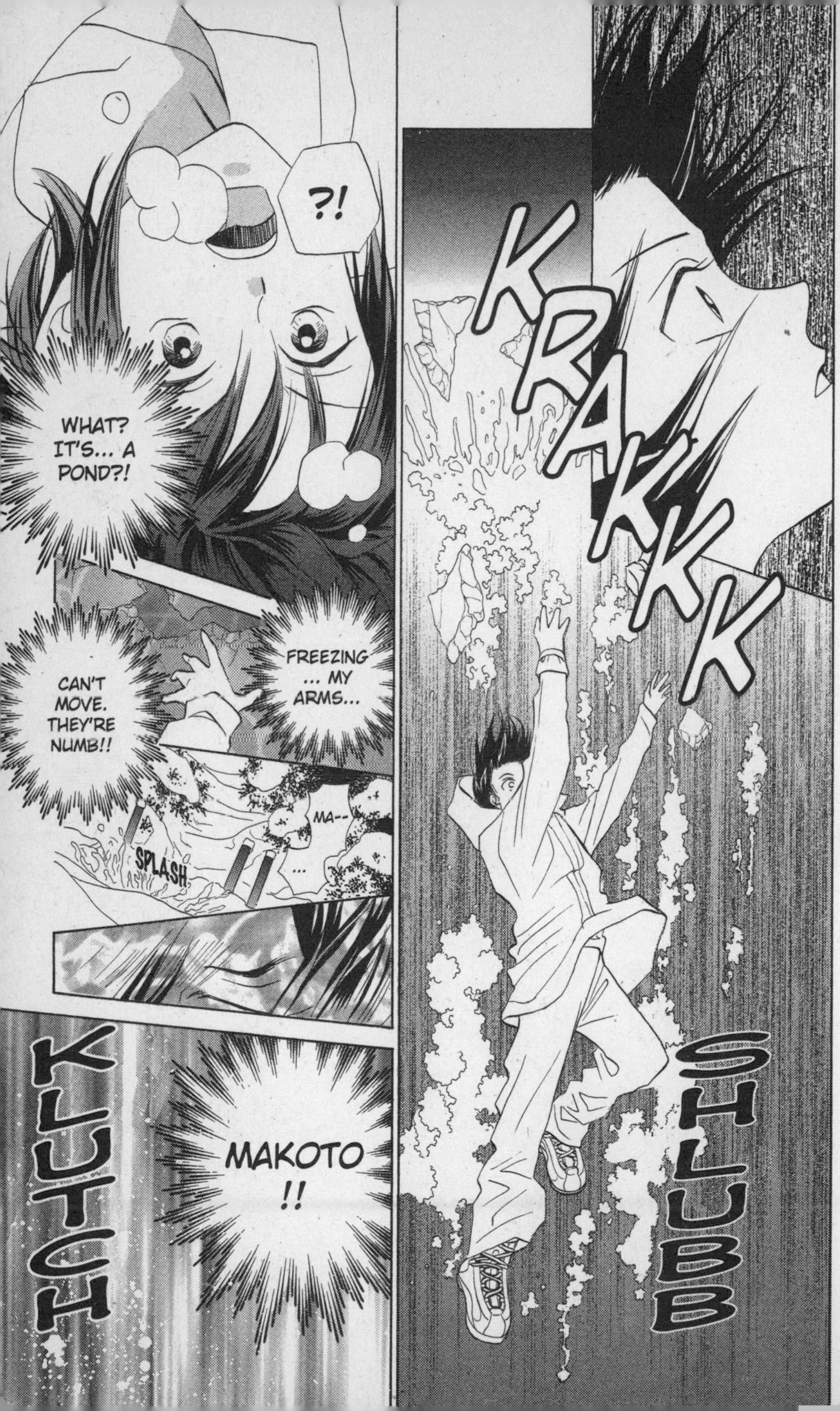
KRAKKKK
SHLUBB
?!
WHAT? IT'S... A POND?!
FREEZING ... MY ARMS...
CAN'T MOVE. THEY'RE NUMB!!
MA--
...
SPLASH
MAKOTO !!
KLUTCH

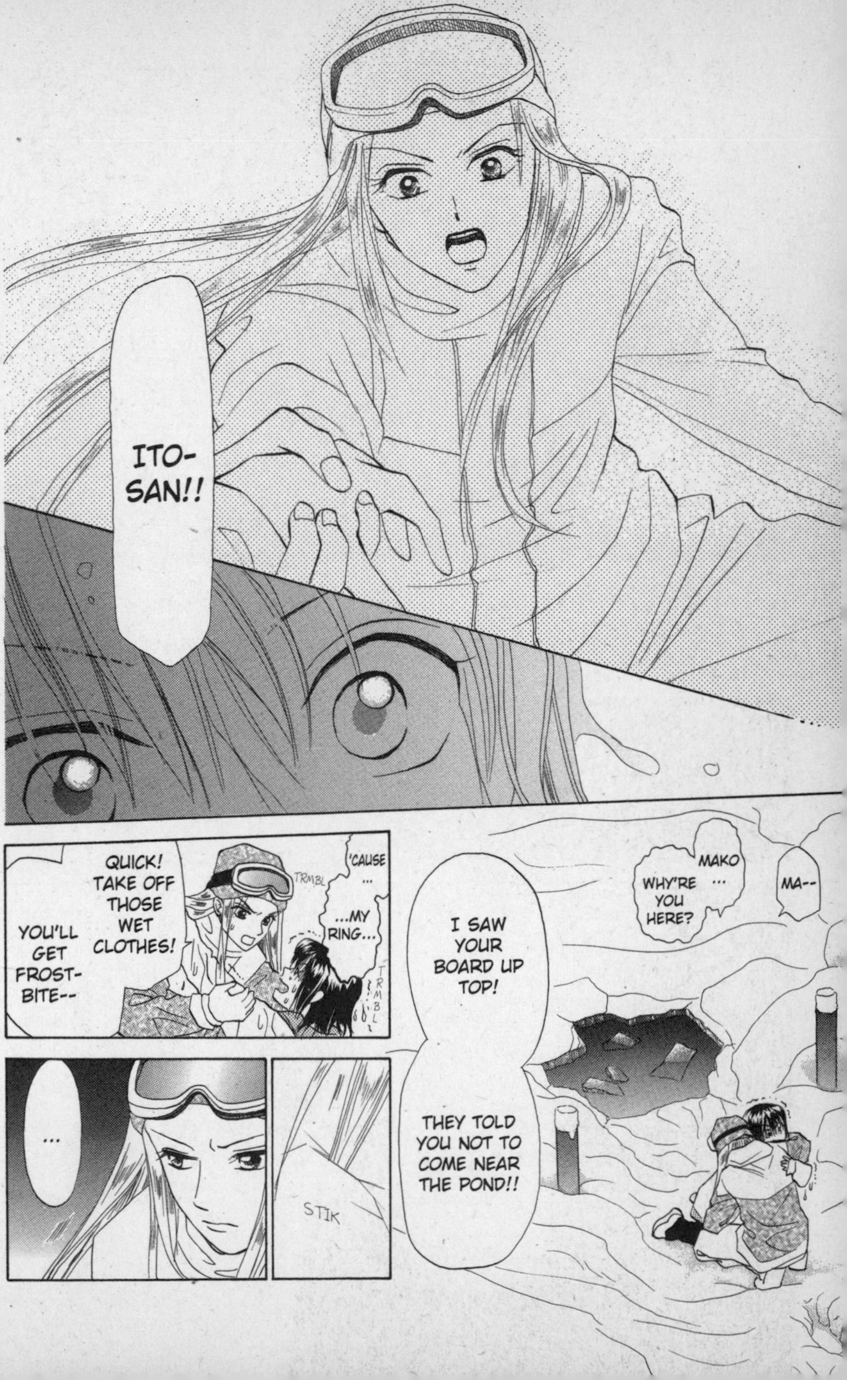
ITO-SAN!!
MA--
MAKO ... WHY'RE YOU HERE?
I SAW YOUR BOARD UP TOP!
THEY TOLD YOU NOT TO COME NEAR THE POND!!
'CAUSE ...
...MY RING...
TRMBL
TRMBL
QUICK! TAKE OFF THOSE WET CLOTHES!
YOU'LL GET FROST-BITE--
STIK
...

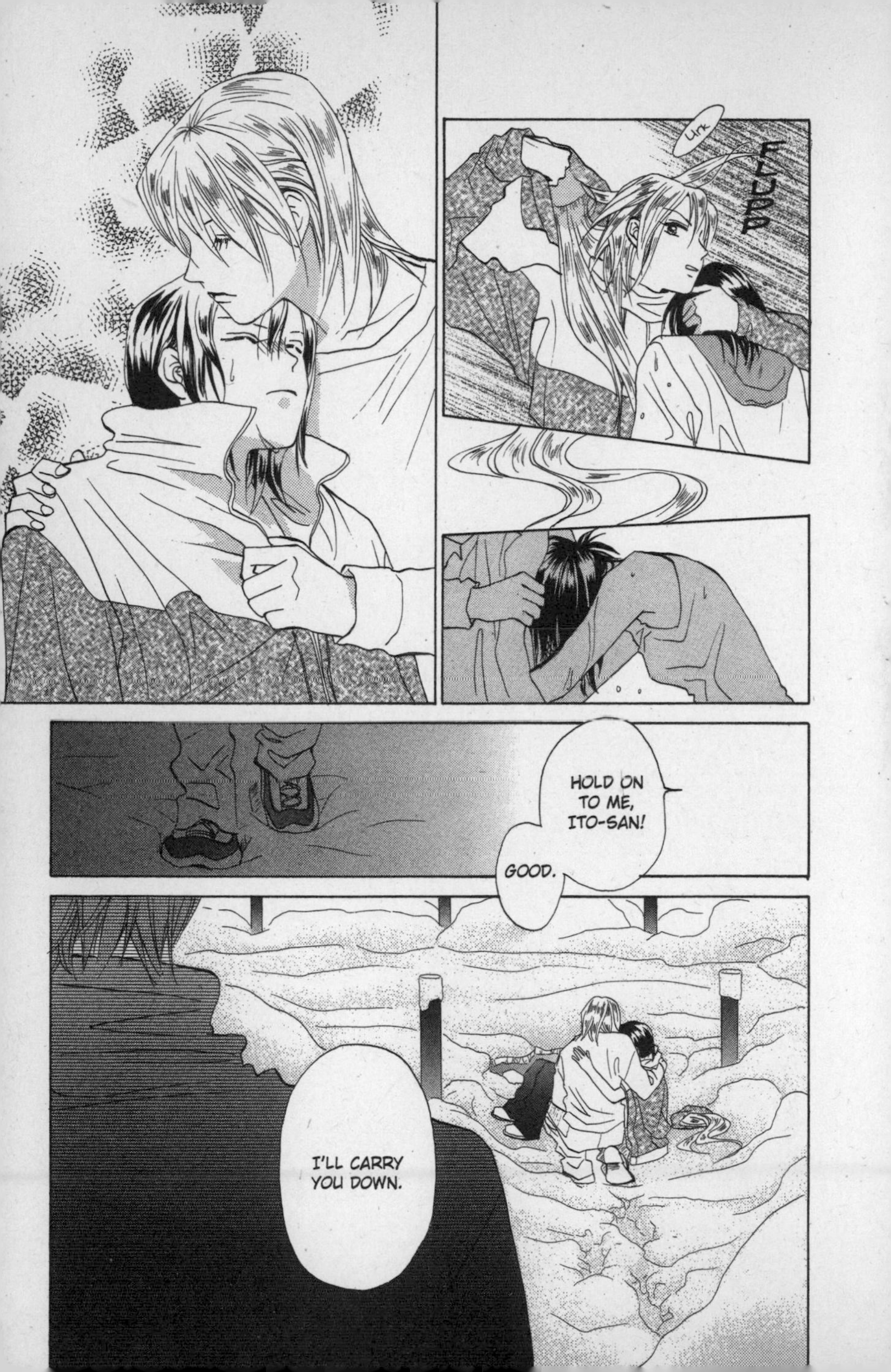
Urk
FLUPP
HOLD ON TO ME, ITO-SAN!
GOOD.
I'LL CARRY YOU DOWN.

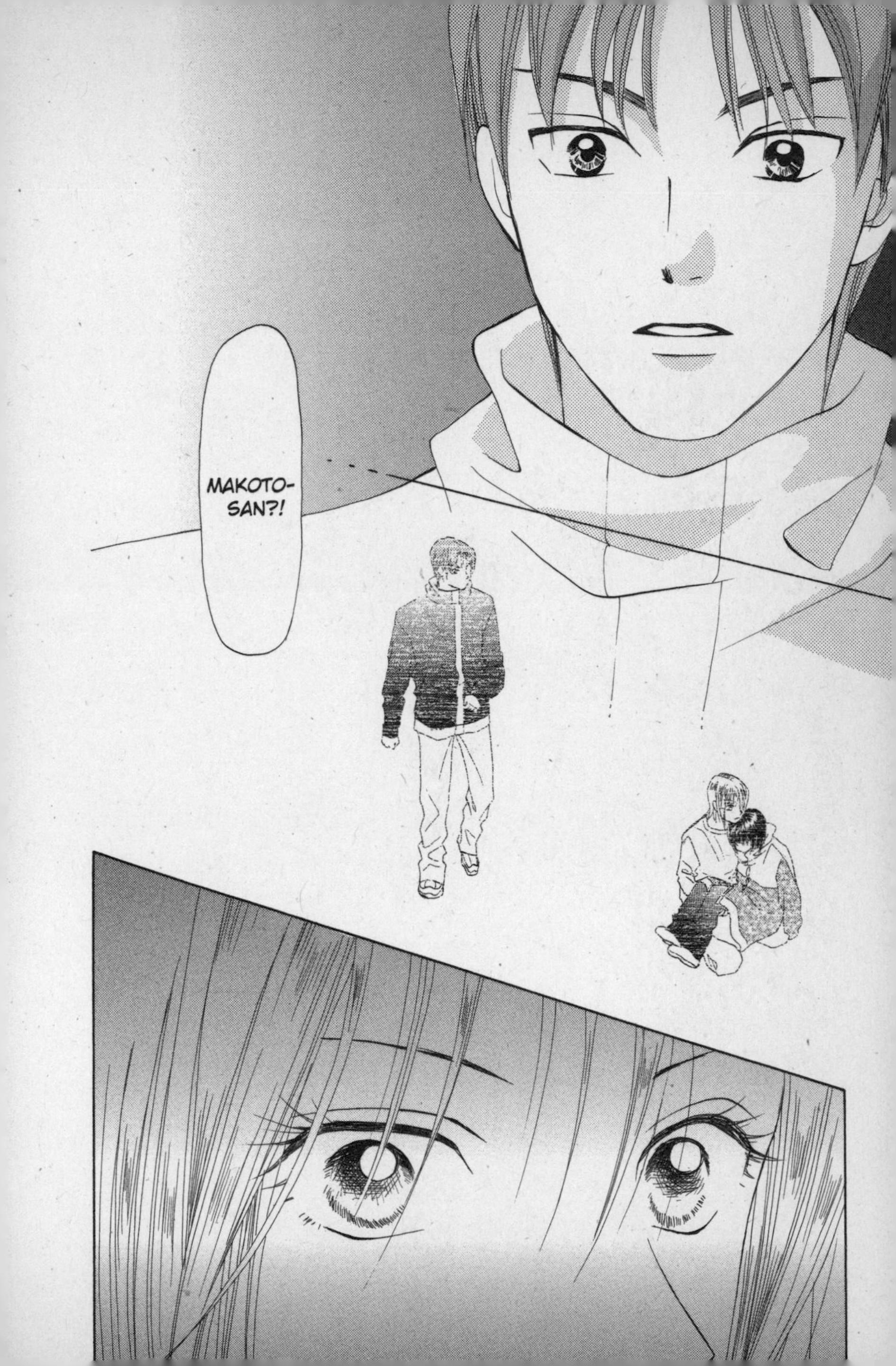
MAKOTO-SAN?!

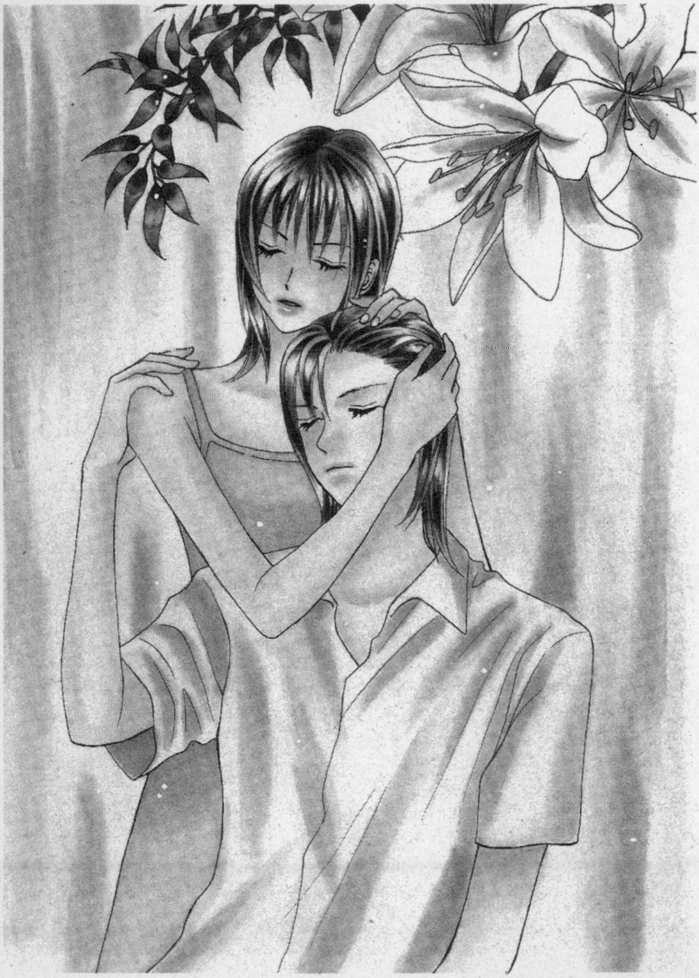

← 2002
Hana to Yume No. 18,
opening page, draft

Doodle ②

An image that
can never be
used for an
opening page.
There's no space
for the title.
(Laugh)

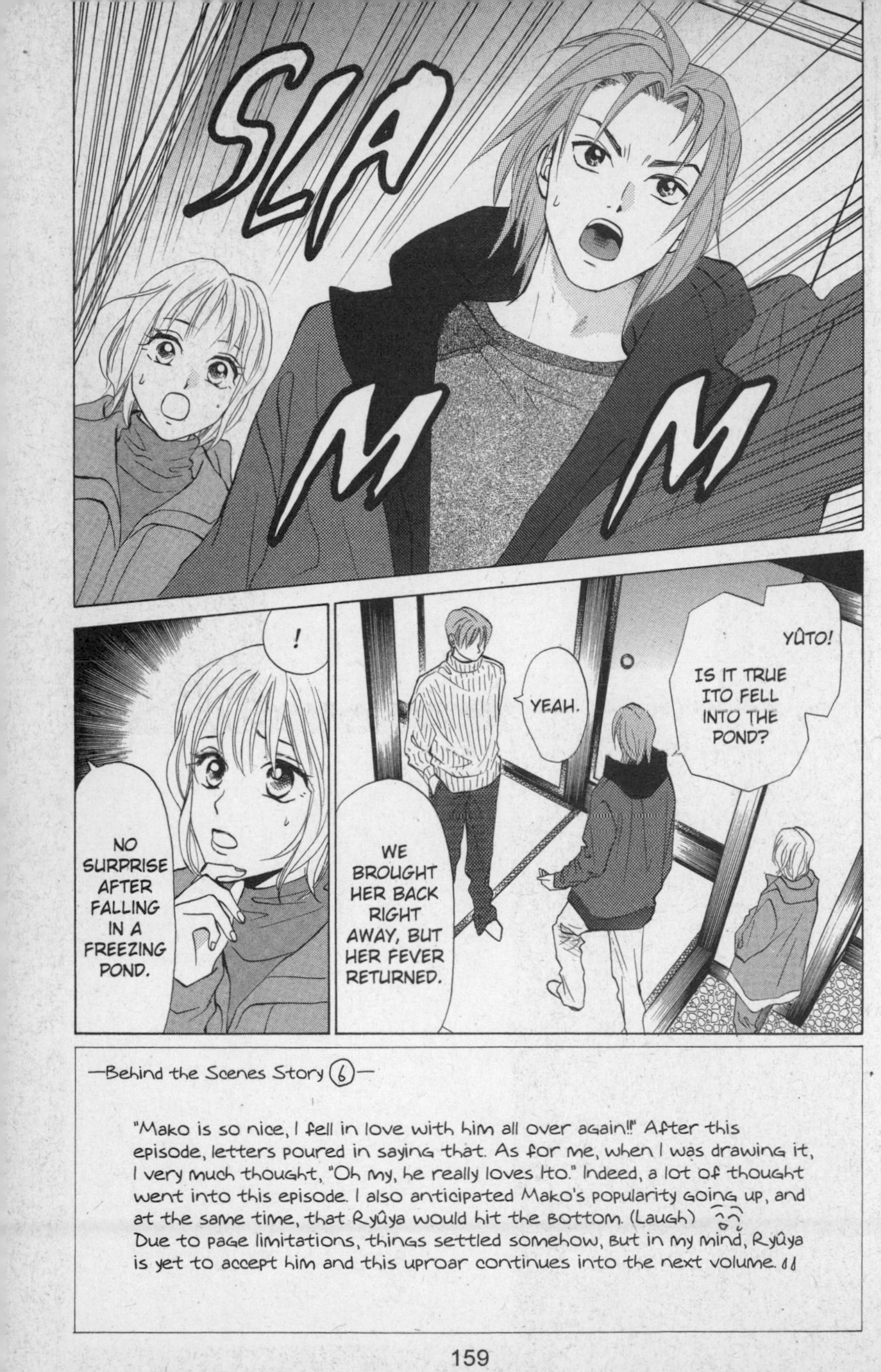
SLAM
YÛTO!
IS IT TRUE ITO FELL INTO THE POND?
YEAH.
WE BROUGHT HER BACK RIGHT AWAY, BUT HER FEVER RETURNED.
!
NO SURPRISE AFTER FALLING IN A FREEZING POND.

—Behind the Scenes Story ⑥—

"Mako is so nice, I fell in love with him all over again!!" After this episode, letters poured in saying that. As for me, when I was drawing it, I very much thought, "Oh my, he really loves Ito." Indeed, a lot of thought went into this episode. I also anticipated Mako's popularity going up, and at the same time, that Ryûya would hit the bottom. (Laugh)
Due to page limitations, things settled somehow, but in my mind, Ryûya is yet to accept him and this uproar continues into the next volume.

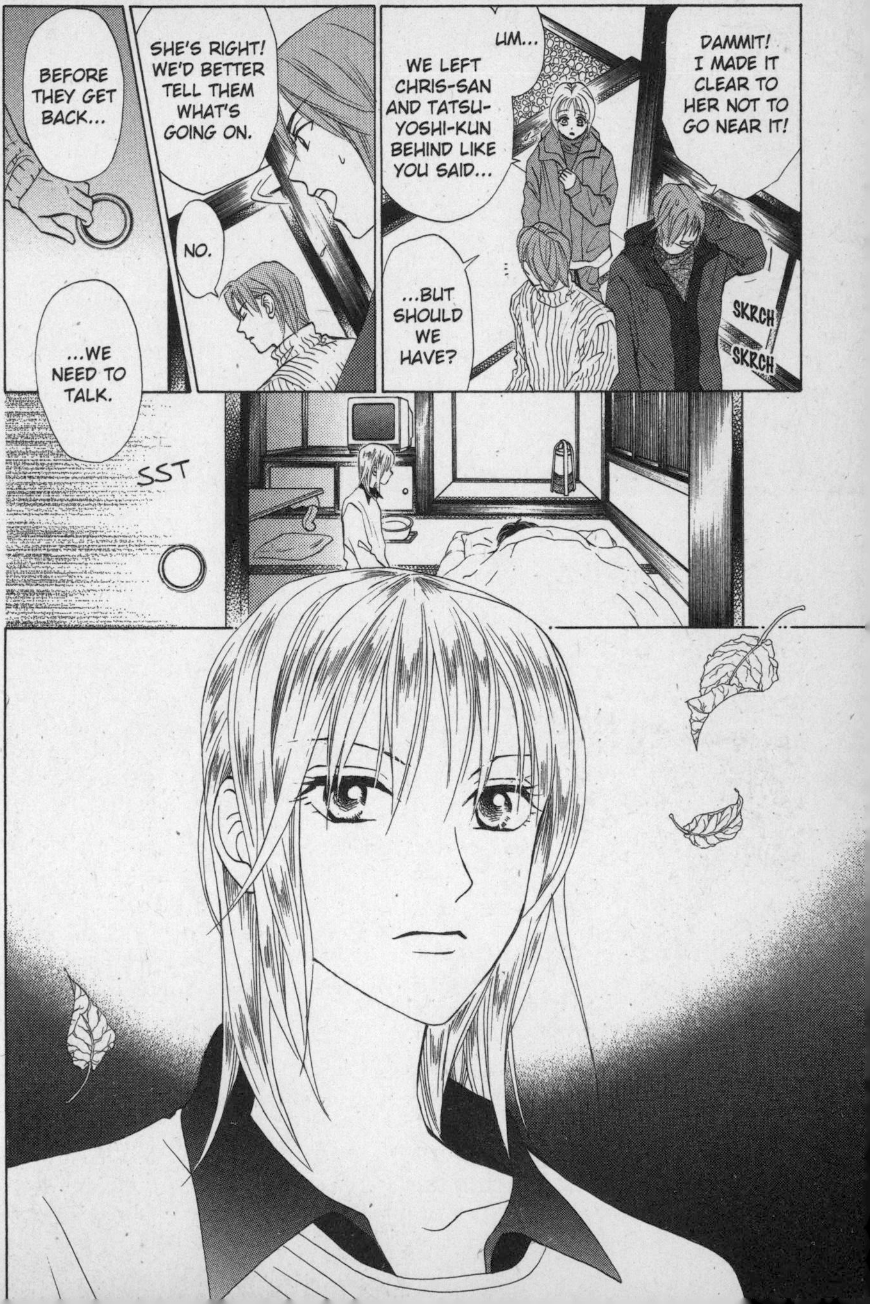
DAMMIT! I MADE IT CLEAR TO HER NOT TO GO NEAR IT!
UM...
WE LEFT CHRIS-SAN AND TATSU-YOSHI-KUN BEHIND LIKE YOU SAID...
SKRCH
SKRCH
...BUT SHOULD WE HAVE?
SHE'S RIGHT! WE'D BETTER TELL THEM WHAT'S GOING ON.
NO.
BEFORE THEY GET BACK...
...WE NEED TO TALK.
SST

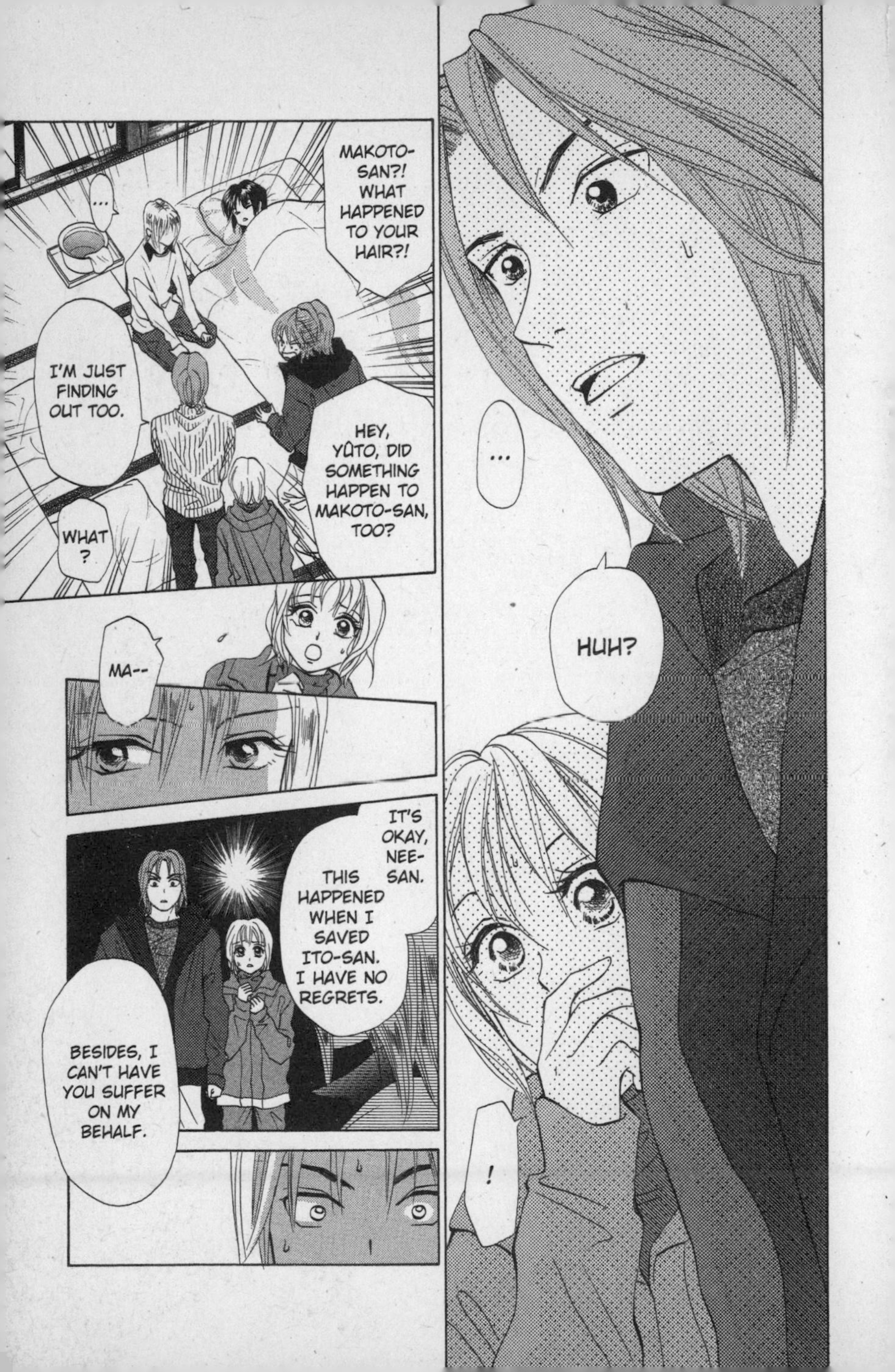
...
HUH?
!
MAKOTO-SAN?! WHAT HAPPENED TO YOUR HAIR?!
...
HEY, YÛTO, DID SOMETHING HAPPEN TO MAKOTO-SAN, TOO?
I'M JUST FINDING OUT TOO.
WHAT?
MA--
IT'S OKAY, NEE-SAN.
THIS HAPPENED WHEN I SAVED ITO-SAN. I HAVE NO REGRETS.
BESIDES, I CAN'T HAVE YOU SUFFER ON MY BEHALF.

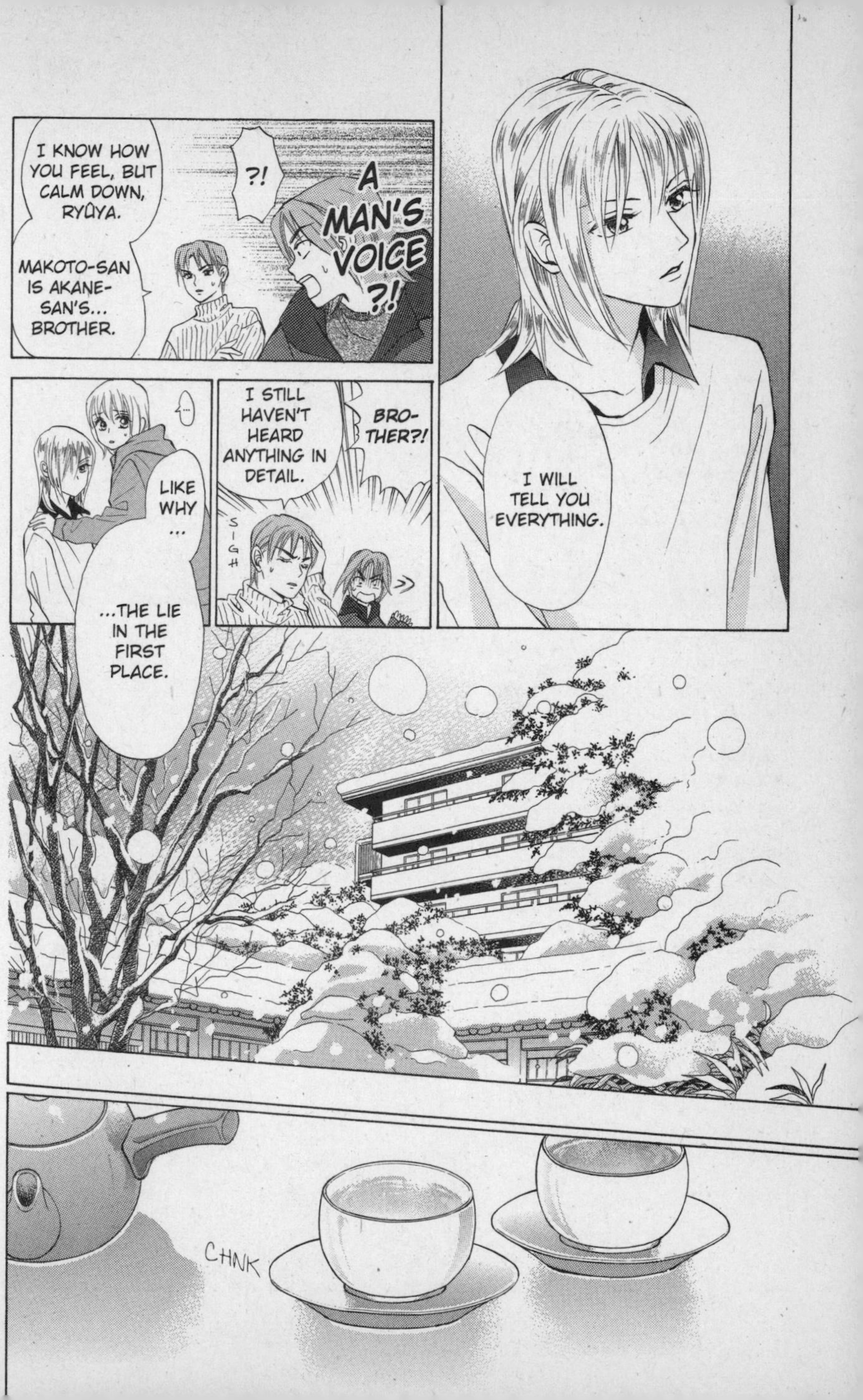
I WILL TELL YOU EVERYTHING.
?!
A MAN'S VOICE ?!
I KNOW HOW YOU FEEL, BUT CALM DOWN, RYÛYA.
MAKOTO-SAN IS AKANE-SAN'S... BROTHER.
BRO-THER?!
I STILL HAVEN'T HEARD ANYTHING IN DETAIL.
SIGH
...
LIKE WHY ...
...THE LIE IN THE FIRST PLACE.
CHNK

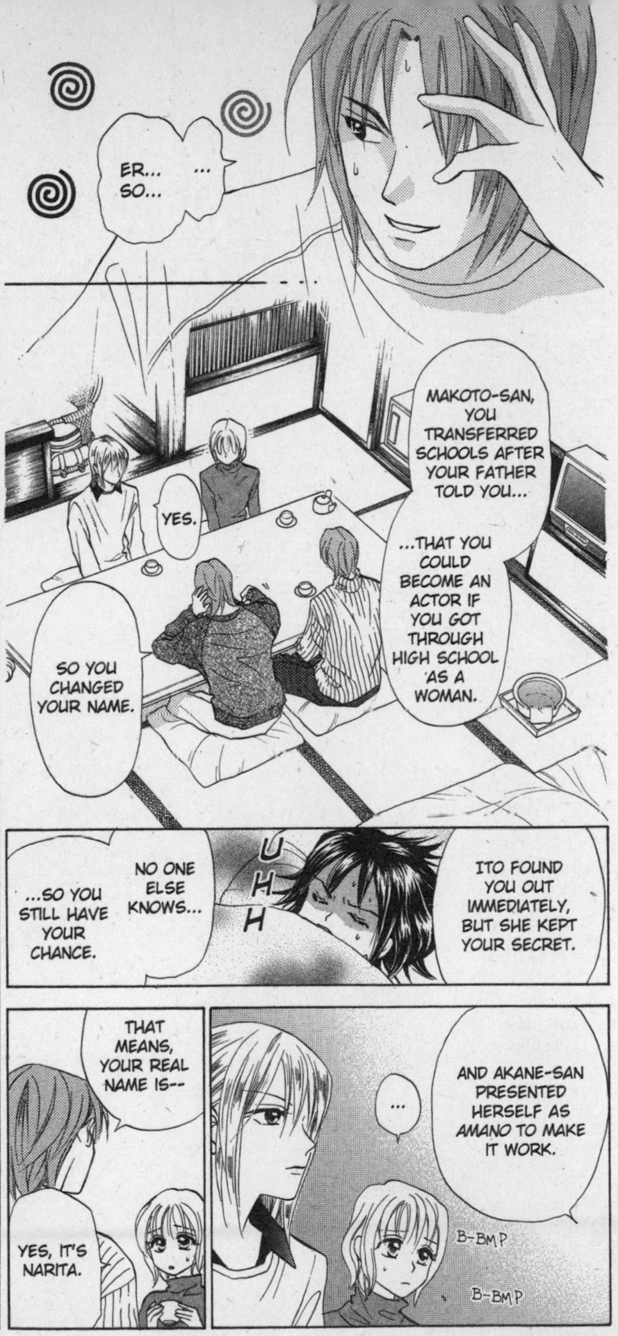
ER... ... SO...
MAKOTO-SAN, YOU TRANSFERRED SCHOOLS AFTER YOUR FATHER TOLD YOU...
...THAT YOU COULD BECOME AN ACTOR IF YOU GOT THROUGH HIGH SCHOOL AS A WOMAN.
YES.
SO YOU CHANGED YOUR NAME.
ITO FOUND YOU OUT IMMEDIATELY, BUT SHE KEPT YOUR SECRET.
UHH
NO ONE ELSE KNOWS...
...SO YOU STILL HAVE YOUR CHANCE.
AND AKANE-SAN PRESENTED HERSELF AS AMANO TO MAKE IT WORK.
...
B-BMP
B-BMP
THAT MEANS, YOUR REAL NAME IS--
YES, IT'S NARITA.

● Tsubaki-chan is so different inside and out. Which of her parents did she take after?

Ⓔ She is a mutant.

● Why is the princess a beast instead of a human in volume ⑨'s Swan Lake?

Ⓔ Is that a beast?! That look was my concoction based on the original story.

The explanation of the original story is described in volume ②. Incidentally, volume ⑨'s Swan Lake and volume ②'s signing assembly are linked.

By the way, my family and friends call that swan a "duck."

Anyhow, this ends the Question Corner. See you!

2002.12.10

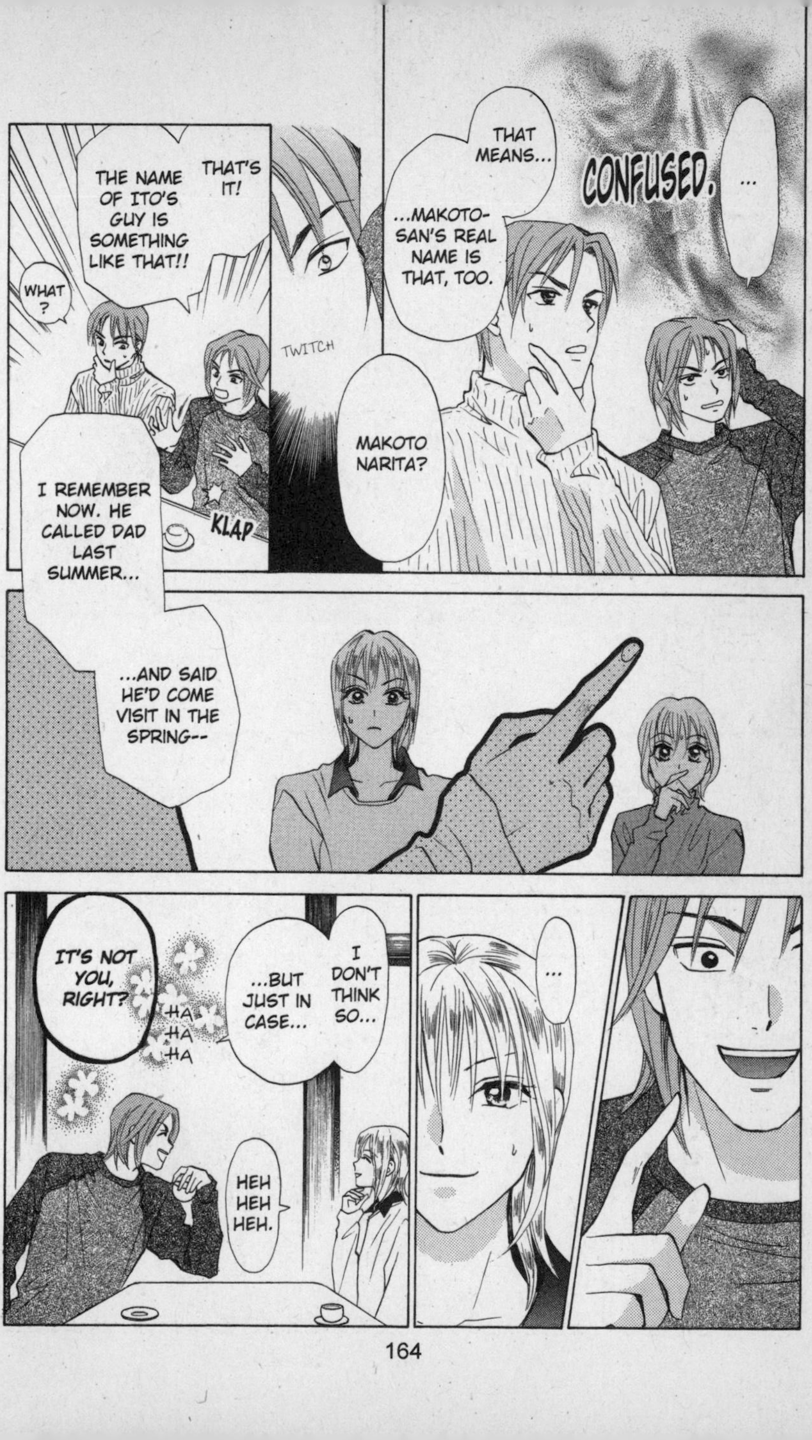
CONFUSED.
...
THAT MEANS...
...MAKOTO-SAN'S REAL NAME IS THAT, TOO.
TWITCH
MAKOTO NARITA?
THAT'S IT!
THE NAME OF ITO'S GUY IS SOMETHING LIKE THAT!!
WHAT?
KLAP
I REMEMBER NOW. HE CALLED DAD LAST SUMMER...
...AND SAID HE'D COME VISIT IN THE SPRING--
...
I DON'T THINK SO...
...BUT JUST IN CASE...
IT'S NOT YOU, RIGHT?
HA HA HA
HEH HEH HEH.

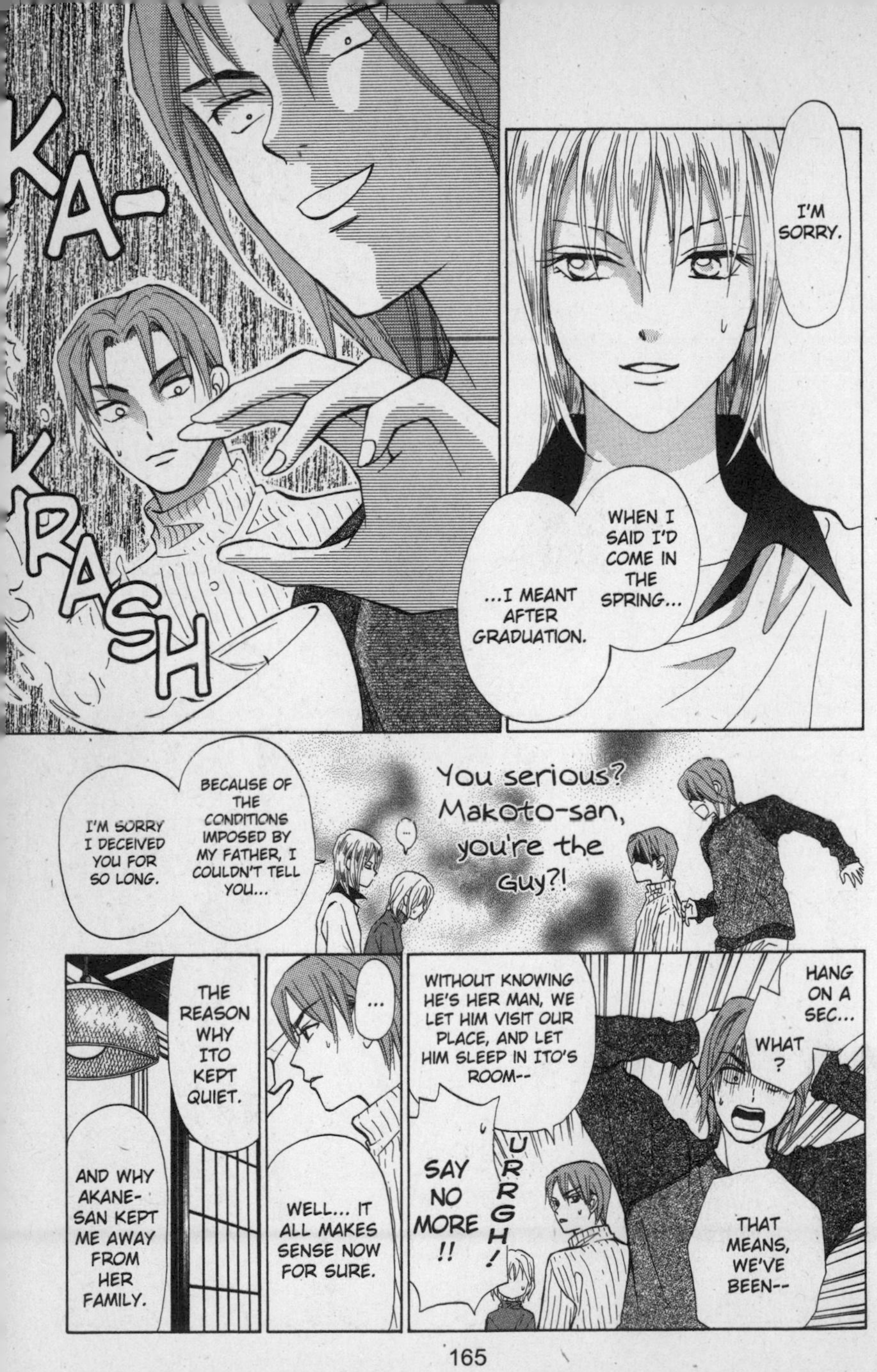
I'M SORRY.
WHEN I SAID I'D COME IN THE SPRING...
...I MEANT AFTER GRADUATION.
KA-KRASH
You serious? Makoto-san, you're the guy?!
...
BECAUSE OF THE CONDITIONS IMPOSED BY MY FATHER, I COULDN'T TELL YOU...
I'M SORRY I DECEIVED YOU FOR SO LONG.
HANG ON A SEC...
WHAT?
THAT MEANS, WE'VE BEEN--
WITHOUT KNOWING HE'S HER MAN, WE LET HIM VISIT OUR PLACE, AND LET HIM SLEEP IN ITO'S ROOM--
URRGH!
SAY NO MORE!!
...
WELL... IT ALL MAKES SENSE NOW FOR SURE.
THE REASON WHY ITO KEPT QUIET.
AND WHY AKANE-SAN KEPT ME AWAY FROM HER FAMILY.

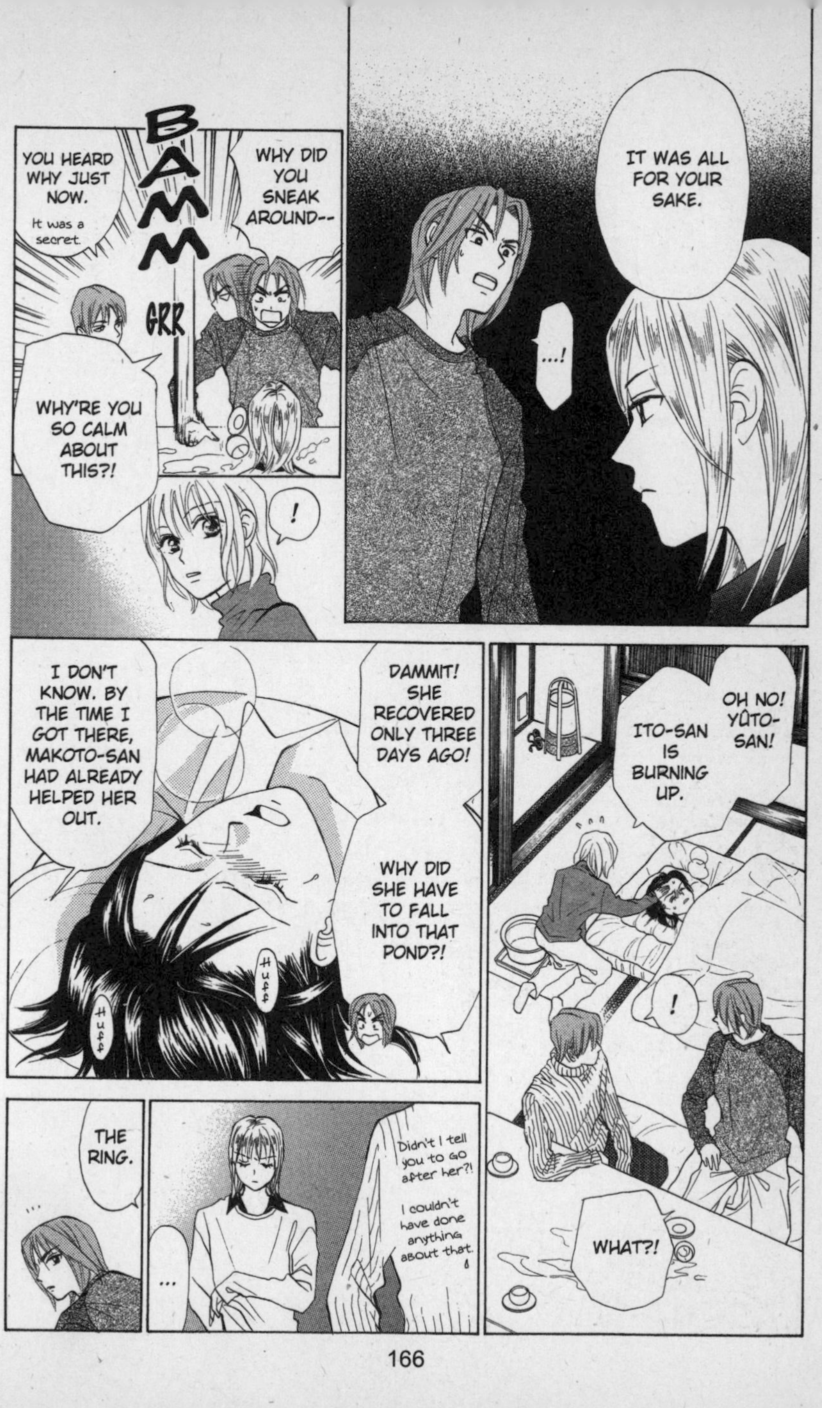
IT WAS ALL FOR YOUR SAKE.
...!
WHY DID YOU SNEAK AROUND--
BAMM
YOU HEARD WHY JUST NOW.
It was a secret.
GRR
WHY'RE YOU SO CALM ABOUT THIS?!
!
OH NO! YÛTO-SAN!
ITO-SAN IS BURNING UP.
!
WHAT?!
DAMMIT! SHE RECOVERED ONLY THREE DAYS AGO!
WHY DID SHE HAVE TO FALL INTO THAT POND?!
Huff
Huff
I DON'T KNOW. BY THE TIME I GOT THERE, MAKOTO-SAN HAD ALREADY HELPED HER OUT.
Didn't I tell you to go after her?!
I couldn't have done anything about that.
...
THE RING.
...

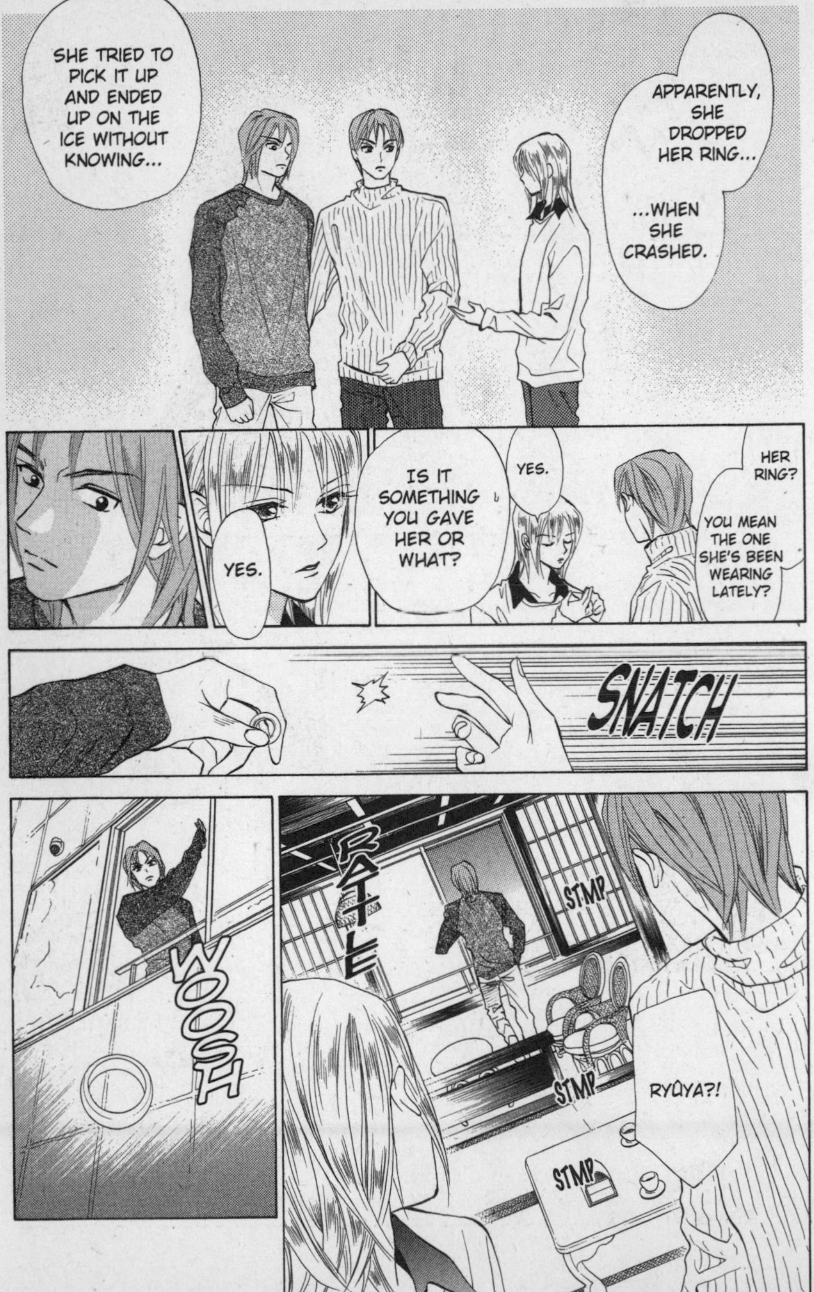
APPARENTLY, SHE DROPPED HER RING...
...WHEN SHE CRASHED.
SHE TRIED TO PICK IT UP AND ENDED UP ON THE ICE WITHOUT KNOWING...
HER RING?
YOU MEAN THE ONE SHE'S BEEN WEARING LATELY?
YES.
IS IT SOMETHING YOU GAVE HER OR WHAT?
YES.
SNATCH
RATTLE
STMP
STMP
STMP
RYÛYA?!
WOOSH

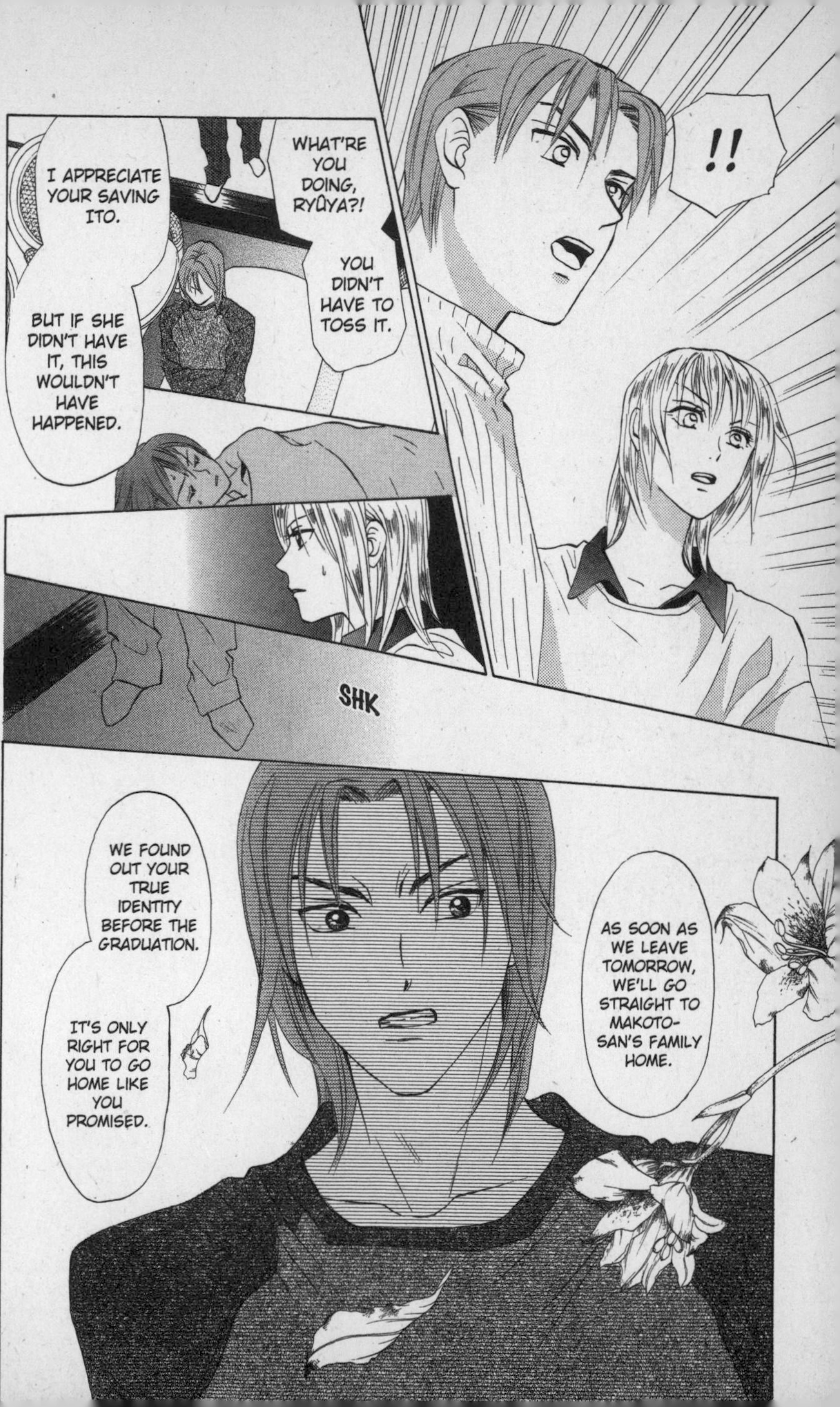
!!
WHAT'RE YOU DOING, RYŪYA?!
YOU DIDN'T HAVE TO TOSS IT.
I APPRECIATE YOUR SAVING ITO.
BUT IF SHE DIDN'T HAVE IT, THIS WOULDN'T HAVE HAPPENED.
SHK
AS SOON AS WE LEAVE TOMORROW, WE'LL GO STRAIGHT TO MAKOTO-SAN'S FAMILY HOME.
WE FOUND OUT YOUR TRUE IDENTITY BEFORE THE GRADUATION.
IT'S ONLY RIGHT FOR YOU TO GO HOME LIKE YOU PROMISED.

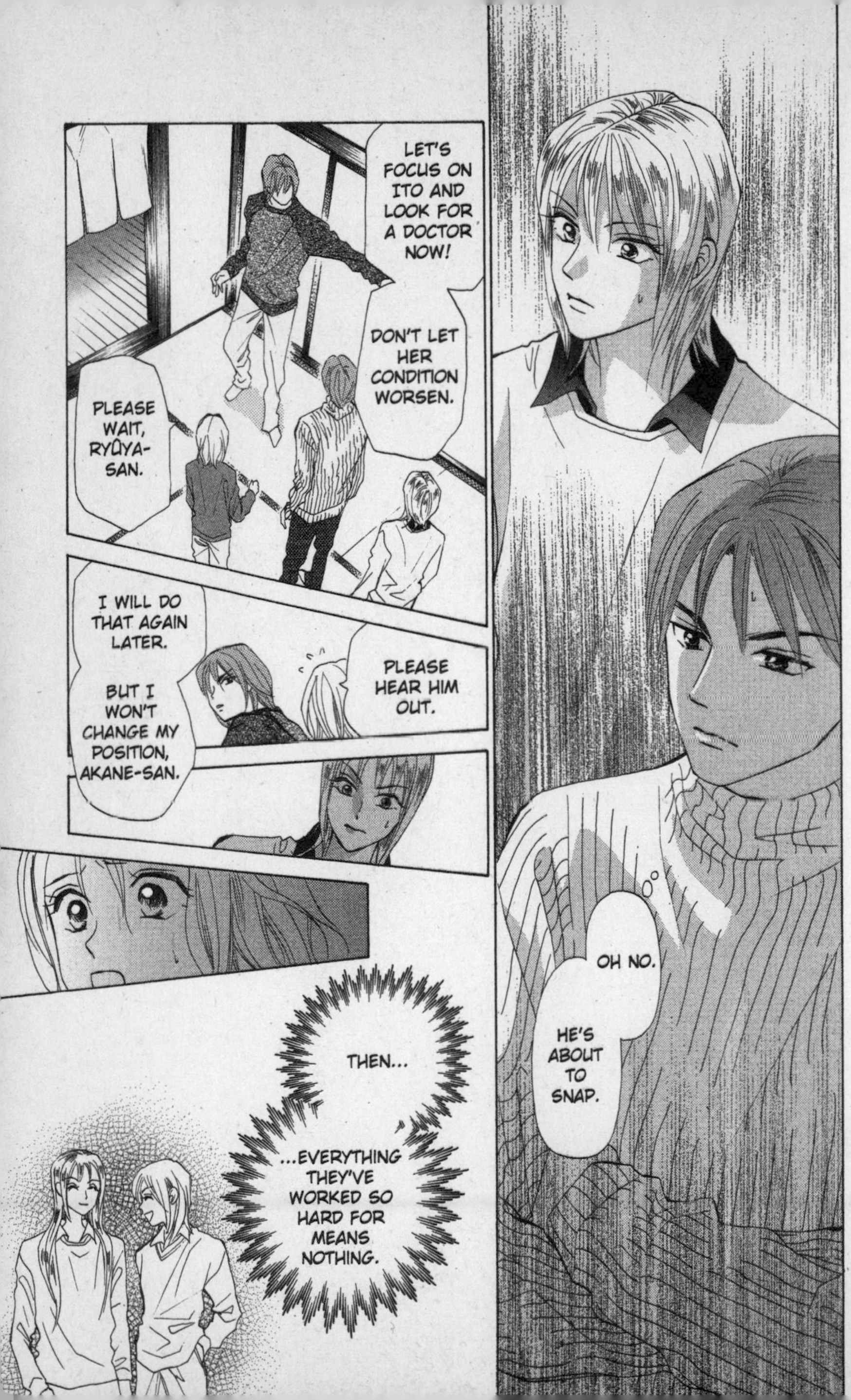
OH NO.
HE'S ABOUT TO SNAP.
LET'S FOCUS ON ITO AND LOOK FOR A DOCTOR NOW!
DON'T LET HER CONDITION WORSEN.
PLEASE WAIT, RYŪYA-SAN.
PLEASE HEAR HIM OUT.
I WILL DO THAT AGAIN LATER.
BUT I WON'T CHANGE MY POSITION, AKANE-SAN.
THEN...
...EVERYTHING THEY'VE WORKED SO HARD FOR MEANS NOTHING.

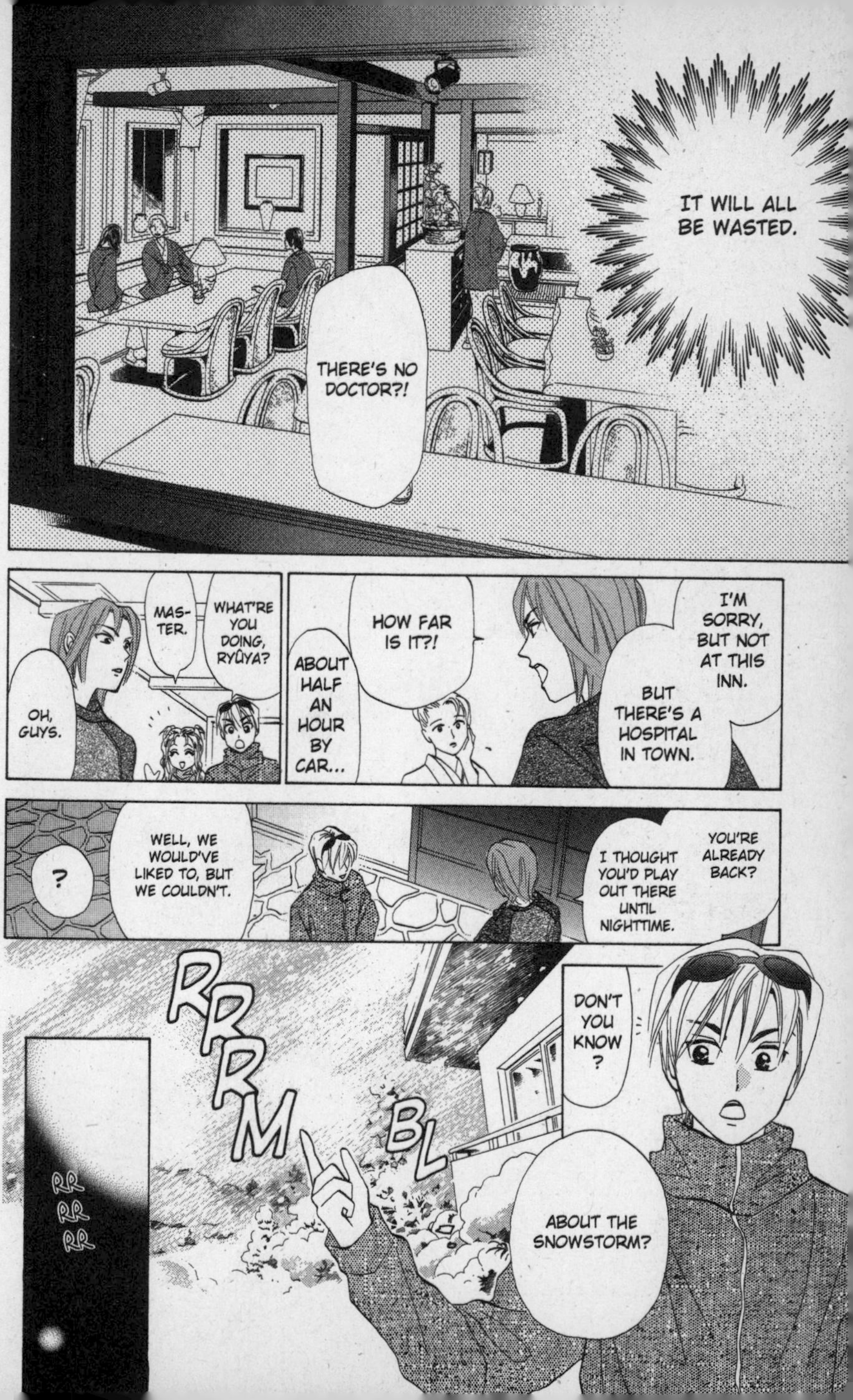

IT WILL ALL BE WASTED.
THERE'S NO DOCTOR?!
I'M SORRY, BUT NOT AT THIS INN.
BUT THERE'S A HOSPITAL IN TOWN.
HOW FAR IS IT?!
ABOUT HALF AN HOUR BY CAR...
WHAT'RE YOU DOING, RYŪYA?
MAS-TER.
OH, GUYS.
YOU'RE ALREADY BACK?
I THOUGHT YOU'D PLAY OUT THERE UNTIL NIGHTTIME.
WELL, WE WOULD'VE LIKED TO, BUT WE COULDN'T.
?
DON'T YOU KNOW?
ABOUT THE SNOWSTORM?
RRRM
BL
RR RR RR

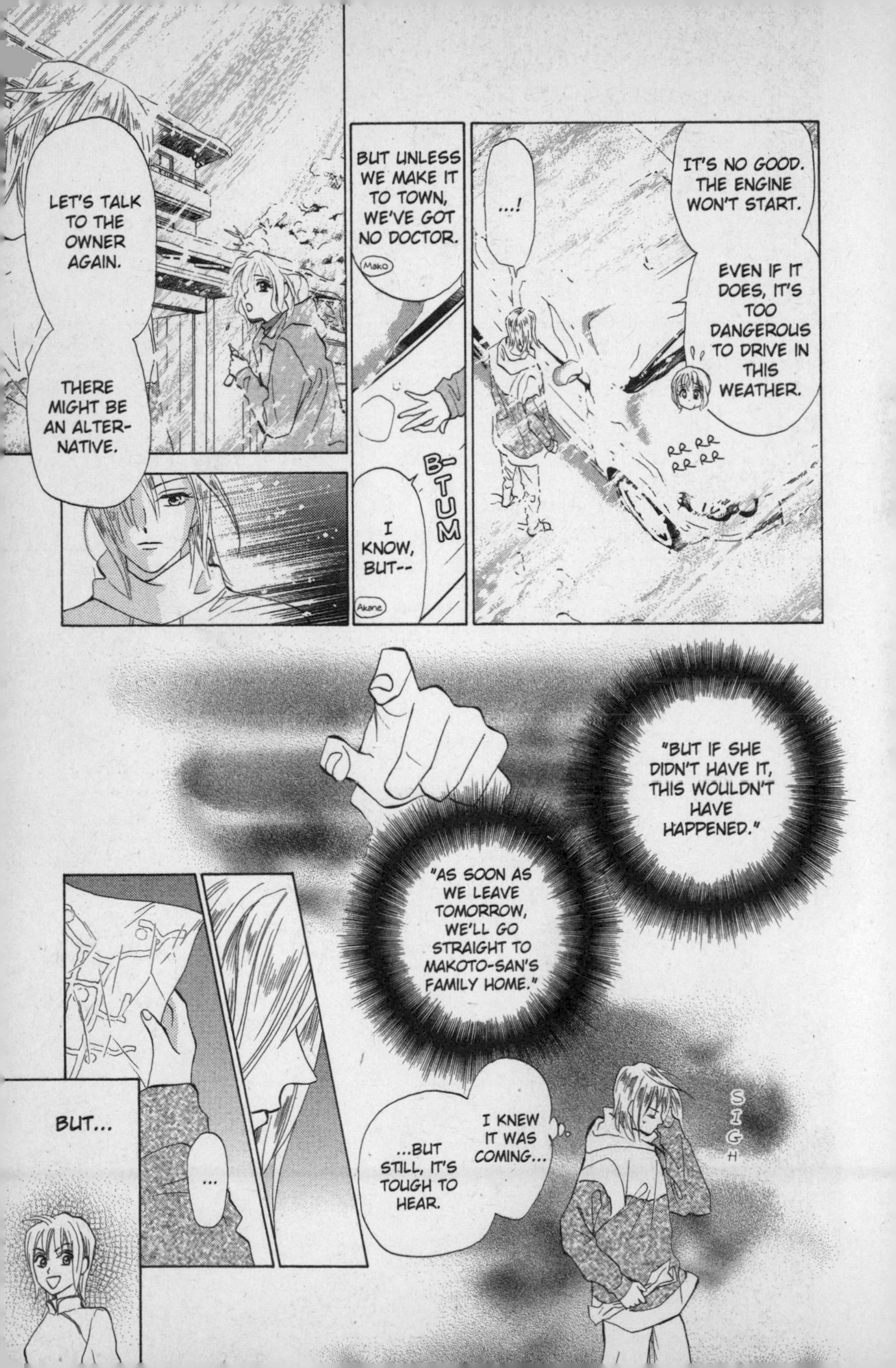
IT'S NO GOOD. THE ENGINE WON'T START.
EVEN IF IT DOES, IT'S TOO DANGEROUS TO DRIVE IN THIS WEATHER.
RR RR RR RR
...!
BUT UNLESS WE MAKE IT TO TOWN, WE'VE GOT NO DOCTOR.
Mako
B-TUM
I KNOW, BUT--
Akane
LET'S TALK TO THE OWNER AGAIN.
THERE MIGHT BE AN ALTER-NATIVE.
"BUT IF SHE DIDN'T HAVE IT, THIS WOULDN'T HAVE HAPPENED."
"AS SOON AS WE LEAVE TOMORROW, WE'LL GO STRAIGHT TO MAKOTO-SAN'S FAMILY HOME."
SIGH
I KNEW IT WAS COMING...
...BUT STILL, IT'S TOUGH TO HEAR.
...
BUT...

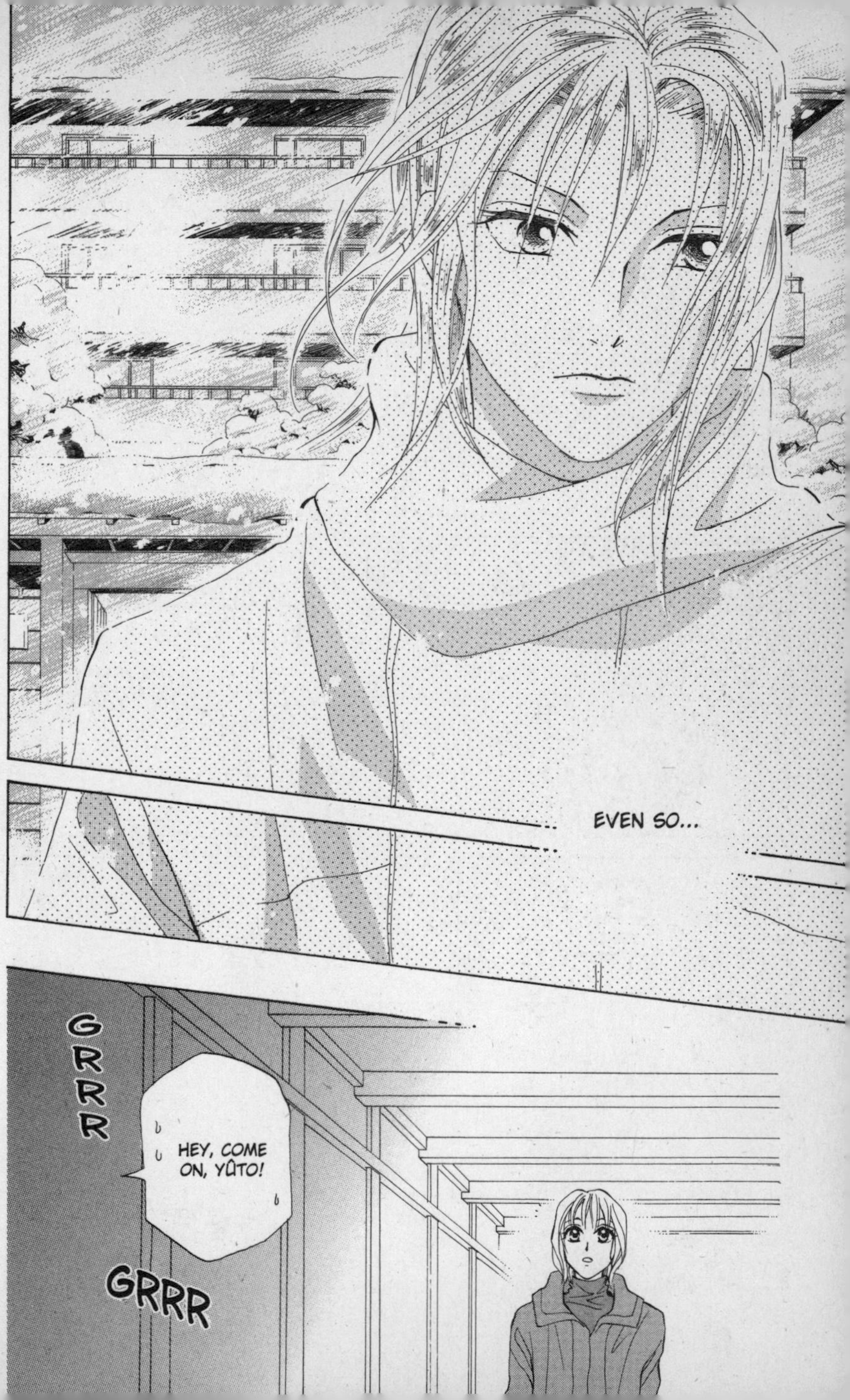
EVEN SO...
HEY, COME ON, YÛTO!
GRRR
GRRR

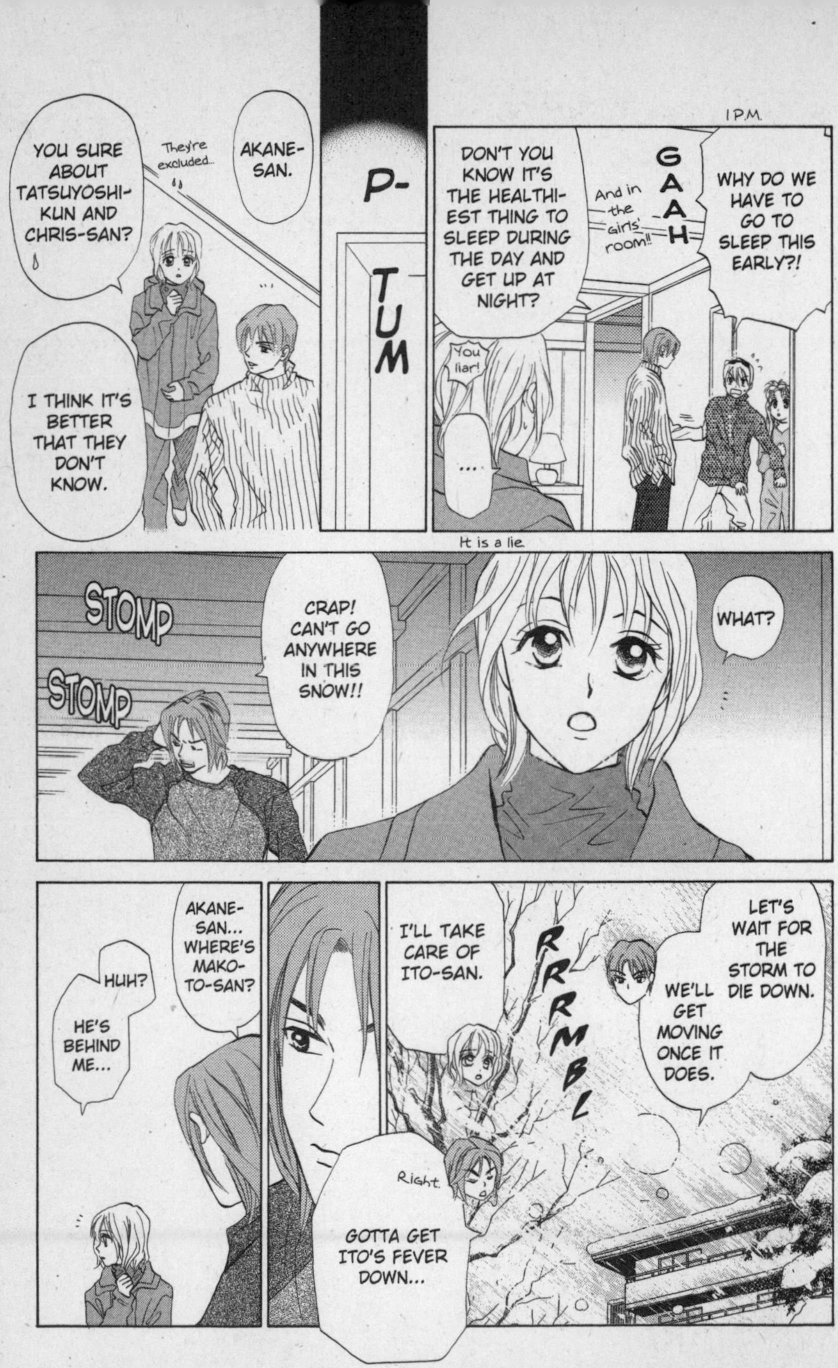
1 P.M.
WHY DO WE HAVE TO GO TO SLEEP THIS EARLY?!
GAAH
And in the girls' room!!
DON'T YOU KNOW IT'S THE HEALTHIEST THING TO SLEEP DURING THE DAY AND GET UP AT NIGHT?
You liar!
...
It is a lie.
P-TUM
AKANE-SAN.
They're excluded...
YOU SURE ABOUT TATSUYOSHI-KUN AND CHRIS-SAN?
...
I THINK IT'S BETTER THAT THEY DON'T KNOW.
WHAT?
CRAP! CAN'T GO ANYWHERE IN THIS SNOW!!
STOMP
STOMP
LET'S WAIT FOR THE STORM TO DIE DOWN.
WE'LL GET MOVING ONCE IT DOES.
RRRMBL
I'LL TAKE CARE OF ITO-SAN.
Right.
GOTTA GET ITO'S FEVER DOWN...
AKANE-SAN... WHERE'S MAKO-TO-SAN?
HUH?
HE'S BEHIND ME...

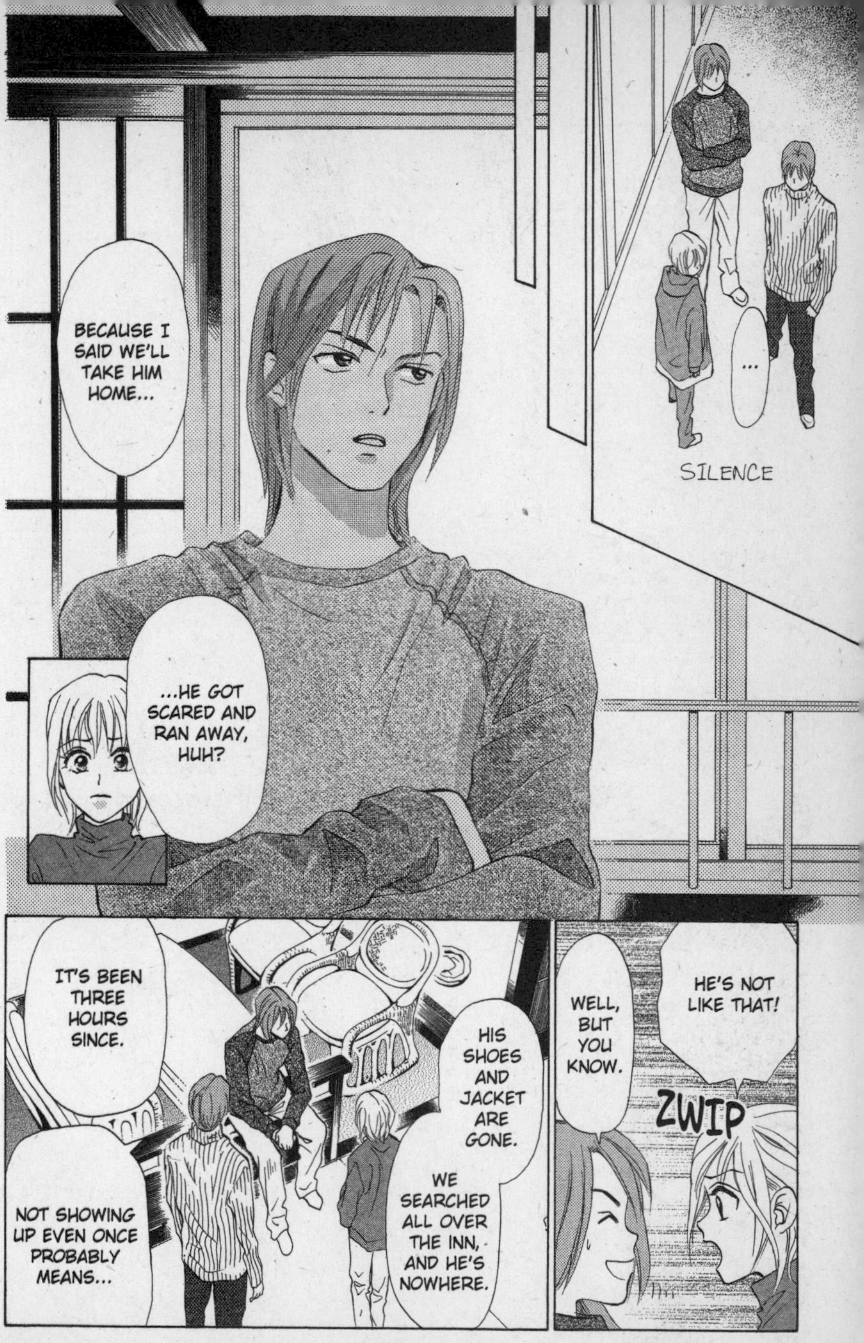
...
SILENCE
BECAUSE I SAID WE'LL TAKE HIM HOME...
...HE GOT SCARED AND RAN AWAY, HUH?
HE'S NOT LIKE THAT!
ZWIP
WELL, BUT YOU KNOW.
HIS SHOES AND JACKET ARE GONE.
WE SEARCHED ALL OVER THE INN, AND HE'S NOWHERE.
IT'S BEEN THREE HOURS SINCE.
NOT SHOWING UP EVEN ONCE PROBABLY MEANS...

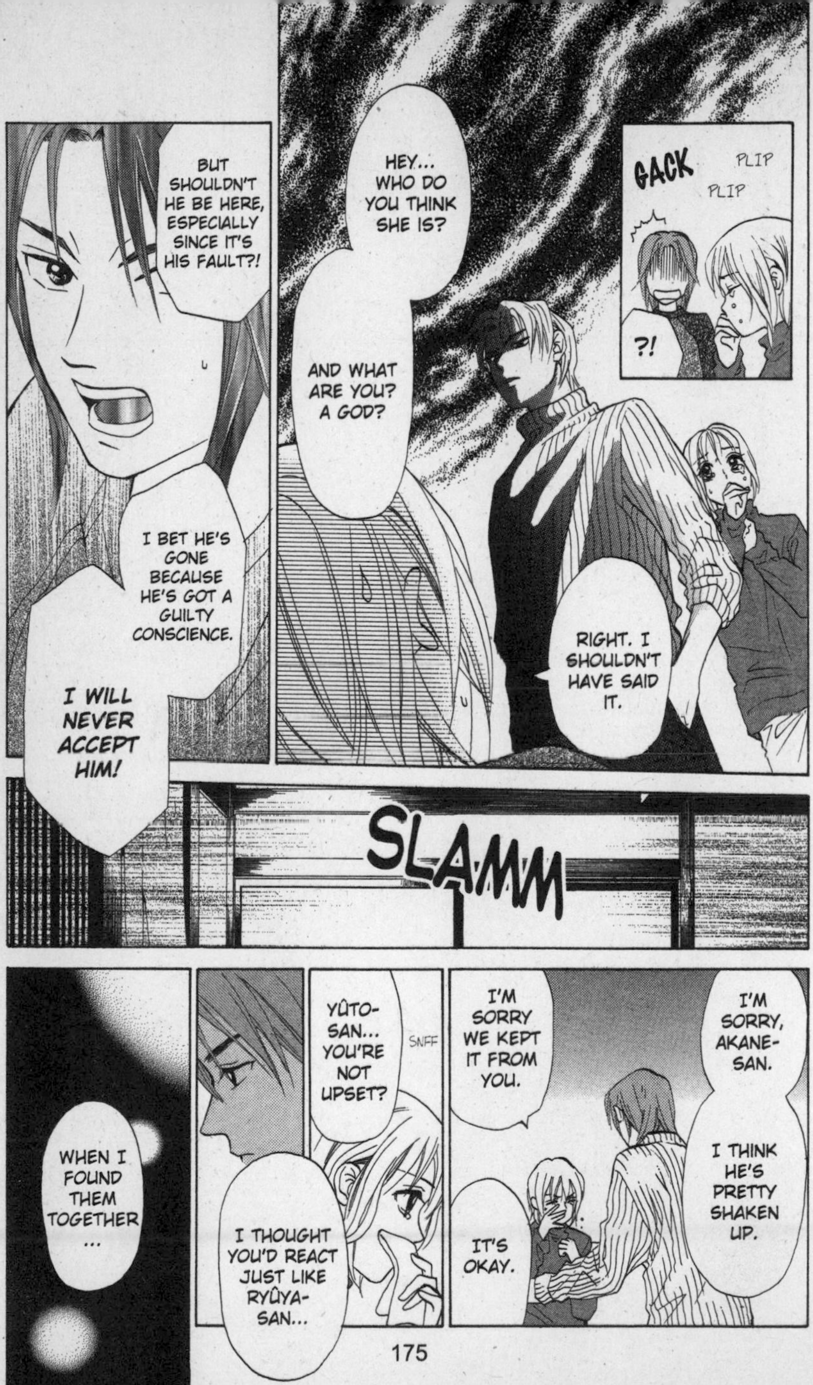
GACK
PLIP
PLIP
?!
HEY... WHO DO YOU THINK SHE IS?
AND WHAT ARE YOU? A GOD?
RIGHT. I SHOULDN'T HAVE SAID IT.
BUT SHOULDN'T HE BE HERE, ESPECIALLY SINCE IT'S HIS FAULT?!
I BET HE'S GONE BECAUSE HE'S GOT A GUILTY CONSCIENCE.
I WILL NEVER ACCEPT HIM!
SLAMM
I'M SORRY, AKANE-SAN.
I THINK HE'S PRETTY SHAKEN UP.
I'M SORRY WE KEPT IT FROM YOU.
IT'S OKAY.
SNFF
YÛTO-SAN... YOU'RE NOT UPSET?
I THOUGHT YOU'D REACT JUST LIKE RYÛYA-SAN...
WHEN I FOUND THEM TOGETHER...

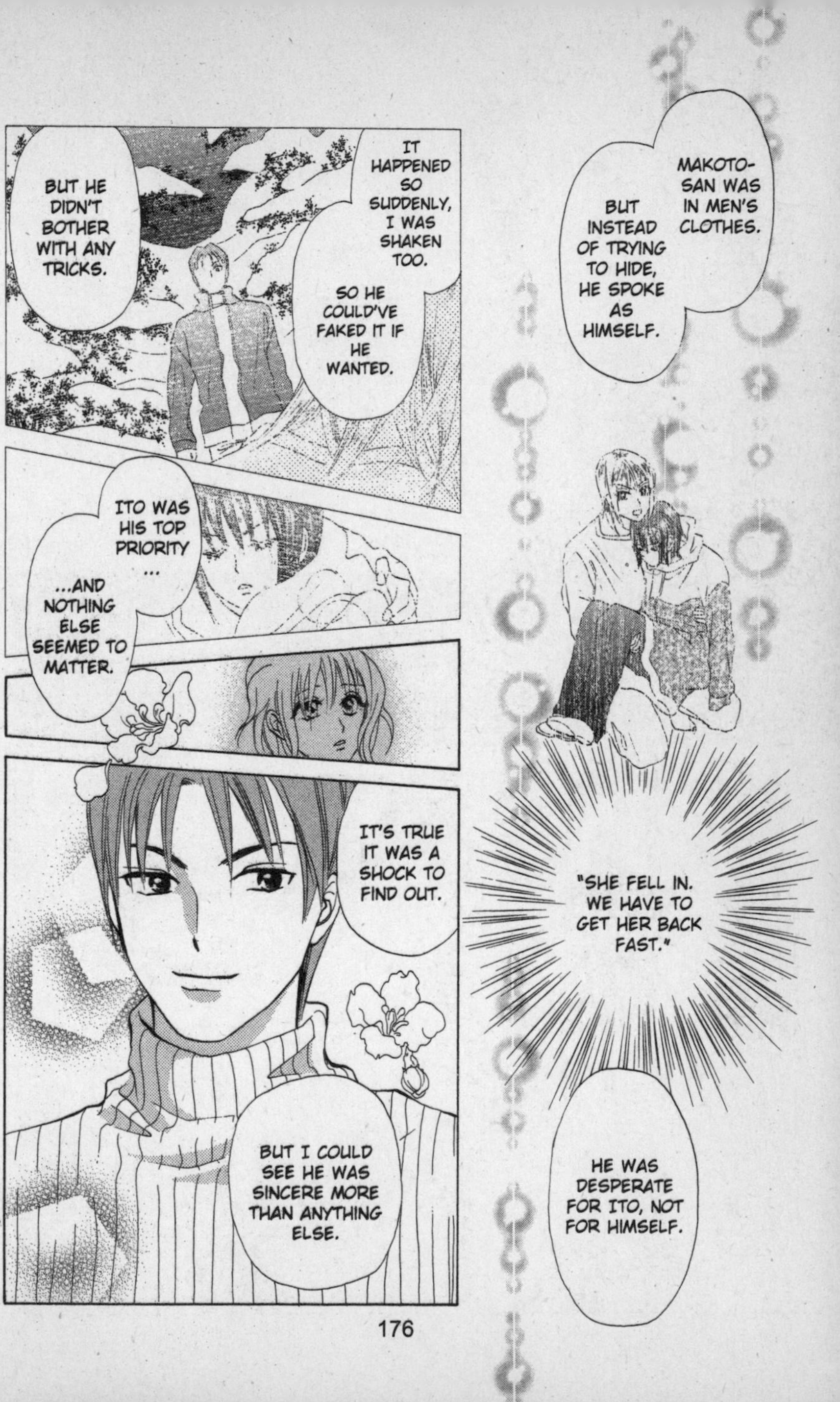
MAKOTO-SAN WAS IN MEN'S CLOTHES.
BUT INSTEAD OF TRYING TO HIDE, HE SPOKE AS HIMSELF.
"SHE FELL IN. WE HAVE TO GET HER BACK FAST."
HE WAS DESPERATE FOR ITO, NOT FOR HIMSELF.
IT HAPPENED SO SUDDENLY, I WAS SHAKEN TOO.
SO HE COULD'VE FAKED IT IF HE WANTED.
BUT HE DIDN'T BOTHER WITH ANY TRICKS.
ITO WAS HIS TOP PRIORITY ...
...AND NOTHING ELSE SEEMED TO MATTER.
IT'S TRUE IT WAS A SHOCK TO FIND OUT.
BUT I COULD SEE HE WAS SINCERE MORE THAN ANYTHING ELSE.

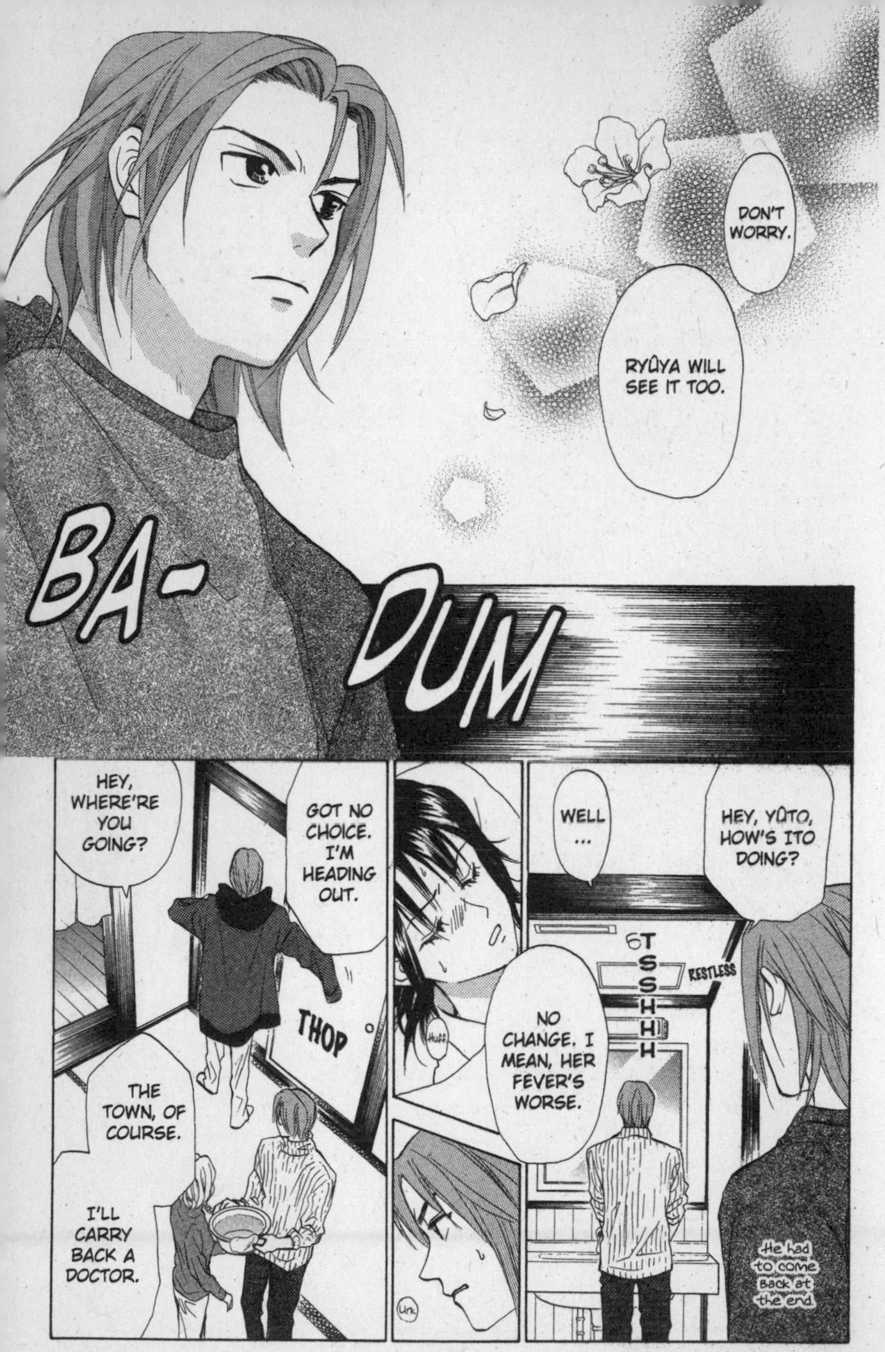
DON'T WORRY.
RYÛYA WILL SEE IT TOO.
BA-
DUM
HEY, YÛTO, HOW'S ITO DOING?
WELL ...
TSSHHH
RESTLESS
NO CHANGE. I MEAN, HER FEVER'S WORSE.
Huff
He had to come back at the end
Urk
GOT NO CHOICE. I'M HEADING OUT.
HEY, WHERE'RE YOU GOING?
THOP
THE TOWN, OF COURSE.
I'LL CARRY BACK A DOCTOR.

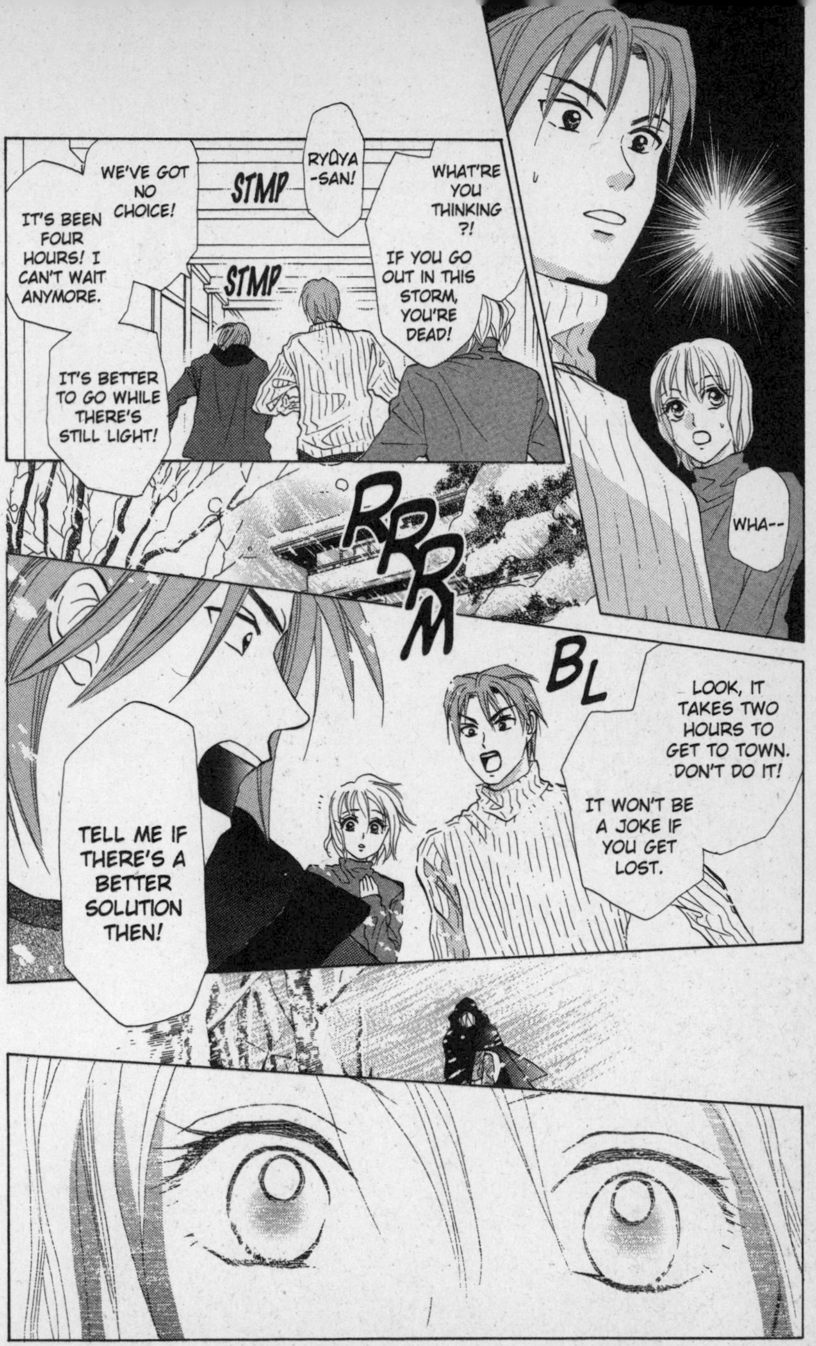
WHA--
WHAT'RE YOU THINKING?!
IF YOU GO OUT IN THIS STORM, YOU'RE DEAD!
RYŪYA-SAN!
STMP
WE'VE GOT NO CHOICE!
IT'S BEEN FOUR HOURS! I CAN'T WAIT ANYMORE.
STMP
IT'S BETTER TO GO WHILE THERE'S STILL LIGHT!
RRRM
BL
LOOK, IT TAKES TWO HOURS TO GET TO TOWN. DON'T DO IT!
IT WON'T BE A JOKE IF YOU GET LOST.
TELL ME IF THERE'S A BETTER SOLUTION THEN!

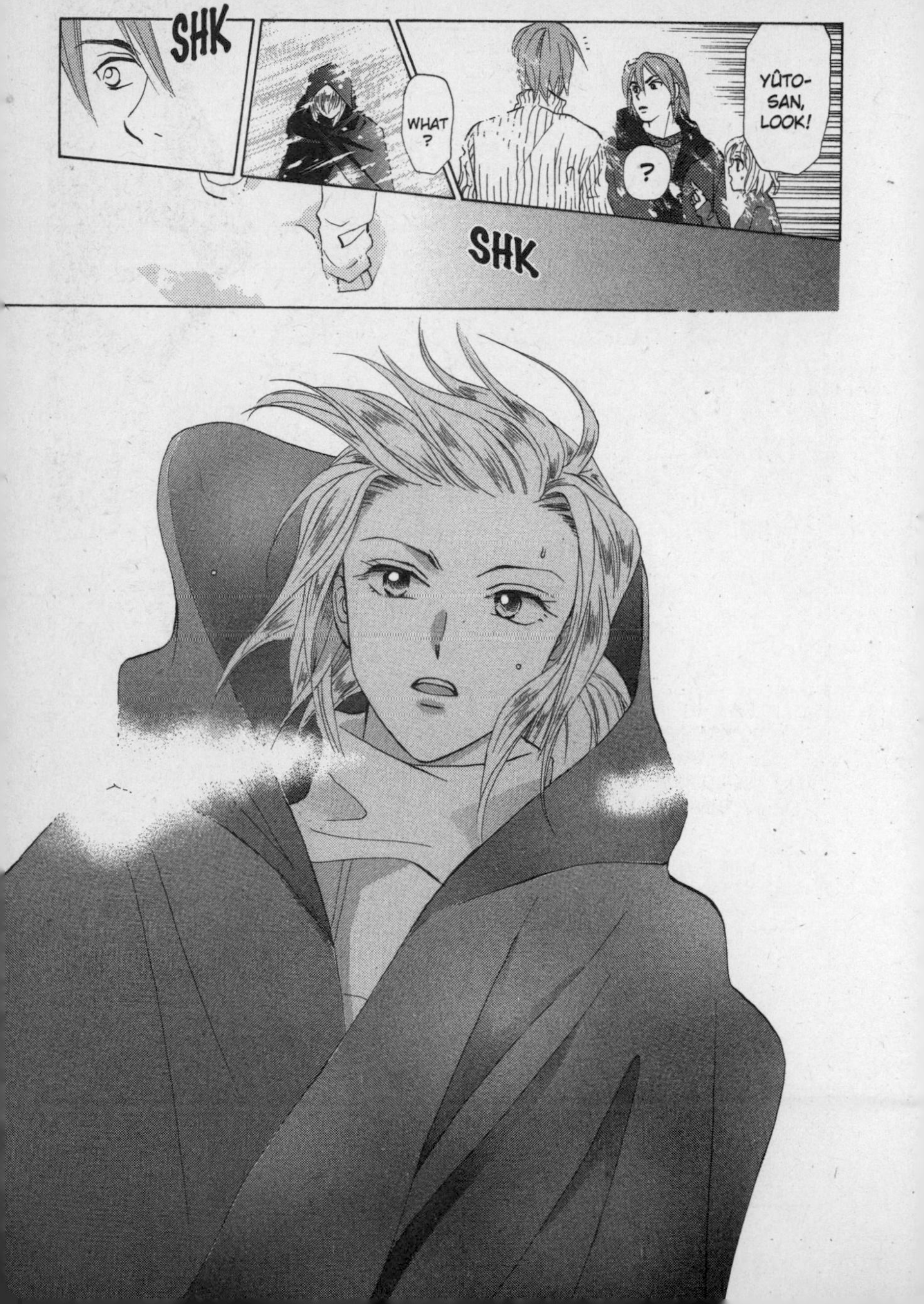
YÛTO-SAN, LOOK!
?
WHAT ?
SHK
SHK

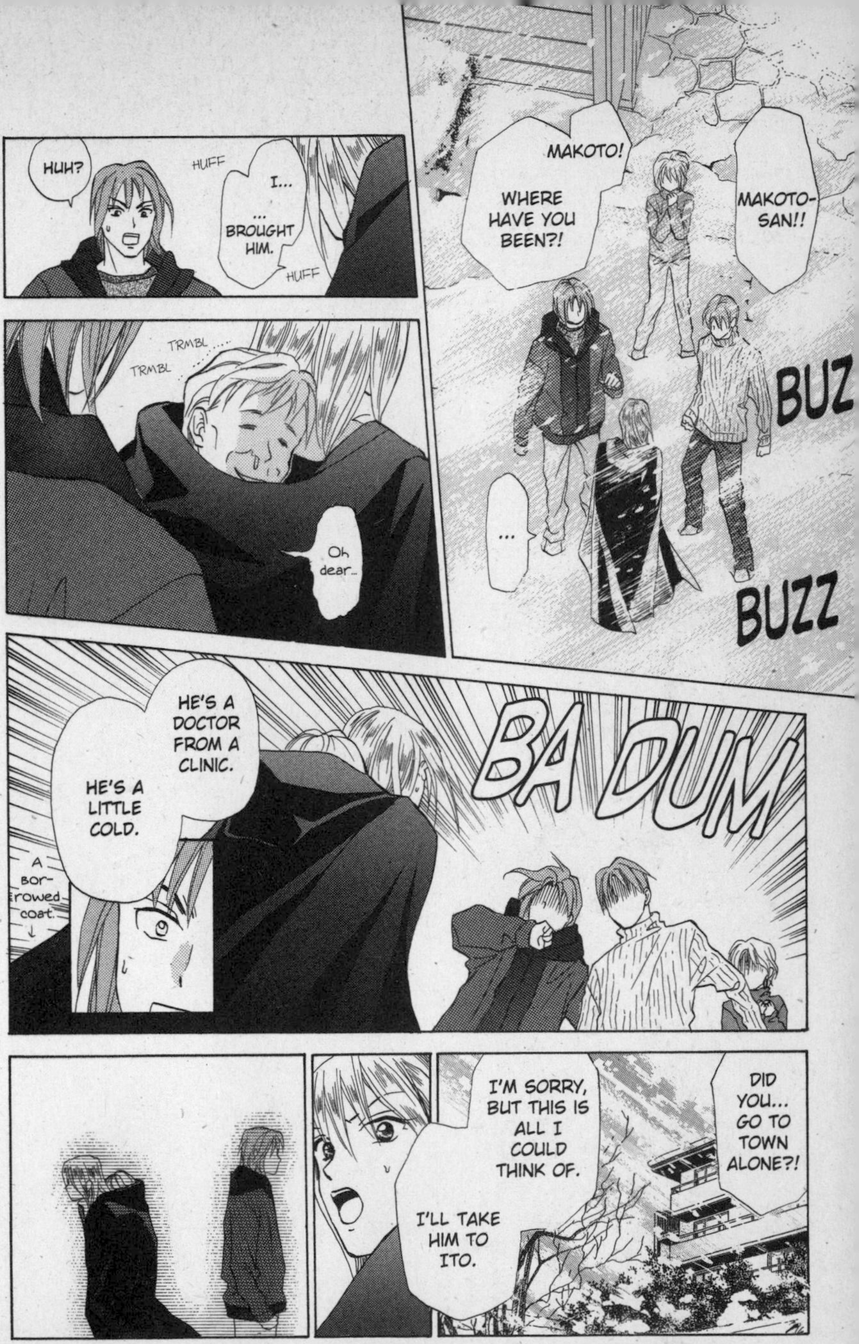
MAKOTO-SAN!!
MAKOTO!
WHERE HAVE YOU BEEN?!
BUZ
BUZZ
...
HUFF
I...
... BROUGHT HIM.
HUFF
HUH?
TRMBL
TRMBL
Oh dear...
BA DUM
HE'S A DOCTOR FROM A CLINIC.
HE'S A LITTLE COLD.
A borrowed coat.
DID YOU... GO TO TOWN ALONE?!
I'M SORRY, BUT THIS IS ALL I COULD THINK OF.
I'LL TAKE HIM TO ITO.

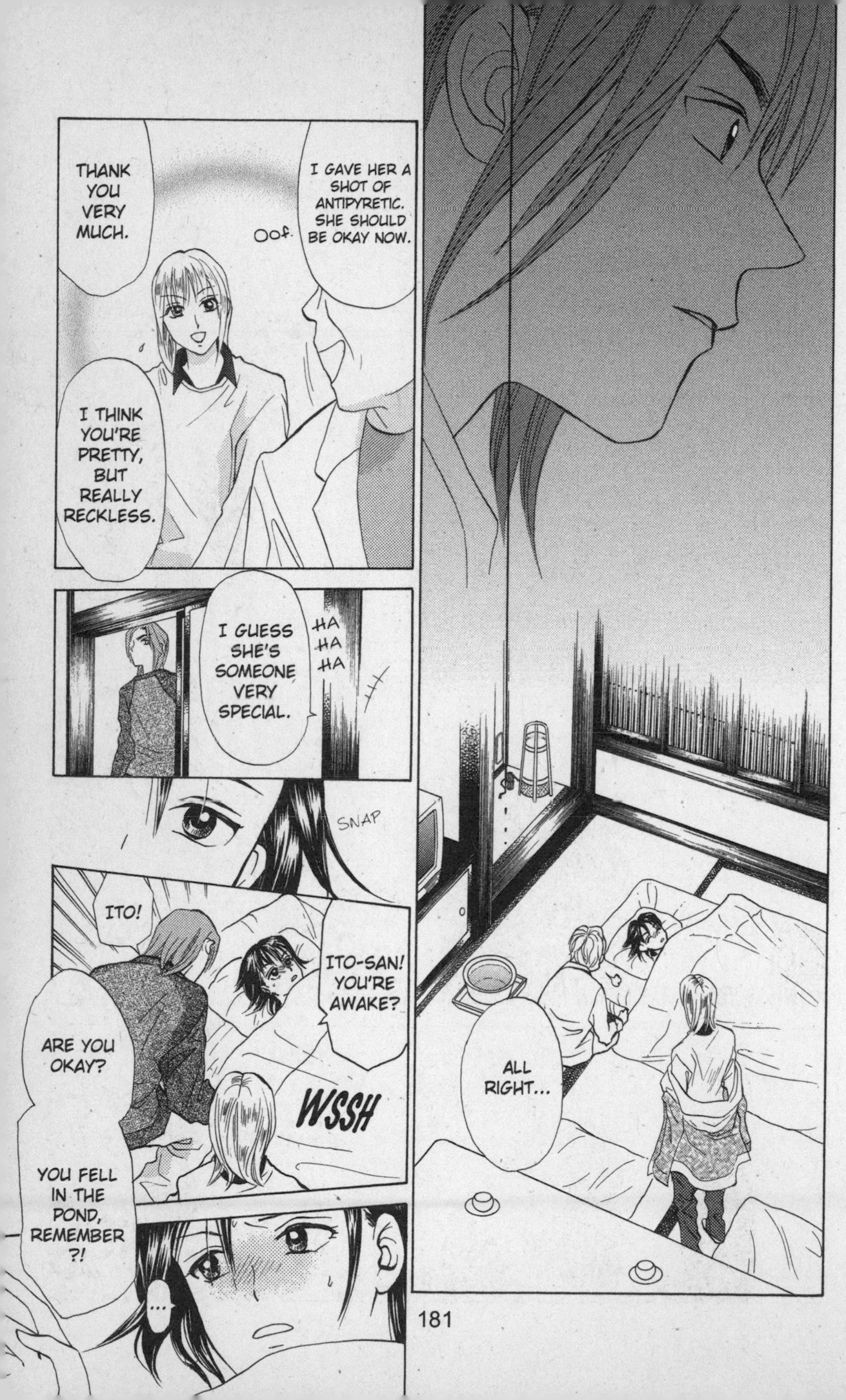
ALL RIGHT...
I GAVE HER A SHOT OF ANTIPYRETIC. SHE SHOULD BE OKAY NOW.
Oof.
THANK YOU VERY MUCH.
I THINK YOU'RE PRETTY, BUT REALLY RECKLESS.
HA HA HA
I GUESS SHE'S SOMEONE VERY SPECIAL.
SNAP
ITO-SAN! YOU'RE AWAKE?
ITO!
WSSH
ARE YOU OKAY?
YOU FELL IN THE POND, REMEMBER?!
...

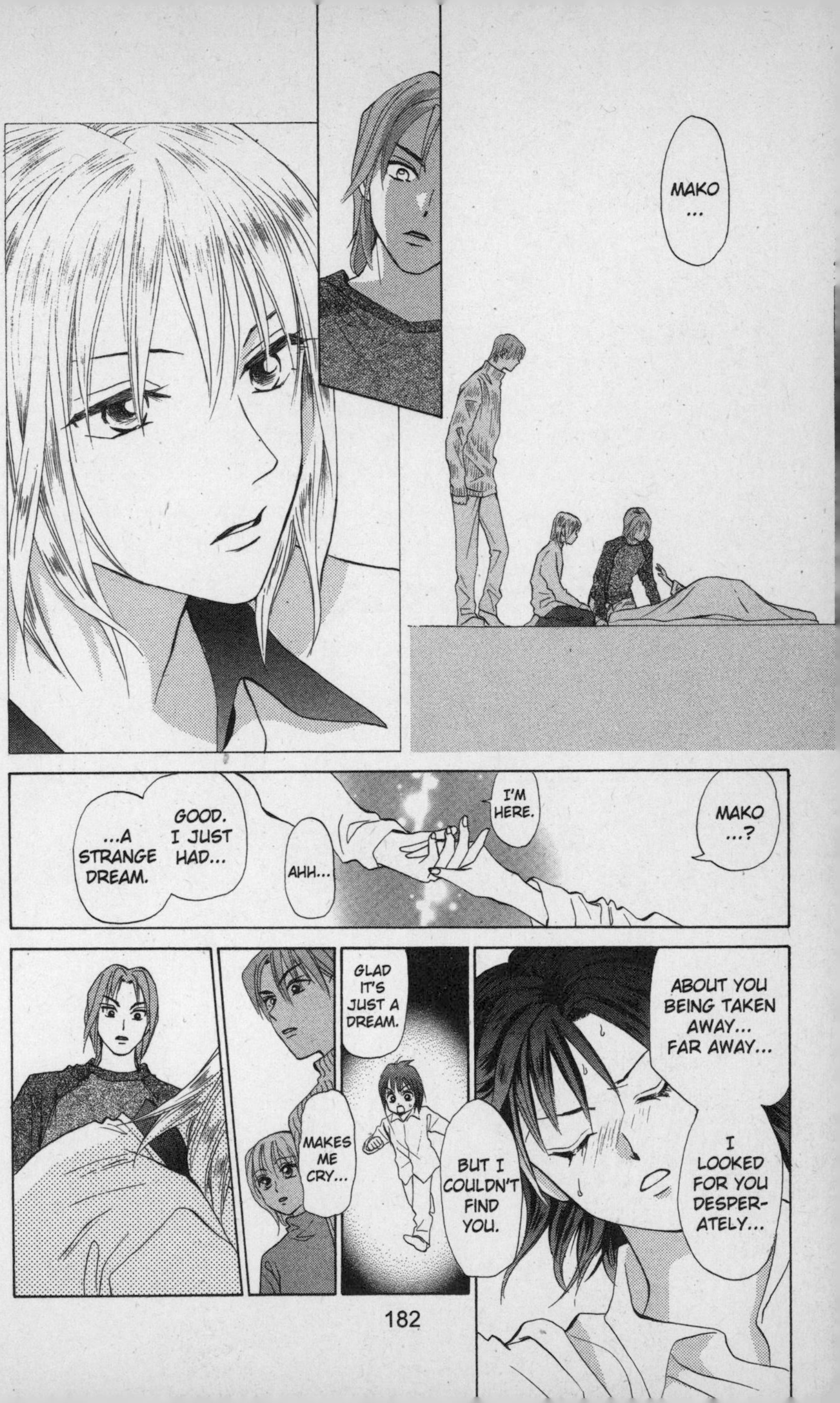
MAKO ...
MAKO ...?
I'M HERE.
AHH...
GOOD. I JUST HAD...
...A STRANGE DREAM.
ABOUT YOU BEING TAKEN AWAY... FAR AWAY...
I LOOKED FOR YOU DESPERATELY...
BUT I COULDN'T FIND YOU.
GLAD IT'S JUST A DREAM.
MAKES ME CRY...

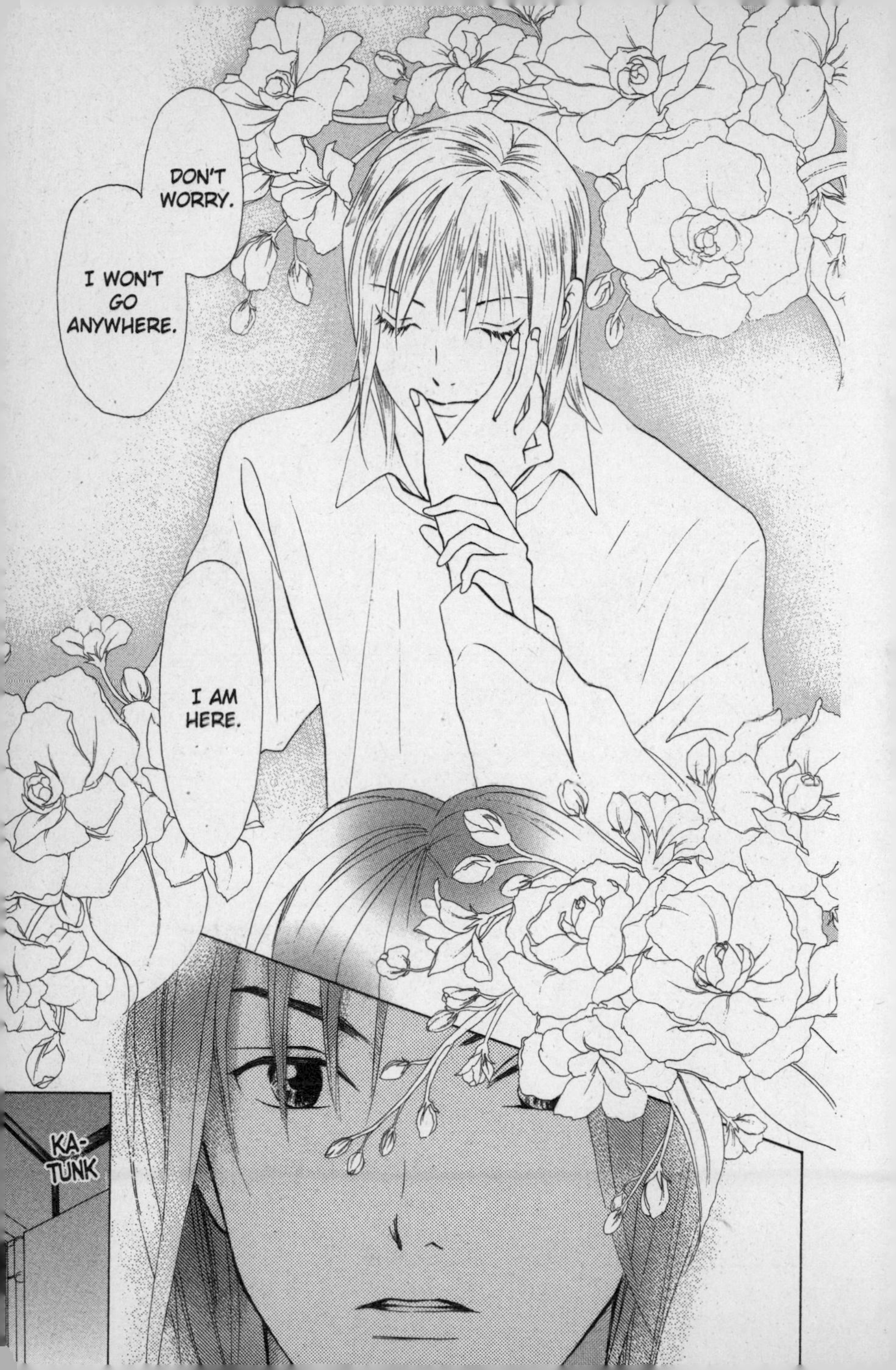
DON'T WORRY.
I WON'T GO ANYWHERE.
I AM HERE.
KA-TUNK

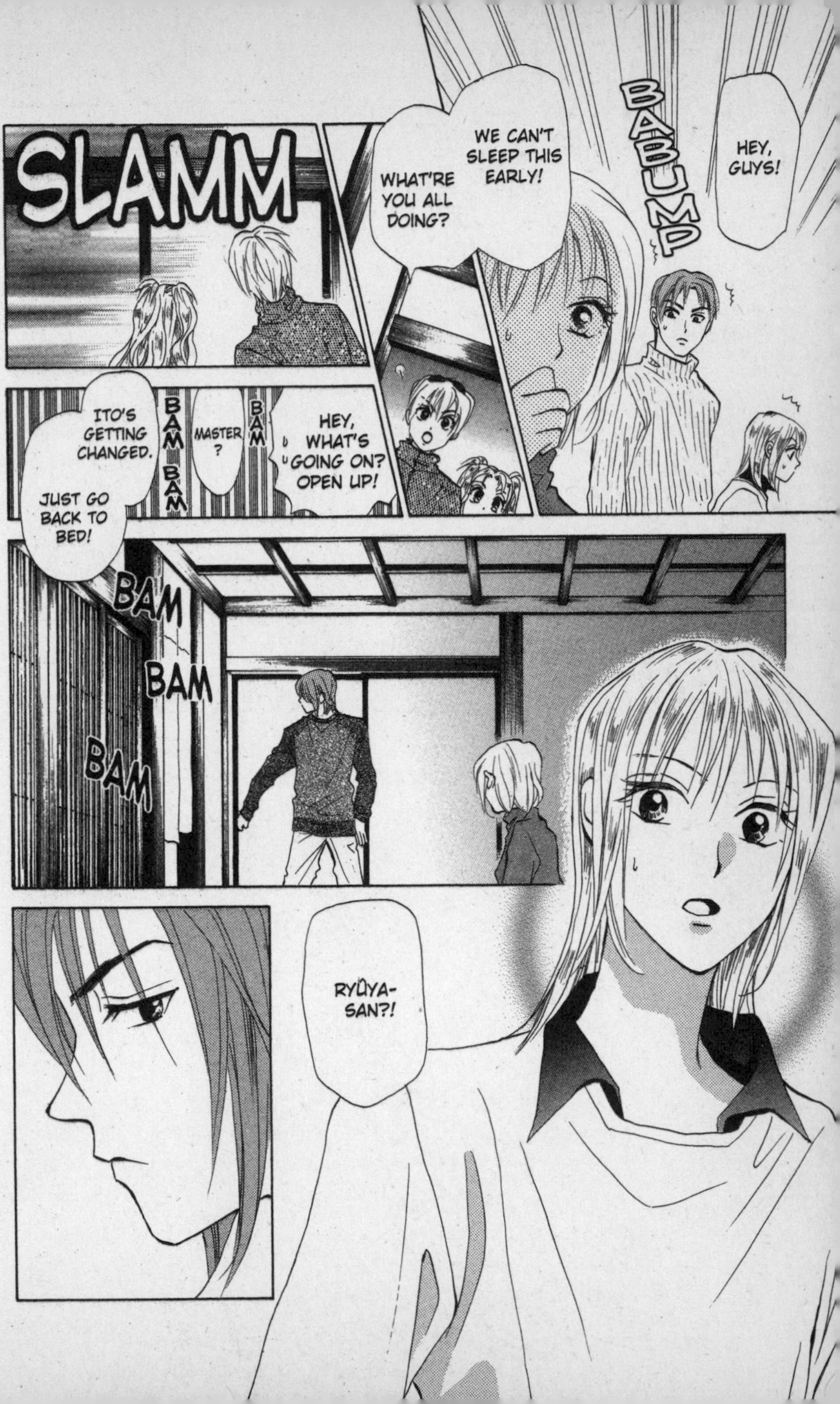
HEY, GUYS!
BABUMP
WE CAN'T SLEEP THIS EARLY!
WHAT'RE YOU ALL DOING?
SLAMM
HEY, WHAT'S GOING ON? OPEN UP!
BAM
MASTER?
BAM BAM
ITO'S GETTING CHANGED.
JUST GO BACK TO BED!
BAM
BAM
BAM
RYŪYA-SAN?!

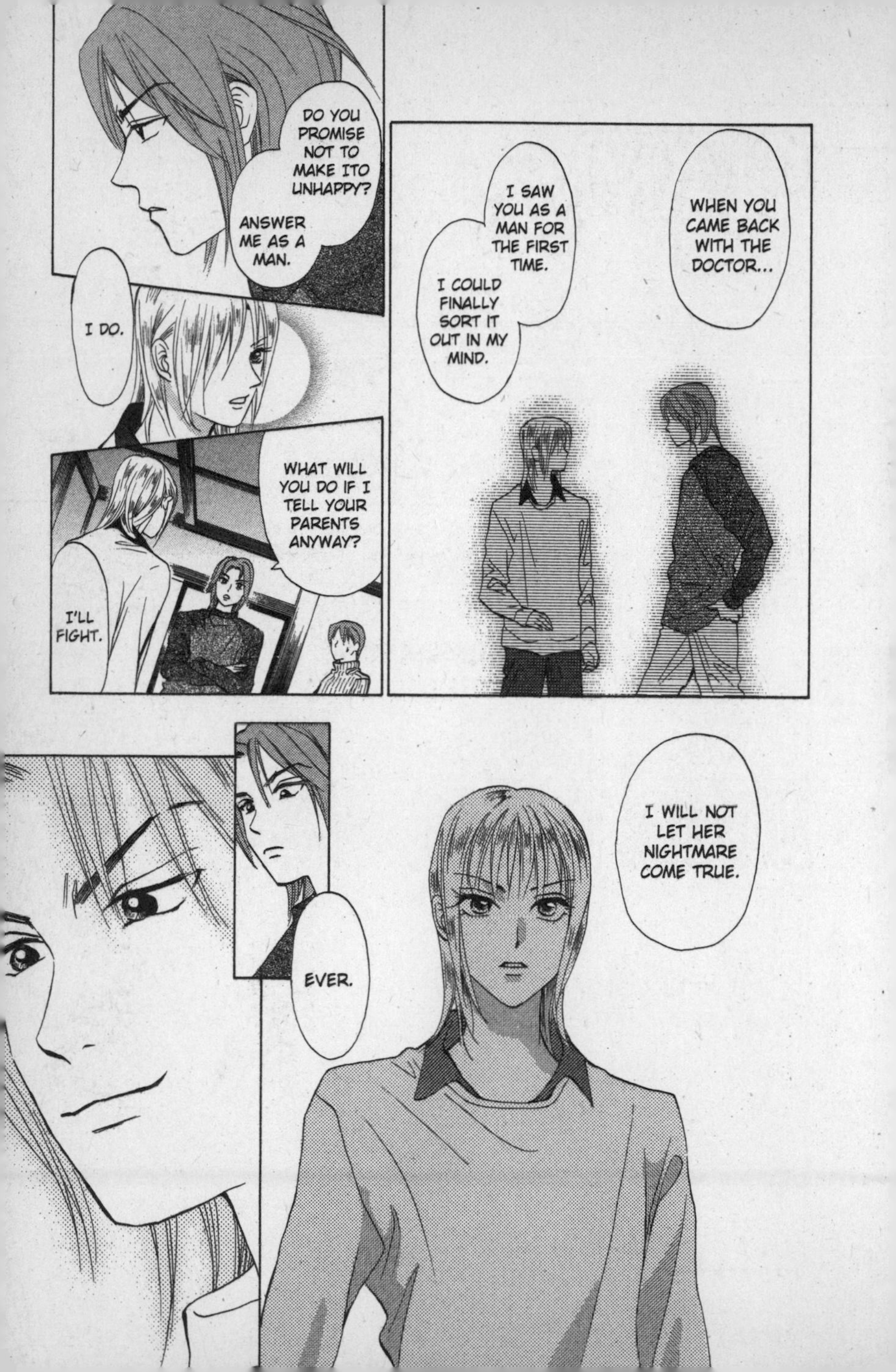
WHEN YOU CAME BACK WITH THE DOCTOR...
I SAW YOU AS A MAN FOR THE FIRST TIME.
I COULD FINALLY SORT IT OUT IN MY MIND.
DO YOU PROMISE NOT TO MAKE ITO UNHAPPY?
ANSWER ME AS A MAN.
I DO.
WHAT WILL YOU DO IF I TELL YOUR PARENTS ANYWAY?
I'LL FIGHT.
I WILL NOT LET HER NIGHTMARE COME TRUE.
EVER.

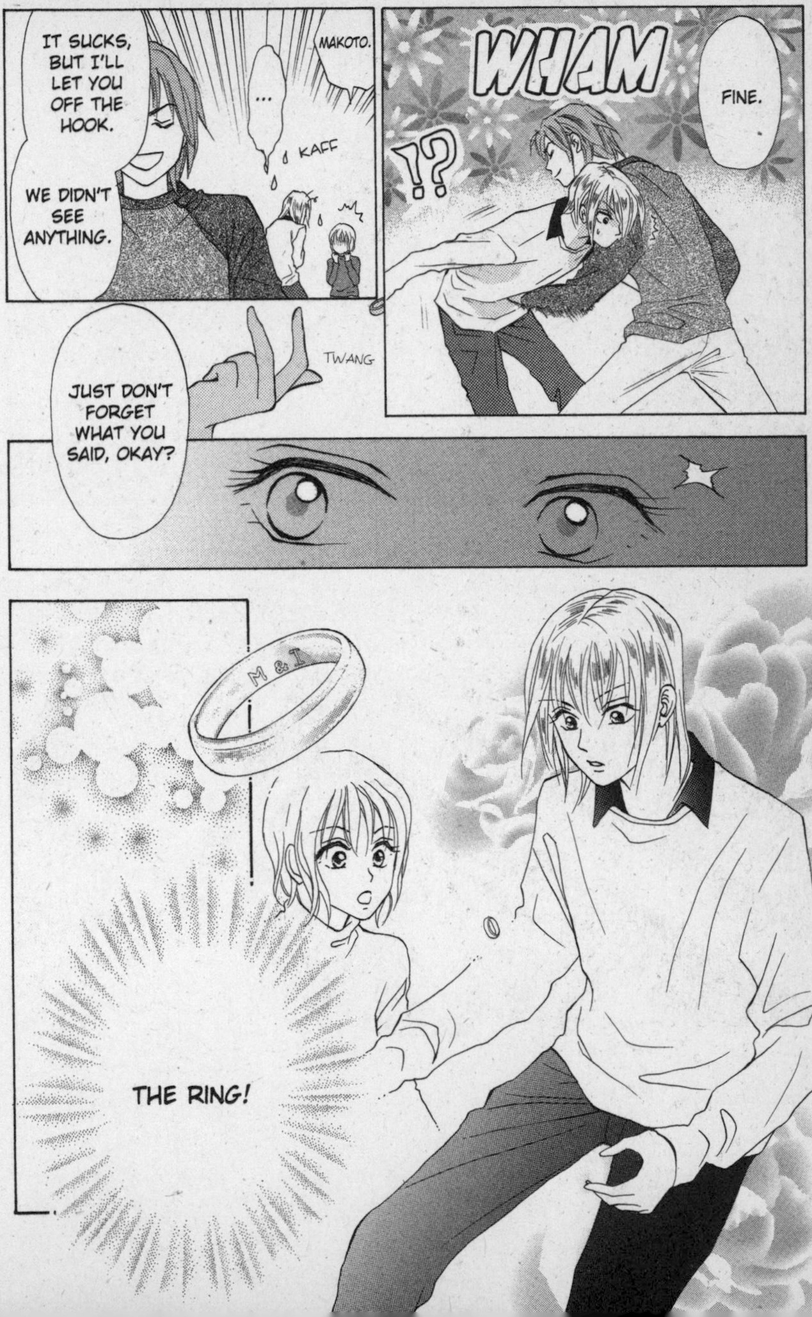
FINE.
WHAM
!?
MAKOTO.
...
KAFF
IT SUCKS, BUT I'LL LET YOU OFF THE HOOK.
WE DIDN'T SEE ANYTHING.
TWANG
JUST DON'T FORGET WHAT YOU SAID, OKAY?
M & I
THE RING!

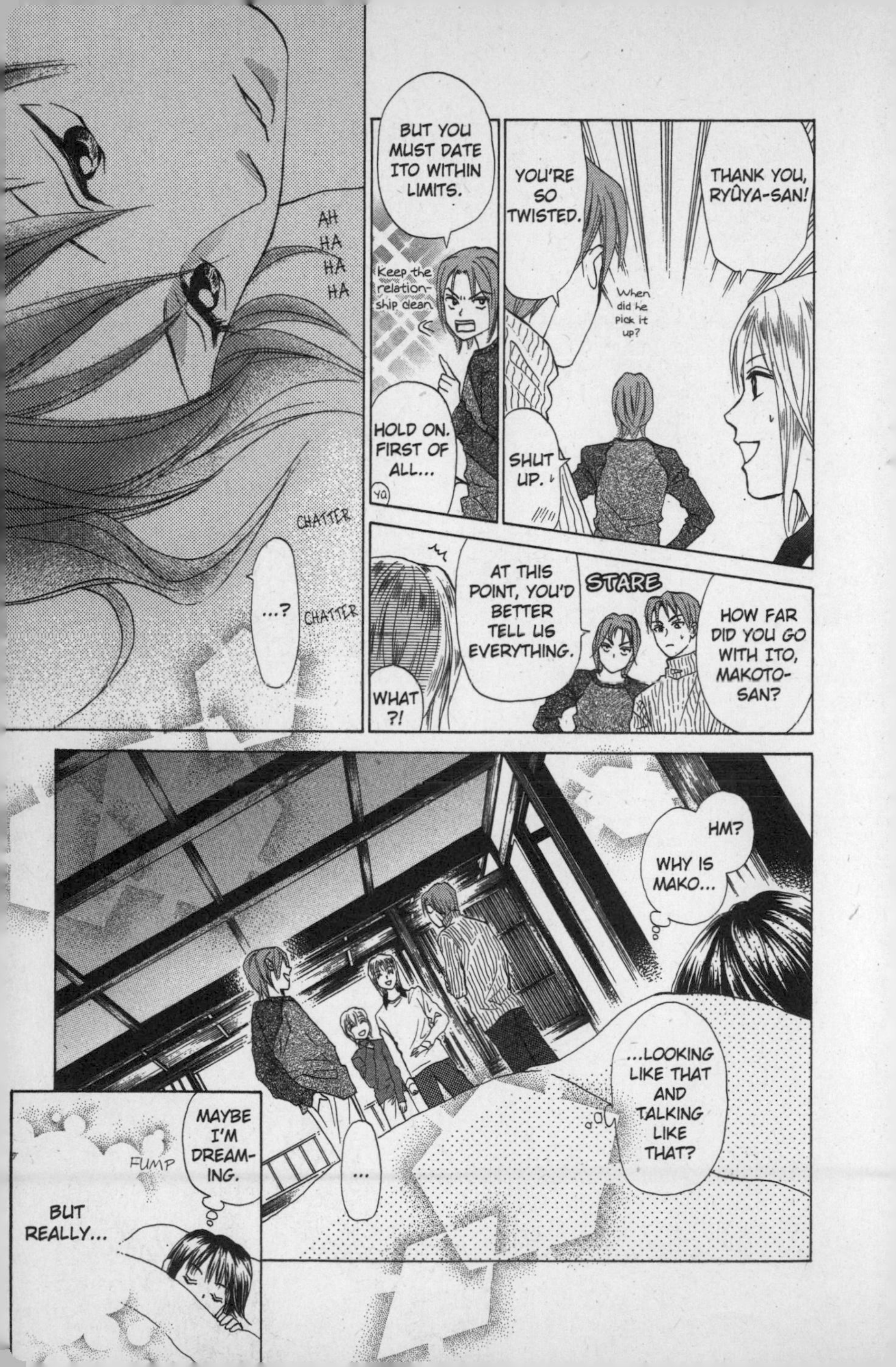
THANK YOU, RYÛYA-SAN!
YOU'RE SO TWISTED.
When did he pick it up?
SHUT UP.
BUT YOU MUST DATE ITO WITHIN LIMITS.
Keep the relationship clean.
HOLD ON. FIRST OF ALL...
YA
HOW FAR DID YOU GO WITH ITO, MAKOTO-SAN?
STARE
AT THIS POINT, YOU'D BETTER TELL US EVERYTHING.
WHAT ?!
AH HA HA HA
CHATTER
...?
CHATTER
HM?
WHY IS MAKO...
...LOOKING LIKE THAT AND TALKING LIKE THAT?
...
MAYBE I'M DREAMING.
FUMP
BUT REALLY...

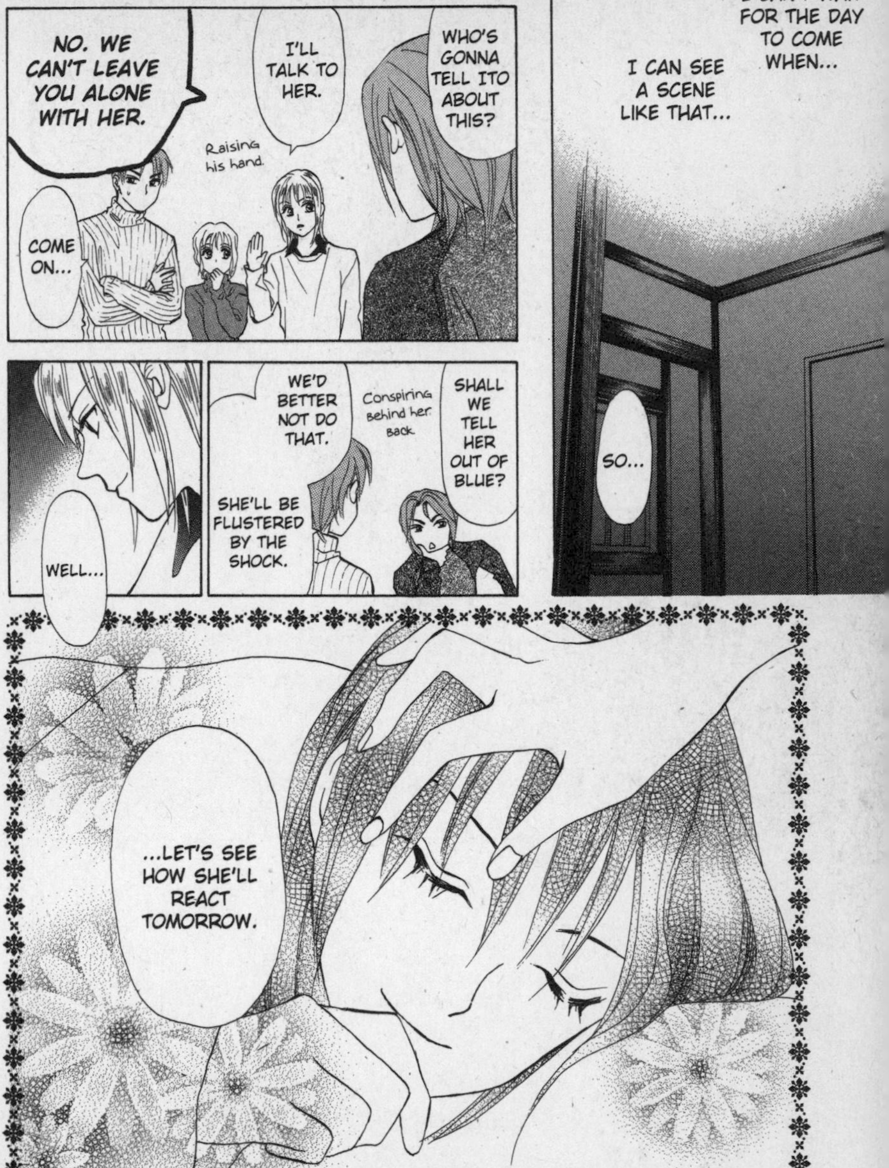
I CAN'T WAIT FOR THE DAY TO COME WHEN...
I CAN SEE A SCENE LIKE THAT...
SO...
WHO'S GONNA TELL ITO ABOUT THIS?
I'LL TALK TO HER.
Raising his hand.
NO. WE CAN'T LEAVE YOU ALONE WITH HER.
COME ON...
SHALL WE TELL HER OUT OF BLUE?
Conspiring behind her back
WE'D BETTER NOT DO THAT.
SHE'LL BE FLUSTERED BY THE SHOCK.
WELL...
...LET'S SEE HOW SHE'LL REACT TOMORROW.

W Juliet ⑬ / The End

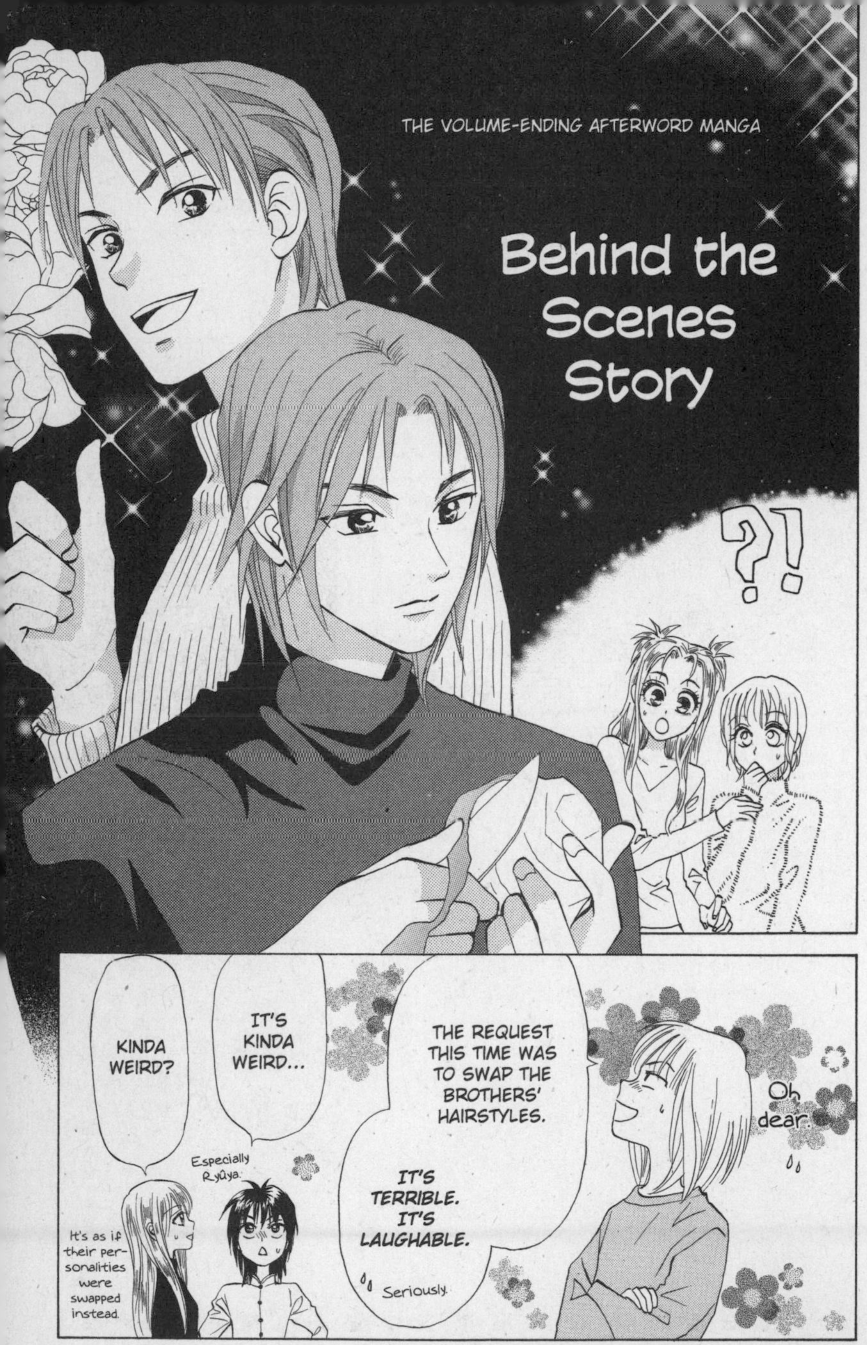
THE VOLUME-ENDING AFTERWORD MANGA
Behind the Scenes Story
?!
Oh dear.
THE REQUEST THIS TIME WAS TO SWAP THE BROTHERS' HAIRSTYLES.
IT'S TERRIBLE. IT'S LAUGHABLE.
Seriously.
IT'S KINDA WEIRD...
Especially Ryûya.
KINDA WEIRD?
It's as if their personalities were swapped instead.

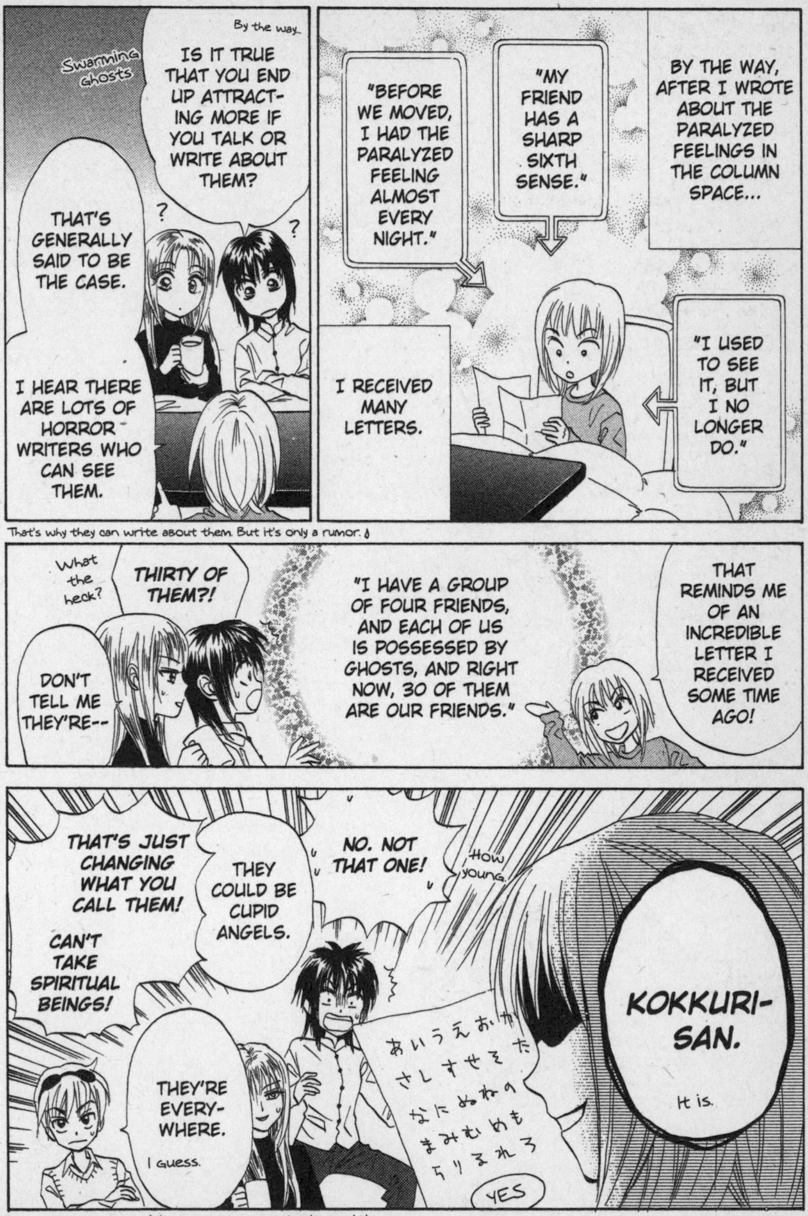

BY THE WAY, AFTER I WROTE ABOUT THE PARALYZED FEELINGS IN THE COLUMN SPACE...
"MY FRIEND HAS A SHARP SIXTH SENSE."
"BEFORE WE MOVED, I HAD THE PARALYZED FEELING ALMOST EVERY NIGHT."
"I USED TO SEE IT, BUT I NO LONGER DO."
I RECEIVED MANY LETTERS.
By the way...
IS IT TRUE THAT YOU END UP ATTRACTING MORE IF YOU TALK OR WRITE ABOUT THEM?
Swarming Ghosts
THAT'S GENERALLY SAID TO BE THE CASE.
I HEAR THERE ARE LOTS OF HORROR WRITERS WHO CAN SEE THEM.
That's why they can write about them. But it's only a rumor.
THAT REMINDS ME OF AN INCREDIBLE LETTER I RECEIVED SOME TIME AGO!
"I HAVE A GROUP OF FOUR FRIENDS, AND EACH OF US IS POSSESSED BY GHOSTS, AND RIGHT NOW, 30 OF THEM ARE OUR FRIENDS."
THIRTY OF THEM?!
What the heck?
DON'T TELL ME THEY'RE--
KOKKURI-SAN.
It is.
How young.
NO. NOT THAT ONE!
THEY COULD BE CUPID ANGELS.
THAT'S JUST CHANGING WHAT YOU CALL THEM!
CAN'T TAKE SPIRITUAL BEINGS!
あいうえおか
さしすせそた
なにぬねの
まみむめも
ちりるれろ
YES
THEY'RE EVERYWHERE.
I guess.
It's dangerous, so don't try it!

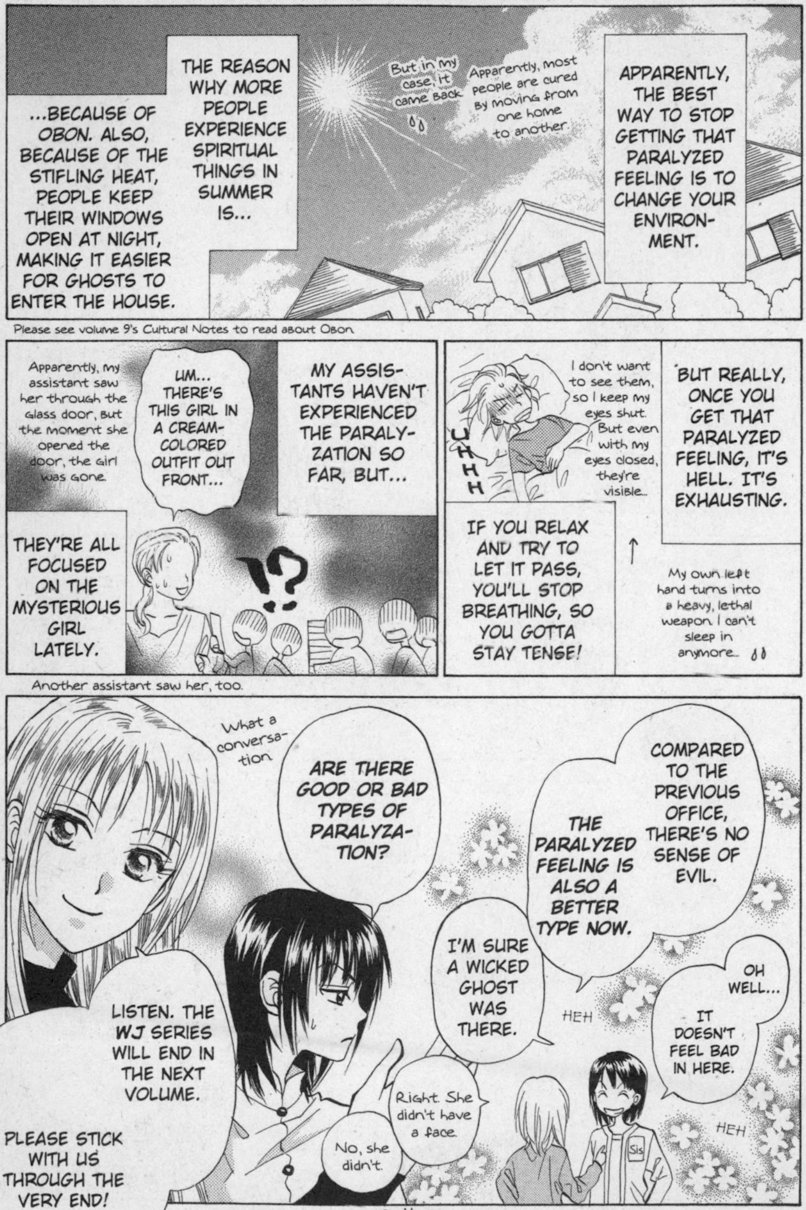
APPARENTLY, THE BEST WAY TO STOP GETTING THAT PARALYZED FEELING IS TO CHANGE YOUR ENVIRON-MENT.
Apparently, most people are cured by moving from one home to another.
But in my case, it came back
THE REASON WHY MORE PEOPLE EXPERIENCE SPIRITUAL THINGS IN SUMMER IS...
...BECAUSE OF OBON. ALSO, BECAUSE OF THE STIFLING HEAT, PEOPLE KEEP THEIR WINDOWS OPEN AT NIGHT, MAKING IT EASIER FOR GHOSTS TO ENTER THE HOUSE.
Please see volume 9's Cultural Notes to read about Obon.
BUT REALLY, ONCE YOU GET THAT PARALYZED FEELING, IT'S HELL. IT'S EXHAUSTING.
I don't want to see them, so I keep my eyes shut. But even with my eyes closed, they're visible...
UHHH
My own left hand turns into a heavy, lethal weapon. I can't sleep in anymore...
IF YOU RELAX AND TRY TO LET IT PASS, YOU'LL STOP BREATHING, SO YOU GOTTA STAY TENSE!
MY ASSIS-TANTS HAVEN'T EXPERIENCED THE PARALY-ZATION SO FAR, BUT...
UM... THERE'S THIS GIRL IN A CREAM-COLORED OUTFIT OUT FRONT...
Apparently, my assistant saw her through the glass door, but the moment she opened the door, the girl was gone.
!?
THEY'RE ALL FOCUSED ON THE MYSTERIOUS GIRL LATELY.
Another assistant saw her, too.
COMPARED TO THE PREVIOUS OFFICE, THERE'S NO SENSE OF EVIL.
OH WELL... IT DOESN'T FEEL BAD IN HERE.
HEH
THE PARALYZED FEELING IS ALSO A BETTER TYPE NOW.
HEH
I'M SURE A WICKED GHOST WAS THERE.
ARE THERE GOOD OR BAD TYPES OF PARALYZA-TION?
What a conversa-tion.
Right. She didn't have a face.
No, she didn't.
Sis
LISTEN. THE WJ SERIES WILL END IN THE NEXT VOLUME.
PLEASE STICK WITH US THROUGH THE VERY END!

2002. 12. 3. 絵夢羅.
Emura.

Cultural Notes

Osechi

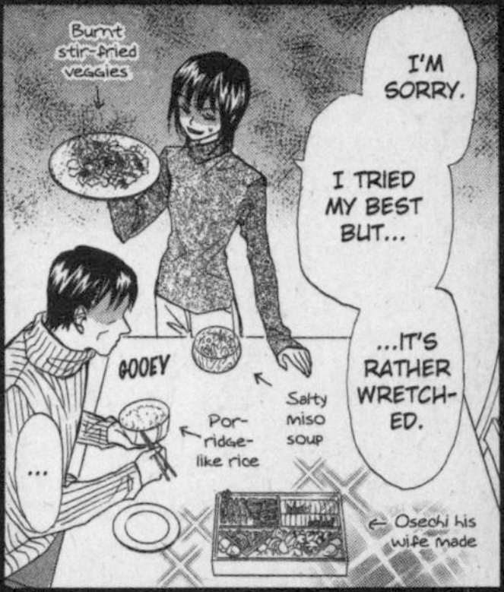
I'M SORRY.
I TRIED MY BEST BUT...
Burnt stir-fried veggies
...IT'S RATHER WRETCHED.
GOOEY
Salty miso soup
Por-ridge-like rice
...
Osechi his wife made

[reference page 51] *Osechi* is a traditional Japanese meal eaten during the New Year's holidays. It includes such foods as fish cakes, sweet potato mashed with chestnuts, black beans, tuna fish wrapped in seaweed, herring roe, omelets with fish paste or mashed shrimp, and vegetable soup with sticky rice cakes. Except for the vegetable soup, traditional osechi dishes are prepared before New Year's Day, and many of them are sweet, salty or sour because they keep better. Nowadays, however, sashimi and sushi are also eaten, as well as Western food such as pizza and fried chicken.

Omiyage

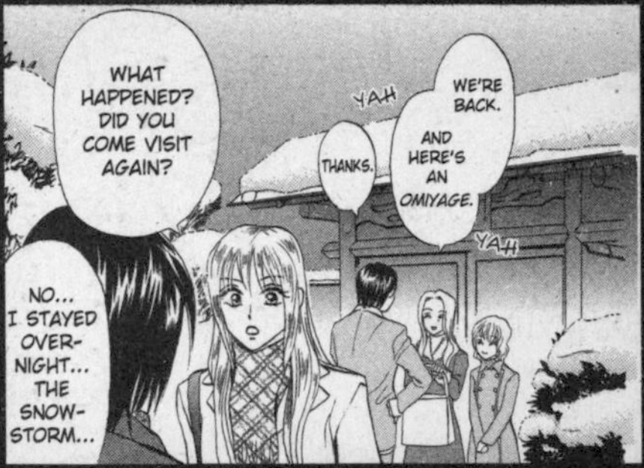
WE'RE BACK.
AND HERE'S AN OMIYAGE.
YAH
THANKS.
WHAT HAPPENED? DID YOU COME VISIT AGAIN?
YAH
NO... I STAYED OVER-NIGHT... THE SNOW-STORM...

[reference page 60] *Omiyage* is a small gift customarily brought home by those returning from a trip.

Kokkuri-san

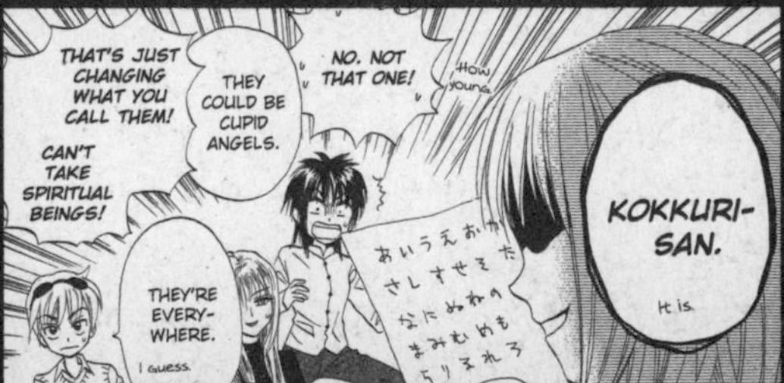
KOKKURI-SAN.
It is.
How young.
NO. NOT THAT ONE!
THEY COULD BE CUPID ANGELS.
THAT'S JUST CHANGING WHAT YOU CALL THEM!
CAN'T TAKE SPIRITUAL BEINGS!
YES
THEY'RE EVERY-WHERE.
I guess.

[reference page 190] *Kokkuri-san*, a type of divination game, is the Japanese equivalent of the Ouija board.

Konyoku (mixed-sex bath)

WOW! IT'S HUGE!

AND NO ONE'S HERE. IT'S ALL OURS!

I'LL HELP YOU WASH YOUR BACK, ITO-SAN.

[reference pages 128 and 134] Although separate-sex baths are sure to be offered at most *ryokan* (a Japanese-style inn), it is not uncommon to find mixed-sex baths, too. *Konyoku* is a tradition that dates back at least 1,300 years. Wearing swimsuits is not allowed at most of the better hot spring resorts, so nudity is the norm—with men, women, young and old all sharing a large bath together, butt-naked and steaming pink. Even if you find the idea unappealing, you might be surprised at how quickly one can get used to being naked among naked strangers—and realize that the idea isn't about looking at other naked people, but about steeping in the blissfully hot water, completely relaxed. Like the ryokan where Ito and Makoto stayed, some places offer private konyoku baths, too.

Goemonburo

What a weird thing to rent.

Goemonburo

[reference page 128] *Goemonburo* is a traditional Japanese bath that looks like a huge cauldron of cast iron. The word "goemon" comes from an infamous burglar named Goemon Ishikawa who was boiled alive in a metal pot as punishment for his crimes. It's rare for Japanese households to have goemonburo in their bathrooms nowadays, and for most people, it's a rare and fun experience to visit a hot spring and try to fold oneself into an old-fashioned iron cauldron.

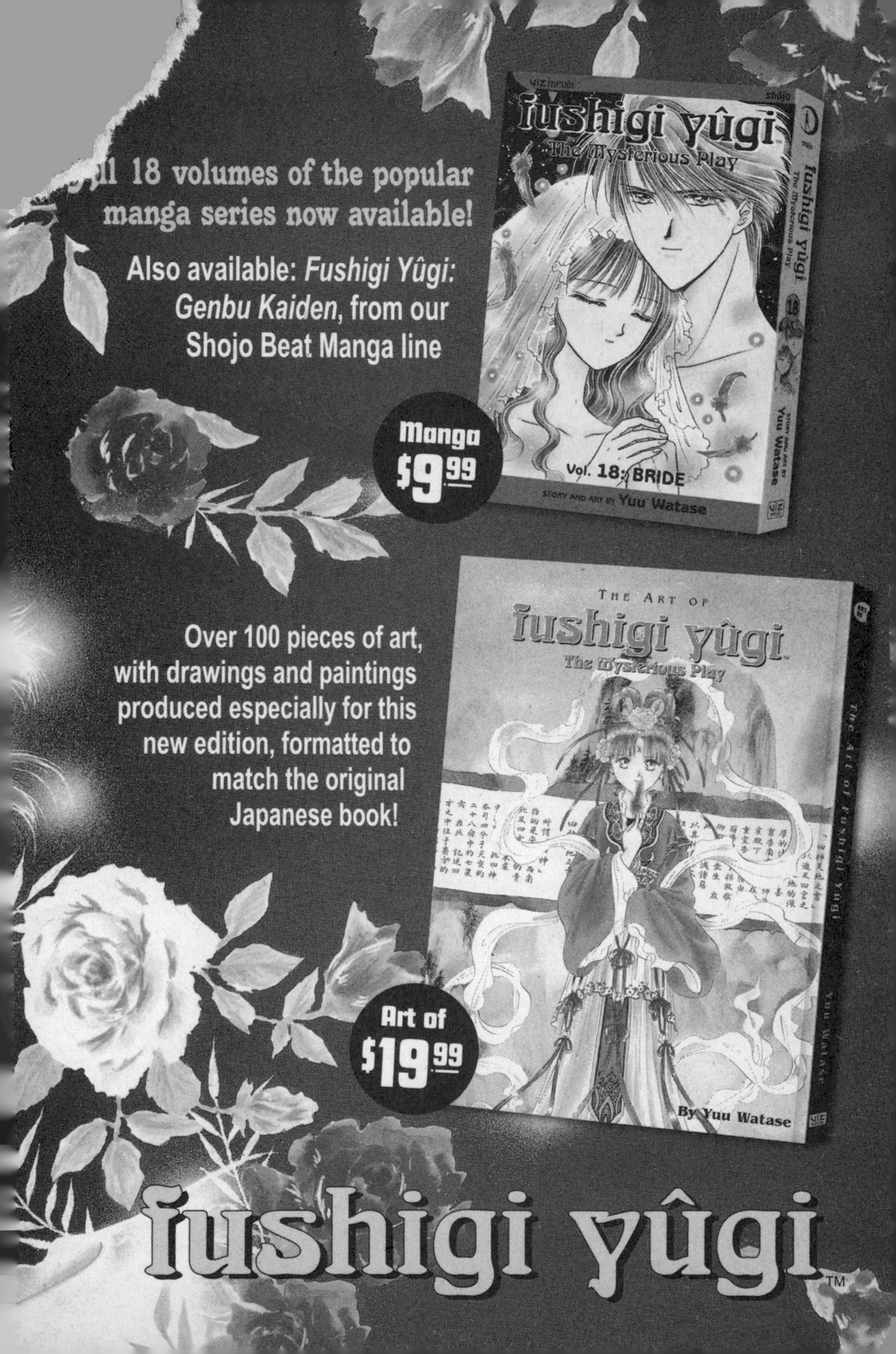

All 18 volumes of the popular manga series now available!
Also available: *Fushigi Yûgi: Genbu Kaiden*, from our Shojo Beat Manga line
fushigi yûgi
The Mysterious Play
Vol. 18: BRIDE
STORY AND ART BY Yuu Watase
Manga $9.99
Over 100 pieces of art, with drawings and paintings produced especially for this new edition, formatted to match the original Japanese book!
THE ART OF
fushigi yûgi
The Mysterious Play
By Yuu Watase
Art of $19.99
fushigi yûgi™

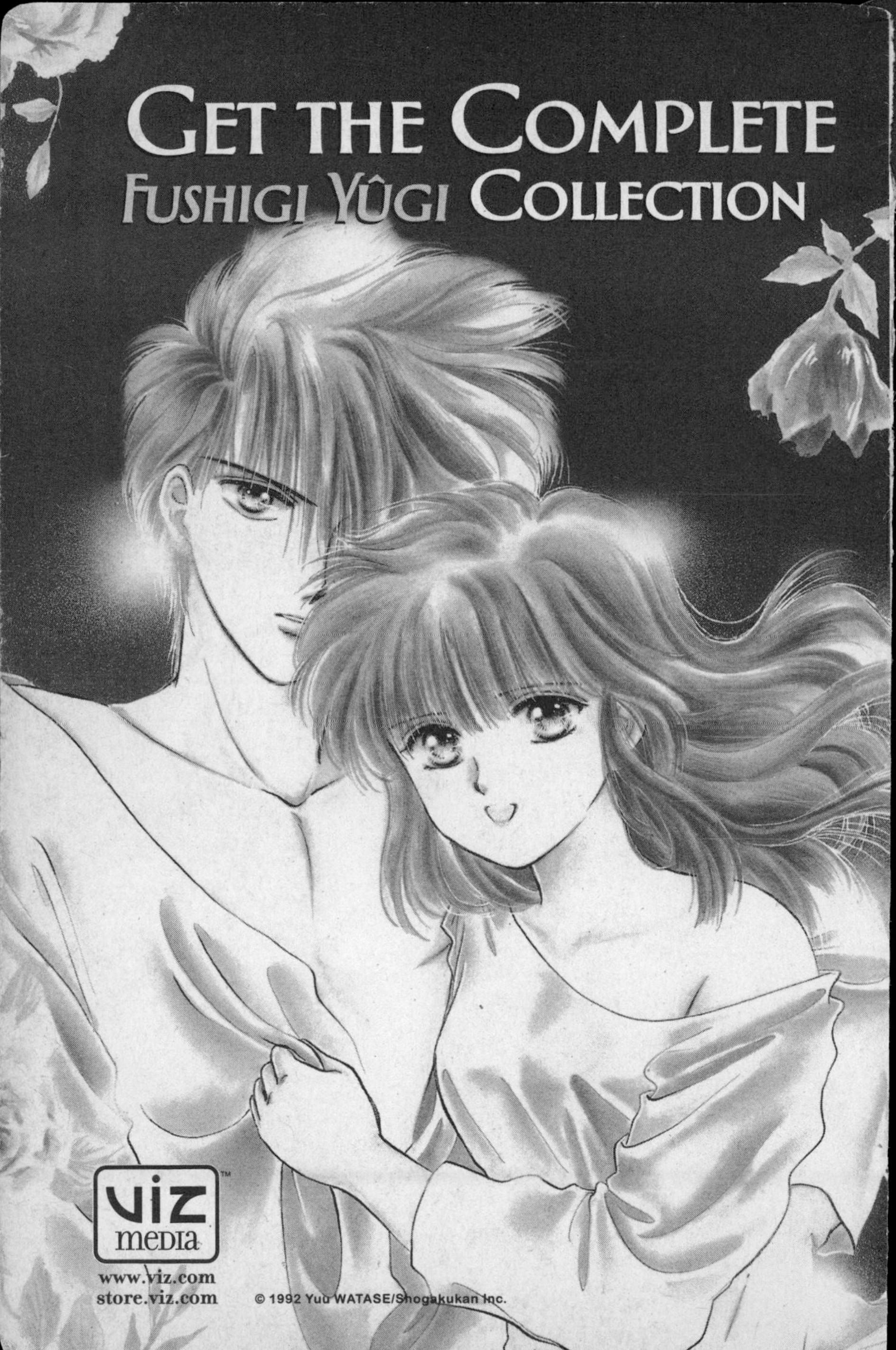